THE L.M. MONTGOMERY READER

Volume 1: A Life in Print

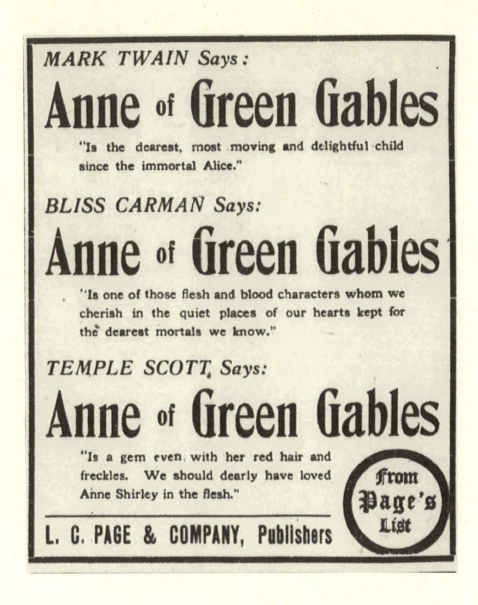

Advertisement for *Anne of Green Gables*, by L.M. Montgomery,
The Sun (New York, NY), 21 November 1908, 7

THE
L.M. MONTGOMERY
READER

Volume 1: A Life in Print

Edited by Benjamin Lefebvre

UNIVERSITY OF TORONTO PRESS
Toronto Buffalo London

© University of Toronto Press 2013
Toronto Buffalo London
www.utppublishing.com
Printed in Canada

ISBN 978-1-4426-4491-5 (cloth)

∞

Printed on acid-free, 100% post-consumer recycled paper
with vegetable-based inks.

Library and Archives Canada Cataloguing in Publication

The L.M. Montgomery reader / edited by Benjamin Lefebvre.

Includes bibliographical references and indexes.
Contents: v. 1. A life in print.
ISBN 978-1-4426-4491-5 (v. 1 : bound)

1. Montgomery, L.M. (Lucy Maud), 1874–1942 – Criticism and interpretation.
I. Lefebvre, Benjamin, 1977–, editor of compilation.
II. Title: Life in print.

PS8526.O55Z63538 2013   C813'.52   C2013-905295-X

University of Toronto Press acknowledges the financial assistance to its publishing
program of the Canada Council for the Arts and the Ontario Arts Council.

Canada Council   Conseil des Arts
for the Arts   du Canada

ONTARIO ARTS COUNCIL
CONSEIL DES ARTS DE L'ONTARIO
50 YEARS OF ONTARIO GOVERNMENT SUPPORT OF THE ARTS
50 ANS DE SOUTIEN DU GOUVERNEMENT DE L'ONTARIO AUX ART!

This book has been published with the help of a grant from the
Canadian Federation for the Humanities and Social Sciences, through the
Awards to Scholarly Publications Program, using funds provided by the
Social Sciences and Humanities Research Council of Canada.

University of Toronto Press acknowledges the financial support of the
Government of Canada through the Canada Book Fund for its publishing activities.

Contents

Acknowledgments xi

Abbreviations xiii

Introduction: A Life in Print 3
BENJAMIN LEFEBVRE

A Note on the Text 29

1 [Such a Delightful Little Person] (1908) 31

2 Author Tells How He Wrote His Story (1908) 33

3 Origin of Popular Book (1908) 35

4 The Author of *Anne of Avonlea* (1909) 37

5 Miss Montgomery, the Author of the "Anne" Books (1909) 40
A. WYLIE MAHON

6 A Trio of Women Writers (1909) 44
DONALD B. SINCLAIR

7 Canadian Writers on Canadian Literature –
A Symposium (1910) 48

8 Says Woman's Place Is Home (1910) 50

Contents

9   Want to Know How to Write Books?
    Well Here's a Real Recipe (1910)   53
    PHOEBE DWIGHT

10 Miss Montgomery's Visit to Boston (1910)   57

11 Four Questions Answered (1910)   59
    LUCY MAUD MONTGOMERY

12 Miss L.M. Montgomery,
    Author of *Anne of Green Gables* (1910)   62

13 How I Began to Write (1911)   67
    L.M. MONTGOMERY

14 [Seasons in the Woods] (1911)   73
    L.M. MONTGOMERY

15 With Our Next-Door Neighbors:
    Prince Edward Island (1911)   98
    THOMAS F. ANDERSON

16 [The Marriage of L.M. Montgomery] (1911)   101

17 A Canadian Novelist of Note Interviewed (1911)   105

18 Interviews with Authors (1911)   110
    ANNE E. NIAS

19 The Old Minister in *The Story Girl* (1912)   114
    A. WYLIE MAHON

20 L.M. Montgomery: Story Writer (1913)   120
    MARJORY MACMURCHY

21 L.M. Montgomery at Women's Canadian Club (1913)   126

22 L.M. Montgomery of the Island (1914)   129
    MARJORY MACMURCHY

23 What Twelve Canadian Women Hope to See
    as the Outcome of the War (1915)   134

24 The Way to Make a Book (1915)   137
    L.M. MONTGOMERY

25 How I Began (1915)   144
    L.M. MONTGOMERY

Contents

26 [This Hideous War] (1915)   148

27 What Are the Greatest Books
    in the English Language? (1916)   151

28 My Favorite Bookshelf (1917)   154
    L.M. MONTGOMERY

29 The Author of Anne (1919)   157
    ETHEL M. CHAPMAN

30 The Gay Days of Old (1919)   163
    L.M. MONTGOMERY

31 Introduction to *Further Chronicles of Avonlea*,
    by L.M. Montgomery (1920)   169
    NATHAN HASKELL DOLE

32 One Little Girl Who Wrote to L.M. Montgomery
    and Received a Reply (1920)   174

33 A Sextette of Canadian Women Writers (1920)   177
    OWEN MCGILLICUDDY

34 Blank Verse? "Very Blank," Said Father (1921)   180
    L.M. MONTGOMERY

35 "I Dwell among My Own People" (1921)   182
    L.M. MONTGOMERY

36 Bits from My Mailbag (1922)   185
    L.M. MONTGOMERY

37 From *Fiction Writers on Fiction Writing: Advice, Opinions
    and a Statement of Their Own Working Methods
    by More Than One Hundred Authors* (1923)   189

38 Novel Writing Notes (1923)   197
    L.M. MONTGOMERY

39 Proud That Canadian Literature Is Clean (1924)   199

40 Canadian Public Cold to Its Own Literature (1924)   202

41 Thinks Modern Flapper Will Be Strict Mother (1924)   204

42 Symposium on Canadian Fiction in Which
    Canadian Authors Express Their Preferences (1924)   207

Contents

43 Something about L.M. Montgomery (1925)   209

44 L.M. Montgomery's *Rilla of Ingleside*:
    A Reader's Journal (1925)   217
    ALTAIR

45 Famous Author and Simple Mother (1925)   224
    NORMA PHILLIPS MUIR

46 The Day before Yesterday (1927)   230
    L.M. MONTGOMERY MACDONALD

47 Who's Who in Canadian Literature:
    L.M. Montgomery (1927)   237
    V.B. RHODENIZER

48 About Canadian Writers: L.M. Montgomery,
    the Charming Author of "Anne" (1927)   241
    KATHERINE HALE

49 On Being of the Tribe of Joseph (1927)   244
    AUSTIN BOTHWELL

50 Minister's Wife and Authoress (1928)   249
    C.L. COWAN

51 An Autobiographical Sketch (1929)   254
    L.M. MONTGOMERY

52 Modern Girl Defined by Noted Writer (1929)   260

53 L.M. Montgomery's Ideas (1930)   262

54 The 'Teen-Age Girl (1931)   273
    L.M. MONTGOMERY

55 Anne of Green Gables at Home (1931)   283
    A.V. BROWN

56 An Open Letter from a Minister's Wife (1931)   288
    L.M. MONTGOMERY

57 Life Has Been Interesting (1933)   293
    MRS. L.M. MACDONALD (L.M. MONTGOMERY)

58 The Importance of Beauty in Everything (1933)   295
    L.M. MONTGOMERY

Contents

59 From *Courageous Women* (1934)   298
    L.M. MONTGOMERY

60 Author to Get No Profit as *Green Gables* Filmed (1934)   316

61 Film Preview of Noted Novel Honors
    Canadian Woman Writer (1934)   320

62 Is This My Anne (1935)   323
    L.M. MONTGOMERY

63 Foreword to *Up Came the Moon*,
    by Jessie Findlay Brown (1936)   328
    L.M. MONTGOMERY

64 Come Back with Me to Prince Edward Island (1936)   330
    L.M. MONTGOMERY

65 Memories of Childhood Days (1936)   341
    L.M. MONTGOMERY

66 The Mother of the Anne Series –
    Lucy M. Montgomery (1937)   343
    EVA-LIS WUORIO, TRANSLATED BY VAPPU KANNAS

67 The Book and the Film (1937)   347

68 For and about Girls (1937)   350
    L.M. MONTGOMERY

69 Prince Edward Island (1939)   352
    L.M. MONTGOMERY, O.B.E.

70 Beloved Writer Addresses Several Aurora Gatherings (1940)   356

71 Noted Author Dies Suddenly at Home Here (1942)   359

72 Lucy Maud Montgomery (1942)   363

73 L.M. Montgomery's "Anne" (1942)   365

74 Body of Island's Beloved Authoress Home for Burial (1942)   367

75 Island Writer Laid to Rest at Cavendish (1942)   369

76 The Creator of "Anne" (1942)   373

77 [L.M. Montgomery's Last Poem] (1942)   375

Contents

78 L.M. Montgomery / Mrs. (Rev.) Ewen Macdonald (1942)   378

79 L.M. Montgomery as a Letter-Writer (1942)   385
   E. WEBER

80 L.M. Montgomery's "Anne" (1944)   400
   E. WEBER

Epilogue: *Anne of Green Gables* –
The Story of the Photoplay (1920)   411
ARABELLA BOONE

Sources   421

Bibliography   427

Index   441

Acknowledgments

This first volume of *The L.M. Montgomery Reader* owes so much to a number of people who assisted and encouraged me through several years of research. I am grateful to Vanessa Brown, Mary Beth Cavert, Cecily Devereux, Kelly Norah Drukker, Melanie Fishbane, Irene Gammel, Carole Gerson, Andrea McKenzie, Cynthia Soulliere, Meg Taylor, and Lorraine York, whose advice and feedback helped with the final shape of the volume, and to several people who tracked down a number of items at libraries across North America: Joshua Ginter in Winnipeg, Katharine MacDonald in Charlottetown, Sarina Annis and Yuka Kajihara in Toronto, Christy Woster in Minnesota, and Emily Woster in Illinois. Tracking down Eva-Lis Wuorio's article in *Sirkka* led to a collaborative search that involved Linda Boutilier, Mary Beth Cavert, and Sandy Wagner, and leads for additional items were given to me by Donna J. Campbell and Carolyn Strom Collins. As with all projects involving L.M. Montgomery's periodical career, this one draws on the earlier research of the late Rea Wilmshurst, whose findings appear in what remains an invaluable resource, *Lucy Maud Montgomery: A Preliminary Bibliography* (1986).

At University of Toronto Press, I am grateful to Siobhan McMenemy for her editorial expertise, sharp eye, encouragement, and collegiality, and to Frances Mundy, Ani Deyirmenjian, and Matthew Kudelka for their expertise throughout the volume's production stages. Archivists, librarians, and their colleagues were likewise generous with their help and knowledge: Linda Amichand, Lorne Bruce, Kathryn Harvey, and

Acknowledgments

Darlene Wiltsie, Archival and Special Collections, University of Guelph Library; Mark Leggott, Simon Lloyd, and Pauline MacPherson, Robertson Library, University of Prince Edward Island; Cecile W. Gardner and Henry F. Scannell, Boston Public Library; Jannah Toms, Public Archives and Records Office, Charlottetown; Joel Cyr, Jean Matheson, and Jocelyne Potyka, Library and Archives Canada; Kelly Casey, Dalhousie University Archives; and the staff at the University of Guelph Storage Annex and at the interlibrary loan departments at the Wilfrid Laurier University and the University of Winnipeg Libraries.

This project began during a two-year postdoctoral fellowship funded by the Social Sciences and Humanities Research Council of Canada, held at the University of Alberta between 2007 and 2009, for a project entitled "Branding a Life: The Case of L.M. Montgomery.™" I gratefully acknowledge SSHRC for its research and travel support, as well as the Leverhulme Trust for a visiting fellowship at the University of Worcester (UK) and the Macdonald Stewart Foundation for supporting the Visiting Scholar position at the L.M. Montgomery Institute, University of Prince Edward Island.

My special thanks are for the members of my family: my mother, Claire Pelland Lefebvre; my siblings, Melanie and Jeremy, and their families; and especially my partner, Jacob Letkemann, who read through portions of the manuscript and generously shared ideas and comments throughout the editing of this volume. I dedicate this volume to the memory of my father, Gerald M. Lefebvre (1934–2008), who taught me so much about hard work, scholarly integrity, and the importance of humour in everything.

Abbreviations

The following abbreviations refer to sources attributed to L.M. Montgomery:

AA   *Anne of Avonlea*. 1909. Toronto: Seal Books, 1996.

AfGG   *After Green Gables: L.M. Montgomery's Letters to Ephraim Weber, 1916–1941*. Edited by Hildi Froese Tiessen and Paul Gerard Tiessen. Toronto: University of Toronto Press, 2006.

AGG   *Anne of Green Gables*. 1908. Toronto: Seal Books, 1996.

AHD   *Anne's House of Dreams*. 1917. Toronto: Seal Books, 1996.

AIn   *Anne of Ingleside*. 1939. Toronto: Seal Books, 1996.

AIs   *Anne of the Island*. 1915. Toronto: Seal Books, 1996.

AP   *The Alpine Path: The Story of My Career*. 1917. Don Mills, ON: Fitzhenry and Whiteside, n.d.

AWP   *Anne of Windy Poplars*. 1936. Toronto: Seal Books, 1996.

BC   *The Blue Castle*. 1926. Toronto: Seal Books, 1988.

BQ   *The Blythes Are Quoted*. Edited by Benjamin Lefebvre. Toronto: Viking Canada, 2009.

CA   *Chronicles of Avonlea*. 1912. Toronto: Seal Books, 1993.

CJLMM, 1   *The Complete Journals of L.M. Montgomery: The PEI Years, 1889–1900*. Edited by Mary Henley Rubio and Elizabeth Hillman Waterston. Don Mills, ON: Oxford University Press, 2012.

Abbreviations

CJLMM, 2	*The Complete Journals of L.M. Montgomery: The PEI Years, 1901–1911*. Edited by Mary Henley Rubio and Elizabeth Hillman Waterston. Don Mills, ON: Oxford University Press, 2013.
EC	*Emily Climbs*. 1925. Toronto: Seal Books, 1998.
ENM	*Emily of New Moon*. 1923. Toronto: Seal Books, 1998.
EQ	*Emily's Quest*. 1927. Toronto: Seal Books, 1998.
FCA	*Further Chronicles of Avonlea*. Boston: The Page Company, 1920.
GGL	*The Green Gables Letters from L.M. Montgomery to Ephraim Weber, 1905–1909*. Edited by Wilfrid Eggleston. 1960. Ottawa: Borealis Press, 1981.
GR	*The Golden Road*. 1913. Toronto: Seal Books, 1987.
MDMM	*My Dear Mr. M: Letters to G.B. MacMillan from L.M. Montgomery*. Edited by Francis W.P. Bolger and Elizabeth R. Epperly. 1980. Toronto: Oxford University Press, 1992.
MM	*Magic for Marigold*. 1929. Toronto: Seal Books, 1988.
MP	*Mistress Pat*. 1935. Toronto: Seal Books, 1988.
RI	*Rilla of Ingleside*. 1921. Edited by Benjamin Lefebvre and Andrea McKenzie. Toronto: Viking Canada, 2010.
RV	*Rainbow Valley*. 1919. Toronto: Seal Books, 1996.
SG	*The Story Girl*. 1911. Toronto: Seal Books, 1987.
SJLMM	*The Selected Journals of L.M. Montgomery*, Volume 1: *1889–1910*; Volume 2: *1910–1921*; Volume 3: *1921–1929*; Volume 4: *1929–1935*; Volume 5: *1935–1942*. Edited by Mary Rubio and Elizabeth Waterston. Toronto: Oxford University Press, 1985, 1987, 1992, 1998, 2004.
SR	"Scrapbook of Reviews from Around the World Which L.M. Montgomery's Clipping Service Sent to Her, 1910–1935." L.M. Montgomery Collection, University of Guelph archives.
WOP	*The Watchman and Other Poems*. Toronto: McClelland, Goodchild, and Stewart, 1916.

THE L.M. MONTGOMERY READER

Volume 1: A Life in Print

Introduction: A Life in Print

BENJAMIN LEFEBVRE

In the field of L.M. Montgomery Studies, the genesis story of Montgomery criticism goes something like this: although the novels of L.M. Montgomery (1874–1942) have been extraordinarily popular with all types of readers worldwide since the publication of her first book, *Anne of Green Gables* (1908), her work was virtually ignored by the academy throughout and beyond her lifetime, except for occasional disparaging comments by prominent male critics such as Archibald MacMechan (1862–1933), Arthur L. Phelps (1887–1970), William Arthur Deacon (1890–1977), E.K. Brown (1905–1951), and Desmond Pacey (1917–1975), all of whom tended to sideline popular and female authors in their quest to construct a canon of high modernism for Canadian literature and literary criticism. Finally, in 1966, Elizabeth Waterston contributed a pioneering chapter on Montgomery to the collection of essays *The Clear Spirit: Twenty Canadian Women and Their Times*. The tide continued to turn thanks to the founding in 1975 of the academic journal *Canadian Children's Literature*, which focused one of its inaugural issues on Montgomery's work and which, for the duration of its existence, continued to publish editorials, articles, and reviews pertaining to Montgomery's work and its afterlives.

According to this story, it was not until late 1985 that what Carole Gerson has called a "discernible turning point" occurred: the release of the first volume of *The Selected Journals of L.M. Montgomery*, edited by Mary Rubio and Elizabeth Waterston and published by Oxford University Press, a publishing venture that coincided with the Canadian premiere of Kevin Sullivan's first *Anne of Green Gables* television miniseries.[1] While a range of television productions throughout the 1980s and 1990s ensured that Montgomery's name and characters remained anchored in popular culture both in Canada and worldwide, the publication of Montgomery's journals startled those who had known her personally, by reputation, or simply as the author of *Anne of Green Gables*. Not only have the journals proven to be a unique cultural document, providing a first-hand account of the daily life of a well-read and articulate woman during a period of profound social change, but the person who emerges from its pages comes across as a far more introspective, critical, irritable, and sometimes vindictive figure than readers of her primary work tend to expect. Moreover, this shift in tone had an unanticipated effect on her critical reputation, because scholars began to use her journals as a lens through which they reread Montgomery's fiction, finding what Rubio and Waterston later called "secret messages of rebellion and resistance against authority (especially patriarchal authority) in[] her sunny stories."[2] This reconsideration of Montgomery and her work occurred in the midst of disciplinary shifts throughout the 1980s and 1990s, which saw a gradual breakdown of the barriers between "high" and "low" culture and a reclaiming of authors who, like Montgomery, had been marginalized due to their gender, their popularity, and the genres in which they wrote.[3] Today, more than a century after *Anne of Green Gables* first became a best-selling novel, scholarship on L.M. Montgomery focuses as much on the primary work published within her lifetime as on the range of adaptations of that work and on the forms of life writing that have appeared since her death. These scholars, working from all over the world, continue to find new ways to study this body of work – in terms of empire and nation, sexuality and repression, performance and resistance, parody and allusion, space and place, memory and forgetting, nature and culture, authorship and legislation, and national and international appeal and reception.[4]

While this straightforward narrative of Montgomery criticism is familiar and compelling, it nevertheless pushes to the sidelines a surprisingly vast array of additional materials that originated beyond the walls of the ivory tower and that appeared in "middlebrow" venues such as trade books, newspapers, and popular magazines that valued popularity and accessibility.[5] *The L.M. Montgomery Reader* gathers a selection of these neglected materials in three volumes in order to broaden our understanding of the ways in which Montgomery's work has been received since *Anne of Green Gables* made her an international celebrity author. Most of these items – from Canada, the United States, the United Kingdom, Australia, South Africa, New Zealand, and the Netherlands – are reprinted in these volumes for the first time. They have been gathered together as a result of two streams of research: the work of scholars and collectors who have searched through libraries and archival repositories by hand for lost items related to Montgomery,[6] and the ongoing digitization and indexing of print materials, a project that is revitalizing humanities research in the twenty-first century. If these two streams have taught us anything so far, it is that there is always something new to discover about L.M. Montgomery.

This first volume, subtitled *A Life in Print*, gathers together ninety pieces published from the immediate aftermath of the publication of *Anne of Green Gables* to a few years after Montgomery's death. Among the highlights of this volume are a number of essays and letters by Montgomery as well as several interviews with her from across her career. These pieces show her at her best, discussing a range of topics with wit, wisdom, and humour: the natural landscape of Prince Edward Island, her wide readership, anxieties about modernity (including the figure of the "modern girl"), the role of minister's wives in rural communities, the future of Canadian literature, her methods and ambitions as a writer, and her career as a best-selling author with an international reputation. While Montgomery's published journals shocked readers by revealing a woman who at times could be depressed, agitated, ecstatic, livid, judgmental, and even malicious, the items in this volume show her to be in total control of herself: as a rising celebrity author, as a minister's wife, as a reluctant feminist, as an established authority in Canada and beyond. As evidence of a more public Montgomery, these pieces complement and complicate the poetics of self-representation that scholars have traced in past published sources, including ten volumes of journals and letters. Moreover, this public voice adds a new layer to a figure that Irene Gammel has aptly referred to as "Canada's most enigmatic literary icon."[7]

As a way to trace the critical reception and the perceived literary value of Montgomery's work throughout this period, this volume also includes a range of profiles of the author as well as early responses to her work. These materials follow her thirty-year public career and include extensive media coverage of her death and funeral. Joining MacMechan, Deacon, and their ilk are a range of additional voices whose detailed commentaries on Montgomery's work have fallen through the cracks of the dominant narrative of Montgomery criticism. Montgomery rarely lost the opportunity to respond to these items in her journals and letters, and while her comments indicate that she did not always agree with these insights into her work, she nevertheless was careful to gather a vast range of these materials in scrapbooks for future generations to ponder.

Volume 2, subtitled *A Critical Heritage*, continues the story of Montgomery's critical reception in the seventy years since her death. It traces a number of milestones in the field, including the publication of Waterston's chapter on Montgomery in *The Clear Spirit* in 1966, the centenary of Montgomery's birth in 1974, the founding of *Canadian Children's Literature* in 1975, the publication of Montgomery's journals beginning in 1985, the founding of the L.M. Montgomery Institute at the University of Prince Edward Island in 1993, and the worldwide celebration of the centenary of *Anne of Green Gables* in 2008, and it includes a sample of twenty contributions to the field from 1966 to 2012. Volume 3, subtitled *A Legacy in Review*, considers another neglected forum for discussion of Montgomery's work in the mass media, namely, book reviews in newspapers, magazines, and journals – an additional treasure trove of materials that so far have rarely been part of the conversation.

It is my hope that the materials gathered here – most of which will be new even to longtime readers and scholars in the field – will add to the ongoing conversation about Montgomery's life and work and how they continue to be meaningful to readers all over the world. When I started digging through old reference books and periodicals as a graduate student for materials pertaining to Montgomery's work and legacy, I was motivated by a desire, shared by most of her readers, to keep on reading, to delay inevitably the final "the end" to her work. What I have found over the course of this research is that, even under the guise of absolute frankness, her journals and letters rarely tell the whole story. In a journal entry dated 6 March 1901, for instance, she reported that the day's Charlottetown *Patriot* contained an article on popular Prince Edward Island poets, but although she mentioned that the article offered "several paragraphs of compliments and quotations," she focused instead on her irritation that it referred to her by her full name, Lucy Maud Montgomery ("which I detest!") and on the self-pitying conviction, in her grief over the recent death of her father, that she had no one to share in her success.[8] What she omitted from her journal was that the article, entitled "Our Island Poets," was gushing in its praise for her: "Among the younger writers of to-day perhaps the name of first repute is Lucy Maud Montgomery, who is a frequent contributer [*sic*] to magazines of the first class. Miss Montgomery[,] although a young writer, shows marked ability and promise. She has an easy, graceful, charming style, coupled with excellent descriptive powers, which make her poems so fascinating and make them linger in one's mind. She is impressed with the beauty of her native Province and delights to paint it in descriptive verse. The thought, too, is wholesome, for the writer has a correct understanding of life and its meaning." Moreover, although at the time Montgomery was more than seven years away from publishing her first book, the unsigned editorial added, "much is still expected of her."[9] The journal form allowed Montgomery to retain absolute control over the version of her life that she wanted preserved for posthumous publication, but at the same time, she saw these journals as "grumble book[s]" in which she "work[ed] off all [her] revolutionary tendencies."[10] The items presented in this volume were for the most part beyond her control: filled sometimes with praise and admiration, sometimes with misinformation and conjecture, but always demonstrating a shared conviction that Montgomery and her work were worth talking about.

"The Bare Facts" vs. "The Real *Me*"

Soon after the publication of *Anne of Green Gables* in mid-June 1908, Montgomery began to encounter four aspects of authorship that she had rarely before experienced, despite having published hundreds of poems and short stories in North American periodicals for nearly two decades: celebrity endorsements, reviews, requests for interviews and biographical information, and spite. Although she was pleased with the novel's warm reception – within two months of its publication she had received sixty-six reviews of the book, sixty of them "kind and flattering beyond my highest expectations" – she was dismayed when the public's attention started to shift away from her work and to focus on her. Confiding in her two principal correspondents, G.B. MacMillan in Scotland and Ephraim Weber in western Canada, that she was besieged with requests from tourists to meet the author, she reported that she made a point of turning them down: "I don't want to be 'met.'" By then, she had been living with her maternal grandmother in Cavendish for a decade (save for a nine-month stint in Halifax), and while the isolation had been a boon for her writing career, it made socializing with crowds of strangers a daunting prospect. To Weber, she added that she also had to contend with animosity within her own community: "If you want to find out just how much *envy* and *petty spite* and *meanness* exists in people, even people who call themselves your friends, just write a successful book or do something they can't do, and you'll find out!" Too diplomatic or embarrassed to provide specific examples, she recorded in her journal that this kind of treatment made her feel "a sort of nausea with human nature."[11]

A private and pragmatic woman, Montgomery responded to this unwanted attention by seizing control of it where she could. Presumably she was also keen to correct misconceptions about her and her work, such as those appearing in a notice in the *Boston Herald* in late October 1908: "Miss Montgomery is a Canadian, her home being in the village of Cavendish, Prince Edward Island, where she teaches the village school. Many of the incidents in her delightful story are transcripts from her own experience, Avonlea being a picture of Cavendish."[12] Due to her remote location in rural Prince Edward Island, her earliest requests for interviews and personal information arrived in the form of letters: in November 1908, less than a month after getting a request from her publisher for "a personal sketch of how 'Anne' came to be" for the benefit of "inquisitive editors," she received a letter from a Toronto journalist who wanted details about "my birth, education, early life, when and how I began to write etc." for an article in preparation. Having already grown weary of this media attention, she wrote in her journal about how she planned to comply: "I'll give him the bare facts he wants. He will not know any more about the real *me* or my real life for it all, nor will his readers. The only key to *that* is found in this old journal."[13] She wrote nothing more about this request for information, but a short article published in the *Boston Journal* eleven days later and a second letter appearing in the *Brooklyn Daily Eagle* that December (see chapters 2 and 3 in this volume) show the author keeping the focus squarely on the "bare facts" of her writing life. In these two letters – her earliest known public responses to the media's interest in the author of *Anne of Green Gables* and the prototype for all future renditions of her "how I began" narrative – Montgomery responded politely and even amiably to this interest in her work while refusing to reveal even the most basic details about herself: her age, her location, her education, and her past writing credits. Indeed, one of these articles is entitled "Author Tells How He Wrote His Story."

In tandem with this initial refusal to open up about her personal life, Montgomery provided in such letters details about the creative process that she omitted from her journal: in fact, some of the most revealing details about Montgomery's strategies and methods as a writer are found in the essays, letters, and interviews published in her lifetime. At times, rather than reveal too much about herself, she resorted to sharing her fan mail with the press instead, as in a *Boston Herald* report that December:

"When an old man falls in love with a young girl," wrote a correspondent to L.M. Montgomery, the author of "Anne of Green Gables," the other day, "it is usually evidence of his dotage, but there are exceptions: such as in my case. I don't mind confessing that I am an old man and that the girl is 'Anne of Green Gables.'" Miss Montgomery's mail is replete with similar epistles, coming from readers of all ages. A "red-headed" girl wrote that she "never expected to see her inmost thoughts put into print"; and at the other end of the scale is a woman of 61 who "though a grandmother understands exactly the feelings of Anne."[14]

E. Holly Pike has noted that Montgomery's "willingness to share information about herself shows that she had accepted and actively shaped her role as a celebrity,"[15] but as the items collected in this volume show, her willingness increased only as she gradually became more accustomed or perhaps simply more resigned to her fame. During a rare business trip to Boston in November 1910, she consented to several in-person interviews, and after her marriage and move to southern Ontario in 1911, she was in high demand as a public speaker. Yet, partly because she valued her privacy and partly because as a minister's wife she had to be especially careful about what was said about her in print, she presented herself as far more socially conservative than she did in her journals and letters and omitted even mildly controversial details about her life. For instance, after writing a 25,000-word memoir entitled "The Alpine Path: The Story of My Career" for publication in the Toronto periodical *Everywoman's World* in 1917, she noted in her journal that she had snubbed the editor's request for an additional thousand words on her romantic relationships: "The dear public must get along without this particular tid-bit ... My grandchildren may include what they like in my biography. But while I live these things are arcana."[16] At the same time, as many of the items in this volume demonstrate, Montgomery was always careful to remain friendly and accessible to interviewers, no matter what drama was brewing behind the scenes: an article in the *Saskatoon Star–Phoenix* in 1930 mentioned that, "with her dignity and charm, her girlish slenderness and twinkly eyes," not to mention "a gracious manner and a pleasant smile," Montgomery came across to the unidentified reporter as "a friend of the family whom one had not seen for years and years."[17]

Montgomery's stance about the firm line between public and private pervades most of the items from the first decade of her career as a celebrity author. In an essay published in July 1912 in *The Editor: The Journal of Information for Literary Workers*, she began by deploying the patina of feminine modesty that had already become central to her public persona: "There isn't really much to say regarding my literary career. It has been made up of two elements: 'hard work' and 'stick to it.'"[18] On several occasions, however, concerned that certain assumptions about her or her work would be repeated until they became fact, she did not hesitate to intervene in what was being written about her. In a letter published in the *Toronto World*, also in 1912, in response to a comment made in a review of her short story collection *Chronicles of Avonlea*, Montgomery was quick to correct the expectation that she would maintain the frantic publication schedule of her first five books:

> I don't want you to remain under the mistaken impression that I've been writing a book every year (although it may look that way from the road). *Green Gables* was written three years before it was published and *Avonlea* was written the last of those years. *Kilmeny* was a serial written a couple of years before *Green Gables* and the short stories in my latest book have been written at intervals in the past ten years. So, you see, that at least two years have intervened between the writing of all my books, tho [*sic*] not between the publishing of them. If I should bring out another book next year, it will be two years since the writing of *The Story Girl*. I take a year to write a book and a year to rest in.[19]

In this instance as well, she kept the focus squarely on her writing life and made no mention of the fact that recent changes in her personal life – which by 1912 included marriage, new responsibilities as the wife of a Presbyterian minister, and motherhood – understandably had an impact on her writing career. She quickly saw, however, that she could not control what was written about her or her work: a 1912 article in *The Family Herald and Weekly Star*, a Montreal farm paper, claimed that Montgomery had submitted the opening chapters of *Anne of Green Gables* to a publisher "for use as magazine matter; but the head of the firm, after reading the proofs, communicated with her, advised her to elaborate the matter and to make a book of it, as it deserved." According to this article, her "near relative, Mr. D. Montgomery," testified to the fact that all her main characters were "drawn from life" and "could vouch for the accuracy of the delineation of them by his talented relative." Commenting on this clipping in her journal nearly three decades later, Montgomery was more amused than annoyed: "Poor Cousin Dan!"[20]

In many cases, too, direct quotations of Montgomery's words need to be met with skepticism, such as a reported "conversation" between her and an unidentified "well-known literary editor" that was also published in 1912, first in the *Boston Herald*, then in *The Writer: A Monthly Magazine for Literary Workers*, and then in slightly different form in the *Western Mail*, an Australian newspaper. Although it may have originated in a letter by Montgomery, as an actual conversation it is likely fictional, if only because she was seven months pregnant at the time it was first published:

"Now, just how do you set to work at writing a book?" asked the literary editor.

"Well," came the reply, "my stories are all thought out before I set them on paper. I write out the first chapter of a book, criticise it, twist and turn it a bit. Then, I write my second chapter. Immediately this is finished, I start back again at the first chapter and polish this up along with the new chapter. With the third, fourth and even the 18th chapter I work in just the same way, going over each and every chapter I have written as many times as a new one is added. So you see that when I had completed the 38 chapters in my *Anne of Green Gables*, the first chapter had been edited at least 39 times and perhaps a few more."

"But what a tremendous amount of labor!" said the literary editor.

"You think so?" was the questioned answer. "Well, it's only my way of writing a book."

Indeed, by the time this item appeared in abridged form in the *Los Angeles Times* less than a month later, it was the first chapter of *Anne of Avonlea* that had been edited thirty-nine times "and perhaps a few more."[21]

As Lorraine York observes in *Literary Celebrity in Canada* (2007), "Montgomery was unusually articulate about and aware of the conditions and ironies of her celebrity," and in fact "was well able to diagnose her own condition as a public commodity."[22] Now that we know so much more about the woman behind the legend, thanks to the publication of ten volumes of journals and letters, we are able to appreciate better the extent to which Montgomery strove to maintain a clear division between public and private. In an interview published in the *Toronto Globe* in November 1936, while vacationing in Prince Edward Island, she publicly stated her enthusiasm over the creation of a national park:

"I'm having a good time and rest here. 'The Island' is very lovely in its autumn coloring. The farm where the scene of *Anne of Green Gables* was laid is part of the block of land being purchased by the Government for a National Park, so Anne's haunts will be preserved as they are and my dear old woods will never be sold to someone who might not care for them when the present owner passes on.

"I had forgotten that my Island was so lovely. It is always a fresh revelation when I come back to it."

As Gerson has noted, however, privately Montgomery "mourned the desecration of her 'dear woods' by 'hordes of sight seers and by pleasure hunters.'"[23] Moreover, Montgomery's speeches during the 1930s also started to focus more and more on the importance of preserving the past: "Don't let the wonderful tales and legends told you by your grandparents and the old people of today die," she declared in a 1935 speech reported on in the Toronto *Globe*. "Even if you have no literary ability yourself, write them down and preserve them – they will give color to our native Canadian history and literature." In a similar speech two years later, also reported on in the *Globe* (which in 1936 merged with the *Mail and Empire* to become the *Globe and Mail*), she encouraged her listeners to record the "tremendous amount of literary material in Canada which will pass away when those who know the stories pass away." In this 1937 speech, she added that "when I came to Ontario – I was a minister's wife – I thought it was not safe to lay the scene in Ontario lest all my husband's congregation think they were in the book."[24]

Montgomery's self-awareness about her own celebrity is also evident in a number of letters published in the 1920s, at a time when she was taking advantage of the fact that her fame and her readership were at their peak to help her promote the importance of Canadian literature. In a letter appearing in *Successful Authorship*, a "handbook" for writers published by Shaw Schools in Toronto around 1922, Montgomery responded favourably to their invitation to join their advisory board: "Your letter came to-day, together with the synopsis of your Course in Story Writing and some lessons. I think the idea is an excellent one and, judging from the synopsis, your course should be of great value to beginners in literature. I am especially pleased with the lesson on 'Style.' I think that the greatest want in our Canadian writers, with sadly few exceptions, is style. If your Course did nothing more than teach young writers how to acquire a good and distinctive style, it would be of inestimable benefit to Canadian literature." In a 1923 article in the Regina *Morning Leader* entitled "Do We Canadians Need a School of Manners?" Laura Mason noted that Montgomery's response, "which, amid the distractions of a double career, she has generously made time to send, carries the sanction of a close observer of life in one of our best-mannered provinces, supplemented by the experience of the mistress of an Ontario manse": "I can only say that, as far as my observation goes, I haven't noticed any special deterioration of manners. Of course we have not the 'finished' manners of older civilizations. But as for real kindness, courtesy and consideration I think the present generation has quite as much of it as any preceding one. I do not see that a 'school of manners' is required. The said verities of courtesy and consideration should be taught as a matter of course in our homes and schools. Compared with them mere conventional etiquette matters very little." Always keen to show off her literary prowess, Montgomery closed this letter with a quotation from Tennyson's "Idylls of the King": "Manners are not idle but the fruit / Of loyal nature and of noble mind."[25]

Furthermore, in *The House of Stokes 1881–1926*, a book of "letters from authors on the forty-fifth anniversary of the establishment of the publishing house of Frederick A. Stokes Company," Montgomery's contribution not only reveals her gratitude to her second American publisher on her tenth anniversary with the firm but indirectly speaks volumes about the shabby treatment she had received from her first publisher, L.C. Page and Company, with whom she was still embroiled in a series of lawsuits: "In those ten years I have never once regretted our 'partnership.' Your unfailing courtesy, consideration, and 'square dealing' have made our connection one of pleasure as well as profit to me and I sincerely hope that this pleasant relationship will continue as long as I am afflicted with the incurable disease of *cacoethes scribendi*." Although the subtext of this letter would not be made apparent in her lifetime, she had already given a number of talks containing "some good advice born of my sorrows with the Page Co.," with whom she had parted company under bad terms in 1919. One clipping covers a speech in which she "told something of herself as a writer and the difficulties which she had earlier encountered."[26] And in one instance, Montgomery wrote a letter of inspiration to the Rainbow Club, a popular newspaper column for children by *Halifax Herald* reporter Laura P. Carten, who wrote under the pseudonym "Farmer Smith." In a letter dated 15 March 1927, Montgomery offered her readers a sentiment that would anticipate an observation she would make in her journals about herself more than two years later: "I like to leave people laughing":

I had met a certain woman. She wasn't young, she wasn't beautiful, she wasn't clever. Not even very modern. She didn't say a brilliant thing all the time we talked together. But somehow, she made me feel so nice and cheerful and hopeful – as if the world were really a decent place full of nice people. After she had gone someone said; "Mrs. A. always makes you feel so much happier."

Now, isn't that a lovely thing to have said about you – that you always left the people you had been talking to "feeling happier"? I don't think there could be a finer ideal for a Rainbow to have. And everyone does – or should – feel happier when he sees a rainbow. So please live up to your name.

Here's wishing everyone of you luck and a pot of gold. You know there's always a pot of gold at the end of every rainbow. Only, it's fairy gold and folks aren't always wise enough to know it when they see it. So they throw it away and are sorry ever after.[27]

Letters reproduced in full in this volume – on anticipated outcomes of the Great War for Canadian women, on the future of Canadian literature, and on her six favourite novels in the English language and her three favourite Canadian novels (both of which involved difficult decisions, although for opposite reasons) – indicate that Montgomery's opinion was actively sought in the mainstream media of the time. Even letters to unidentified friends and fans made the news, as happened with a letter about the Canadian war effort published in an American newspaper prior to the involvement of the United States in the Great War (see chapter 26 in this volume) and a 1919 response to a fan letter (see chapter 32 in this volume). In a letter dated around 1932, Montgomery even mentioned that "this summer a party of Americans hunted all through the graveyard at Cavendish, P.E.I., for my monument! Isn't that gruesome?" As well, an unidentified clipping from around 1929 quotes what is apparently a letter from Montgomery written while she was vacationing in Prince Edward Island:

Yesterday down at the beach I met an old Irishman, a grizzled old chap whom no one would ever suspect of reading a book in his life. He came up to me exclaiming, "Shure and it's meself never thought to have the honor of shaking hands wid ye. I've read every book ye ever wrote, and it's hoping I am ye'll live forever and go on writing books. Ye're the bright star of Prince Edward Island and we're all proud of ye, Lord bless ye."

However, lest this should give me "swelled head," the next person we encountered looked very black when I was introduced as "L.M. Montgomery."

"Have you ever read any of her books?" asked my introducer, a little dashed.

"No!" said the lady. "Is she a Baptist?"

I have not been able to puzzle out the connection. Had she registered a solemn vow to read nothing save what was written by a Baptist? Or did she believe that nobody but a Baptist could write anything worth reading? Or did she just think I looked like a Baptist? I shall never know.[28]

It is not always clear whether these letters were published with her consent or not: an article quoting Montgomery's letter in which she declined to enter a PEI literary competition on the grounds that it would "scarcely be fair to the other competitors for a professional writer to answer" added that Montgomery's "words, above quoted, although not intended for publication, are an inspiration also and we commend them to our readers."[29] But at least they are likely to be a more accurate transcript of her words than speeches that were covered in newspapers, for which reporters used longhand notes to reconstruct direct quotations after the fact. For instance, although part of the lore of *Anne of Green Gables* is that Montgomery typed her manuscript on an "old second-hand typewriter that never makes the capitals plain and won't print 'w' at all,"[30] in a 1935 speech at the Royal York Hotel this typewriter suddenly "wouldn't print the 'm's' at all, and had a crooked 'y.'"[31] As well, in her essays and interviews Montgomery frequently provided specific distances between Cavendish and the nearest railway, town, or telephone to emphasize the isolation of her rural community, but the exact figures were rarely consistent. Montgomery occasionally made corrections in her journals and scrapbooks – once even writing in her scrapbook in ink that a particular interview had never actually occurred (see chapter 18, "Interviews with Authors," by Anne E. Nias, in this volume) – so in the absence of a correction in her copies of these items, we can be reasonably sure that her words were reported accurately or, at the very least, that she was not sufficiently bothered by an inaccuracy to correct it. But while Montgomery continued to receive excellent coverage in the mainstream press till the end of her life, there was another form of media attention over which she had no control and little recourse – academic and journalistic criticism.

"A Good Deal of Nonsense"

Although it has been generally assumed that Montgomery's work was either ignored or denigrated by academic critics throughout her lifetime, such a statement tells only part of the story. An early sign of Montgomery's endurance as an author occurred in a report, published in the *Manitoba Free Press* in May 1910, of comments made about Canadian authors by Arthur Spurgeon, managing director of Cassels Publishing in London: the article reported his belief that "great things might be expected from Miss Montgomery," and that "she would be one of the powers that would count in the days to come." Twelve extracts from *Anne of Green Gables* and *Anne of Avonlea* appeared in *Canadian Days: Selections for Every Day in the Year from the Works of Canadian Authors*, a book compiled by the Toronto Women's Press Club and published around 1911. An entry on Montgomery appeared in Henry James Morgan's *The Canadian Men and Women of the Time* in 1912; although the entry appears under the name "McDonald, Mrs. Lucy Maud" and lists an erroneous birth date of 1877, it includes extracts from glowing reviews of her books. In Thomas Guthrie Marquis's *English-Canadian Literature*, published the following year, Montgomery is referred to as an author "who was to make Prince Edward Island, its inhabitants and external nature, known to the world as they never had been before ... Sympathy with child life and humble life, delight in nature, a penetrating, buoyant imagination, unusual power in handling the simple romantic material that lies about every one, and a style direct and pleasing, make these books delightful reading for children and, indeed, for readers of all ages."[32]

The question of whether Montgomery wrote for children or for adults was never settled conclusively even during these early years (a matter that returns in the reviews collected in Volume 3 of *The L.M. Montgomery Reader*), but whether they saw Montgomery's books as intended for adults or for children or for both, commentators at the time were for the most part lavish with their praise. In an unidentified clipping from around 1918, a Miss Lillian Leveridge of Brighton, Ontario, contributed an article entitled "Some Canadian Women in Song and Story":

> L.M. Montgomery's work is quite unique, and literary critics eminently capable of judging, have praised it very highly. This young author, of whom we are justly proud, has been characterized as "the Jane Austen of Canada," in that her work, like that of the famous English author, is a truthful portrayal of rural domestic life. For she

does not go abroad for her themes, but expends her rare gifts of imaginative and creative genius in revealing to us the beauty, humor and pathos of simple everyday life as she knows it. Her work is not strong in plot – it does not need to be – but because it so faithfully mirrors Canadian country life, with just enough idealism to make it a work of art rather than a photograph, it has a high value, not only in Canadian, but in wider fields of literature. A love of nature and of beauty in every form, and an overflowing spring of fresh enthusiasm and love of life are noticeable in all her work. Those readers who are overfed on romance and look for thrills on every page may find her books unsatisfying; but those who delight in simple literary beauty and the fresh, sweet spirit of youth – the beauty and spirit of Nature's own landscape garden rather than of the symmetrical city plot – will be grateful to our young author for the real pleasure she has afforded.[33]

An article on "Women in Canadian Literature" published in the Toronto *Globe* in 1919 offered a list of "characteristics" of Montgomery's fiction: "Delight in nature, buoyant imagination, and a direct and pleasing style. She makes us feel that Prince Edward Island is indeed an Island of the Blest, and that its young people are the most charming of the species to be met with anywhere on earth." Finally, in an article published in *The Canadian Bookman* that same year, E.J. Hathaway (1871–1930) declared that "there is perhaps no more winsome child in all fiction than Anne Shirley," and that while Anne had already appeared in three sequels by then, "the author has not even yet exhausted her infinite variety."[34]

In the 1920s, a number of critics, editors, and authors mobilized to disseminate Canadian literature, firstly by founding the Canadian Authors' Association in 1921 (Montgomery was active in the Toronto branch despite living in the rural community of Leaskdale),[35] and secondly by publishing several book-length studies of Canadian literature. Of the "six literary surveys" from the 1920s mentioned in W.H. New's *A History of Canadian Literature* (2003), Montgomery is mentioned in detail in five – and the sixth, by Ray Palmer Baker, ends at Confederation.[36] *Highways of Canadian Literature* (1924) was written jointly by J.D. Logan, who according to Montgomery had gone up to her at a social function the year before exclaiming "Hail, Queen of Canadian Novelists," and Donald G. French, who in 1921 had published a short article in the *Globe* commenting on Montgomery's "creative gifts in portraying the beauty, the humor and the pathos that lies about our daily paths" and praising *Rilla of Ingleside* to the skies.[37] In addition to providing a biographical sketch and a summary of her books to date and including her on a list of authors who had produced "aesthetically satisfying poetry," Logan and French noted that, although "her life has been spent chiefly within the limits of the little island province and the bounds of an Ontario country parish," this fact "does not narrow her outlook although she confines herself to themes bounded by rural experiences, for her forte is the portrayal of what she has seen and knows. She has imaginative and creative gifts, but she uses these in enabling us to see the beauty, the humour, and the pathos that lies about our daily paths." Calling Anne "an entirely new character in fiction," they echoed the suggestion that Montgomery's novels were not big on plot, but added that "the community type of fiction does not demand thrilling plots. Other writers can write plot stories, but most other writers do not hold before us the mirror of Canadian country life."[38]

Montgomery's work also received attention in Archibald MacMechan's *The Headwaters of Canadian Literature*, published the same year. Montgomery had taken a course with MacMechan at Dalhousie College in 1895–96 (referring to him in her journal as "rather a weak man"), but his enthusiasm for Montgomery's work was decidedly more tepid than Logan and French's. After describing the character Anne and the book's popularity extensively, MacMechan concluded that "the Canadian book just misses the kind of success which convinces the critic while it captivates the unreflecting general reader. The story is pervaded with a sense of reality; the pitfalls of the sentimental are deftly avoided; Anne and her friends are healthy human beings; their pranks are engaging; but the 'little more' in truth of representation, or deftness of touch, is lacking; and that makes the difference between a clever book and a masterpiece."[39] Although Waterston relies on MacMechan's remarks to suggest that "critical respect for the work of L.M. Montgomery dimmed" by the 1920s, it is worth considering exactly what MacMechan actually had in mind by "little more." The same year that Montgomery praised Canadian literature for being "clean" (see chapter 39, "Proud That Canadian Literature Is Clean," in this volume), MacMechan vilified it – all of it – for being "tame. It bears everywhere the stamp of the amateur. Nowhere can be traced that fiery conviction which alone brings forth a masterpiece. Modern problems are as yet untouched, unapproached. Direct, honest realism is also sadly to seek, though subjects are crying aloud for treatment on every side ... So far Canadian fiction is conventional, decent, unambitious, *bourgeois*. It has nowhere risen to the heights or plumbed the depths of life in Canada."[40] MacMechan's criticism of Montgomery's "clever book" was thus not about her book at all; rather, it emerged out of his yearning for a form of Canadian realism that – in his view at least – did not yet exist. As for Montgomery, her only response to this commentary was to "raise[] a laugh" in her journal over MacMechan's suggestion that her writing was informed by her marriage to a Presbyterian minister: "Critics generally imagine a good deal of nonsense."[41]

Waterston adds that Lionel Stevenson's *Appraisals of Canadian Literature* (1926) "reinforced the patronizing tone,"[42] a stance certainly borne out by his remark that a "juster reflection of Canadian life, although tinged with sentimentalism of a conventional sort dear to numerous readers," could be found in Montgomery's depictions of "placid rural life of the older maritime provinces," not to mention his backhanded observation that the "passages of splendid farce" in her novels "give a very strong impression of being events from real life introduced arbitrarily into the narrative." Elsewhere in his book, he divided the "rest of Canadian fiction" into two groups, each "typified by the authors who have won the greatest success in practising them," naming one after Ralph Connor (1860–1937), the author of numerous popular westerns and adventure stories, and one after Montgomery (whose books "deal chiefly with character"). While this is hardly a shining endorsement of her work, it is worth noting that, unlike the more comprehensive *Headwaters* and *Highways*, Stevenson's study was "concerned only with literature that is inherently of some distinctive Canadian quality," so the very inclusion of Montgomery's work in his book is indicative of his positive view of its worth.[43] Moreover, Stevenson's mixed messages are certainly much more encouraging than Isabel Paterson's unambiguously negative comments in a 1922 article in the New York *Bookman*: "One does not foresee any further development for L.M. Montgomery. Her spun sugar creations are immaterial to the progress of the Canadian novel. Immensely popular though they are, they cannot even do any harm, because the peculiar kind of very real talent needed to confect such pleasant and pretty trifles is much rarer than the mechanical ingenuity and platitudinous piety required for a Bindloss or a Ralph Connor."[44] Here she is lumping Montgomery not only with Connor's popular westerns but also with those of Harold Edward Bindloss (1866–1945), an English author who wrote forty novels set in western Canada between 1902 and 1943. Even so, she later gave glowing reviews of Montgomery's *Emily of New Moon* and *Emily Climbs* (included in Volume 3 of *The L.M. Montgomery Reader*), indicating that her opinion of Montgomery's work evolved over time.

Montgomery received her most negative treatment in her lifetime from William Arthur Deacon, with whom she was active in the Toronto branch of the Canadian Authors' Association (CAA) and whose 1926 book *Poteen: A Pot-Pourri of Canadian Essays* compared Montgomery's "series of girls' sugary stories" to the "quick popularity" of Connor: "Canadian fiction was to go no lower; and she is only mentioned to show the dearth of mature novels at the time." Deacon's animosity toward Montgomery and Connor extended further when he even denigrated fellow critics who saw their work as worthy of study: "a critic who would divide between Ralph Connor and Lucy M. Montgomery ... a quarter of the space devoted to the last 30 years, is not to be taken altogether seriously."[45] As Mary Henley Rubio has noted, Deacon's animosity toward Montgomery's writing emerged as part of his attempt to build for himself a reputation not only as a literary journalist but also as a powerful critic in the field of Canadian literature, first as literary editor of *Saturday Night* between 1922 and 1928 (Montgomery had published a number of poems in this periodical, although not between these dates) and later as book review editor of the *Mail and Empire* (later the *Globe and Mail*) between 1928 and 1961. As Rubio suggests, "Deacon enjoyed flying in the face of the prevailing public opinion (and most critical opinion) with his complete dismissal of Maud's books," and, moreover, his "ongoing hostility to her and her writing seemed more personal than professional," given that they knew each other through their work with the CAA. This animosity culminated in Deacon snubbing Montgomery publicly at Canada's National Book Week in November 1935 and elbowing her out of the CAA executive in April 1938.[46]

Yet it would be a mistake to assume that Deacon's pronouncements on Montgomery's fiction set the tone for what followed. In 1927, Lorne Pierce (1890–1961) made two positive albeit tentative comments about Montgomery's work in *An Outline of Canadian Literature (French and English)*, noting first that *Anne of Green Gables* was "deservedly a classic of its kind, not because of its excellence of style or plot, but because of the altogether charming character, Anne," and second, regarding Montgomery's *The Watchman and Other Poems* (1916), that her "long list of successful novels contain many passages of fine imaginative prose; while her poems are simple and sincere, it is as a storyteller that she will be remembered."[47] Also in 1927, Vernon Blair Rhodenizer (1886–1968) published a glowing overview of Montgomery's body of work in the "Who's Who in Canadian Literature" series of essays published in *The Canadian Bookman*, an official CAA publication (see chapter 47 in this volume).

Rhodenizer extended his admiration for Montgomery's work in a review of *Emily's Quest* (reproduced in Volume 3 of *The L.M. Montgomery Reader*) and in his 1930 book *A Handbook of Canadian Literature*, in which he added that "a reading of *The Blue Castle* ... will convince the student of L.M. Montgomery's works that her future fame depends upon her stories of children."[48] That same year, a brief, descriptive entry for *Anne of Green Gables* ("The setting of this Canadian story is laid in Prince Edward Island") appeared in the first edition of *Books for Boys and Girls*, a compendium compiled by the Toronto Public Library. As Leslie McGrath notes, this brief entry was "a coded endorsement," because, as with Stevenson's *Appraisals*, the inclusion of the novel in this study "is itself indicative of the book's quality."[49]

Even Montgomery's poetry – largely unknown to today's readers and largely ignored by today's scholars – received high praise during her lifetime. In an article entitled "Sweet Singers of Canada" and published in *The Methodist Review*, a New York periodical, in July 1920, Rudolf A. Clemens profiled Montgomery alongside Charles G.D. Roberts (1860–1943), Wilfred Campbell (1860–1918), Bliss Carman (1861–1929), and Pauline Johnson (1861–1913), making her by far the youngest of the group. As Clemens noted in his opening remarks, "Canadian poets ... are poets of Nature to a degree not often excelled in other literatures. 'Our Lady of the Snows,' as Canada is called, has impressed her people with the moods of her wonderful landscapes. Besides being simply the expression of nature in Canada the best Canadian literature has often sprung out of significant events in the country's history. Indeed, in a word, Canadian literature is a distinctly national literature." Quoting extracts from Montgomery's poems "The Old Home Calls" and "When the Dark Comes Down," the article continued:

> The last poet we consider here is Miss L.M. Montgomery, whom one could never leave out, for her fame is secure as the creator of Anne of Green Gables ... Knowing the novelist one is not surprised at her being a poet. One with her joyous outlook in [*sic*] life, vivid imagination, instinct for words and facility of expression could not help being a poet. More than that, she has lived nearly all her life in Prince Edward Island, where the fairies are said to live. In truth Miss Montgomery, or Mrs. MacDonald [*sic*] as she is now, was a poet long before she began to write prose. Indeed it is doubtful if she has ever been anything else, for Anne Shirley is essentially a creature of sentiment and imagination and of those qualities of heart and

brain which are the product of the poetic mind. Her verse is quite as perfect as her prose, and her lyrics, especially those dealing with the smiling aspects of her native forest, its fragrant fields of red earth and the "blue sea coming up on every side," are of rare quality, delicate, lilting, and full of music.[50]

Two additional publishing patterns indicate further that Montgomery's critical reputation and popularity were not yet waning in the 1920s. As the academic and middlebrow conversations continued in Canada during this period, Montgomery's earliest books were being published in new, standard editions in England and Australia beginning in 1925; this marked a "turning-point in L.M. Montgomery's climb to fame" in those two countries.[51] In addition, Montgomery's work was still being widely anthologized. "Dog Monday's Vigil," a self-contained story adapted from a subplot in *Rilla of Ingleside*, appeared in *Our Canadian Literature: Representative Prose and Verse* (1922), compiled by Albert Durrant Watson and Lorne Albert Pierce. Montgomery's poem "Love's Prayer" appeared in *Canadian Singers and Their Songs: A Collection of Portraits and Autograph Poems* (1919) and in a revised edition, subtitled *A Collection of Portraits, Autograph Poems and Brief Biographies* (1925), both compiled by Edward S. Caswell. Four extracts from *Anne's House of Dreams* and the poem "Off to the Fishing Ground" were included in *Standard Canadian Reciter: A Book of the Best Readings and Recitations from Canadian Literature* (1921), compiled by Donald Graham French.[52] Her poem "Our Women," first published in John W. Garvin's *Canadian Poems of the Great War* (1918), was reprinted in *Songs of the Maritimes* (1931), edited by Eliza Ritchie. Garvin's anthologies *Canadian Poets* (1916) and *Canadian Verse for Boys and Girls* (1930) contain a total of eight poems by Montgomery.[53] An extract from the initial chapter of *Emily of New Moon* appeared in *The Voice of Canada: Canadian Prose and Poetry* (1926), edited by A.M. Stephen. Although academic critics were ambivalent about including Montgomery's work in their vision for a canon of Canadian Literature, the presence of her work in so many anthologies indicates that this ambivalence was far from consistent.

Montgomery's critical reputation in the 1930s is less straightforward to determine, primarily because the kind of survey of Canadian literature offered in *Headwaters* and *Highways* was not redone during this decade. Yet, as the materials collected in Volume 3 of *The L.M. Montgomery Reader* demonstrate, her work continued to be reviewed prominently and favourably throughout the final decade of her life, in such periodicals as the *Globe, Punch,* the *New York Times Book Review, The Canadian Bookman,* the *Los Angeles Times, University of Toronto Quarterly, Saturday Night,* and the *Times Literary Supplement.* Entries on Montgomery appeared in the 1934 *Who's Who* (where her recreations included "reading, walking and motoring") and in the 1934 *Junior Book of Authors,* and she even copied out her standard autobiographical sketch "shortly before her death" for inclusion in *Twentieth Century Authors: A Biographical Dictionary of Modern Literature* (1942).[54]

As well, *Anne of Green Gables* appeared third in a 1937 poll on favourite books and their authors in *The Family Herald and Weekly Star,* a Montreal farm paper, behind Charles Dickens's *David Copperfield* and the Judeo-Christian Bible, an achievement that led columnist Roderick Kennedy to make a bold proclamation about her work:

> She tells a good story which holds interest from start to finish. She draws heroines who seem to live, and who are distinguished by fundamental sweetness, cheerfulness, and courage. Those qualities of the heart are more highly valued than any others among men and women of the country-side, and consequently they love L.M. Montgomery's characters ... Her books are not great literature, but they are sincere and wholesome, and in spite of her tendency to make people too perfect and to gloss over the fact that the sweetest kindliness cannot conquer every problem, there is something permeating her work which makes it enjoyable to a large number of sophisticated readers. And, in spite of the essential femininity of her books they yet have an appeal even to husky, red-blooded young men, such as I was when I fell in love with "Anne of Green Gables," at college![55]

Moreover, one of her last published pieces, an essay on "Prince Edward Island" that had been solicited for *The Spirit of Canada* (1939), a commemorative booklet in honour of the Royal Visit of George VI and Queen Elizabeth (later known as the Queen Mother) and that appears as chapter 69 in this volume, was accompanied by a biographical note that identified her as "the outstanding interpreter of Prince Edward Island and the Canadian Girl."[56]

When L.M. Montgomery died in April 1942, her death and funeral received extensive coverage in a number of newspapers across Canada, as well as tributes in two Toronto periodicals, *Saturday Night* and *The Presbyterian Record,* all of which are included in full in this volume.

In a third tribute essay published in *The Maritime Advocate and Busy East* shortly after Montgomery's death, Aida B. McAnn declared that "many such delightful Island 'characters' are charmingly portrayed in Miss Montgomery's books, along with a cheerful, wholesome, happy, healthful way of life that seems well-nigh Utopian to our present war-plagued generation. There is no pleasanter 'escape literature' than the Anne Books." But in the same article, McAnn referred to Green Gables House erroneously as "the same neat white farmhouse with the green trimmings that it had been sixty-six years ago, when a little girl, one year old, came there to live with her grandparents." Attempting to correct such mistakes in the tourist sites related to *Anne of Green Gables* proved to be uphill work, however. In 1945, Montgomery's eldest son, Chester Macdonald, responded to a newspaper article in the *Tillsonburg News* about the Prince Edward Island National Park that stated that the "Lake of Shining Waters" was in Cavendish – a recurring misconception that Montgomery had noted in her journals as early as 1911 (what had inspired her, she wrote, was the pond at Park Corner). Responding to the article's blending of fact and fiction, Macdonald wrote concerning his mother: "in the mind of the author there never was a 'real' Green Gables ... It is true that the lane through the woods at Ernest Webb's farm, which is the present so-called Green Gables, was the original of the 'Lovers' Lane' immortalized in the books ... but certain it is that the 'Lake of Shining Waters' ... is not at Cavendish, where the Travel Bureau has placed it in the middle of the Green Gables Golf Course, and never was."[57]

As I show in Volume 2 of *The L.M. Montgomery Reader*, the recovery of Montgomery's work as worthy of scholarly attention occurred within a larger evolution in the creation of a canon of Canadian literature, a project started in the 1920s and pursued with renewed energy in the 1960s and 1970s. In the meantime, what would keep Montgomery's name alive after her death were her readers: whether they saw her books as "escape literature," harmless girls' books, sophisticated writing for adults, or a combination of all three, these readers continued to buy her books in sufficient quantities to keep them in print. Presumably they found, as did McAnn in her 1942 essay, that "the spirit of L.M. Montgomery is imperishable; and Anne of Green Gables, the child of her brain, is immortal."[58]

NOTES

1 Gerson, *"Anne of Green Gables,"* 18; see also Gerson, "Seven Milestones," 27–28. For further iterations of this genesis story, see Rubio, "Why L.M. Montgomery's Journals," 474–75; Rubio, *Lucy Maud Montgomery*, 2–8; Epperly, "L.M. Montgomery"; Åhmansson, *A Life and Its Mirrors*, 13–25; Reimer, "Introduction," 2; Gammel, "Introduction," 3–4; Steffler, "Anne in a 'Globalized' World," 152; Waterston, *Kindling Spirit*, 19–24.
2 Rubio and Waterston, *Writing a Life*, 12.
3 Rubio, "Introduction," 5–6; Gammel, "Making Avonlea," 8–10.
4 See the website for L.M. Montgomery Online at http://lmmonline.org for a comprehensive resource of scholarly contributions on L.M. Montgomery's work and its afterlives.
5 For more on the middlebrow and the work of female authors such as Montgomery, see Hammill, *Women, Celebrity, and Literary Culture*, 9–13.
6 Chief among these is Rea Wilmshurst (1941–1996), who spent countless hours in libraries searching for Montgomery's periodical pieces long before the digital age, publishing *Lucy Maud Montgomery: A Preliminary Bibliography* (1986) in collaboration with Ruth Weber Russell and D.W. Russell as well as eight collections of Montgomery's short stories.
7 Gammel, "Introduction," 4.
8 Montgomery, 6 March 1901, in *SJLMM*, 1: 257.
9 *The Patriot*, "Our Island Poets," 2.
10 Montgomery, 16 March 1904, in *SJLMM*, 1: 294; Montgomery, 22 December 1900, in *SJLMM*, 1: 255.
11 Montgomery to MacMillan, 31 August 1908, in *MDMM*, 39, 40; Montgomery to Weber, 10 September 1908, in *GGL*, 75; Montgomery, 15 October 1908, in *SJLMM*, 1: 340.
12 *The Boston Herald*, "Week-End Book Notes," 9. In 1930, responding to this allegation that she taught school in Cavendish, she wrote in her journal, "Not guilty" (Montgomery, 1 March 1930, in *SJLMM*, 4: 41).
13 Montgomery, 10 November 1908, in *SJLMM*, 1: 342.
14 *The Boston Herald*, "Mid-Week Book Notes," 7.
15 Pike, "Mass Marketing, Popular Culture," 246.
16 Montgomery, 5 January 1917, in *SJLMM*, 2: 202, 206.
17 *The Saskatoon Star–Phoenix*, "Author of 'Anne' Books," 8.
18 Montgomery, "Letters from the Literati," 4.
19 "L.M. Montgomery: An Explanation Regarding the Publication of Her Different Books," *Toronto World*, undated clipping, in SR, 39. The review to which she responds appears in Volume 3 of *The L.M. Montgomery Reader*.

20 Chesterfield, "Men and Women We Read About," 4; Montgomery, 1 March 1930, in *SJLMM*, 4: 42.

21 *The Boston Herald*, "With Books and Authors," 4; Ford, "Women's Work, Women's Clubs," 16; see also *The Writer*, "Montgomery," 4; *The Western Mail*, "Miss Montgomery's Methods," 36.

22 York, *Literary Celebrity in Canada*, 75, 78.

23 *The Globe*, "Anne of Windy Poplars," 21; Gerson, "Seven Milestones," 23; Montgomery, 15 October 1936, in *SJLMM*, 5: 99–100; Montgomery, 30 September 1936, in *SJLMM*, 5: 94; *The Guardian*, "Famous Island Authoress," 3; see also *The Gazette*, "Author Revisits P.E.I."

24 *The Globe*, "English Union Hears Author," 9; *The Globe and Mail*, "Old-Timers' Stories Source for Author," 5; also in Montgomery, Black Scrapbook, 2: 77; see also "Old Tales Are Not to Be Lost," unidentified and undated clipping, in SR, 389.

25 Montgomery to Shaw Correspondence School, undated letter, in *Successful Authorship*, 22; Mason, "Do We Canadians," Magazine Section 1.

26 Montgomery to "Mr. [Maynard] Dominick," 14 August 1926, in *The House of Stokes*, 72. The term *"cacoethes scribendi"* is Latin for "scribbling itch." Montgomery pasted photographs of both Stokes and Dominick in SR, 247. Montgomery, 27 January 1922, in *SJLMM*, 3: 37; untitled, unidentified, and undated clipping, in SR, 169.

27 Montgomery, 3 October 1929, in *SJLMM*, 4: 15; *Halifax Herald*, "Author of 'Anne of Green Gables,'" 7.

28 "The Anne Books," unidentified and undated clipping (ca. 1932), in SR, 371; untitled, unidentified, and undated clipping (ca. 1929), in SR, 330. Both anecdotes from the 1929 clipping appear in Montgomery, 22 September 1929, in *SJLMM*, 4: 8.

29 "Notes," unidentified and undated clipping (ca. 1911), quoting an undated letter from "Mrs. L.M. Montgomery McDonald [*sic*]," in SR, 43.

30 Montgomery, 16 August 1907, in *SJLMM*, 1: 331; see also *AP*, 75.

31 *The Globe*, "English Union Hears Author," 9.

32 *Manitoba Free Press*, "Bright Future for Canadian Letters," 16; Morgan, *The Canadian Men and Women*, 760; Marquis, *English-Canadian Literature*, 564–65.

33 Lillian Leveridge, "Some Canadian Women in Song and Story," unidentified and undated clipping (ca. 1918), in SR, 121. Montgomery was first referred to as "the Jane Austen of Canada" in a review of *Chronicles of Avonlea* that appears in Volume 3 of *The L.M. Montgomery Reader*.

34 *The Globe*, "Women in Canadian Literature," 20; Hathaway, "How Canadian Novelists," 19.

35 The Canadian Authors' Association (later the Canadian Authors Association) is a national organization devoted to the protection and development of Canadian authors, with branches across the country. It became responsible for *The Canadian Bookman*, a periodical that published several poems by Montgomery as well as reviews of her books, as well as *The Canadian Author*, to which Montgomery contributed an essay in 1937 (see chapter 67, "The Book and the Film," in this volume). The two periodicals eventually merged to form *Canadian Author and Bookman* and, later, *Canadian Author & Bookman and Canadian Poetry*.

36 New, *A History of Canadian Literature*, 132.

37 Montgomery, 30 April 1923, in *SJLMM*, 3: 128; French, "Rilla, Daughter of 'Anne'"; also in SR, 180.

38 Logan and French, *Highways of Canadian Literature*, 278, 298, 299, 300, 301.

39 Montgomery, 25 September 1895, in *SJLMM*, 1: 145; MacMechan, *The Headwaters of Canadian Literature*, 211.

40 Waterston, *Kindling Spirit*, 19; MacMechan, *The Headwaters of Canadian Literature*, 215.

41 Montgomery, 1 February 1925, in *SJLMM*, 3: 217. Montgomery also pasted in her scrapbook an unidentified and undated clipping that comments on both *Highways* and *Headwaters* and that criticizes the latter text for "treating the last two decades as 'the era of the best-seller,' ignoring writers of consequence in that epoch in favor of extended consideration of Ralph Connor and Lucy M. Montgomery" (SR, 222).

42 Waterston, *Kindling Spirit*, 20.

43 Stevenson, *Appraisals of Canadian Literature*, 31–32, 157, 128, vii; see also 131, 134–35. Stevenson's comments on Montgomery first appeared in near identical form in a 1924 article published in *English Review*.

44 Paterson, "The Absentee Novelists of Canada," 138; also in SR, 187.

45 Deacon, *Poteen*, 169, 210.

46 Rubio, *Lucy Maud Montgomery*, 356, 461; see also 464–65, 530–31.

47 Pierce, *An Outline of Canadian Literature*, 38, 107.

48 Rhodenizer, *A Handbook of Canadian Literature*, 102.

49 *Books for Boys and Girls*, 154; McGrath, "Reading with Blitheness," 104.

50 Clemens, "Sweet Singers of Canada," 610, 619–20. The phrase "blue sea coming up on every side" is apparently an allusion to Marjory MacMurchy's article "L.M. Montgomery: Story Writer," reproduced in this volume. It is worth noting that most of these introductory remarks appear with only minor variations in John W. Garvin's anthology *Canadian Poets* (1916), which also includes both of these poems, and are attributed to

E.J. Hathaway. Both poems excerpted in Clemens's article are also included in Garvin's anthology.

51 "Publisher's Postscript," 142. The new edition of *Anne of Green Gables* even called for a slightly revised and updated text (see Devereux, "A Note on the Text," 44–45). To date, textual studies of Montgomery's published texts have been limited to *Anne of Green Gables*, so it is not yet possible to determine whether any of the later texts have likewise been altered since their first edition.

52 See Montgomery, "Captain Jim's Enjoyment," "A Disappointment," "Miss Cornelia Makes a Call," and "Miss Cornelia's Startling Announcement."

53 "Sunrise along Shore," "Off to the Fishing Ground," "An Old Man's Grave," "When the Dark Comes Down," and "The Old Home Calls" appear in the former volume, and "The Way to Slumbertown," "Canadian Twilight," and "Oh, We Will Walk with Spring To-Day!" appear in the latter one.

54 *Who's Who 1934*, 2085; Montgomery, "L.M. Montgomery"; "Montgomery, Lucy Maude [*sic*]," 974.

55 *The Family Herald and Weekly Star*, "Five Favorite Books"; Kennedy, "Authors of Today," 38.

56 "Notes on Contributors," 58.

57 McAnn, "Life and Works of L.M. Montgomery," 20, 19. Montgomery, 27 February 1911, in *SJLMM*, 2: 40; Macdonald, Letter to the Editor; see also *The Tillsonburg News*, "Green Gables Included." The L.M. Montgomery Collection at the University of Guelph contains a number of Chester Macdonald's papers, including a diary kept from March to November 1945 and typescripts of short stories that have not been found in published form, with titles such as "Karnath of the Apes" (signed "C.C. 'Jerry' Macdonald"), "The Fighting Prince of Mars," "Jerry Mills and the Rangers," and "Doubling in Brass: A Jerry Mills Tale." For a glimpse of his professional life, see the article "Lawyer Son Tells about Writing of Authoress Mother" in the *Fort Williams Daily Times–Journal* in July 1946.

58 McAnn, "Life and Works of L.M. Montgomery," 19.

A Note on the Text

This volume is based on ninety-one items published in journals, magazines, newspapers, and books in Canada and the United States across a thirty-five-year period. In her own essays and letters, Montgomery frequently recycled extracts, quotations, and entire paragraphs from one publication to the next, sometimes repeating the same text with only minor variations decades after a first publication. In selecting material for this volume, I have tried to avoid excessive duplication and have omitted material that is already available elsewhere, particularly Montgomery's "The Alpine Path: The Story of My Career," a memoir published in six instalments in *Everywoman's World* in 1917 and reprinted in book form in 1974. Because I have opted whenever possible to include pieces in their entirety, some duplication has been unavoidable. Additional items that were better excerpted than reproduced in full are mentioned in the headnotes and explanatory notes that accompany each chapter.

In addition to journals and letters, Montgomery kept over a dozen scrapbooks filled with poems, short stories, articles, clippings, photographs, and reviews pertaining to her professional and personal lives. These scrapbooks indicate that Montgomery felt a need to document her life and her career; yet, although she took great care to preserve these items for posterity, in most instances she omitted bibliographical information and disrupted the chronology so that it is usually impossible to ascertain where or when these items first appeared. After several years of combing through old periodicals, sitting in front of microfilm readers, searching online databases, and relying on the assistance and discoveries of fellow researchers, I have tracked down many of these items to their original published sources, which are identified here for the first time. In many cases, this identification entailed matching typefaces or looking for internal clues in the text, but often it was the result of persistence (or what Montgomery would call "stick-to-it-iveness") or just dumb luck.

Because the pieces in this volume first appeared in a range of periodicals, I have retained the inconsistent use of American and Canadian spellings and styles. For ease of reading, I have silently corrected obvious errors in spelling and punctuation and standardized the capitalization of titles and subheads. I have italicized the titles of books and films as well as words and phrases that were bolded, underlined, or capitalized for emphasis in the copy texts. I have also corrected misspellings of names ("MacDonald" and "McDonald" instead of Macdonald, "Ann" and "Annie" instead of Anne, "Valancey" instead of Valancy, "MacNeil," "Macneil," "Macniell," "MacNeill," and "McNeil" instead of Macneill, "Ewen" and "Evan" instead of Ewan, "Wollner" instead of Woolner) and places ("Alvonlea," "Cavandish," "Leaksdale," "Leaskvale," "Prince Edward's Island"), but I comment on these corrections in the notes. All ellipses and phrases in parentheses or square brackets appear in the original publications; my occasional omissions are noted with [* * *]. If Montgomery makes a handwritten correction in a copy found in her scrapbooks, I treat it as authoritative and mention it in the notes. All other substantive corrections are likewise identified in the notes.

Titles of chapters appearing in square brackets are mine. Each chapter begins with a headnote that places the item in Montgomery's overall career. In the notes, I have tried whenever possible to identify literary allusions, quotations from Montgomery's own work, historical personages, archaic words and terms, misquotations, and factual errors, as a way of providing cultural and historical context to the primary texts. Readers who have been interested in tracing the literary allusions in her fiction will be pleased to see that Montgomery likewise peppers her essays and even her speech with allusions to past work. Unless stated otherwise, all quotations from the Judeo-Christian Bible are from the King James Version (KJV), and all definitions from the *OED* are from the Oxford English Dictionary Online.

For a comprehensive resource pertaining to L.M. Montgomery's legacy – editions, periodical pieces, textual transformations (including stage and screen adaptations, abridgments, rewrites, and parodies), posthumously published work, scholarship, and reviews – see the website for L.M. Montgomery Online at http://lmmonline.org.

1

[Such a Delightful Little Person]

—— 1908 ——

After *Anne of Green Gables* was published in June 1908, her publisher, L.C. Page and Company, promoted the novel aggressively, placing in major newspapers ads that included public endorsements of the book by prominent writers. The best known of these – by American author and humorist Samuel Clemens (1835–1910), otherwise known as Mark Twain – has often been misquoted, and a number of variations can be found in several of the items appearing in all three volumes of *The L.M. Montgomery Reader*. It appeared in a letter from Clemens's secretary to Montgomery in which "Mr. Clemens directs me to thank you for your charming book + says I may quote to you from his letter to Francis Wilson about it: 'In "Anne of Green Gables" you will find the dearest + most moving + delightful child since the immortal Alice.'" By Montgomery's account, she related the quotation to Page, who "worked it to the limit as a publicity morsel."[1] A notice in the *New York Times* provided a different take on the matter, claiming that Montgomery, who, "living in quiet Prince Edward's [*sic*] Island, is unaware of the ways of the advertiser, sent her book to Mark Twain in the innocent hope of amusing him, and was rather overwhelmed by receiving in reply his secretary's statement that in writing to Mr. Francis Wilson of the book, the master of his craft had named Anne 'the dearest and most moving and delightful child since the immortal Alice.' It is unnecessary to say that she was as much delighted as surprised."[2] The second major endorsement, by Canadian-born New England poet Bliss Carman, is not as well known today, although an excerpt appeared alongside the Twain quotation in at least one ad (see frontispiece). The novel was also endorsed by Marguerite Linton Glentworth, Chairman of the New York Women's Press Club, who promised to "recommend it to all as a book to drive away the blues," and by Sir Louis Henry Davies of the Supreme Court of Canada (and formerly Premier of PEI), who stated, "I can hardly tell you how much I enjoyed the book. I have not read anything more delightful than this story in years."[3]

Anne of Green Gables, by L.M. Montgomery, one of the recent publications of L.C. Page & Co., of Boston, has been received with great favor by the press and public. The publishers are in receipt of the following letter from the well-known poet and essayist, Bliss Carman, with regard to the charming story:

"If I have been tardy in making my acknowledgments for Anne of Green Gables, it has not been for lack of appreciation. I notice with satisfaction that she has become one of the popular young ladies of the season. But I can assure you that if she had no one else to love her, I should still be her most devoted admirer. Such a delightful little person and so refreshing after the too numerous and far too sensational heroines of the hour.

"One can bask in such a presence as in a mild salubrious air. And it is no small triumph for an author to make so genuine a success by such simple, straight-forward means – nothing facetious in the book, no strain for effect, no reliance in dialect or novelty – just plain old-fashioned sufficient human nature.

"And I take it as a great test of the worth of the book that while the children are rummaging all over the house looking for Anne, the head of the house has carried her off to read on his way to town. That is real success, isn't it? Henceforth Anne must always remain one of the immortal children of fiction, those characters who are as real as our flesh and blood friends, and whom we treasure in the quiet places of our hearts reserved for the dearest mortals we know."

NOTES

1 J.V. Lyon to Montgomery, 3 October 1908, reproduced in *SJLMM*, 5: 332; Montgomery, 8 May 1939, in *SJLMM*, 5: 331. Francis Wilson (1854–1935), American actor and playwright.
2 *The New York Times*, "The Week's News of Boston Books," SR692.
3 *The Sun*, ad for *Anne of Green Gables*, 8; *The Boston Herald*, "From Page's List," 7.

2

Author Tells How He Wrote His Story

—— 1908 ——

This short article, published in the *Boston Journal* on 21 November 1908, quotes a letter from Montgomery that shows the author already striving to create a public persona that would suit her private nature. While the subhead states that "L.M. Montgomery Says the Tale Grew from a Serial Story into a Novel," she in fact refused to provide even the most basic personal information about herself, to the point that the newspaper editor evidently could not detect that she was a woman.

L.M. Montgomery, the author of *Anne of Green Gables*, tells the following interesting story of the growth of that popular novel:

"Ever since I can remember I wrote stories and verse for my own amusement. When I grew up I began to write them for other people's amusement. One day the editor of a Sunday school weekly asked me to write him a juvenile serial of seven or ten chapters. I looked through an old dog-eared, much abused note book for an idea and came across the following note, written years ago in my teens.

"'Elderly couple decide to adopt a boy from an orphan asylum. By mistake a girl is sent them.'

"I decided this would do for the central idea of my serial. I blocked out ten chapters and hunted out a few suitable incidents from the same old note book. I meant it to be a quiet little yarn with a well-behaved little heroine and a nice little moral snugly tucked away in it. If I had had time to sit right down then and there and write it, that is all it probably would have been and 'Anne' would have begun and ended her career in the pages of the aforesaid Sunday school weekly.

"By the time I was free to get to work I knew that a seven chapter serial could never hold all I wanted to say about her; and for the first time the idea of writing a book came to me.

"The characters in the book are all imaginary – that is, no one person sat for the portrait of any of them. But many of the incidents recorded happened in my childhood to me, or my playmates and many of the places are drawn from life. The 'haunted wood,' with its motley crowd of specters, had a very real and – to a certain trio of children – a very terrifying existence once, and 'lovers' lane' is still as green and beautiful a seclusion as when Anne's girlish feet danced through it. As for the episode of the liniment cake, why, the mistress of a quiet little Methodist parsonage in New Brunswick will remember things about that if she ever reads it."[1]

NOTES

1 In their notes to *The Complete Journals of L.M. Montgomery: The PEI Years, 1889–1900*, Mary Henley Rubio and Elizabeth Hillman Waterston identify the minister's wife in question as Ada Estey of Bideford, PEI (*CJLMM*, 1: 231n1).

3

Origin of Popular Book

—— 1908 ——

Less than a month after the publication of the letter in the *Boston Journal*, a second letter appeared in the *Brooklyn Daily Eagle* on 21 December 1908. After covering much of the same ground regarding the genesis and mapping out of Anne's "career" as a Sunday school serial, Montgomery diverted from her script and offered new details about her work schedule and her creative process. The similarities as well as the differences between the two letters suggest either that Montgomery provided a longer master letter that newspaper editors shortened as they saw fit, or that – more likely – she simply copied out the same material and varied it as needed. Indeed, the downplaying of her work as an author echoes a similar narrative strategy that she deploys in her journals, where she also referred to her novel as "a labor of love"; however, in a letter to Ephraim Weber she was far less self-effacing about the writing process: "I revised and re-wrote and altered words until I nearly bewildered myself."[1]

L.M. Montgomery, the author of *Anne of Green Gables*, was asked recently as to the origin of her clever book, and the following is her answer:

"Ever since I can remember I wrote stories and verse for my own amusement. When I grew up I began to write them for other people's amusement. One day the editor of a Sunday school weekly asked me to write him a juvenile serial of seven or ten chapters. I looked through an old dog-eared, much abused note book for an idea, and came across the following note, written in my teens: 'Elderly couple decide to adopt a boy from an orphan asylum. By mistake a girl is sent them.'

"I decided this would do for the central idea of my serial. I blocked out ten chapters and hunted out a few suitable incidents from the same old note book. I meant it to be a quiet little yarn, with a well-behaved little heroine and a nice little moral snugly tucked away in it. If I had had time to sit right down then and there and write it, that is all it probably would have been, and 'Anne' would have begun and ended her career in the pages of the aforesaid Sunday school weekly. I did not have the time to begin work on it, however, for several weeks. During these weeks I 'brooded' my story, and somehow Anne began to take possession of me. It is a mistake to say I 'created' her. I didn't. Like Topsey, she 'growed' on her own account,[2] and I had nothing to do with her development save to watch it and describe it. By the time I was free to get to work, I knew that a seven chapter serial could never hold all I wanted to say about her; and for the first time the idea of writing a book came to me. I wrote and sent a suitable serial about a boy to the Sunday school weekly, and then I began Anne. In view of her then uncertain future, I felt that I could not afford to take time from my regular magazine work for it; so I wrote the book in the evenings or at any odd spare time when I felt in the mood. It was a labor of love, and when I finished it I felt as sorry to part with my characters as if they were 'real folks' with whom I had been living.

"As for Anne's name, it was never selected with malice prepense. She was 'Anne' from the start – popping into my fancy, with her red hair and big eyes, all ready christened, even to the all-important 'E.'"[3]

NOTES

1 Montgomery, 16 August 1907, in *SJLMM*, 1: 331; Montgomery to Weber, 10 September 1908, in *GGL*, 73.
2 Cecily Devereux identifies "Topsy" as a reference to Harriet Beecher Stowe's *Uncle Tom's Cabin* (1852), in which Topsy, a young African American slave, responds to questions about her parentage with the claim that she had no mother or father, but rather, "I 'spects I growed." This reference appears again in a "The Author of *Anne of Avonlea*" and "The Way to Make a Book," reprinted below. See Montgomery, *Anne of Green Gables*, edited by Devereux, 365n1.
3 As Irene Gammel has noted in *Looking for Anne*, Montgomery never admitted publicly or privately how indebted she was to popular magazines of her era for sources for her books, which included several long-forgotten stories about earlier characters named "Ann."

4

The Author of *Anne of Avonlea*

—— 1909 ——

This article appeared in the 6 October 1909 issue of *Zion's Herald* (Boston), a progressive Christian periodical, a month after the publication of Montgomery's second novel, *Anne of Avonlea*. It includes extracts from the "personal sketch" that Page had requested from her the year before in the immediate aftermath of the unexpected success of *Anne of Green Gables*, a book that this periodical had called "delightful in every sense of the word" in their overview of "Noteworthy Books" of 1908.[1] Although the article suggests that the editors first saw Montgomery as a poet, her earliest known contribution to this periodical was a short story, "A Helping Hand," which appeared in July 1900 and which was followed by twenty-seven additional stories, the last appearing in 1914. She also published forty-four poems in this magazine between 1901 and 1916, beginning with "Southernwood" in September 1901. Repeating the strategy used in her two autobiographical letters of 1908 appearing in the preceding two chapters, this article limits the biographical details to the "bare facts" that Montgomery had claimed she was prepared to offer nosy journalists.[2]

Several years ago – twelve or more, possibly – as the editor of the Family Department of the *Herald* was sorting her exchanges, she accidentally came across a manuscript in an ordinary newspaper wrapper, which had been thrown into the paper basket by the editor-in-chief on the natural supposition that it was only one in the weekly avalanche of papers and pamphlets. On examination it proved to be a poem, neatly type written, sent from Cavendish, P.E. Island, and signed "L.M. Montgomery." "Oh, dear! another poetry fiend!" sighed the Family Department lady, but conscientiously began the perusal of the verses. The first few lines, however, made her "sit up and take notice," exclaiming: "Ah! here is a fresh note, something sweet and unhackneyed – *real* poetry, in fact. But *who* is L.M. Montgomery – man or woman, young or old, married or single?" Though intuition insisted on youth and the feminine gender, nevertheless a state of mystification prevailed until the publication last year of *Anne of Green Gables*, when a picture of the author in a literary magazine showed L.M. Montgomery to be a remarkably charming young woman. Since that first poem the pages of the *Herald* have been enriched every year by delightful stories and verses from the pen of this gifted writer. On the publication of her first book last winter[3] she won immediate and deserved recognition as an author of superior attainments; and everybody fell in love with *Anne of Green Gables*.

Miss Montgomery was born at Clifton, Prince Edward Island, Canada, where her father was a merchant. Owing to the death of her mother when she was only a few months old,[4] she was brought up by her maternal grandparents in Cavendish, P.E. Island – a seashore farming settlement, much like the "Avonlea" of her book. She attended the "district school" there until she was seventeen, then went to the Prince of Wales Academy in Charlottetown for a year. After this she taught a year, and then took the freshman year at Dalhousie College, Halifax. She taught two more years. Then the death of her grandfather made it necessary for her to stay at home with her grandmother in Cavendish, and she has lived there ever since.

Her literary work began very early. As far back as she can remember she wrote stories and verse for her own amusement. Her first plunge into the sea of journalism was taken when she was at Prince of Wales, when she wrote a poem, "To a Violet," and it was accepted by an American household magazine. In referring to this she naïvely says: "I was given two subscriptions to the magazine as payment – and that was quite all the verses were worth."[5]

From that until about three years ago Miss Montgomery has been writing fiction and verse for the magazines and religious papers. In answer to an inquiry as to how she came to write *Anne of Green Gables*, she says: "Three years ago the editor of a Sunday-school weekly asked me to write a short serial of about seven chapters for his paper. I looked through an old notebook and found a faded entry, jotted down many years before: 'Elderly couple apply to orphan asylum for a boy. By mistake a girl is sent them.' I thought this would do for the foundation of my serial. I blocked out a few chapters and hunted through my notebook of 'workable' incidents. I intended to write a nice little tale with a nice little heroine and a nice little moral; and if I had had time to go at it at once, that is likely all it would have been, and 'Anne' would have begun and ended her career in the pages of the Sunday-school weekly. But I did not have the time, and in the weeks that followed I 'brooded' the tale in my mind. 'Anne' began to expand in such a fashion that I soon saw I could never confine her career to a seven-chapter serial. It is really a mistake to say I 'created' 'Anne.' Like 'Topsey,' she 'growed' of her own accord, and I seemed simply to watch and describe that growth.[6] The result was, *Anne of Green Gables*."

In connection with this sketch and a review of her new book, *Anne of Avonlea*, we present a poem and a story by Miss Montgomery, both of which will richly repay reading.[7]

NOTES

1 Montgomery, 15 October 1908, in *SJLMM*, 1: 339; *Zion's Herald*, "Noteworthy Books of the Year," 1638.

2 Montgomery, 10 November 1908, in *SJLMM*, 1: 342.

3 *Anne of Green Gables* was in fact published in June 1908.

4 Montgomery's mother, Clara Macneill Montgomery, died in September 1876, when Montgomery was twenty-one months old.

5 The poem, entitled "The Violet's Spell," was published in *The Ladies' World* (New York) in July 1894. Montgomery had actually published five additional poems prior to this, three of them in Canadian newspapers. See Montgomery, 21 March 1901, in *SJLMM*, 1: 261, in which she mentioned giving the second subscription to her grandmother.

6 Properly, "Topsy." See chapter 3, "Origin of Popular Book," note 2, in this volume.

7 Appearing on the subsequent page of this issue of *Zion's Herald* are Montgomery's poem "On the Hills" and a review of *Anne of Avonlea*, and on the two following pages the short story "A Narrow Escape."

5

Miss Montgomery,
the Author of the "Anne" Books

—— 1909 ——

A. WYLIE MAHON

This profile, with the subhead "A Short Pen Sketch of the Young Prince Edward Island Authoress, Who Has Achieved Distinction as the Creator of a Delightful Character in Fiction," appeared in *The Canadian Bookman* and in identical form in *Bookseller and Stationer*, both Toronto periodicals, in November 1909. It was accompanied by a photograph of the Macneill farm and a caption that claimed that "the gable window on the left gave the inspiration of *Anne of Green Gables*." Its author, Alexander Wylie Mahon (1853–1930), was a Presbyterian minister who held charges in Prince Edward Island and New Brunswick before becoming assistant pastor of St. Andrew's Church (Toronto) from 1918 to 1924. His reference to Montgomery as "Lucy Maud" continued a pattern that would persist throughout her lifetime and beyond; as she noted to G.B. MacMillan in 1928 concerning later write-ups about her, "I was never in my life called 'Lucy Maud.' My friends called me 'Maud' and nothing else."[1] Mahon was also the author of "The Old Minister in *The Story Girl*," the earliest known article-length treatment of Montgomery's work, published in *The Canadian Magazine* in 1911 and reproduced as chapter 19 in this volume.

Few names in Canadian literature are so well known to-day as that of Miss L.M. Montgomery, "Lucy Maud," as the proud Prince Edward Islanders love to call her. It may be partly owing to their insular position – although no one would care to advance this theory too openly whilst sojourning amongst the thrifty, sharp-witted, and delightfully hospitable people of that beautiful little province – that the Islanders are so clannish.

The people as a whole feel that they have a provincial, proprietary right, almost a family interest in those of their number who are distinguishing themselves in the world of life or literature. President J.G. Schurman, of Cornell, will always be "Jacob" to many of them;[2] and Professor D.J. Fraser, of Montreal, will always be "Dan."[3] The more charming and popular books Miss Montgomery writes the more tenaciously will the proud Prince Edward Islanders hold on to "Lucy Maud."

Miss Montgomery's home is at Cavendish,[4] on the north side of the Island, where she can look out upon the broad Gulf of St. Lawrence, and dream dreams and see visions, and exercise her imagination unrestrainedly, no Rachel Lynde daring to make her afraid, although it is hinted that Rachel's original does live and move and have her being in that charming countryside.[5]

Miss Montgomery belongs to an exceptionally clever, brainy family. The Rev. L.G. Macneill, the pastor-emeritus of St. Andrew's Church, St. John, N.B., who is recognized as one of the ablest preachers Canada has produced, is her uncle. Mr. Chester Macneill, so well known on the Pacific coast, is also her uncle; and Professor Macneill, of Dalhousie College, Halifax, is her cousin.[6]

Miss Montgomery showed the bent of her genius for story telling almost as early in life as Sir Walter Scott himself.[7] When a mere child she began to write stories in which her cats with their comical names appeared as the principal characters. Whatever else the cats lacked, they did not lack imagination. They could imagine very much after the manner of Anne Shirley herself.

It would be interesting to-day to read those first attempts at literature on the part of this popular writer, if some one had preserved them as the mother of Charles Kingsley in her place of concealment took down her child's sermons which he preached to the chairs in the nursery.[8]

At a very early age Miss Montgomery began contributing stories and bits of verse to the local papers, some of which attracted a good deal of attention in her Island province. The writer knows one person who came across some verses written by her when she was not very far advanced in her teens which impressed him so favorably that he ventured to prophesy that the larger world would some day know the name of Lucy Maud Montgomery. This man rests his reputation as a literary prophet upon this prediction which is being very rapidly fulfilled these days when *Anne of Green Gables,* and the younger Anne of literature that is the older Anne of life, *Anne of Avonlea,* are amongst the best sellers, and will soon require six figures to represent the number sold.

Miss Montgomery is a prodigious worker, as any one might readily infer from a hasty glance over the popular magazines and periodicals of the day where her name is so frequently to be found. She is now engaged on a new book which her friends believe will rival in interest and popularity the "Anne" books.[9]

A few months ago in a review of the Canadian literature of the Atlantic provinces a writer in one of our weekly journals made some reference to Miss Montgomery. When this appeared in print the "Miss" had been converted into a "Mrs." The writer immediately wrote Miss Montgomery and assured her that he was not to blame for making a "Mrs." of her. He told her that being a clergyman, and properly registered in the province in which he resided, he was legally qualified to make a "Mrs." of her, if she were to appear before him with all the necessary documents, and also a man; but under existing circumstances, the woman and the man and the documents all being absent, he had no power to make a "Mrs." of her.

Miss Montgomery wrote an exceedingly clever and characteristic reply to this letter, assuring the clergyman that far worse things than that had happened to her in print. Some had made a "Mr." of her. That was hard to bear. She said that she had no unovercomable repugnance, such as some mythical females of uncertain age were supposed to have, to the term "Mrs." This, of course, presupposed a kindred spirit. Rachel Lynde, who is an authority in all such matters, whispers that there is a kindred spirit in Miss Montgomery's world, in the realm of divinity. But I must not repeat what Rachel says.[10]

NOTES

1 Montgomery to MacMillan, 6 February 1928, in *MDMM*, 131.
2 Jacob Gould Schurman (1854–1942), who was appointed Sage Professor of Philosophy at Cornell University and president of the university in 1892. Montgomery mentioned him in defence of PEI rural schools in a journal entry dated 1 March 1930, in *SJLMM*, 4: 41.
3 Rev. Daniel James Fraser (1866–1948), a Presbyterian minister who was also a professor of New Testament Literature and Exegesis at the Presbyterian College in Montreal.
4 I have corrected the original, which reads "Cavandish."
5 Although Montgomery admitted that Mrs. Lynde's house was drawn from the home of neighbour Pierce Macneill and that Rachel Lynde and Rachel

Macneill shared a first name, she stressed that there was "no [further] connection whatever between them" (Montgomery, 27 January 1911, in *SJLMM*, 2: 38).

6 Leander George Macneill (1845–1913) and Chester Macneill (1861–1942), the two eldest children of Montgomery's maternal grandparents. Murray Macneill, a professor of mathematics at Dalhousie University from 1907 to 1942 and second eldest son of Leander Macneill. Although Montgomery disliked Murray, he apparently sent her a kind letter congratulating her on *Anne of Green Gables*, to which she responded in July 1909. See Gillen, *The Wheel of Things*, 79–80. I have corrected the original, which reads "L.G. Macneil" and "Chester Macniell."

7 Sir Walter Scott (1771–1832), Scottish novelist and poet whose novels included *Waverley* (1814) and *Anne of Geierstein* (1829).

8 Charles Kingsley (1819–1875), English novelist and Church of England priest.

9 *The Story Girl* was published in May 1911, but the writing of it was interrupted when Montgomery's publisher asked her to expand a five-part serial, "Una of the Garden," into what would become her third novel, *Kilmeny of the Orchard*, published in May 1910.

10 A sly reference to Ewan Macdonald (1870–1943), whom Montgomery had agreed to marry in October 1906 on the condition that they wait until after her grandmother's death. Their engagement was supposedly a secret.

6

A Trio of Women Writers

—— 1909 ——

DONALD B. SINCLAIR

This article appeared in the 27 November 1909 issue of *The Canadian Courier*, a Toronto magazine that had published Montgomery's short story "The Great Actor's Part" earlier that year; she would publish another fourteen stories in this magazine by 1921, as well as a poem, "Genius," in 1910. The full article also profiles Nellie L. McClung, whose 1908 novel *Sowing Seeds in Danny* appeared slightly ahead of *Anne of Green Gables* and *Anne of Avonlea* in the 1909 list of national best-sellers in Canada,[1] and Alice Ashworth Townley (1870–1941), author of the novel *Opinions of Mary* (1909). Three decades later, commenting on this article's "report" on her teaching methods, she noted in her journal that "this of course was all moonshine."[2]

Woman is to the fore in letters to-day. Her rise has been contemporaneous with the ascendancy of the novel as the chief form of expression of the literary art. In the palmy days of poetry and the drama and history woman did not do much writing. She could not wholly comprehend the intricate problems of history; and her attitude toward the drama and poetry was more sympathetic and interpretative than creative. So she preferred to lean back and provide the inspiration for the verse-making. But in the novel she found a vehicle suitable for the conveyance of her ideas. She realised at once that her feminine qualities of rapid intuition, delicate insight into character and motive, and super-sensitiveness enabling an innate recognition of the finer and more subtle touches of feeling, were the very requisites for success in the new branch of literature. From a dormant one, she became an active factor in the book world. She strove with men and equalled and beat them at the game of story-writing. To-day, who enjoys among masculine wielders of the pen, a larger audience in England than Mrs. Humphry Ward or Marie Corelli, or in America than Mrs. Wharton or Mrs. Deland?[3] We in Canada have not been behind. One of the signs of the times in the Dominion is the majority of women among those whose vocation is the making of the books of the land.

In the last two years three women writers, who before then were comparatively unknown beyond their own tea tables, have commanded the attention of the Continent.

Miss L.M. Montgomery is the Prince Edward Island lady who wrote a story about a winsome little girl called Anne, sent it to a publisher across the line, and awoke to hear Mark Twain telling her that he had found *Anne of Green Gables* the "best ever" since the chronicles of the renowned Alice. Miss Montgomery lives at Cavendish, Prince Edward Island. She was brought up there among the tillers of the soil of the "Million Acre Farm,"[4] and the toilers on the shore of the sea. She is an orphan and resided with her grandparents. Her education went as far as the freshette stage at Dalhousie. Then she went into school-teaching. That only lasted two years. From report, Miss Montgomery's pupils had not a very strenuous time of it. Their teacher was more inclined to be delighted at their vagaries than proud of their scholastic virtues. When she found teaching uncongenial, Miss Montgomery retired from the profession after the example of Archibald Lampman at Orangeville,[5] and did a lot of thinking. Her contemplations found expression upon paper. She dreamed of writing. Now, when a Canadian girl gets literary notions, her first efforts are invariably along the line of verse. Miss Montgomery versified. The editors called her creations poetry, and paid her for them. One of them conceived the idea that she might write a story. He was a Sunday School editor and wanted a Sunday School story. Miss Montgomery thus relates the account of her attempts:

"I looked through an old notebook and found a faded entry written many years ago: 'Elderly couple apply to Orphan Asylum for a boy, a girl is sent them.' I thought that would do for the foundation of my serial. I blocked out a few chapters and hunted through the aforesaid notebook for suitable incidents. I intended to write a good little yarn with a good little heroine and a good little moral, and, if I had had time to go at it at once, that is all it would have been, and Anne would have begun and ended her career in the pages of a Sunday School weekly. But I did not have the time, and in the weeks that followed, as I 'brooded' over the tale in my mind, Anne began to expand in such a fashion that I soon saw I would never confine her career to a seven chapter serial. It is really a mistake to say that I created Anne. Like Topsy she 'growed' of her own accord, and I simply seemed to watch her growth. The result was *Anne of Green Gables*."

Anne was such an attractive young lady, and was received so generally, especially in the United States, that Miss Montgomery was prevailed upon to promise a further account of her heroine.[6] Fagged out folks who this Christmas find *Anne of Avonlea* in their Santa Claus stocking will discover in Anne's latest piquant philosophy a sure tonic to help them tide over another year.

[* * *]

NOTES

1 According to Mary Vipond, *Sowing Seeds in Danny* placed fourth on the 1909 list, followed by *Anne of Green Gables*, which tied for sixth place with Mrs. Humphry Ward's *Marriage à la Mode*, and by *Anne of Avonlea*, at eighth place (Vipond, "Best Sellers in English Canada," 115).

2 Montgomery, 1 March 1930, in *SJLMM*, 4: 41.

3 Mary Augusta Ward (1851–1920), also known as Mrs. Humphry Ward, Australian-born English novelist best known for *Robert Elsmere* (1888) and a founder of the Women's National Anti-Suffrage League. Marie Corelli (1855–1924), English novelist whose work included the 1895 novel *The Sorrows of Satan* (which Montgomery read) and whose popularity lasted until the First World War. "Mrs. Wharton" refers to Edith Wharton (1862–1937), American author whose work included the 1905 novel *The House of Mirth* (which Montgomery read). "Mrs. Deland" refers either to Margaret Deland (1857–1945), American author best known for the 1888 novel *John Ward, Preacher* (which Montgomery read), or to Ellen Douglas Deland (1860–1923), the author of books for girls including *The Friendship of Anne* (1907).

4 "Million acre farm" remains a popular phrase for promoting the agricultural fecundity of PEI.

5 Archibald Lampman, one of the Confederation Poets and frequently cited as Canada's finest English-language poet of the nineteenth century. He taught high school unsuccessfully for a few months in Orangeville, Ontario, before finding employment in the Post-Office Department in Ottawa.

6 A recurring misconception is that the runaway success of *Anne of Green Gables* prompted Montgomery to write a sequel, when in fact she was asked to write a sequel upon acceptance of her first manuscript by Page, a standard practice for a publisher who saw sequels and series as financially lucrative. See Montgomery, 16 August 1907, in *SJLMM*, 1: 331; see also Gerson, "'Dragged at Anne's Chariot Wheels.'"

7

Canadian Writers on Canadian Literature –
A Symposium

—— 1910 ——

The longer article, published in the Toronto *Globe* in January 1910 about the ability of Canadian literature to express "national life," features a number of letters from prominent historians, essayists, fiction writers, and poets, including Andrew Macphail (1864–1938), Nellie L. McClung (1873–1951), Arthur Stringer (1874–1950), Marjorie Pickthall (1883–1922), Ethelwyn Wetherald (1857–1940), and Virna Sheard (1865–1943). Montgomery's letter leads the section on "Writers of Fiction." In a 1919 journal entry, Montgomery commented on her letter after coming across it in one of her scrapbooks: "When I wrote that I had no premonition of the Great War. But if I had known what was coming I could hardly have described it better ... The great Canadian literature will come from the generation born of this conflict not from the generation that fought through it."[1] At the time of this journal entry, she had just started writing her Great War novel *Rilla of Ingleside* (1921), for which she would select lines from Sheard's poem "The Young Knights" for its epigraph.

It was not with the amateur gardener's desire to pull up the plant to look at the roots that the following symposium on Canadian literature was planned. Rather was it a wish that when the crop yields, the lumber output and other signs of progress were being weighed the literary wares of the Dominion should be considered also. The critics have their say from week to week, but it is seldom that the men and women who are writing our books and contributing to our magazines have an opportunity to estimate their own collective work. It will be seen from the following opinions, representing nearly all the leading present-day writers of Canada, that, while there is a certain amount of satisfaction at progress made, the writers are on the whole moved by a healthy impatience for better work and by a jealousy – if that is not too strong a word – for the prominence which commerce now achieves over literature.

The questions submitted by the Literary Editor of *The Globe* were as follows:

(1) Is Canadian literature making satisfactory progress as an expression of national life?

(2) If so, in what direction is the most progress being made?

(3) What field shows the greatest opportunity for development?

The replies, every one of which is worth reading, are as follows: [* * *]

Miss L.M. Montgomery, Cavendish, P.E.I., author of *Anne of Green Gables* and *Anne of Avonlea*: –

"I do not think that, so far, our Canadian literature is an expression of our national life as a whole. Our literature is sectional. This is not saying anything against it. Some of the best literature in the world has been sectional but it is not national – that is, as I understand the word. Its perusal by an inhabitant of Mars would not give him any real notion of Canadian life and development. He would get a notion of Canada in spots, not as a whole.

"I think this is because we have only very recently – as time goes in the making of nations – had any real national life. Canada is only just finding herself. She has not yet fused her varying elements into a harmonious whole. Perhaps she will not do so until they are welded together by some great crisis of storm and stress. That is when real national literature will be born. The 'piping times of peace'[2] are not favorable to its development; and I do not believe that the 'great Canadian' novel or poem will be ever written until we have had some kind of a baptism by fire to purge away all our petty superficialities and lay bare the primal passions of humanity."

NOTES

1   Montgomery, 27 August 1919, in *SJLMM*, 2: 340.
2   Properly, "this weak piping time of peace." From *Richard III* (ca. 1591), by William Shakespeare (ca. 1564–1616), English playwright and poet.

8

Says Woman's Place Is Home

—— 1910 ——

In October 1910, Lewis Page invited L.M. Montgomery to be his guest for a week in Boston the following month. Her third novel, *Kilmeny of the Orchard*, had appeared the preceding May, and she was about to send him the finished typescript of her fourth novel, *The Story Girl*, scheduled for publication in spring 1911. For Montgomery, after several years of living a monotonous existence with her grandmother in Cavendish, the trip to Boston was her first opportunity to experience the "other side" of fame – as her account in her journal documents in detail, she was "besieged with invitations and telephone calls" for the duration of her trip.[1] In the first of four known interviews that occurred during this visit, published in the *Boston Post*, the "Authoress Gives Views on Suffrage," as the subhead announces, referring to a movement whose objective was to extend voting rights to women. Although she is wrongly identified as "Louise" Maud Montgomery, the questions she answers about suffrage and authorship reveal the extent to which she was called upon as a literary celebrity. Publicly, she adopted a patina of feminine modesty by asserting that a woman's place was at home – a stance she would repeat throughout her career. Her public views expressed here were much more conservative than those she expressed in private, however: repeating her general disinterest in suffrage in a 1909 letter to Ephraim Weber, she stated emphatically that "I *do* believe that a woman with property of her own should have a voice in making the laws. Am I not as intelligent and capable of voting for my country's good as the Frenchman who chops my wood for me, and who may be able to tell his right hand from his left, but cannot read or write?"[2] While here she objected to a double standard that disadvantaged her because of her sex, she was less sensitive to double standards based on literacy, language, and class. Similarly, while the best-selling author was careful to indicate that she wrote for love, not money, she had told MacMillan in 1903 that, "frankly," she wrote "to make [her] living out of it."[3]

Louise Maud Montgomery, who wrote *Anne of Green Gables*,[4] and other "Best Sellers," was the guest of honor yesterday at the afternoon tea which is held each day at the Boston Authors' Club.[5] Miss Montgomery, who lives in Prince Edward Island, "The Island," as she calls it, with emphasis on "The," has never met any kindred spirits[6] in her profession, and so yesterday, Mrs. L.C. Page of Brookline,[7] with whom Miss Montgomery is stopping, took her to the Authors' Club.

When a reporter arrived at the club, a group of literary folk were ensconced in a corner sipping tea with Miss Montgomery in the centre, the whole being flanked by piles of cakes.

Miss Montgomery was informed that a newspaper man wished to speak to her, and she immediately left Charles Follen Adams and Nathan Haskell Dole,[8] who were discussing the high cost of living, and rustled over to where the reporter waited. Her gown was some sort of pink stuff which shimmered and dazzled one. "I never met any authors before, you know," said Miss Montgomery, "which is the reason I am here. I didn't know I was coming until this afternoon."

"Now that you have met them, Miss Montgomery, have you changed your mind any in regard to being an author?"

Not a Suffragette

"Oh, I find them much like human beings," she replied. "No, I am not a suffragette.[9] Do you know I was told that question would be asked me just as soon as I arrived in Boston. I am a quiet, plain sort of person, and while I believe a woman, if intelligent, should be allowed to vote, I would have no use for suffrage myself. I have no aspirations to become a politician. I believe a woman's place is in the home.

"I began to write so many years ago I really can't say when I did start. My first public writings, however, commenced 10 years ago, and were in the form of juvenile stories. Three years ago my first book, *Anne of Green Gables*, was published, and since that time I have written *Anne of Avonlea*, *Kilmeny of the Orchard*, and my latest book in regard to which I am in Boston, *The Story Girl*. That I expect will be published next spring.

"I write for the love of it, and I should continue even though my books were never published.

"I haven't had much opportunity to see Boston, as I arrived but a short time ago, and leave for my home next Thursday. I did visit the Museum of Fine Arts.[10]

"In regard to Boston I can only say I like it very much, but as I have been to no other large cities I cannot compare it with them.[11] The people I have met in Boston are very nice, and I regret I have such a short time to stay."

NOTES

1 Montgomery, 29 November 1910, in *SJLMM*, 2: 23, 28. For additional samples of the newspaper coverage of Montgomery's visit to Boston, see three society pieces that appeared on the same day as this article: *The Boston Herald*, "Authors' Club Reception"; *The Boston Herald*, "Personal and Social News"; *The Boston Journal*, "Canadian Writer."

2 Montgomery to Weber, 2 September 1909, in *GGL*, 91.

3 Montgomery to MacMillan, 29 December 1903, in *MDMM*, 3.

4 I have corrected the original, which reads "'Annie of Green Gables.'"

5 Founded in 1899, the Boston Authors Club held its first meeting in January 1900 and is still in existence today.

6 A key phrase popularized in *Anne of Green Gables*. For its etymology, see Montgomery, *Anne of Green Gables*, edited by Devereux, 84–85n1.

7 Montgomery learned in 1917 that Mildred Page was actually Lewis Page's third wife and that she had divorced him the preceding year (Montgomery, 24 October 1917, in *SJLMM*, 2: 226). Brookline, a town in Norfolk County, Massachusetts, borders on the city of Boston.

8 Charles Follen Adams (1842–1918), American poet; Nathan Haskell Dole (1852–1935), American author, editor, and translator. Dole would write the introduction to the first edition of *Further Chronicles of Avonlea* (1920), reprinted as chapter 31 in this volume.

9 The term "suffragette" refers to "a female supporter of the cause of women's political enfranchisement, *esp.* one of a violent or 'militant' type" (*OED*). The earliest known usage of this term is 1906.

10 This museum, one of the largest in the United States, had moved to its current location on Huntington Avenue in 1909.

11 Montgomery had actually stopped in Ottawa, Montreal, Toronto, and Winnipeg on her train rides to Saskatchewan and back again in 1890–91.

9

Want to Know How to Write Books?
Well Here's a Real Recipe

—— 1910 ——

PHOEBE DWIGHT

In this interview, published in the *Boston Traveler*, Montgomery presents herself as a best-selling author who has little use for suffrage yet who writes to please herself instead of bowing to the demands of a mainstream reading audience. The article is accompanied by a photograph of Montgomery dressed to the nines, with the caption "Louise M. Montgomery, Noted Author, Now in Boston" and a subhead: "Author of *Anne of Green Gables* Tells the Right Time to Mount Pegasus and Give Him the Rein."[1] In her journal, she referred to the reporter as "a girlish little creature who looked too young to be a journalist but who was quite an expert in her line, as her consequent write-up showed."[2]

Would you like to know how to write novels?

Here is a recipe:

Miss Louise Maud Montgomery, the author of *Anne of Green Gables*, *Anne of Avonlea*, *Kilmeny of the Orchard*, and other stories, gave it to me today.

"An old woman once said to me, 'My dear, never get married as long as you can possibly help it, for when the right man comes along, you can't help it.'[3]

"That is just about the way with novel writing. 'Never write as long as you can possibly help it, for when the writing fever seizes you, you can't help it.'

"That's my recipe," she smiled.

Tells about Her Newest Tale

Miss Montgomery is petite, with the fine, delicate features of an imaginative woman. She has said that she is soon to bring out a novel called *The Story Girl*. I hastened to ask her about it.

"It is a simple little tale about children,[4] not unlike the others I have written," she answered. "That is about the only kind of story I write, for that is the phase of life I know. I am sure you cannot write convincingly about anything you do not understand from having lived it.

"Ever since I was a little kiddie I have scribbled verse or stories on every scrap of paper I could find. Of course I began, as very young writers do, by planning all kinds of elaborate novels with the most complicated plots." Miss Montgomery smiled at her childish attempts. "But the older I grow the more I see the enduring charm of simplicity in writing, as in everything else. Children are refreshing. Stories about them are."

"Then you do not attempt society novels, or problem stories?"[5]

"No, never," said Miss Montgomery. "My home is in Prince Edward Island. When I tell you that I live four miles from a telephone and 11 miles from a railway, you may know that there are few problems and little society with a capital S. there. Life in the island is not at all complex. But it is the most splendid place to write, if you are fond of simple characters. And I am."

Writers Who Look On

"I have a feeling," went on Miss Montgomery, "that many of the stories written about society are written by people who look on from the outside. You must be really inside to understand it all, and be impartial. It is so easy to mistake one aspect for the whole. And it is so inaccurate. I have never written suffrage stories, either. As everyone does, I can see the truth of the arguments, but I am not at all ardent about it. As for the problem novels, well, – the problems are never settled by them, often scarcely helped.

"I remember the first bit I succeeded in selling. It was a little magazine verse. I cannot dignify it by calling it poetry. I sold it to *Golden Days* for three dollars.[6] I never was so rich before or again as I was with those three beautiful dollars." Miss Montgomery's voice fairly gloated over the little "fortune."

Then she laughed at herself and went on:

"For a long time I wrote stories that would sell to semi-religious papers. But it was a forced kind of writing. All the tales had to have a plot that would furnish a moral. The good little boy must always triumph and the naughty boy must always be frustrated. I grew very tired of it all.

"One day an editor of one of the Sunday School magazines asked me to write a seven-part serial story for him. I looked through my note book and discovered this line, 'An old couple send to an orphan asylum to adopt a boy, and a girl is sent them by mistake.'

"So I started on the story. The more I thought of it, the more it grew and the fonder I became of the little girl. I couldn't bear to fit it to the Sunday school scheme. Finally I sent another story to the editor, and amused myself in winter evenings with this novel. The result was *Anne of Green Gables*.[7] The more you give your imagination free play the more there is in it for you," ended Miss Montgomery.

"And is Anne purely a child of your imagination, or is she founded on some little girl you know?" I asked.

"Purely imagination," Miss Montgomery replied. "At least, she is not patterned after any especial child. I suppose that there is in her some of myself. I was a solitary child, and what I couldn't have I imagined, and I found that almost as good."

Miss Montgomery was silent for a moment.

Then she said, contentedly:

"When I began I used to have to write what the public wanted, regardless of what I wanted. Now I can write what pleases me to write, what gives me joy in the doing.

"I am certain that if a woman writes what she sees and what appeals to her, if she does it convincingly, that there are enough people in the world fashioned in her mould, to enjoy reading the book as much as she did in writing it."

NOTES

1 I have corrected the title, which in the original reads "Want to Know How to Write Book?" Pegasus, a fantastical creature in Greek mythology, is a winged divine horse that is eventually tamed by Bellerophon, a Greek hero who rides Pegasus in order to defeat a monster but is dismounted by Zeus when attempting to reach Mount Olympus.

2 Montgomery, 29 November 1910, in *SJLMM*, 2: 30.

3 I have corrected the original, which reads "comes along you, you can't help it."

4 Here Montgomery echoes a 1908 journal entry in which she referred to *Anne of Green Gables* as "such a simple little tale" (Montgomery, 15 October 1908, in *SJLMM*, 1: 339).

5 A problem story is a work of fiction that uses characters and incidents to broach or work through a particular social problem, often one concerning current or controversial subject matter.

6 According to her journals, Montgomery received five dollars for her second published short story, "Our Charivari," which was published in *Golden Days for Boys and Girls* (Philadelphia) in May 1896 under the pseudonym "Maud Cavendish."

7 I have corrected the original, which reads "'Ann of Green Gables.'"

10

Miss Montgomery's Visit to Boston
—— 1910 ——

This article, part of a column called "Latest Gossip of Book World" in the *Boston Herald*, grew out of an interview conducted by a "Mr. Alexander," whom Montgomery called in her journal "a canny delightful old Scotchman."[1] Here, the author reports the details that Montgomery had apparently shared with him about her process of outlining, writing, and editing her books.

Lucy Maud Montgomery, the author of *Anne of Green Gables*, *Anne of Avonlea*, and still more recently *Kilmeny of the Orchard*, is visiting Boston as the guest of her publisher, Mr. Page of L.C. Page & Company. Her home, as many know, is located in a quiet nook of Prince Edward Island, the atmosphere of which pervades all her stories. It will be of interest to her many readers to know that she is putting the finishing touches to a new story which will appear in the spring. A title has not yet been given to it, but once more an interesting young girl fills the role of honor in the dramatis personae, differing from the previous heroines of the author, but quite as instinct with pure human passion and fine ideal. Miss Montgomery has been at work on this volume for nearly three years, devoting to it much painstaking labor. The story presumably has the same environment as that of her other books. She leaves our city for Charlottetown, P.E.I., on Saturday morning of this week.

It may interest many of our readers to know something of Miss Montgomery's method of writing her tales. First of all she thinks out her story; then drafts it on paper, working out the principal characters.

When all of this has been done she takes up the initial chapter, usually dreaming out its elaboration in a twilight walk. In the morning she is ready to begin with the pen. When finished she goes over it critically to make corrections or changes. Chapter two is taken up in the same way; then chapters one and two are rewritten. Chapters three and four have analogous treatment, with this difference that when the rewriting takes place it begins with chapter one, and so with five and six and all the rest of them. The manuscript is practically written over as many times as there are chapters in it, the author writing over the later divisions sufficiently often to make up the difference. This is painstaking in the extreme. It is doubtful whether you have ever known of one so self-exacting. But nothing less than this will satisfy the author of the "Anne" books, and when one becomes conscious of their charm, the daintiness of their touch, the attractive humanness of their character delineation, one can appreciate just what the whole of that has cost in labor.

NOTES

1   Montgomery, 29 November 1910, in *SJLMM*, 2: 29.

11

Four Questions Answered

—— 1910 ——

LUCY MAUD MONTGOMERY

This short essay by Montgomery appeared in the "Topics Worth While" column of the *Boston Herald*, with a biographical note identifying her as "the author of *Anne of Green Gables*, *Anne of Avonlea* and still more recently *Kilmeny of the Orchard*, who is now in Boston." Montgomery claimed that this form of journalistic writing was "beyond" her ability, but she was actually being coy: she had spent a year working at the Halifax *Daily Echo*, where her responsibilities included writing a column, "Around the Table," under the pseudonym "Cynthia."[1] Furthermore, although she stated that she could not make her home except on Prince Edward Island, her future husband, Ewan Macdonald, was stationed at the time in Leaskdale, Ontario, so Montgomery knew at this point that she would most likely leave PEI after her marriage.

I have been asked to write for *The Herald* on "my impressions of Boston." Had the editor asked me to write a novel I could have done it. Had he asked me to write a theological essay I should have rushed in where angels fear to tread[2] and had a try at it. But an editorial contribution is beyond me – at least, if it be what it was supposed to be in my early days – a weighty, ex cathedra[3] utterance for the grinding and shaping of public opinion.

I am just going to answer the four questions which have been asked me repeatedly ever since I arrived here. The first is – "How do you like Boston?" Now, how could I help liking Boston very, very much, where everybody I have met here has been so nice to me? I have met unceasing kindness and the most delicate consideration on every hand. To the stranger within their gates your people have given such a cordial welcome that she does not feel as if she were among strangers, but among old and valued friends and "kindred spirits." Of course, Boston has, for me, the drawbacks which any large city must have. But in a brief sojourn one does not mind them. Yes, Boston is a very nice place to visit.

The second question is: "What do you think of woman suffrage?" Well, I do not think very much about it at all. I think women should be allowed to vote, if they wish it, and I think they soon will vote; but I question if it will make such a change in anything as both its champions and its opponents imagine that it will in everything. I do not think it will add much to the sum total of human happiness, and therefore I frankly confess that it does not seem to me worth while to worry about it.

The third question isn't a question at all, but a calm, maddening statement with a slightly rising inflection. It is: "I suppose you are completely frozen up down there by this time?" "Down there" means Prince Edward Island, and "frozen up" means that steamship communication with the mainland is interrupted. Frozen up in November! Heaven grant me patience. In the worst of years we are never "frozen up" until February. Then for a week or 10 days the ice in the strait way is so thick that the steamers cannot cut through it, and the "ice boats" are put on to carry passengers and mails. But this happens in only about one winter out of three. We rarely have lasting snow until after Christmas. Last winter, as I remember, wheels ran every month, and the snow never stayed long enough to make good roads for sleighing. Of course, we have an occasional severe and stormy winter; but we are never frozen up in November.

The fourth question is: "Wouldn't you like to live up here?" To that I must answer "No." I have enjoyed my sojourn among you most heartily; but noble as your land is, it is not my land; friendly and delightful as your people are, they are not "mine own people";[4] beautiful as your starry banner is, it is not my old flag that has "braved a thousand years the battle and the breeze."[5] Only in the shadow of that old flag could I wish to make my home.

But, oh, you are nice to visit!!!

NOTES

1 See McCabe, "Lucy Maud Montgomery's Table Talk."

2 Properly, "For Fools rush in where Angels fear to tread." From *An Essay on Criticism* (1709), by Alexander Pope (1688–1744), English poet.

3 The Latin term "ex cathedra," literally "from the chair," refers in Catholic theology to a teaching or pronouncement made under the guise of papal infallibility.

4 An allusion to 2 Kings 4:13 in the Hebrew Bible: "I dwell among mine own people." Montgomery would adapt this quotation for the title of a later article in the 1920s, reprinted as chapter 38, in this volume.

5 Properly, "Whose flag has braved, a thousand years, / The battle and the breeze!" From "Ye Mariners of England" (1800), by Thomas Campbell (1777–1844), Scottish poet.

12

Miss L.M. Montgomery,
Author of *Anne of Green Gables*

—— 1910 ——

In this final interview during her stay in Boston, published in the Boston *Republic*, Montgomery discusses her impressions of the city, some of the sources for her books, her views on women's work, and her reluctance to write another sequel to *Anne of Green Gables*. In her journal, she mentioned how much she liked the reporter who had interviewed her – a "Miss Conway," who was "a most charming woman. I liked her 'write-up' better than any of the others."[1]

During the week just ending authors and book-lovers in and about Boston have had the pleasure of meeting Miss L.M. Montgomery, author of *Anne of Green Gables, Anne of Avonlea* and *Kilmeny of the Orchard*, who has been the guest of Mr. and Mrs. L.C. Page at their charming home on Pewell street, Brookline.

Less than three years ago the name of L.M. Montgomery was unknown to the reading public of the United States. Today she is in the forefront of our popular authors, not only in this country but in England, Canada and Australia. It is true, of course, that the author had a modest repute for excellent 'prentice work,[2] so to speak, and was known as a student and book-lover in her secluded home in the beautiful little town of Cavendish, Prince Edward Island;[3] but doubtless those who knew her best little dreamed that her bud of promise was to have so early and splendid development.

Miss Montgomery's success is as honorable to human nature as to her own fine, pure instincts and splendid literary training and to the discernment of her publishers. She came to the heartfelt welcome of the reading public not over the thin ice of a dangerous "problem" novel, nor a bit of uncanny sensationalism, but through the quiet green fields and woods of her own lovely island, with the simple story of a little country girl, finding "scope for her imagination"[4] in the life of a picturesque farming village. But "Anne of Green Gables," sweet, innocent and fragrant as a branch of apple blossoms, took her place as by right in palatial city home and at country fireside, with every family of one mind as to her enduring charm. Father and mother followed the little orphan's bettering fortunes with delight, and made them free to the little daughter of nine or ten years.

Every discerning critic realized that in *Anne* a new and original character had come into the world of fiction, and would abide until she had become a classic. In these fickle days when of making books there is literally no end, six months is a long popularity for a book, but after over two years *Anne of Green Gables*, now in its twenty-fifth large edition, is selling as well as ever, and is known in every land of English speech. Those who had followed Anne through her childhood wanted to continue her friendship into her 'teens; so Miss Montgomery had to gratify them with a sequel, *Anne of Avonlea*, in the spring of 1909.[5] It met equal favor, and is now in its fourteenth edition. The author's book of the present year (all her books are published by L.C. Page & Company of Boston) is a delightful bit of unmixed romance; and while "Anne's" lovers find nothing of their favorite in it but the "imagination," it has within a few months run into its seventh edition. Still another book is coming, *The Story Girl*, but that will not appear until the spring.

We have, however, discussed all of Miss Montgomery's books in *The Republic*.[6] Now the question is, "What of the author?" During her far too brief stay, she has been entertained with the proverbial hospitality of these parts, alike in social circles, by literary associations, etc. It was the present writer's misfortune to be unable to attend the hastily arranged reception to Miss Montgomery on the part of the Boston Authors on the afternoon of November 11.[7] But this was compensated for by a quiet little visit with her and her hosts at an hour when there were no others to claim her attention. As the young author entered the Pages' beautiful library one thought came to us: "It is a repetition of history: Charlotte Brontë coming up to London."[8] By-and-by we found we were not alone in the idea.

Miss Montgomery is short and slight, indeed of a form almost childishly small, though graceful and symmetrical. She has an oval face, with delicate aquiline features, bluish-grey eyes and an abundance of dark brown hair. Her pretty pink evening gown somewhat accentuated her frail and youthful aspect.

It would not be easy to exaggerate the retiring manner and untouched simplicity of this already famous woman; nor was it easy to induce her to talk about herself or her books. Her attitude on the subject was clearly of extreme surprise at the success of the latter and the interest of Bostonians in their author.

Yes, Boston is the first big city she has ever visited.

"But wouldn't you like to see more of the United States and of lands beyond the sea?"

Yes, she would like to verify the impressions formed by reading; it was something one ought to do, if possible; but it was very clear that her heart was in her island, and that nothing gave her so much happiness as the pride and pleasure of her lifetime friends and neighbors in her early success.

Miss Montgomery told the writer, further, that she lived with her aged grandmother, but had no end of cousins. Cavendish was long ago settled by three families, whose descendants had ever since been intermarrying, so that every one is related to every one else;[9] much the same description as James Jeffrey Roche, who came from Prince Edward Island and attained literary success in Boston, was wont to give of the parts of the island which he knew best.[10]

"Is there anything of real life in *Anne of Green Gables*?"

"The background is real, the 'haunted wood' is real, the little girl and her chum are leaves out of other lives, and, yes, I used to name the places that I especially loved, just as 'Anne' did, 'the lake of shining waters, the white way of delight,' and so on, but except for this last there is nothing of autobiography in the book."

"I am commissioned by a little lover of 'Anne' to entreat you for another book about her and Gilbert Blythe."

"Oh, yes, indeed, Miss Montgomery. We must have Anne's love story," added another of the little company.

"But I want to leave 'Anne' just as she is forever; in her young girlhood," said the author earnestly. "Besides, I know so little of college life. I made but a year of the course at Halifax."

"But one needs not be a college woman to write a good story," we remonstrated, remembering the many successful literary workers of our acquaintance or close friendship who never had the college, but supplemented the ordinary school course by private study and experience in the university of life in later years.

"Oh, I don't claim the necessity of the college for the literary worker," said the young author; and then we branched off into a discussion of various subjects pertaining to women's work and ideals which revealed Miss Montgomery as distinctly conservative. More and more her individuality came out, until we remembered the word of the first eminent literary man of our own experience who was wont to declare that the strong, original characters usually develop in the small secluded places till the unconscious shining of their light attracts attention, and then the big city clamors for them.

We fancy, however, that any big city will clamor in vain for Miss Montgomery as a permanent resident. For all of her gentleness and marked feminity[11] of aspect and sympathies, she impressed the writer as of a determined character, with positive convictions on the advantage of the secluded country life with its opportunities for long reflection and earnest study. It is not probable that henceforward she will be able to escape breaks in the quietude of her life of steady literary productiveness, but she impresses us as one who, whithersoever called from the abode of her love and choice, will still go back to it with "heart untravailed."[12]

She has no favor for woman suffrage; she believes in the home-loving woman; we could not imagine her as "a woman of affairs," or aught but the modest, quiet, little, gentlewoman of the warm heart and the vigorous, creative brain that she is.

Bostonians are charmed with her unique personality not less than with her books; but for ourselves we should be more interested to know just how the pageant of our strenuous life has recast itself on the mind of this quiet but observant and philosophical sojourner. Perhaps Boston, in which not a few natives of Miss Montgomery's beloved island have attained distinction in various professions and even in public office, may be suggestive for that third "Anne" book which at present she has no desire to write; but we shall never know till we have it in our hands.

NOTES

1 Montgomery, 29 November 1910, in *SJLMM*, 2: 30.
2 This apprentice work included the publication of several hundred poems and short stories in Canadian and American periodicals from 1890 onward,

some of which Montgomery mentioned in detail in later accounts of her early career.

3 Here and throughout, I have corrected the original, which reads "Prince Edward's Island."

4 The term "scope for the imagination" recurs throughout *Anne of Green Gables* and its sequels, and its origins can be found in a range of British texts from the late eighteenth and nineteenth centuries (see Montgomery, *Anne of Green Gables*, edited by Devereux, 62n1).

5 *Anne of Avonlea* was actually published in September 1909.

6 The *Republic*'s review of *The Story Girl* appears in Volume 3 of *The L.M. Montgomery Reader*.

7 See Montgomery, 29 November 1910, in *SJLMM*, 2: 29.

8 Charlotte Brontë (1816–1855), English novelist who lived in rural Yorkshire with her father and who was invited by her publisher to visit London on occasion following the success of her novel *Jane Eyre* (1847) in order to nurture literary friendships there. I have corrected the original, which reads "Bronte."

9 As Montgomery later remarked in her journal, a local joke circulated in her youth concerning those three families: "From the conceit of the Simpsons, the pride of the Macneills and the vainglory of the Clarks Good Lord deliver us" (Montgomery, 2 June 1931, in *SJLMM*, 4: 125). This joke appears with different surnames in *AHD*, 29. See also chapter 17, "A Canadian Novelist of Note Interviewed," in this volume.

10 James Jeffrey Roche (1847–1908), Irish-born newspaperman who grew up in Prince Edward Island and whose books include *Ballads of Blue Water and Other Poems* (1895).

11 An archaic form of "femininity" or possibly a typographical error. Montgomery uses "femininity" when quoting this extract in her journal (see Montgomery, 29 November 1910, in *SJLMM*, 2: 30).

12 Properly, "heart untravell'd." From "The Traveller" (1764), by Oliver Goldsmith (1730–1774), Anglo-Irish poet.

13

How I Began to Write

—— 1911 ——

L.M. MONTGOMERY

Published in January 1911, less than two months after her trip to Boston, this article in the Toronto *Globe*, part of the "Circle of Young Canada" column edited by "Rose Rambler," repeats some of the anecdotes that Montgomery had already recounted in her journals and that she would write about again in her longer memoir, "The Alpine Path," in 1917.[1] While she certainly is not boastful about her success, she nevertheless resists the kind of self-deprecation that is characteristic of her later narratives about her development as an author.

"Tell your young Canadians that I wish for them one and all the best gift life can give them – a happy youth, in which is laid the foundation for a noble and useful maturity."

This is Miss Montgomery's message to the Circle of Young Canada, together with the charming little personal story given below. It will be read with the greatest pleasure. – Rose Rambler.

"When did I begin to write?" I wish I could remember. I cannot recall the time when I was not writing, and when I did not fondly dream of being a "really, truly author" when I grew up. From the time I first tried to guide a pen I was a most indefatigable little scribbler, and stacks of MSS.[2] – long ago reduced to ashes, alas! – bore testimony to the same. Sometimes I wrote prose; and then all the little incidents of my not very exciting existence were described. I wrote descriptions of my favorite haunts, "biographies" of my pets, accounts of visits and school affairs – and even "critical" reviews of books I had read. Sometimes I broke out in verse, and wrote "poetry" about flowers and months, or addressed "lines" to my friends, and enthused over sunsets. I remember the very first "poetry" I ever wrote. I was nine years old, and I had been reading Thomson's "Seasons,"[3] of which a little curly-covered, atrociously-printed copy had fallen into my hands. So I composed a poem called "Autumn," in blank verse, in imitation thereof. I wrote it, I remember, on the back of one of the long red "letter bills" then used in the post-office service. It was seldom easy for me to get all the paper I wanted, and those jolly old "letter bills" were positive boons.[4] My grandparents, with whom I lived, kept the post office,[5] and three times a week a discarded letter bill came my delighted way. As for "Autumn," I can recall only the opening lines: –

"Now Autumn comes, laden with peach and pear:
The sportsman's horn is heard throughout the land.
And the poor partridge, fluttering, falls dead."

True, peaches and pears were not abundant in Prince Edward Island at any season, and I am sure nobody ever heard a "sportsman's horn" in this Province – though dear little partridges are shot mercilessly. But in those glorious days my budding imagination declined to be hampered by facts. Thomson had sportsmen's horns, and so forth; therefore I must have them, too.

"Autumn" had many successors. Once I had found out that I could write poetry, I overflowed in verse about everything. Writing came as easily and naturally to me as breathing or eating. Other children found their recreation in games and romps. I found mine in creeping away into some lonely corner with a pencil and a "letter bill," and writing verses or sketches in a cramped, schoolgirl hand.

I remember – who could ever forget it? – the first commendation my writings received. I was about twelve, and I had a stack of poems written out, and hidden jealously from all eyes – for I was very sensitive about my scribblings, and could not bear the thought of having them seen by those who would probably laugh at them. Nevertheless, I wanted to know what others would think of them – not from vanity, but from a strong desire to find out if an impartial judge would see any merit in them. So I employed a ruse to find out. It seems very funny, and a little pitiful, to me now; but then it seemed to me that I was at the bar of judgment for all time. It would be too much to say that, had the verdict been unfavorable,

I would have forever surrendered my dreams. But they would certainly have been frosted for a time!

A school teacher was boarding with us then.[6] She was a rather sweet singer, and one evening I timidly asked her if she had ever heard a song called "Evening Dreams."

The said "Evening Dreams" was no less than a long poem of my own, which I then considered my masterpiece. It is not now extant, and I can recall only the first two verses. I suppose they were indelibly imprinted on my memory by the fact that the teacher asked me if I knew any of the words of the "song." Whereupon I, in a trembling voice, repeated the two opening verses: –

> "When the evening sun is setting
> Quietly in the west,
> In a halo of rainbow glory,
> I sit me down to rest.

> "I forget the present and future;
> I live over the past once more,
> For I see before me crowding
> The beautiful days of yore."

Strikingly original! Also, a child of twelve would have a long "past" to live over!

I finished up with a positive gasp, but the teacher was busy sewing, and did not notice my pallor and general shakiness. For I was pale – it was a moment of awful import to me. She placidly responded that she had never heard the song, but that "the words were very pretty."

The fact that she was sincere must certainly detract from her reputation for literary discrimination. But to me it was the sweetest morsel of commendation that had ever fallen to my lot – or that ever has fallen since, for that matter. Nothing has ever surpassed that delicious moment. I went out of the house – it wasn't big enough to contain my joy; I must have all outdoors for that – as if I trod on the amber air of the clear summer evening, and danced down the lane under the birches in a frenzy of delight, hugging to my heart the remembrance of those words.

Perhaps it was this which encouraged me, sometime during the following winter, to write out my "Evening Dreams" very painstakingly – on both sides of the paper, alas! – and send them to the editor of *The*

Household, an American magazine which we took.[7] The idea of being paid for them never entered my head. Indeed, I am not at all sure that I knew at that time that people were ever paid for writing. At least, my early dreams of possible fame were untarnished by any mercenary speculations.

Alack! The editor of *The Household* was less complimentary, but more discriminating, than my teacher. He sent my verses back – although I had not enclosed a stamp for that purpose, being in blissful ignorance of any such requirement.

My aspirations were nipped in the bud for a time. It was a year before I recovered from the blow. Then I essayed a more modest flight. I copied out my "Evening Dreams," in which I still had some faith, despite the cruel editor, and sent them to a Charlottetown weekly. It was not called *The Standard*, but that name will do.[8] I felt quite sure it would print them – for it often printed verses which I honestly thought, and, for that matter, still think, were no better than mine.

For a week I dreamed delicious dreams of seeing my verses in the poets' corner, with my name appended thereto. When *The Standard* came I opened it with trembling eagerness. Alas! there was not a sign of an evening dream about it.

I drained the cup of failure to the very dregs. It seems very amusing to me now, but it was horribly real and tragic to me then. I was crushed in the very dust of humiliation, and I had no hope of ever rising again. I burned my "Evening Dreams," and, though I still continued to write because I couldn't help it, I sent no more stuff to the editor.

After this mortifying experience three years passed. I still wrote "poems." They were pretty bad, but they were an improvement on "Evening Dreams." By this time my long-paralyzed ambition was beginning to recover and lift its head again. I wrote an old north-shore legend up in rhyme, and sent it to – let us say – *The Charlottetown Enterprise*.[9] No more of *The Standard* for me!

Well, *The Enterprise* printed the piece! It was the first sweet bubble on the cup of success, and it intoxicated me! To be sure, there were some fearful printers' errors in it, which made the flesh creep on my bones; but it was mine, in black type. The moment we see our first darling brain-child in print is a very wonderful one!

During the following year several more of my effusions, on "June" and kindred subjects, were printed in that long-suffering *Enterprise*.[10] Then I sighed for new worlds to conquer. The demon of filthy lucre began to creep into my heart. I wrote a story and sent it to *The New York Sun*, because I had been told that it paid for contributions. *The Sun* sent it back. I flinched, as from a slap in the face – and went on writing. I had learned the first, last and middle lesson of success – "never give up."

I went on sending things away and getting them back. But one day, when I was seventeen, I got a thin letter, with the address of a fourth-rate American periodical in the corner thereof. In it was a brief note accepting a poem, "Only a Violet," and offering in payment two subscriptions to the magazine.[11] I kept one for myself, and gave the other to a friend, and those magazines, with their vapid little stories, were the first tangible recompense my pen brought me.

During the next two years I wrote a good deal, and learned a good deal – but still my stuff came back, except from two periodicals, which evidently thought that literature was its own reward, and quite independent of monetary considerations.[12]

Then came another wonderful day, when I received a check from an American juvenile for a short story. It was for five dollars. Never in my life, before or since, have I felt so rich![13]

Then followed several years, in which I wrote hundreds of stories for Sunday school publications and juvenile periodicals generally. They were well enough in their way, I suppose; but I wanted to do more enduring work. Of course, like every other scribbler, I meant to write a book some day. I knew just what kind of a book – a very serious affair, with a complicated plot and a Dickensian wealth of character. But I never seemed to get ready to tackle it. Then the editor of a Sunday school weekly asked me to write a short serial of seven chapters for his paper. I looked through my notebook of "ideas," and found a faded entry, written many years before: "Elderly couple apply to orphan asylum for a boy; by mistake, a girl is sent them." I thought this would do for the central idea of my serial. I blocked out a few chapters, and hunted through my notebook for suitable incidents. I intended to write a nice little yarn about a good little girl, with a snug little moral tucked away in it, like a pill in a spoonful of jam. And if I had had time to go at it at once that is likely all it would have been. But I did not have the time, and in the weeks that followed I "brooded" the tale in my mind. Anne – she was not so named of malice aforethought, but flashed into my fancy all ready christened, even to the all-important "e" – began to expand in such a fashion that I soon saw I could never confine her career to a seven-chapter serial. The result was *Anne of Green Gables* – a very different book from that which I had fondly dreamed of writing. But *Anne* has won love, where the "big" book would probably have failed to win even interest.

"There's a divinity that shapes our ends,
Rough-hew them as we will."[14]

NOTES

1 The majority of this essay, from the anecdote about "Evening Dreams" to
the acceptance of her first short story, first appeared in different form in
Montgomery, 21 March 1901, in *SJLMM*, 1: 258–62.
2 An abbreviated form of the word "manuscripts."
3 "The Seasons" (1730), by James Thomson (1700–1748), Scottish poet and
playwright. Here and below, I have corrected the original, which reads
"Thompson."
4 These "letter bills" would also be a boon to Montgomery's future protagonist, the emerging author Emily Byrd Starr, beginning in *Emily of New
Moon* (1923).
5 I have corrected the original, which reads "postoffice."
6 Montgomery's description in her journal of the animosity between her and
said teacher, Izzie Robinson, is omitted here. See Montgomery, 21 March
1901, in *SJLMM*, 1: 259.
7 This Kansas periodical would publish two short stories by Montgomery:
"Miss Marietta's Jersey" in July 1899 (which was eventually reworked as
an episode in *Anne of Avonlea*) and "One Clear Call" in August 1928. See
Montgomery, 21 March 1909, in *SJLMM*, 1: 259.
8 According to her journal, the actual newspaper in question was the Charlottetown *Examiner*. Montgomery, 21 March 1901, in *SJLMM*, 1: 260.
9 This fictional Charlottetown newspaper is mentioned in *Anne of Avonlea*,
The Story Girl, *Rilla of Ingleside*, *Anne of Ingleside*, and *The Blythes Are
Quoted*. Montgomery discusses her poem "On Cape Le Force" in chapter
34, "Blank Verse? 'Very Blank,' Said Father," in this volume.
10 Her poem "June!" was published in the Charlottetown *Patriot* in 1891.
11 Her poem "The Violet's Spell" appeared in *The Ladies' World* (New York)
in July 1894.
12 Montgomery published seventeen poems in *The Ladies' Journal*, a Toronto
magazine, between 1895 and 1898.
13 Montgomery's first short story, "A Baking of Gingersnaps," signed Maud
Cavendish, was published in *The Ladies' Journal* in July 1895 and in *The
American Farmer*, a Baltimore periodical, in September 1895.
14 Properly, "Rough-hew them how we will." From *Hamlet* (ca. 1599–1601),
by William Shakespeare.

14

[Seasons in the Woods]

—— 1911 ——

L.M. MONTGOMERY
Author of *Anne of Green Gables*, etc.[1]

These four nature essays outlining four seasons in the woods were published in *The Canadian Magazine* (Toronto), which by 1911 had published eleven stories and eleven poems by Montgomery, most recently "The Story of a Love" and the poem "An April Night" in the March and April 1911 issues respectively. Although they are not set in a particular locale, for Elizabeth Rollins Epperly these essays are "memory pictures of her favourite home in nature, Lover's Lane"[2] – a place near her Cavendish home that Montgomery had identified in 1899 as "the dearest spot in the world to me."[3] As she had noted to MacMillan five years earlier, in 1906, "The woods always seem to me to have a delicate, subtle life all their own that epitomizes the very spirit of all the seasons in turn and is never out of harmony with the time o' year ... I always feel so utterly and satisfyingly at home in the woods."[4] To Weber, mentioning that she had written these essays in mid-1909, she stated that "I put a good deal of blood into them but don't know whether they're worth while after all ... I enjoyed writing them so perhaps people will enjoy reading them."[5] Her tribute to her attachment to Lover's Lane is especially poignant given that, by the time the first essay was published, Montgomery had already left Cavendish for Park Corner, twenty-two kilometres away, within days of the funeral for her maternal grandmother, who had died on 5 March. As she mentioned in a letter to MacMillan, "When these long beautiful spring evenings come it seems to me that I shall *die* if I cannot go to Lover's Lane and wander through it."[6]

As Epperly notes further, Montgomery relied on these essays when writing her Ontario novel *The Blue Castle*, published fifteen years later in 1926: as she notes, "All six John Foster descriptive passages, together with half a dozen of the narrator's comments, are taken from [the] Lover's Lane–inspired articles."[7] Perhaps for this reason Montgomery included in her Muskoka novel another "Lover's Lane," although this one is populated by "canoodling" couples and "young girls in pairs" rather than by the solitary rambler described in these essays.[8] The recycling of this material does not end there, however. She repeated phrases, sentences, and often entire paragraphs with only minor modifications in several of her later books, beginning with *The Golden Road* (1913) and ending with the last novel published in her lifetime, *Anne of Ingleside* (1939). Chapter 28 of the former book, "The Path to Arcady," describing a ramble in the woods, borrows liberally from these essays, particularly in the words spoken by Blair Stanley, a man who, we are told by the narrator, could "talk like a book."[9] Given that *The Golden Road* was the first novel that Montgomery would write after leaving PEI for Ontario, these borrowings reveal an attempt on her part to recapture a delightful "spot" that lived on in her memory.

Spring in the Woods

The woods are so human that to know them we must live with them. An occasional saunter through them, keeping, it may be, to the well trodden paths, will never admit us to their intimacy. If we wish to be near friends we must seek them out and win them by frequent reverent visits at all hours, by morning, by noon, and by night, and at all seasons, in spring and in summer, in autumn and in winter. Otherwise, we can never really know them, and any pretence we can make to the contrary will never impose on them. They have their own effective way of keeping aliens at a distance and shutting their heart to mere casual sight-seers.

Believe me, it is of no use to seek the woods from any motive except sheer love of them; they will find us out at once and hide all their sweet, world-old secrets from us. But if they know we come to them because we love them they will be very kind to us and give us such treasure of beauty and delight as is not bought or sold in market nor even can be paid for in coin of earthly minting; for the woods when they give at all give un- stintedly and hold nothing back from their true worshippers. We must go to them lovingly, humbly, patiently, watchfully, and we shall learn what poignant loveliness lurks in the wild places and silent intervals, lying un- der starshine and sunset, what cadences of unearthly music are harped on aged pine boughs or crooned in copses of fir, what delicate savours exhale from mosses and ferns in sunny corners or on damp brooklands, what dreams and myths and legends of an older time haunt them, what unsuspected tintings glimmer in their dark demesnes and glow in their alluring by-ways; for it is the by-ways that lead to the heart of the woods, and we must not fail to follow them if we would know the forests and be known of them.[10]

Spring is the best time to walk in the woods; at least, we think so in spring; but when summer comes it seems better still; and autumn woods are things quite incomparable in their splendour; and sometimes the winter woods, with their white reserve and fearlessly displayed nakedness, seem the rarest and finest of all.[11] For it is with the forest as with a sweetheart of flesh and blood, in every changing mood and vesture she is still more adorable in her beloved's eyes.

But it is certain that there is more of frank friendliness in the woods in spring than at any other season. In summer they are very busy about their own concerns; in autumn they are so gorgeous and imperial that we feel they have no particular need of us, even though they may like us as well as ever; and in winter their chaste aloofness inspires us with more of the awe of a worshipper than the ardour of a lover.

But in the spring they have so much time before them, and are so well pleased with themselves and the exquisite things that are budding in and about their bailiwick,[12] that they take us into full companionship and make us free of all their crafts and mysteries, from the potent, unutterable charm of a dim spruce wood to the grace of flexile mountain ashes fringing a lonely glen.[13]

The spring woods have a fashion of flowers, dainty, spirit-fine things, akin to the soul of the wilderness. Here is a westward sloping hill, lying under white drifts of cloud, feathered over with lisping young pines and firs that cup little hollows and corners where the sunshine gets in and never gets out again, but stays there and grows mellow, coaxing dear things to bloom long before they would dream of wakening up elsewhere. This is the spot for mayflowers; we are certain to find them here, on this little russet knoll for choice, where at first sight there is not a hint of blossom. Wait; the mayflowers never flaunt themselves; they must be sought and wooed as becomes them. See, we stoop, we pull aside the brown leathery leaves, and behold! The initials of spring's first lettering, trails and clusters of star-white and dawn-pink that have in them the very soul of all the springs that ever were, reincarnated in something which it seems gross to call perfume, so exquisite and spiritual will it prove to be.[14]

Now that we have learned the art of finding mayflowers we can gather them all over this hill. It is the only place where they grow, for they do not like luxurious surroundings, they extract all their sweetness out of sandy, inhospitable soil, and offer it to the wet, leafless world before the forests have fairly begun to waken up and preen themselves.

After the mayflowers have gone the woods open eyes of blue violets. We find them almost everywhere; the thick spruce woods are the only places where we can venture fearlessly. Elsewhere we must walk most delicately, lest our feet crush the dear, sky-tinted things.[15] Wherever a bit of grass finds sunshine enough on which to thrive there we find violets, along the lanes, and about the roots of slim birches, and in the dappled pasture corners overhung with beechen boughs; but to find the place where they grow most thickly we must wander into a tiny, sequestered valley of a western hill; beyond it there is a pool which is not known to summer days, but in spring is a glimmering green sheet of water on whose banks nymphs might dance as blithely as ever they did on Argive hill or in Cretan dale.[16] Certes,[17] they would have rare footing of it, for here violets grow so thickly that all the grass is enskied with them; and in just one corner we find the rarer white violets, tiny blossoms with purple pencillings in their little urns, which are filled with the most subtly distilled incense.

This pool is a witching spot near which to linger on spring evenings. Somewhere through the lissome willows and poplars that fringe it faint hues of rose and saffron from the far bourne of sunset steal across its pearly shimmer. It is unruffled by a breath, and every leaf and branch is mirrored in it, to the very grasses that sway on its margin.[18] The willows are decked with glossy silver catkins, the maples are mistily red-budded, and that cluster of white birches, a meet home for a dryad, is hung over with golden tassels.

When the violets begin to leave us we have the white garlands of the wild cherry flung out everywhere, against the dark of the spruces and in the hedges along the lanes; and will you please look at that young wild pear which has adorned herself after immemorial fashion as a bride for her husband, in a wedding veil of fine lace. The fingers of wood pixies must have woven it, for nothing like it ever came from an earthly loom. I vow the tree is conscious of its own loveliness; it is trembling and bridling before our very eyes, as if its beauty were not the most ephemeral thing in the woods, as it is the rarest and most exceeding, for to-day it is and to-morrow it is not. Every south wind purring gently through the boughs will winnow away a shower of slender petals. But what matter? To-day it is queen of the wild places, and it is always to-day in the woods, where there is neither past nor future but only the prescience of immortality.[19]

Of course, there are dandelions in the woods, because there are dandelions everywhere. They have no sense of the fitness of things at all;[20] they
are a cheerful, self-satisfied folk, firmly believing that they are welcome
wherever grass can grow and sunshine beckon. But they are alien to the
ancient wood. They are too obvious and frank; they possess none of the
mystery and reserve and allurement of the real wood flowers; in short,
have no secrets. Still, nothing, not even the smug dandelion, can live long
in or near the woods without some sort of psychic transformation coming over it; and presently all the obtrusive yellowness and complacency
are gone, and we have instead misty, phantom-like globes that hover over
the long grasses in full harmony with the traditions of the forests.[21]

The open spaces in the woods, washed in a bath of tingling sunshine,
visited of all the winds of heaven, with glimpses of faraway hills and
home meadows where cloud shadows broaden and vanish, are dear to
our hearts; and dearer still the place of hardwoods, hung with their mist
of green, where elfin lights frolic; but dearest of all is the close wood,
curtained with fine-spun purple gloom,[22] through which only the most
adventurous sunbeams may glide, looking pale as if with fear over their
own daring. This is where the immortal heart of the wood will beat
against ours and its subtle life will steal into our veins and make us its
own forever, so that no matter where we go or how wide we wander in
the noisy ways of cities or over lone paths of sea, we shall yet be drawn
back to the forest to find our most enduring kinship.[23]

Those who have followed a dim, winding, balsamic path to the unexpected hollow where a wood spring lies, have found the rarest secret the
woods can reveal. Here it is, under its pines, a crystal-clear thing, with
lips unkissed by so much as a stray sunbeam. It is easy to dream that it is
one of the haunted springs of old romance, an enchanted spot where we
must go softly and speak, if we dare speak at all, in the lowest of whispers, lest we disturb the rest of a white, wet naiad or break some spell
that has cost long years of mystic weaving. Come, let us stoop down on
the brink and ever so gently drink from our hollowed hands of the living
water, for it must have some potent quality of magic in it, and all our
future lives we shall have better understanding of the wood and its lore
by reason of drinking from the cup it offers.[24]

A brook steals away from the spring. At first it goes deeply and darkly
and softly, as becomes its birth; but as soon as we follow it from that
somewhat uncanny locality we see that, though born of the spring, it was
begotten by the spirit of the wild, and is more its father's child than its
mother's, becoming promptly what all brooks are, a gay, irresponsible

L.M. Montgomery

vagabond of valley and wilderness.[25] Let us take it for a boon companion and follow it in all its windings and doublings and tricksy surprises.
A brook is the most changeful, bewitching, lovable thing in God's good
world. It is never in the same mind or mood two minutes. Here it creeps
around the roots of the birches, with a plaintive little murmur and sigh,
as if its heart were broken. We feel that we must sympathise with its old
sorrow and nameless woe. But listen, a curve further on and the brook is
laughing, a long, low gurgle of laughter, as if it were enjoying some capital joke all by itself;[26] and so infectious is its mirth that we must laugh
too and forget old sadness as the brook forgets.

Here it makes a pool, dark and brooding and still, and thinks over
its secrets with a reticence savouring of its maternity; but anon it grows
communicative and gossips shallowly over a broken pebble bed, where
there is a diamond-dance of sunbeams, and no minnow or troutling can
glide through without being seen.

Sometimes its banks are high and steep, hung with slender ashes and
birches; then they are mere low margins green with delicate mosses,
shelving out of the wood. Here we come to a little precipice, the brook
flings itself over undauntedly in an indignation of foam and gathers itself
up rather dizzily among the mossy stones below. It is some time before
it gets over its vexation; and it goes boiling and muttering along, fighting with the rotten logs that lie across it and making far more fuss than
is necessary over every root that interferes with it.[27] But the brook is
sweet-tempered and cannot be angry long; and soon it is twinkling ever
so good-naturedly in and out among the linked shadows, and presently it
leads us out of the woods into the meadows.

It is a spring evening and the earth smells good. All the birds, which
have been so busy nest-building through the day, have gone to sleep,
except the robins, which are just beginning to whistle, clearly, melodi-
ously, enchantingly, as they never whistle at any time save just after a
spring sunset. "Horns of elfland" never sounded so sweetly around hoary
castle and ruined tower as do the vesper calls of robins in a twilit wood
of spruces and across dim green pastures lying under the pale radiance of
a young moon.[28]

The frogs sing us homeward. From every pool in the valleys and swamp
in the forests come their "flute-throated voices." In that silvery, haunting
chorus the music of all the springs that have been since the days of Eden
finds its ever-renewed reincarnation.

Here the wood gives us a last sweet amazement for its guerdon.[29] Before us is a young poplar, the very embodiment of youth and spring in

78

its litheness and symmetry and grace and aspiration. Its little leaves are hanging tremulously, but are not yet so fully blown as to hide its delicate development of bough and twig, making poetry against the spiritual tints of a spring sunset.[30] It is so beautiful that it hurts us, with the pain inseparable from all perfection. Why is it so? Is it the pain of finality, the realisation that there can be nothing beyond but retrogression? Or is it the prisoned infinite in us calling out to its kindred infinite expressed in that visible perfection?[31]

The Woods in Summer

The spring woods are all spiritual. They charm us through the senses of eye and ear – delicate tintings and aerial sounds, like a maiden's dreams set to music. But the summer woods make a more sensuous appeal. They know that they have lost the freshness of their first youth, that something is gone for which all their luscious shadows and mellow lightings can never quite atone. So they offer us delectable things to tickle our palates. Who that has eaten strawberries, grass-new, from the sunny corners of summer woods, can ever forget them?

Strawberries are very delicious, even when eaten with cream and sugar, among the haunts of men. But would you know the real flavour of the strawberry in its highest perfection? Then come with me to a certain sunlit dell, along which white birches grow on one side and on the other the still, changeless ranks of the spruces. There are long grasses here at the roots of the trees, combed down by the winds, and wet with morning dew, long into the afternoon. Here we shall find berries, fit for the gods on high Olympus, great ambrosial sweetnesses, hanging like rubies to long, rosy stalks. Lift them by the stalk and eat them from it while they are uncrushed and virgin, tasting each berry by itself, with all its wild fragrance ensphered within. If you try to carry it home that elusive essence escapes, and then it is nothing more than a common berry of the fields and sunshine, very kitchenly good, indeed, but not as it should be when gathered and eaten in its uncharted haunts until our fingers are stained as pink as Aurora's eyelids.[32]

There are blueberries, too, growing on the sandy hill where we gathered May flowers in the spring. The blueberries are not sung in song or enshrined in romance; but I do not see why they should not be, for they are beautiful to behold; and, if eaten in their native haunts, are delicious enough as well, although, of course, not to be mentioned in the same paragraph as the strawberries. Perhaps it is because they are somewhat too lavish of themselves, in their great, heavily-hanging, plainly-seen clusters. They lack the charm of comparative rarity and exclusiveness; they need not to be eaten one by one, like the strawberries, but may be crunched together in generous mouthfuls. See how pretty they are – the dainty green of the unripe berries, the glossy pinks and scarlets of the half-ripe, the misty blue of the fully matured. To sit on this hill, steeped in languid summer sunshine, rife with odours of fir and of nameless growing things in their golden prime, with the sough of winds in the shaking tree-tops, and eat blueberries, is something that the mighty ones of earth might envy us. The poor inhabitants of palaces, how we can pity them, from this, our hill throne of the wilderness, fronting the gateways of the west![33] The afternoon is a great, dulcet, golden dream of peace, through which the heart of summer throbs with lazy rhythm.

Pigeon-berries are not to be eaten. They are woolly, tasteless things.[34] But they were created to be looked at and they have the beauty that is its own excuse for being. They grow in the places of shadow, preferably the fibrous banks under the boughs of the spruces, knowing, perhaps, how the green and the gloom set off their glowing scarlet. Such scarlet! They, too, are true children of the wood, in that they lose their beauty elsewhere. Dare to take them home with you, and they seem hard, flaunting, obvious things, void of all charm. But in the spruce wood they are vivid and brilliant, the jewels with which the sombre forest of conebearers loves to deck its brown breast.

The woods are full of summer flowers, and rich spoil may be ours for the seeking; but it is a pity to gather wood flowers. They do not bear it well, not even so well as the strawberries. They lose half their witchery away from the shadow and the green and the flicker. The gay ones look too gay and crude when unsoftened by the backgrounds of the ancient wood; and the little, shy, sweet things seem lost and timid and homesick. No, we shall not pluck the wood flowers. The way to enjoy them most is to track them down to their remote haunts, gloat over them there, and then leave them, with backward glances, taking with us only the beguiling memory of their grace and fragrance.[35]

In late June and early July the spruce woods are given over to the June-bells, which have another and more scientific name, of course.[36] But who wants a better name than June-bells? They are so perfect in their way that they seem to epitomise the very secret and charm of the forest, as if the old wood's daintiest thoughts had materialised in blossom, and all the roses by Bendameer's stream are not so fragrant as a shallow sheet of June-bells under the boughs of fir.[37]

Starflowers grow here, too, spirit pale and fair; and ladies' lips are found in abundance by those who know just where to look for them, but never reveal themselves to the casual passer-by. They are not, as their name might suggest, red, but creamy tinted. Perhaps it is their surpassing sweetness which accounts for the name. Their perfume is richer than that of the June-bells and every whit as haunting and mystical.

In July the waste places of the wood, which axe has scarred and flame scorched, are aglow with the purple pomp of the fireweed, which depends, and not vainly, on its colouring alone for its beauty. The fire that defaced and blackened must have awakened some answering glow and fervour in the veins of the wood, which has outbroken in this wave of royal magnificence, surging against the pine hill and overflowing the brushwood to our very feet.

The ladies' eardrops are twinkling jewel-like from hanging boughs on all the brooklands; and along the lanes and among the birches the buttercups are smiling at us, quite as much at home here as on the breezy uplands.

In August the goldenrod makes glad the sunny woodways, and the asters shake out their frilled lavender gowns. The country people have such a pretty name for them; they call them "farewell-summers," because they come when summer is beginning to walk westering. She is with us still, but her face is turned from us.

Look, I pray you, at the tints on the trunk of that birch tree before us, whence some vandal hand has torn away the white-skin wrapper in several places. They range from the purest creamy white through exquisite golden tones, growing deeper and deeper until the inmost layer reveals the ripest, richest brown, as if to tell us that all these birches, so maiden-like and cool exteriorly, have yet warmly hued feelings at their hearts.[38]

It is so easy to love your neighbours when your neighbours are all trees; and it is so easy to live with trees. They are the most friendly things in God's good creation. To hold converse with pines, to whisper secrets with mountain ashes, to listen to the tales of old romance that beeches have to tell, to walk in eloquent silence with self-contained firs is to learn what real companionship is.[39] And then, too, trees, unlike so many humans, always improve on acquaintance. No matter how much you like them at the start you are sure to like them much better further on, and best of all when you have known them for years and enjoyed intercourse with them in all seasons, staunch, loyal friends that they are.

Trees have as much individuality as human beings to those who love and learn them. Not even two spruces are alike. There is some kink or curve, or bend of bough to single each one out from its fellows. Some trees love to grow sociably together, branches intertwining, like girls with their arms about each other, whispering interminably of their secrets. There are more exclusive groups of four or five, and there are hermits of trees who like to stand apart in solitary majesty and hold commune only with the winds of heaven. Yet these trees are often the best worth knowing, and have all the charm that attaches to the strong and lonely and reserved. It is more of a triumph to win their confidence than that of easier trees.[40]

Pines are the trees of myth and legend. They strike their roots deep into the traditions of an older world, but wind and star love their lofty tops. What music when old Aeolus draws his bow across the branches of a pine![41] What a sense of two majesties meeting when a pearl white planet seems resting on its very crest! Have you ever witnessed a thunderstorm in a pine wood, especially when evening is drawing on? I have, once. And since then I think I have known what God's voice must have been speaking to Job out of the whirlwind.[42]

We are not going to have a thunderstorm on our walk of this evening, but I verily believe a shower of rain is coming up. Have you noticed the veiled hush that has fallen over the woods lately, while we have been wandering from tree to tree? All the young breezes that were whispering and rustling so importantly a while ago have folded their wings and are motionless and soundless. Not a leaf rustles, not a shadow flickers. The maple leaves yonder turn wrong side out, until the tree looks as if it were growing pale from fear.[43] And now a cool shade falls over the woods; the cloud has reached us; it is not a big cloud; there is crystalline, untroubled sky below and above it. 'Twill be but a passing shower, and the thick boughs of this fir copse are all the protection that we shall need. Creep under and sit at ease, on the dusky soil, compact of many dead and gone generations of fir needles, which no passing shower can moisten.

Ha, there is the rain now, with a rush and sweep of wind, really more noise than anything else! Yet the shower is a good, smart one while it lasts. It patters down sharply on the maples and dimples the faces of the wood pools. It dances along the lanes and byways and pelts the brook right merrily. It makes quite a fuss for the time being, this impertinent, important shower. But not a drop touches us through our staunch fir, and presently it is all over. The cloud is away and the low sun is shining out on the wet, glistening trees. Far away we see a hill still dim with rain, but below us the cup of the valley seems brimming over with peach-tinted mists. The woods are all pranked out with the sparkle and glitter of jewels, and a bird begins to sing overhead as if he were cheated into believing it is springtime again, so wondrously fresh and sweet is the world all at once.[44]

The rain is a marvellous alchemist. It has extracted the aroma from tree and shrub and blossom, and flung it lavishly on the cool, moist air. It has taken from the firs the tang of their balsam, from the lanes the warm breath of the asters and grasses, from the blueberry hill its savour of ripening fruit, and the wind comes down from the wild places spiced and poignant with the breath of drenched and tangled fern.

A bird comes tiptoeing along the lane, with a worm in her mouth. After a shower is the blessed time for birds. It is a robin, a plump, reddish-breasted thing, that is not even afraid of us. I know her nest is near by, for I found it last week, half-built. Let us look to see if any eggs are in it. Ha, Madam Robin, this disturbs your complacency somewhat, does it? Even the worm is dropped and forgotten, and you fly to a bough above us, chirping frantically. Dear, we are not going to hurt your little home, nor yet this most wonderful egg in it, though we touch it with reverent fingers.

Think what is penned within those fragile, pale-blue walls ... not, perhaps, "the music of the moon," but an earthlier, homelier music, compact of wholesome sweetness and the joy of living. This egg will some day be a robin, to whistle us blithely home in the afterlights.[45]

It is afterlight now, for the sun has set. Out in the open there is still much light of a fine, emerald-golden sort.[46] But the wood is already wrapping itself in a dim, blue twilight and falling upon rest in bosk and dell.[47] It will be quite dark before we reach the end of this long, wetly-fragrant lane. There goes the first firefly, or is it a pixy out with a lantern? Soon there are hundreds of them, flashing mysteriously across the dusk, under the boughs and over the ferns. There is certainly something a little supernatural about fireflies. Nobody pretends to understand them. Did anyone ever see a firefly in daylight? They are akin to the tribes of faery, survivals of the olden time, when the woods and hills swarmed with the little green folk. It is still very easy to believe in fairies when you see those goblin lanterns glimmering among the fir tassels.[48]

The full moon has been up for some time, and now, as we come out to the clearing, she is gleaming lustrously from a cloudless sky across the valley. But between us and her stretches up a tall, tall pine, far above the undergrowth, wondrously straight and slender and branchless to its very top, where it overflows in a crest of dark boughs against the silvery splendour behind it. Beyond, the uplands and the homesteads are lying in a suave, white radiance,[49] but here the spell of the woods is still on us, and the white magic of the moonlight behind the pine speaks the last word of the potent incantation.

The Woods in Autumn

Maples are trees that have primeval fire in their souls. It glows out a little in their early youth, before the leaves open, in the redness and rosy-yellowness of their blossoms, but in summer it is carefully hidden under a demure, silver-lined greenness. Then, when autumn comes, the maples give up trying to be sober and flame out in all the barbaric splendour and gorgeousness of their real natures, making of the ancient wood a thing out of an Arabian Nights dream in the golden prime of good *Haroun Alraschid*.[50]

You never may know what scarlet and crimson really are until you see them in their perfection on an October hillside under the unfathomable blue of an autumn sky. All the glow and radiance and joy at earth's heart seem to have broken loose in a splendid determination to express itself for once before the frost of winter chills her beating pulses. It is the year's carnival ere the dull Lenten days of leafless valleys and penitential mists come.[51]

The maples are the best vehicle for this hidden, immemorial fire of the earth and the woods, but the other trees bear their part valiantly. The sumacs are almost as gorgeous as the maples; the wild cherry trees are, indeed, more subdued, as if they are rather too reserved and modest to go to the length the maples do, and prefer to let their crimson and gold burn more dully through overtints of bronzy green.

I know a dell, far in the bosky deeps of the wood, where a row of maiden birches fringe a deeply-running stream, and each birch is more exquisite than her sisters.[52] And, as for the grace and goldenness of the young things, that cannot be expressed in terms of the dictionary or symbols of earth, but must be seen to be believed or realised. I stumbled on that dell the other day quite by accident ... if, indeed, there can be such a thing as accident in the woods, where I am tempted to think we are led by the Good People along such of their fairy paths as they have a mind for us to walk in.[53] It was lying in a benediction of amber sunshine, and it seemed to me that a spell of eternity was woven over it ... that winter might not touch it, nor spring evermore revisit it. It must continue forever so,[54] the yellow trees mirrored in the placid stream, with now and then a leaf falling on the water to drift away and be used, mayhap, as a golden shallop for some adventurous wood sprite, who had it in mind to fare forth to some wonderful far-off region where all the brooks run into the sea.[55]

I left the dell while the sunshine still shone on it, before the shadows had begun to fall. And I shall never, if I can help it, revisit it again. I wish to remember it always as in that one vision and never see it changed or different.[56] I think it is one of the places where dreams grow;[57] and hereafter whenever I have a dream of a certain kind … a golden, mellow, crimson-veined dream, a very dream of dreams, I shall please my fancy with the belief that it came from my secret dell of birches, and was born of some mystic union between the fairest of the sisters and the genius of that crooning brook.[58]

The woods are full of purple vistas, threaded with sunshine and gossamer.[59] Down drop the tinted leaves, one by one, with the faintest of sighs, until our feet rustle most silverly through their fallen magnificence. The woods are as friendly as ever; but they do not make the advances of spring, nor do they lavish attentions on us as in summer. They are full of a gentle, placid indifference. We have the freedom of their wonders, as old friends, but we are not any longer to expect them to make much fuss over us; they want to dream and remember, undisturbed by new things. They have spread out a spectacle that cannot be surpassed … have flung all their months of hoarded sunlight into one grand burst of colour, and now they wish to take their rest.

The conebearers hardly know what to make of the transformation that has come over their deciduous neighbours, who comported themselves so discreetly and respectably all through the earlier months of the year. The pines and hemlocks and spruces seem to wrap their dark mantles around them, with a tinge of haughty disapproval. No change of fashion for them, and it please ye, no flaunting in unseemly liveries of riotous hue. It is theirs to keep up the dignity of the forest. Only the firs are more tolerant. Indeed, here and there a fir seems trying to change its sober garments also, and has turned a rich red-brown. But, alas! The poor fir pays for its desertion of fir tradition by death. Only the dying fir can change its colour … and exhale that haunting, indescribable odour,[60] which steals out to meet us in shadowy hollows and silent dingles.

There is a magic in that scent of dying fir. It gets into our blood like some rare, subtly-compounded wine, and thrills us with unutterable sweetnesses, as of recollections from some other, fairer life, lived in some happier star. Compared to it, all other scents seem heavy and earth-born, luring to the valleys instead of the heights. But the tang of the fir summons upward and onward to some "far-off, divine event" ... some spiritual peak of attainment, whence we shall see with unfaltering, un-clouded vision the spires of some aerial city beautiful, or the fulfilment of some fair, fadeless land of promise.[61]

Autumn woods give us another rare fragrance also – the aroma of frosted ferns. The morning is the best time for it – a morning after a sharp frost, when the sunshine breaks over the hollows in the woods; but sometimes we may catch it in the evenings after the afternoon sun has steeped the feathery golden sheets of a certain variety of fern and drawn out their choicest savour.

I have a surprise for you if you will but walk with me through these still, stained mazes and over the enclosed harvest field beyond, and up this dour hill of gnarled spruces and along this maple-fringed upland meadow. There will be many little things along our way to make us glad. Joyful sounds will "come ringing down the wind"; gypsy gold will be ours for the gathering;[62] I can promise you a glimpse now and then of a shy partridge, scuttling away over the fallen leaves; as the evening deepens there will be nun-like shadows under the trees; and there will be squirrels, chattering in the beeches where the nuts are. Squirrels, you know, are the gossips and busybodies of the woods, not having learned the fine reserve of its other denizens. But there is a certain shrill friendliness in their greet-ing, and they are not really half such scolds as one might imagine from appearances. If they would but "take a thought and mend" their shrewd-like ways they would be dear, lovable creatures enough.[63]

Ah, here is my promised surprise. Look you ... a tree ... an apple tree ... an apple tree laden with fruit ... as I live, a veritable apple-bearing apple tree here in the very heart of the woods, neighboured by beeches and pines, miles away from any orchard. Years ago it sprang from some chance sown seed; and the alien thing has grown and flourished and held its own. In the spring I wandered this way and saw it white amid wildness with its domestic blossom. Pluck and eat fearlessly, I pray you. I know these apples of old and fruit of Hesperides hath not a rarer flavour, nor the fatal apple of Eden.[64] They have a tawny skin, but a white, white flesh, faintly veined with red; and, besides their own proper apple taste, they have a certain wild, delicious flavour no orchard-grown apples ever possessed or can possess. Let us sit here on this fallen tree, cushioned with mosses, and eat our fill, while the shafts of sunshine turn crimson and grow remote and more remote, until they vanish altogether and the early autumn twilight falls over the woods.[65] Surely, there is nothing more for our quest, and we may as well go home.

Nothing more? Look you, I pray you, over yonder, through the mist of this mild, calm evening. Beyond the brook valley, halfway up the opposite slope, a brush fire is burning clearly and steadily in a maple grove. There is something indescribably alluring in that fire, glowing so redly against the dark background of forest and twilit hill. A wood fire at night has a fascination not to be resisted by those of mortal race. Come, let us arise and go to it. It may have been lighted by some good, honest farmer, bent on tidying up his sugar orchard, but it may also, for aught we know, have been kindled by no earthly woodman, a beacon or a summons to the tribes of færy.[66] Even so, we shall seek it fearlessly, for are we not members of the immemorial free-masonry of the woods?

Now we are in the grove. Is it not beautiful, O comrade of my wanderings? So beautiful that it makes us perfectly happy; we could sit down and cry for pure, unearthly joy; and we desire fervently some new language, rich in unused, unstained words, to express our rapture.

The fire burns with a clear, steady glow and a soft crackle; the long arcades beneath the trees are illuminated with a rosy radiance, beyond which lurks companies of enticing gray and purple shadows. Everything is very still and dreamy and remote. It is impossible that out there, just over the hill, lies a village of men, where tame household lamps are shining. We must be thousands of miles away from such things. It is an hour and place when and where anything might come true … when men in green might creep out to join hands and foot in fealty around the fire, or wood nymphs steal from their trees to warm their white limbs, grown chilly in autumn frosts, by the blaze. I don't think we would feel much surprise if we should see something of the kind … the flash of an ivory shoulder through yonder gloom, or a queer little elfin face peering at us around a twisted gray trunk. Oh, I think I do see it … but one cannot be sure. Mortal eyesight is too slow and clumsy a thing to match against the flicker of a pixy-litten fire.[67]

Everything is in this hour – the beauty of classic myths, the primal charm of the silent and the open, the lure of mystery, the beguilement of gramarye.[68] It has been a pure love match 'twixt light and dark, and beautiful exceedingly are the off-spring thereof.[69]

We go home by the old fir lane over the hill, though it is somewhat longer than the field way. But it always drags terribly at my heart to go past a wood lane if I can make any excuse at all for traversing it.[70] Sometimes

I like to walk in this lane alone, for I know it well and can tryst here with many shapes of old dreams and joys. But to-night I am glad to have a comrade ... for the dark is coming down, and I am just a wee bit afraid, with a not unpleasant fear. The whole character of the lane seems changed. It is mysterious ... eerie ... almost sinister. The trees, my old, well-known friends, are strange and aloof. The sounds we hear are not the cheery, companionable sounds of daytime ... they are creeping and whispering and weird, as if the life of the woods had suddenly developed something almost hostile ... something, at least, alien and unacquainted and furtive. I could fancy that I hear stealthy footsteps all around us ... that strange eyes were watching us through the boughs.[71] I feel all the old primitive fear known to the childhood of the race – the awe of the dark and shadowy, the shrinking from some unseen menace lurking in the gloom.[72] My reason quells it into a piquant watchfulness, but were I alone it would take but little – nothing more than that strip of dried bark keening so shilly on the rail fence – to deliver me over to a blind panic, in which I should turn and flee shamelessly. As it is, I walk more quickly than my wont, and feel, as we leave the lane behind, that I am escaping from some fascinating, but not altogether hallowed, locality – a place still given over to paganism and the revels of fauns and satyrs. None of the wild places are ever wholly Christian in the darkness, however much they may seem so in daylight. There is always a lurking life in them that dares not show itself to the sun, but regains its own with the night. Comrade, I vow I am right glad to see the steady-gleaming homelight below us, shining on homely, mortal faces. It is a good thing after the uncanny enchantment of the autumn forest.[73]

The Woods in Winter

Last night it snowed. I had been waiting for this first snowfall before I went again to the woods. I did not wish to spy upon their nakedness. It seems like taking an unfair advantage of old friends to visit them when they are unclad, with all the little ins and outs of their realm laid pitifully bare. There is always a November space, after the leaves have fallen, when it seems almost indecent to intrude on the forest, for its glory terrestrial has departed, and its glory celestial ... of spirit and purity and whiteness ... has not yet come upon it.[74] Of course, there are dear days sometimes, even in November, when the woods are beautiful and gracious in a dignified serenity of folded hands and closed eyes ... days full of a fine, pale sunshine that sifts through the firs and glimmers in the gray beech-wood, lighting up evergreen banks of moss and washing the colonnades of the pines ... days with a high-sprung sky of flawless turquoise, shading off into milkiness on the far horizons ... days ending for all their mildness and dream in a murky red sunset, flaming in smoky crimson behind the westering hills, with perhaps a star above it, like a saved soul gazing with compassionate eyes into pits of torment, where sinful spirits are being purged from the stains of earthly pilgrimage.[75]

But such days are an exception in late November and early December. More commonly they are dour and forbidding, in a "hard, dull bitterness,"[76] with sunless gray skies. The winds that still go "piping down the valleys wild" are heartbroken searchers, seeking for things loved and lost, wailing in their loneliness, calling in vain on elf and fay; for the fairy folk, if they be not all fled afar to the southlands, must be curled up asleep in the hearts of the pines or among the roots of the ferns;[77] and they will never venture out amid the desolation of winter woods where there is no leafy curtain to screen them, no bluebell into which to creep, no toadstool under which to hide.

But last night the snow came ... enough to transfigure and beautify, but not enough to spoil the walking; and it did not drift, but just fell softly and lightly, doing its wonder-work in the mirk of a December night. This morning, when I awakened and saw the world in the sunlight, I had a vision of woodland solitudes of snow, arcades picked out in pearl and silver, long floors of untrodden marble, whence spring the cathedral columns of the pines.[78] And this afternoon I went to find the reality of my vision in the woods "that belt the gray hillside" ... ay, and overflow beyond it into many a valley white-folded in immortal peace.[79]

One can really get better acquainted with the trees in winter. There is no drapery of leaves to hide them from us; we can see all their beauty of graceful limb, of upreaching boughs, of mesh-like twigs, spun against the transparent skies. The slenderness or straightness or sturdiness of their trunks is revealed; even the birds' nests ... "there are no birds in last year's nest"[80] ... are hung plainly in sight for any curious eye to see. It does not matter now. The dappled eggs have long ago hatched out into incarnate melody and grace, and the birdlings have flown to lands of the sun far-distant, caring nothing now for their old cradles, which are filled with winter snows.

The beeches and maples are dignified matrons, even when stripped of their foliage; and the birches ... look you at that row of them against the spruce hill, their white limbs gleaming through the fine purple mist of their twigs ... are beautiful pagan maidens who have never lost the Eden secret of being naked and unashamed.[81]

But the conebearers, stanch souls that they are, keep their secrets still. The firs and the pines and the spruces never reveal their mystery, never betray their long-guarded lore.[82] See how beautiful is that thickly-growing copse of young firs, lightly powdered with the new-fallen snow, as if a veil of aerial lace had been tricksily flung over austere young druid priestesses forsworn to all such frivolities of vain adornment.[83] Yet they wear it gracefully enough ... firs can do anything gracefully, even to wringing their hands in the grip of a storm. The deciduous trees are always anguished and writhen and piteous in storms; but there is something in the conebearers akin to the storm spirit ... something that leaps out to greet it and join with it in a wild, exultant revelry. After the first snowfall, however, the woods are at peace in their white loveliness.[84] Today I paused at the entrance of a narrow path between upright ranks of beeches, and looked long adown it before I could commit what seemed the desecration of walking through it ... so taintless and wonderful it seemed, like a street of pearl in the New Jerusalem.[85] Every twig and spray was outlined in snow. The undergrowth along its sides was a little fairy forest cut out of marble. The shadows cast by the honey-tinted winter sunshine were fine and spirit-like.[86] Every step I took revealed new enchantments, as if some ambitious elfin artificer were striving to show just how much could be done with nothing but snow in the hands of somebody who knew how to make use of it. A snowfall such as this is the finest test of beauty. Wherever there is any ugliness or distortion it shows mercilessly; but beauty and grace are added unto beauty and grace, even as unto him that hath shall be given abundantly.[87]

As a rule, winter woods are given over to the empery of silence. There are no birds to chirp and sing, no brooks to gurgle, no squirrels to gossip. But the wind makes music occasionally and gives in quality what it lacks in quantity. Sometimes on a clear starlit night it whistles through the copses most freakishly and joyously; and again, on a brooding afternoon before a storm it creeps along the floor of the woods with a low, wailing cry that haunts the hearer with its significance of hopelessness and boding.[88]

To-day there are no drifts. But sometimes, after a storm, the hollows and lanes are full of them, carved by the inimitable chisel of the northeaster into wonderful shapes. I remember once coming upon a snowdrift in a clearing far back in the woods which was the exact likeness of a beautiful woman's profile. Seen too close by, the resemblance was lost, as in the fairy tale of the Castle of St. John;[89] seen in front, it was a shapeless oddity; but at just the right distance and angle, the outline was so perfect that when I came suddenly upon it, gleaming out against the dark background of spruce in the glow of a winter sunset, I could hardly convince myself that it was not the work of a human hand. There was a low, noble brow, a straight, classic nose, lips and chin and cheek curve modelled as if some goddess of old time had sat to the sculptor, and a breast of such cold, swelling purity as the very genius of the winter woods might display. All "the beauty that old Greece and Rome sang, painted, taught"[90] was expressed in it; yet no eyes but mine saw it.[91]

She is a rare artist, this old Mother Nature, who works "for the joy of the working,"[92] and not in any spirit of vain show. To-day the fir woods on the unsheltered side of the hill, where the winds have shaken off the snow, are a symphony of greens and grays, so subtle that you cannot tell where one shade begins to be the other. Gray trunk, green bough, gray-green moss, above the white floor. Yet the old gypsy doesn't like unrelieved monotones ... she must have a dash of colour. And here it is ... a broken dead fir branch of a beautiful brown swinging among the beards of moss.[93]

All the tintings of winter woods are extremely delicate and elusive. When the brief afternoon wanes, and the low, descending sun touches the faraway hill-tops of the south-west there seems to be all over the waste places an abundance, not of colour, but of the spirit of colour. There is really nothing but pure white after all, but one has the impression of fairy-like blendings of rose and violet, opal and heliotrope, on the slopes and in the dingles, and along the curves of the forest land. You feel sure the tint is there; but when you look directly at it it is gone ... from the corner of your eye you know it is lurking over yonder in a spot where there was nothing but a pale purity a moment ago. Only just when the sun is setting is there a fleeting gleam of real colour; then the redness streams over the snow, and incarnadines the hills and fields, and smites the crest of the firs on the hills with flame. Just a few minutes of trans-figuration and revelation ... and it is gone ... and over the woods falls the mystic veil of dreamy, haunted winter twilight.[94]

To my right, as I stand breathlessly happy in this wind-haunted, star-sentinelled valley, there is a grove of tall, gently waving spruces. Seen in daylight those spruces are old and uncomely ... dead almost to the tops, with withered branches. But seen in this enchanted light against a sky that begins by being rosy saffron and continues to be silver green, and ends finally in crystal blue, they are like tall, slender witch maidens weaving spells of necromancy in a rune of elder days. How I long to share in their gramarye ... to have fellowship in their twilight sorceries![95]

Up comes the moon! Saw you ever such beauty as moonlight in winter woods ... such wondrous union of clear radiance with blackest gloom ... such hints and hidings and revealings ... such deep copses laced with silver ... such aisles patterned with shadow ... such valleys brimmed over with splendour? I seem to be walking through a spellbound world of diamond and crystal and pearl; I feel a wonderful lightness of spirit and a soul-stirring joy in mere existence ... a joy that seems to spring fountain-like from the very deeps of my being and to be independent of all earthy things.[96] I am alone and I am glad of it. Any human companionship, even the dearest and most perfect, would be alien and superfluous to me now. I am sufficient unto myself, needing not any emotion of earth to round out my felicity. Such moments come rarely ... but when they do come they are inexpressibly marvellous and beautiful ... as if the finite were for a second infinity ... as if humanity were for a space uplifted into divinity.[97] Only for a moment, 'tis true ... yet such a moment is worth a cycle of common years untouched by the glory and the dream.[98]

NOTES

1 This tag is omitted from the first essay but appears in the remaining three.
2 Epperly, *Through Lover's Lane*, 160.
3 Montgomery, 8 October 1899, in *SJLMM*, 1: 243.
4 Montgomery to MacMillan, 16 September 1906, in *MDMM*, 26.
5 Montgomery to Weber, 2 September 1909, in *GGL*, 92.
6 Montgomery to MacMillan, 4 May 1911, in *MDMM*, 56.
7 Epperly, *Through Lover's Lane*, 160.
8 *BC*, 27.
9 *GR*, 188.
10 The section from the beginning of the essay till "older time haunt them" appears with minor variations as an extract from John Foster's book *Thistle Harvest* in *BC*, 17–18. The phrase beginning with "what unsuspected tint-ings" appears with minor variations in *AIn*, 8. "Demesnes" is an archaic term that refers to private land used mainly for pleasure, such as a park or a garden. The phrase beginning with "for it is the by-ways" appears with minor variations in *GR*, 188.
11 The phrase beginning with "sometimes the winter woods" appears with minor modifications in *MP*, 92.

12 "One's natural or proper place or sphere" (*OED*).

13 The phrase beginning with "from the potent" appears in *GR*, 187.

14 The majority of this paragraph, beginning with "Here is a westward," appears with minor variations in *GR*, 85.

15 The phrase "the dear, sky-tinted things" appears in *AIs*, 148.

16 Argos and Crete, locations prominent in Greek mythology. The phrase beginning with "a glimmering green sheet" appears in *GR*, 85.

17 An archaic form of "certainly" (*OED*).

18 The last three sentences appear in slightly revised form in *Emily Climbs*: "I went at dusk tonight to that little pearly pool which has always been such a witching spot to linger near on spring evenings. Through the trees that fringed it faint hues of rose and saffron from the west stole across it. It was unruffled by a breath and every leaf and branch and fern and blade of grass was mirrored in it" (*EC*, 325). The word "lissome," a contracted variant of "lithesome," means supple or agile (*OED*).

19 The section between "will you please look" and "to-day in the woods" appears with minor variations in *BC*, 170, in which the "wild pear" becomes a "wild plum-tree."

20 Properly, "the eternal fitness of things." From *Tom Jones* (1749), by Henry Fielding (1707–1754), English novelist and dramatist.

21 Extracts from this paragraph appear in *The Blue Castle* as part of a dialogue between Valancy and Barney, after which she teases him: "That sounds John Fosterish" (*BC*, 170).

22 The phrase "curtained with fine-spun purple gloom" appears in *FCA*, 156.

23 This last sentence appears with minor variations as the last part of the initial extract of John Foster's *Thistle Harvest* in *BC*, 18. It also appears with minor variations as a speech attributed to Blair Stanley in *GR*, 188.

24 The first two sentences in this paragraph appear with minor variations in *GR*, 189. The subsequent sentence and the phrase "some potent quality of magic in it" also appear in speeches attributed to Blair Stanley (ibid.). A naiad is "a nymph of fresh water, thought to inhabit a river, spring, etc., as its tutelary spirit" (*OED*).

25 The phrase "a gay, irresponsible vagabond of valley and wilderness" appears in *GR*, 18.

26 The extract between "A brook is the most changeful" and "some capital joke all by itself" appears with minor variations in *GR*, 190.

27 The preceding paragraph and parts of this one appear with minor variations in *GR*, 190.

28 This sentence appears with minor variations in *GR*, 89. A poem called "Robin Vespers" appears in *The Blythes Are Quoted*. The quotation "The

horns of Elfland" appears in "The Princess" (1847), a poem by Alfred, Lord Tennyson (1809–1892), English poet.

29 Guerdon, an archaic form of reward or recompense (*OED*).

30 The last two sentences appear with minor variations (referring to "an aspen in the orchard") in *GR*, 92.

31 In *Anne's House of Dreams*, Anne refers to an aspen: "It's so beautiful that it hurts me … Perfect things like that always did hurt me – I remember I called it 'the queer ache' when I was a child. What is the reason that pain like this seems inseparable from perfection? Is it the pain of finality – when we realise that there can be nothing beyond but retrogression?" (*AHD*, 152). I have corrected the original, which reads "It is the pain of finality."

32 Most of this paragraph, beginning with the phrase "sunlit dell," appears with minor variations in *BC*, 55. Mount Olympus is the highest mountain in Greece. Aurora is the goddess of dawn in Greek mythology and Latin poetry.

33 The last three sentences appear with minor variations in *BC*, 155; *RV*, 19; *BC*, 152.

34 The last two sentences appear in *GR*, 152.

35 Beginning with the phrase "it is a pity," this paragraph appears in shorter form and with minor variations in *BC*, 87.

36 In her journal, Montgomery identified "the shy sweet mild 'June Bell' – the *Linnea Borealis* – of Prince Edward Island spruce woods" as her favourite wildflower (Montgomery, 15 April 1914, in *SJLMM*, 2: 145).

37 This paragraph appears with minor variations in *GR*, 128. The term "Bendameer's stream" is from *Lulla Rookh* (1817), a work of poetry and prose by Thomas Moore (1779–1852), Irish poet and songwriter.

38 This last sentence appears with minor variations in *AIn*, 8–9.

39 These last two sentences appear with minor variations in *GR*, 188.

40 Parts of the last two paragraphs appear with minor variations in *EC*, 249.

41 The last three sentences appear with minor variations in *BC*, 195. In Greek mythology, Aeolus is ruler or custodian of the four winds.

42 See, in particular, chapter 38 of the Book of Job, part of the Hebrew Bible.

43 The last four sentences appear in revised form in *AWP*, 127.

44 Parts of this paragraph appear with minor variations in *AWP*, 127–28.

45 This paragraph appears with minor variations in *EQ*, 80. The phrase "the music of the moon" is from "Aylmer's Field" (1793), a poem by Alfred, Lord Tennyson.

46 This sentence appears with minor variations in *GR*, 89.

47 A bosk is a thicket or small wood. The phrase "through bosk and dell" is from the long poem "The Lord of the Isles" (1815) by Sir Walter Scott.

48 The last five sentences appear with minor variations in *GR*, 128–29.

49 Parts of this paragraph, from "gleaming lustrously" to "white radiance," appear with minor variations in *GR*, 193.

50 Hārūn al-Rashīd (763/6–809 CE), the fifth head of state of the Abbasid Caliphate in Iran, appears as a fictional character in *One Thousand and One Nights*, a collection of folk tales compiled in Arabic and published in English as *Arabian Nights* in 1706. In "Recollection of the Arabian Nights" (1830), a poem by Alfred, Lord Tennyson, each stanza except the last ends with the phrase "of good Haroun Alraschid."

51 The last two paragraphs appear with minor variations in *GR*, 186.

52 This sentence appears in different form in *GR*, 190.

53 The phrase beginning with "if, indeed" appears with a minor variation in *GR*, 188.

54 The extract between "a spell" and "forever so" appears with minor variations in *GR*, 191.

55 The extract beginning with "the yellow trees" appears with minor variations in *GR*, 190.

56 Sara Stanley expresses the same wish in *The Golden Road* (*GR*, 191).

57 Emily Byrd Starr makes a similar pronouncement in *Emily of New Moon* (*ENM*, 66).

58 The phrase beginning with "hereafter" appears with minor variations in *AWP*, 17.

59 This sentence appears with minor variations in *AIs*, 15.

60 The phrase "haunting, indescribable odour" appears in *GR*, 191.

61 This paragraph appears with minor variations in *GR*, 191–92. The phrase "far-off, divine event" is from "In Memoriam" (1849), by Alfred, Lord Tennyson.

62 The last two sentences appear with minor variations in *GR*, 187. The phrase "came ringing down the wind" is from *The Miller of Martigne* (1847), by Henry William Herbert (1807–1858), English novelist.

63 The last three sentences appear with minor variations in *GR*, 189. The phrase "take a thought and mend" is from "Address to the Deil" (1786), by Robert Burns (1759–1796), Scottish poet.

64 In Greek mythology, the Hesperides are nymphs that inhabit a beautiful garden in the Arcadian mountains. In the Judeo-Christian tradition, Adam and Eve (the first man and woman created by the God of the Hebrew Bible) are permitted to eat the fruit from any tree in the Garden of Eden, except from the tree of knowledge of good and evil. When Eve is tempted by a serpent to eat fruit from this tree and offers some to Adam, the two are expelled from the Garden by God (see Genesis 2:4–3:24 in the Hebrew Bible).

In the Christian tradition, the story of Adam and Eve forms the basis of the concept of original sin.

65 In *Anne of the Island*, Gilbert surprises Anne with "a veritable apple-bearing apple tree" in the woods, where this paragraph appears in different form (*AIs*, 15). The phrase beginning with "shafts of sunshine" appears with minor variations in *GR*, 191.

66 Extracts from this paragraph, beginning with the phrase "halfway up," appear in different form in *GR*, 192.

67 This paragraph appears in different form in *GR*, 192–93.

68 The phrase ending with "lure of mystery" appears in a speech attributed to Blair Stanley in *GR*, 193. "Gramarye" is an obscure and archaic word for "grammar" (*OED*).

69 An adult Anne murmurs a similar sentence to herself in *AIn*, 75.

70 See Blair Stanley's speech in *GR*, 188.

71 The extract from "eerie … almost sinister" to "through the boughs" appears with minor variations in Emily's diary in *EC*, 246–47. See also Montgomery, 18 November 1907, in *SJLMM*, 1: 332.

72 The phrase "old primitive fear" also appears in *AP*, 44.

73 The phrase "uncanny enchantment" appears in *EQ*, 125; the phrase "ever wholly Christian in the darkness" appears in *EC*, 247.

74 This sentence appears with minor variations in *AWP*, 40.

75 The extract beginning with "beautiful and gracious" and ending in "flawless turquoise" appears with minor variations in *BC*, 159, as does the phrase "murky red sunset, flaming in smoky crimson behind the westering hills." The phrase "shading off into milkiness on the far horizons" appears in *GR*, 167. The extract beginning with "a murky red sunset" and ending in "earthly pilgrimage" appears with minor variations in *EC*, 259.

76 From *Snow-Bound: A Winter Idyl* (1866), a long narrative poem by John Greenleaf Whittier (1807–1892), American poet.

77 Parts of this sentence, beginning with "The winds," appear with minor variations in *EC*, 259. The phrase "piping down the valleys wide" is from the introduction to *Songs of Innocence* (1789), by William Blake (1757–1827), English poet and artist.

78 The phrase beginning with "solitudes of snow" appears with minor variations in *GR*, 54.

79 When Sara Stanley asks her father where he is going, he replies: "To 'the woods that belt the gray hillside' – ay, and overflow beyond it into many a valley purple-folded in immemorial peace" (*GR*, 187). The phrase "that belt the gray hillside" is from "Ode to Memory" (1830), by Alfred, Lord Tennyson.

80 Properly, "There are no birds in last year's nest!" From "It Is Not Always May" (1845), by Henry Wadsworth Longfellow (1807–1882), American poet.

81 This sentence appears in slightly different form in *RI*, 108.

82 This sentence appears in different form in *EC*, 218.

83 This sentence appears with minor variations in *EC*, 132. The narrator adds: "Emily decided she would write that sentence down in her Jimmy-book when she went back."

84 The phrase "at peace in their white loveliness" appears in *MP*, 208.

85 The phrase beginning with "taintless and wonderful" appears in *GR*, 22. In the Christian tradition, the "new heaven and new earth" envisioned for a new Jerusalem includes "one pearl" at each of twelve gates and "the street of the city [was] pure gold." See Revelation 21:21 in the Christian Bible.

86 The last three sentences appear with minor variations in *BC*, 161.

87 The last three sentences appear with minor variations in *MP*, 170.

88 The phrase "given over to the empery of silence" appears in *BC*, 166. The extract from "There are no birds" to "lacks in quantity" appears with minor variations in *AWP*, 156. The phrase "whistles through the copses most freakishly and joyously" appears with minor variations in *BC*, 167. The phrase beginning with "on a brooding afternoon" and ending with "wailing cry" appears in different form in *GR*, 54.

89 A sixteenth-century tower house in southwest Scotland.

90 Properly, "The Beauty which old Greece or Rome / Sung, painted, wrought, lies close at home." From "To –: Lines Written after a Summer Day's Excursion," by John Greenleaf Whittier.

91 Most of this paragraph appears with minor variations in *BC*, 161.

92 From "When Earth's Last Picture Is Painted" (1892), by Rudyard Kipling (1865–1936), English poet and novelist.

93 This paragraph appears with minor variations in *BC*, 162–63.

94 Most of this paragraph appears with minor variations in *BC*, 161–62.

95 Most of this paragraph appears with minor variations in *MP*, 195.

96 The phrase beginning with "a joy that seems to spring" appears with minor variations in *EC*, 271.

97 The last three sentences appear with minor variations in *EC*, 177.

98 This sentence appears with minor variations in *GR*, 193. The phrase "the glory and the dream" is from "Ode: Intimations of Immortality from Recollections of Early Childhood" (1807), by William Wordsworth (1770–1850), English poet. Montgomery uses this quotation for the title of chapter 36 of *Anne of Green Gables*.

15

With Our Next-Door Neighbors:
Prince Edward Island

—— 1911 ——

THOMAS F. ANDERSON

Appearing here are extracts from an article on "'The Garden of the Gulf,' a Picturesque and Fertile Province, Smallest of the Maritime Trinity," part of a longer series of articles about North American vacation destinations published in the *Boston Globe* in spring 1911. It is accompanied by a photograph of Montgomery with a caption that identifies her as "Miss L.M. Montgomery, New Canadian Literary Star." The information on her home in Cavendish is out of date, however, and there is no mention of her newest book, *The Story Girl*, copies of which she would receive a few weeks later.

Recently a new and exceedingly brilliant star arose above the literary horizon in the person of a previously unknown writer of "heart interest" stories, Miss L.M. Montgomery; and presently the astronomers located her in the latitude of Prince Edward Island.

No one, especially those who had read Charles Dudley Warner's descriptions of the place,[1] had ever imagined that such a remote and unassertive speck on the map as Prince Edward Island would ever produce a writer whose first three books should one and all be included in the "six best sellers."

But it was in this unemotional little island that *Anne of Green Gables* was born and sent forth upon the uncertain sea of literature. The story was the work of a modest young woman school teacher, who doubtless was as greatly surprised as any of her neighbors when she found that the sweetly simple tale of the childish joys and sorrows of a diminutive red-haired girl had made the literary hit of the season with the entire American public and was destined to catch the fancy of the people of Europe, likewise.

Miss Montgomery lives in the quiet Prince Edward Island town of Cavendish, and thither the mails carry many an appreciative missive from admiring readers of her two delightful "Anne" stories and *Kilmeny of the Orchard* that followed them. There is a pathetic interest attaching to some of these: for Miss Montgomery tells me that scores of children throughout the United States have somehow become possessed of the idea that Anne Shirley is a real personage, and still living in Prince Edward Island; and so they write friendly letters to her, all of which are turned over to Miss Montgomery by the postmaster at Charlottetown,[2] just as the letters that children in big cities often send to Santa Claus are ofttimes forwarded to some big-hearted man or woman of means, who is glad to enact the role of St. Nicholas.

Miss Montgomery, who is entirely unspoiled by her unexpected stroke of fame and fortune, made her first visit to Boston last winter and was lionized to quite an extent, her pleasing personality making a decidedly favorable impression on all who met her. The Prince Edward Islanders here of course were exceedingly proud of her and did much to entertain her.

It was all very nice and novel, but the young lady confided to her friends that she would be more than glad to get back to her quiet and uneventful country life and that she would far prefer it as a regular thing even to a residence in Boston. One of the most delightful of her Boston experiences was a lunch that was given her by the young women employed in the local publishing house that issues her books, a thoroughly Bostonian idea, as well as a most creditable one.

Britain possesses, as a cherished literary shrine, the isle of Man,[3] but on this side of the ocean we have our isle St. Jean,[4] where, in the good old summer time, as Anne Shirley found it on the day of her arrival, the gulf-cooled air is "sweet with the breath of many apple orchards" and the meadows slope away in the romantic distance "to horizon mists of pearl and purple."[5]

NOTES

1 Charles Dudley Warner (1829–1900), American co-author (with Mark Twain) of *The Gilded Age: A Tale of Today* (1873), who wrote about the Maritime provinces in *Baddeck and That Sort of Thing* (1874).

2 In a 1909 letter to Ephraim Weber, Montgomery mentioned receiving a letter addressed to "Miss Anne Shirley, care of Miss Marilla Cuthbert, Avonlea, Prince Edward Island, Canada, *Ontario*" (Montgomery to Weber, 2 September 1909, in *GGL*, 93; emphasis in original).

3 Isle of Man is a self-governing island located between Great Britain and Ireland but not part of the United Kingdom.

4 Prince Edward Island was called Île Saint-Jean in 1534 by Jacques Cartier, as part of the French colony of Acadia, replacing the Mi'kmaq name that was transcribed by Europeans as "Abegweit," a name Montgomery used on occasion; it later became known at St. John's Island when it was ceded to the British. In 1798, it was renamed Prince Edward Island after Prince Edward Augustus, the Duke of Kent (1767–1820), a son of King George III and later the father of Queen Victoria.

5 Properly, "The air was sweet with the breath of many apple orchards and the meadows sloped away in the distance to horizon mists of pearl and purple" (*AGG*, 9).

16

[The Marriage of L.M. Montgomery]
—— 1911 ——

Staying at the home of her Uncle John and Aunt Annie Campbell in Park
Corner since the death of her grandmother, Montgomery prepared for her
marriage to Ewan Macdonald after a five-year engagement. The write-up in the
Charlottetown *Guardian* neglected to make any mention at all of her career,
presumably on the assumption that readers would be more interested in the details of the bride's clothing. Notices of her marriage appeared everywhere, from
the *Manitoba Free Press* to *The Bookseller, Newsdealer and Stationer* and *The
Christian Science Monitor*,[1] but they all appeared a few weeks after the fact. Indeed, it was the *Boston Herald* that revealed the lengths to which Montgomery
went to keep the ceremony private. As with most wedding announcements,
none of these told the entire story: according to a journal entry dated 1912 but
not published until 1987, Montgomery felt so miserable at her wedding banquet that she had to repress the urge to rip the ring off her finger.[2]

From *The Guardian* (Charlottetown, PE)

The marriage of Miss Lucy Maud Montgomery to Rev. Ewan
Macdonald,[3] pastor of St. Paul's Presbyterian Church, Leaskdale, Ontario, was solemnized at the home of the bride's uncle and aunt John
and Mrs. Campbell, Park Corner, P.E. Island on Wednesday July 5th.
At twelve o'clock the bridal party entered the parlor while "The voice
that breathed o'er Eden" was being sung.[4] The marriage ceremony was
performed by the Rev. John Stirling of Cavendish, P.E. Island.[5] The bride

who was unattended was gowned in ivory silk crepe de chene and lace with tunic of chiffon and pearl and crystal garniture. She wore a tulle veil with coronet of orange blossoms, and a pearl and amethyst necklace, the gift of the groom and carried a bouquet of white roses, lilies of the valley and maiden hair fern. Many beautiful wedding gifts were received among which was a silver tea service presented to Mrs. Macdonald by the Cavendish Presbyterian Church in which she has been a worker for many years. In the afternoon Mr. and Mrs. Macdonald left for Montreal whence they will sail on the White Star liner Megantic for a three months tour in England and Scotland. The bride travelled in a suit of steel gray serge with chiffon blouse and hat to match of steel grey braid trimmed with satin rosebuds.

From *The Boston Herald* (Boston, MA)

It will be news to many that Lucy Maud Montgomery, the popular author of *The Story Girl*, *Kilmeny of the Orchard*,[6] and the "Anne" books, has at length surprised her friends by acting the part of heroine in a very real comedy – not one of "Errors." As a blushing bride, presumably, she was led to Hymen's altar[7] in the Arcadia of her own stories, by the Rev. Ewan Macdonald,[8] B.A., a Presbyterian minister of Prince Edward Island, on July 5, 1911, and has sailed with her latest hero to spend a honeymoon in the vicinity of Alloa's "auld haunted kirk." By this time, doubtless, their eyes have feasted on that

> Winnock bunker in the east
> (Where) sat Auld Nick in shape o' beast.[9]

But under such clerical guidance there is little danger that either the vision or fate of Tam o' Shanter will mar the nuptial bliss.

How splendidly our douce and clever "Down-East" author kept her little secret. Who would have dreamed, after looking into her keen, but innocent, eyes, during her recent visit to Boston, that she was so vulnerable to Cupid's dart? It is true she had an excellent opinion of ministers, particularly those with whom she was acquainted on the red soil of her native island, but who could have guessed that the image of one of them was already enshrined in the warmest nook of her heart? Prudent Scotch lassie! How well she had taken to heart the advice of Burns:

[The Marriage of L.M. Montgomery]

> Aye, free, aff han' your story tell,
> When wi' a bosom crony;
> But still keep something to yoursel'
> Ye scarcely tell to ony.
> Conceal yoursel' as weel's ye can
> Frae critical dissection;
> But keek through every other man,
> Wi' sharpen'd, sly, inspection.[10]

Well, of course, a time came when she had to share her secret with a few intimate friends outside of her own family. Her publisher, Mr. L.C. Page of Boston, was one of the earliest of these, and naturally he wished to share it with the public. But straightway he received a letter, part of which ran as follows: "As for the 'embargo' – no, it must not be lifted until after the event. I am resolved that no hint of the matter shall get into the 'paper news' until it is over, and I shall be much annoyed if anything of the sort occurs." Mr. Page, we are informed, promptly telegraphed congratulations on the receipt of the above letter, and this is how the telegram was welcomed: "That telegram of yours nearly set the leather on fire. (We think she meant heather, which isn't quite so tough and is more flammable, 'forbye' making it conformable to a common Scotch phrase). It was telephoned out from K– to the P– C– Cheese Factory and taken by Mrs. C–, who is one of the noted gossips of the settlement. Fortunately, I caught her before she had time to tell and bound her to secrecy, and she seems to have kept her promise, though it must have been pretty hard on her."

Now, of course, all that is over, and there is no interest to be conserved by preventing the heather from going on fire. We wish the author of *The Story Girl* and her husband a large measure of happiness, and we shall remain curious until her next novel appears. We surmise that a parson will figure as the hero of the story.[11] Why not?

NOTES

1 See *Manitoba Free Press*, "Authoress Weds"; *The Bookseller, Newsdealer and Stationer*, "About Authors"; *The Christian Science Monitor*, "Among Books and Their Writers."
2 Montgomery, 28 January 1912, in *SJLMM*, 2: 68.

3　I have corrected the original, which reads "Ewen McDonald," and have corrected "McDonald" twice more in this paragraph.

4　Nineteenth-century hymn with lyrics by John Keble (1792–1866), a professor of poetry at Oxford University. The hymn, for which at least five melodies had been composed by the time of Montgomery's marriage, begins as follows: "The voice that breathed o'er Eden, that earliest wedding day, / The primal wedding blessing, it hath not passed away." According to her journal, the hymn was sung by Montgomery's cousin Stella Campbell and their friends Bruce and Vivian Howatt (Montgomery, 28 January 1912, in *SJLMM*, 2: 67).

5　The Presbyterian minister in Cavendish. He had recently married a close friend of Montgomery's, Margaret Ross. For her impressions of him, which may have shaped the character of Jonas Blake in *Anne of the Island*, see Montgomery, 11 July 1910, in *SJLMM*, 2: 9.

6　I have corrected the original, which reads "'Kilkenny of the Orchard.'"

7　"At Hymen's altar claim the chain / That twines two willing hearts in one!" From *The Welch Heiress, a Comedy*, by Edward Jerningham (1727–1812), English poet.

8　I have corrected the original, which reads "Ewen Macdonald."

9　The phrase "By Alloway's auld haunted kirk," referring to the Alloway kirk (now a ruin) in South Ayrshire, Scotland, appears in "Tam o' Shanter," a poem by Robert Burns, as do the lines "A winnock-bunker in the east / There sat auld Nick, in shape o' beast." The author evidently learned that the married couple would be travelling to Alloa, 115 km northeast of Alloway, and home to Montgomery's correspondent George Boyd MacMillan.

10　From "Epistle to a Young Friend," by Robert Burns.

11　As it happens, two Presbyterian ministers would appear as romantic figures in later Anne books, although not in the way predicted here: Jonas Blake, in *Anne of the Island*, is "the ugliest young man I've ever seen," according to the woman who eventually marries him (*AIs*, 157); and John Meredith, in *Rainbow Valley*, is so absent-minded that he neglects his four motherless children shamelessly.

17

A Canadian Novelist of Note Interviewed

—— 1911 ——

This interview, which evidently took place in Great Britain while Montgomery was on her honeymoon in the summer of 1911, was published within a month of her move to Leaskdale, Ontario. The subhead, "Anna of the Green Gables on Wedding Tour in England Talks of Her Work," conflates the author with her character (and gets Anne's name wrong in the process). Montgomery pasted in one of her scrapbooks an alternative version of this article, published in an unidentified periodical under the title "A Canadian Novelist" and attributed to a Christian Richardson, who perhaps was the "lady journalist and ardent suffragette" mentioned in a 1911 letter to MacMillan.[1]

"Read *Anne of Green Gables*," said a friend, two or three years ago. I began it, and sat up that night till I finished it. Who could turn aside from the thin, little homeless girl whom "nobody ever wanted," yet who had such a faculty of "imagining herself into" all the delights denied her in reality? Did she not at once recognize a "kindred spirit" in old "Matthew"? Did she not storm and rage at the meddlesome neighbor, crack her slate over the head of the handsome boy who called her "carroty," and then so worship the beautiful little "Diana," and "imagine" all the glorious future before her that she ended by sobbing her heart out at the prospect of the inevitable husband who would some time come between them?[2] "Anne, spelled with an 'E'" is irresistible.

That the one who "imagined" her was a Canadian whom no one seemed to have heard of heightened the interest.[3] One ventures now to take special credit for that, since the comment of His Excellency Earl Grey, who paid Miss Montgomery a pretty compliment, to the effect that the Canadians were a very fine people, but one thing he had against them was that they were so apt not to appreciate the work of one of their own until it had been admired by others.[4]

An Unassuming Authoress

Miss Montgomery, or, rather, Mrs. Montgomery Macdonald – for she is just now in England on her wedding tour – is a very unassuming author-ess to outward appearance. Of medium height, slight, pale, and even delicate-looking (though that may easily be more apparent than real), with pointy chin, small mouth, and broad forehead and quiet manner. Her eyes are dark and deep, and the heavy glossy black hair is something good to look at. Sitting in a cosy corner of the hotel drawing-room, out of earshot of the rest, I had a delightful, informal chat, and even enjoyed some "secrets," which will never be told in print.

"It is really all like a dream to me," Mrs. Macdonald said, musingly. "I feel quite as if I were looking on and listening to talk about someone else."

"Was 'Anne's' experience of publishers like that of so many others?"

"Oh, yes," she said; "she was refused by five, one after the other. If the sixth had done the same I should have laid her away and given it up altogether, I think." Then she laughed, and began to tell of the news-paper criticisms of her newest book, *The Story Girl*, with its delightful sketches of child-life in Prince Edward Island. "Most of them are really very kind," she said, "but one is quite vicious – and (is it not curious?) he abuses just the very things that the others praise.[5] Some say they are glad I have gone back to my first style in *Anne*. Now *Anne* was not my first at all, but *Kilmeny of the Orchard*, and that I do not consider at all good. How did I come to write it? Well, you see, I was just a little magazine hack, and had to write what the publishers wanted. I had to earn my liv-ing. One order came for a serial of just seven chapters. I tried *Anne* first, but soon saw I could not make it what he wanted. Then I wrote *Kilmeny*. Later I took up *Anne*, and – it just wrote itself, I think; I really feel as though I had had nothing to do with it. It was only after *Anne* made a hit that the publisher raked up *Kilmeny* out of the old files and got me to pad it out a bit, and make a book of it."[6]

"The Island"

Miss Montgomery was born, and lived her life, till her marriage in June last,[7] in Cavendish, "a little country place on the north shore of Prince Edward Island," and declares "The Island" is the loveliest spot in all Canada. Of course, immigration had for the most part passed it by, but there is a new movement, and many farmers who prefer old settled places are being attracted to it. Her father was Mr. H.J. Montgomery, a merchant of Cavendish. Her mother died when she was a baby, and her grandmother was "all the mother she ever knew," she says, fondly.[8] "She was very pretty, and so young-looking always, and so young in spirit until the very last."

This grandmother, Lucy Woolner, was born in Dunwich, East Suffolk, and came with her parents to Prince Edward Island at the age of 12.[9] Later she married Alexander Macneill, whose grandfather left Argyleshire for Prince Edward Island at the time when the country became uncomfortable for the followers of Charles Stuart.[10] Cavendish, like so many country places, Mrs. Macdonald explained, "has a few principal families" (Macneills, Simpsons and Clarks), all closely intermarried, "because there was no one else to marry."[11] She supposes she inherits her love of writing from her grandfather.[12] He and his brothers all wrote poetry. "It was good, I know," she says, "though there is not a line of it now in existence, for I remember my uncles reciting it to me. My father went to Prince Albert, after my mother's death, and married again. He is dead now. On one occasion a maid with a mania for house-cleaning burned a large bagful of letters and papers which had been hanging for years in the garret. I suppose some poetry, as well as much information about his family, was thus destroyed. The story of Betsey and Nancy Penman in *The Story Girl* is quite true. They were my two grandmothers."[13]

Writing, Housekeeping and Gardening

Mrs. Macdonald loves writing. It never tires her; she does not do enough of it, she says. *Anne* took all one winter, at the rate of an hour in the morning and another in the afternoon. But then the author had her housekeeping and gardening to attend to as well, and she is very fond of both. The advantage of housekeeping and gardening is that they leave your mind free to "imagine" so many other things, and, naturally, the two hours would be used to the best advantage, because what she had to write was always "all thought out" before she sat down.

When Earl Grey came to Charlottetown he sent specially for Miss Montgomery, and was most delightful and unconventional – so genuinely interested in country matters. He said he had "determined when he came to the island to see at least two persons, the authoress of *Anne of Green Gables*, and Dr. Andrew Macphail and his potatoes."[14] Indeed, he jokingly remarked that he had serious thoughts of settling down and growing potatoes himself. "I told him," laughed Mrs. Macdonald, "that he might not enjoy it quite so well, if he had to go out early on a frosty morning and grub the potatoes for his breakfast."

By the way, his excellency, in his criticism of Canadians, must acknowledge one notable exception. The reason why the sixth publisher took "Anne" was that the "reader" to whom it fell happened to be a Prince Edward Islander, who took care to put it into the publisher's own hands and urge him to read it.

Mrs. Macdonald's new home is to be Leaskdale, near Toronto. The Rev. Ewan Macdonald is the Presbyterian minister there.[15] He was formerly stationed in Prince Edward Island. "We have been engaged a long while," she says; then adds simply, "I could not leave my grandmother, could I?"

NOTES

1   Montgomery to MacMillan, 19 September 1911, in *MDMM*, 61. See also *The Patriot*, "Author of Anne of Green Gables."
2   When Anne discovers that Marilla and Matthew actually wanted a boy to help on the farm, she exclaims, "Nobody ever did want me." During Anne's trip home with Matthew, she utters the terms "imagine" or "imagining" twenty-two times. Mrs. Rachel Lynde provokes Anne's rage by calling her "terrible skinny and homely," with "hair as red as carrots." Gilbert Blythe actually teases Anne by calling her "carrots," not "carroty." I have corrected the original, which reads "Dina." In a later scene, eleven-year-old Anne cries bitterly at the prospect of Diana one day marrying and leaving her: "I hate her husband – I just hate him furiously" (*AGG*, 24, 11–20, 64, 111, 119).
3   I have corrected the original, which reads "'imagined' she was a Canadian."
4   Earl Grey, then Governor General of Canada, invited Montgomery as his guest during his trip to Charlottetown in September 1910. See Montgomery, 16 September 1910, in *SJLMM*, 2: 13–17; Rubio, *Lucy Maud Montgomery*, 132–40.

5 For a selection of reviews of *The Story Girl*, see Volume 3 of *The L.M. Montgomery Reader*.

6 "Una of the Garden," the original version of *Kilmeny of the Orchard*, was serialized in five parts in *The Housekeeper*, a Minneapolis publication, beginning in December 1908, six months after the publication of *Anne of Green Gables*. The date of its composition is unknown, whereas *Green Gables* is believed to have been written in 1905.

7 Montgomery's wedding was on 5 July 1911.

8 In the alternate version of this article found in Montgomery's scrapbooks, an additional sentence appears here: "'She was almost young enough to have been my mother too, you know,' she says, fondly" (Christian Richardson, "A Canadian Novelist," unidentified and undated clipping, in SR, 25).

9 I have corrected the original, which reads "Wollner." See Montgomery, 28 January 1912, in *SJLMM*, 2: 56.

10 According to Rubio, "Maud's maternal great-great-grandfather, John Macneill (born circa 1750), had come to Charlottetown from the Kintyre peninsula of Argyllshire, Scotland, around 1772" (Rubio, *Lucy Maud Montgomery*, 22).

11 See chapter 12, "Miss L.M. Montgomery, Author of *Anne of Green Gables*," note 8, in this volume.

12 The original here reads "father," but in the alternate version in her scrapbook Montgomery adds "grand" in the margins in ink.

13 They were, in fact, her two great-grandmothers. For the longer story, see Montgomery, 2 June 1931, in *SJLMM*, 4: 130–32. A similar story is told in *The Story Girl*, but the names are changed to Betty and Nancy Sherman (*SG*, 51–55).

14 Born in Orwell, Prince Edward Island, Andrew Macphail edited *The University Magazine* at McGill University from 1907 to 1920, except for the period in which he served overseas in the First World War. According to Rubio, at this time he was "one of the Island's most famous native sons" (Rubio, *Lucy Maud Montgomery*, 133).

15 I have corrected the original, which reads "Ewen."

18

Interviews with Authors

—— 1911 ——

ANNE E. NIAS

This article, published in *Saturday Night* in October 1911, is included in
Montgomery's "Scrapbook of Reviews" with a note written in her hand:
"This 'interview' is fiction from beginning to end."[1] It was, in fact, part of "a
series of burlesque interviews with celebrities" that appeared in this magazine
throughout the fall of 1911,[2] from the pen of Jean Graham, whose reviews
of *Anne of Avonlea* and *Pat of Silver Bush* appear in Volume 3 of *The L.M.
Montgomery Reader*. It is accompanied by a photograph that identifies the
author as "Louise Montgomery Macdonald."

As I peered timidly through the bars of the manse gate, a pleasant voice
called "Come in!"

"I'm afraid," I admitted.

"But the dog won't hurt you," insisted the Mistress of the Manse,
"he's a very kind creature, and wouldn't hurt even an interviewer."

"I'm not afraid of him. I've always been fond of dumb animals, and
your dog looks remarkably intelligent. But you see the last time I entered
a manse, I got into the most dreadful trouble, and actually appeared in
the *Toronto Globe* the next Monday morning."

"Well, I'll promise not to say one word to the congregation about our
little talk. Besides, this isn't Galt.[3] Then, you must remember that I'm
only the minister's wife, not the minister himself."

"I should like to know why the manse soil seems natural to the successful Canadian novelist."[4]

"But I merely married into the manse. My books don't belong to it, at all."

"That is all very well. The fact remains that you are now an inmate of such an abode – and I shouldn't be surprised if *Anne of Green Gables* would have ever so many new editions. This is the third manse I've visited in the course of my literary pilgrimages. Neither the parsonage nor the rectory seems to break into literature."[5]

"Of course," she said with pride, "you know that I am only a recent resident of Ontario."

"So I believe – but I hope you find yourself at home in Sir James Whitney's favorite province."[6]

"It has its fine points – still, it is not Prince Edward Island."

"That is what all the tourists tell us. Do you know, that charming island province ought to erect a monument in your honor? You have done it more good than all the railroad circulars ever written."

"You are entirely mistaken," she said with quiet hauteur. "Prince Edward Island has no desire to be exploited, and is no paradise for the common or garden variety of tourist."

"Then you shouldn't make it so attractive. Why, one of the midsummer dreams of the Canadian traveller is to find Green Gables and catch a glimpse of Anne."

The creator of Anne smiled forgivingly upon me. "Of course, a literary pilgrimage is a different matter," she admitted. "And you're very kind to speak in such a friendly fashion about Anne. She was rather hard to bring up."

"Anne was a dear," I defended warmly, "but why did you give her red hair? Nearly every modern heroine, young, middle-aged or divorced, has hair of a shade bordering on cerise. A few are allowed to have hair of a brown hue, 'with copper glints in the sun.'[7] But most of them have hair of uncompromising carrots in shade."

"Red hair was inevitable with Anne. Could you imagine such a child with blonde or raven locks? She simply couldn't have written and acted as she did, if she had not possessed a dash of cayenne in her tresses. Anne had temperament."

"Poor dear! I suppose she had, and it's more dangerous than the mumps. I have only one grudge against her. Why did you write that sequel and let her grow up? I cannot become reconciled to a mature Anne. She was too delightful as a Young Person. And please don't marry her to anyone. I've always been so glad that dear old Shakespeare, to say nothing of Bacon, did not allow Romeo and Juliet to marry.[8] Think of Romeo ordering steak or Juliet entertaining the Verona Women's Book Club! It would have been too depressing for anyone but Ibsen."[9]

"I simply had to write that sequel. The public clamored for it and the publishers insisted."[10]

"Sequels are always a sad mistake. It would have been so satisfactory if there had been no sequel to *Little Women*, when we might dream of those four dear girls just as they ought to be. Instead of which, Jo was married to the wrong man, and Amy, horrid, conceited little thing, carried off Laurie.[11] Please don't keep on with Anne until she becomes like the Elsie books."[12]

"Then you don't think she'd better marry and settle down?"

"And hem towels and embroider centrepieces! Never! Let us remember Anne as an immortal red-haired madcap, wandering forever through old-fashioned gardens, with a glimpse of sapphire sea beyond."

"I like her better that way, myself," admitted the Mistress of the Manse. "Anne is not intended for domestic toil and sewing societies. She is a girl who belongs to the gardens, and is a born gad-about. Also, she is a bit romantic, and a girl like that would be sure to order the wrong breakfast food and forget about the dessert. Have you ever been in Prince Edward Island?"

"Not yet – and when I go, it will be solely for the sake of Green Gables."

"There is a beautiful garden near the sea," said the author dreamily, "and on a midsummer night you may see Robin Goodfellow, Peas-Blossom, Cobweb, Moth and Mustard Seed flitting among the flowers in the moonlight. There is no other garden like it, and the ocean's voice is never far away. If you will go there, with a believing heart, you may see Anne and, perhaps, Titania."[13]

"I will go," I said enthusiastically – "and I'm sure that Anne will be waiting near the garden gate, and it will be the very best holiday I ever had. In the meantime, I hope you will find that even Ontario has enchanted spots, far from the Toronto crowd's ignoble strife."[14]

NOTES

1 SR, 26. See also Montgomery, 1 March 1930, in *SJLMM*, 4: 42.
2 Wrenshall, "Jean Graham," 161.
3 Galt, a municipality in southern Ontario, now part of the city of Cambridge, and also the home of R.E. Knowles (1868–1946), a Presbyterian

minister and the author of seven best-selling evangelical novels published between 1905 and 1911.

4 Knowles and Charles W. Gordon (Ralph Connor) were both Presbyterian ministers, as was the husband of Mary Esther MacGregor (Marian Keith).

5 "Manse," "parsonage," and "rectory" are all terms referring to the residence of a Christian cleric. The first term is used mainly by the Scottish Presbyterian church, the second with the Methodist and Lutheran churches, and the third with the Roman Catholic church. Montgomery's short story "Some Fools and a Saint," which she revised for inclusion in *The Blythes Are Quoted*, features a Methodist minister who must board with a local family rather than live in the parsonage (*BQ*, 6).

6 Sir James Whitney (1843–1914), Premier of Ontario from 1905 to 1914.

7 From *The Sovereign Power* (1911), a recent novel by Mark Lee Luther (1872–1951), American author. The character with said "copper glints" is named Ann.

8 Nias refers to the theory, begun in the nineteenth century, that plays attributed to Shakespeare were actually written by Francis Bacon (1561–1626), English philosopher, statesman, and author.

9 Henrik Ibsen (1828–1906), Norwegian playwright and director whose modernist plays were viewed as scandalous at the time they were written.

10 See chapter 6, "A Trio of Women Writers," by Donald B. Sinclair, note 6, in this volume.

11 Louisa May Alcott's *Little Women* (1868) was followed by *Good Wives* in 1869, which depicts the events described here. The two books were published in one volume beginning in 1880 and are most frequently published that way today. Alcott also published *Little Men* (1871) and *Jo's Boys* (1886), featuring the March sisters as adults.

12 *Elsie Dinsmore* (1867), a popular novel for girls by Martha Finley (1828–1909), was followed by twenty-seven sequels about the same character, the last published in 1905.

13 In *A Midsummer Night's Dream* (1590–96), a play by William Shakespeare, Robin Goodfellow (Puck) is a servant to Oberon, King of the Fairies, while Peaseblossom, Cobweb, Moth, and Mustardseed are fairy servants to Titania, Queen of the Fairies.

14 Properly, "the maddening crowd's ignoble strife." From *Elegy Written in a Country Churchyard* (1751), by Thomas Gray (1716–1771), English poet and scholar.

19

The Old Minister in *The Story Girl*
—— 1912 ——

A. WYLIE MAHON

This first sustained article about Montgomery's work – appearing in March 1912 in *The Canadian Magazine*, which had published Montgomery's four "woods" essays the year before as well as reviews of all of her books published up till that point – began a pattern that in many ways continues to this day: namely, a reading of the work that emphasizes biographical elements. In this article, A. Wylie Mahon stresses the historical connections between Montgomery's character "The Rev. Mr. Scott" and the Rev. John Sprott (1780–1869), the Scottish-born Presbyterian clergyman who held the charge in Musquodoboit Valley in Nova Scotia from 1825 to 1849, drawing on the book *Memorials of the Rev. John Sprott*, which had been edited by Sprott's son, George W. Sprott, and published in Edinburgh in 1906. Montgomery made the connection herself in a journal entry published in its entirety only in 2013, in which she called him "a very eccentric person." She also mentioned in a journal entry dated 1930 that "it amused me to read that Uncle Leander was 'the *Uncle Edward* of *The Story Girl*.' I'll tell the world he wasn't!" The Story Girl mentions that she heard the stories of the Rev. Mr. Scott from Uncle Edward, but it is also worth noting the narrator's comment about the plums that continued to grow from the tree named after said reverend: "those plums certainly kept his memory green, as his forgotten sermons could never have done."[1]

Mahon's factual claims about the real-life inspirations for Montgomery's minor characters persisted in a review of *Anne of the Island*, in which he stated categorically that "Redmond College is Dalhousie University" and that the "grumpy old professor of Mathematics, who detested coeds," "was known to the students of his day as 'Charlie.'"[2]

Miss Montgomery's *Story Girl*, whose voice makes words live and carries the most thoughtless listener captive, who can recite the multiplication table with such sweet and varied rhythm and modulation as to bring tears or smiles to the most unimpressionable soul, finds the stories which she tells in local traditions as well as in classic myths and northland folklore. Some of her stories are amusing traditions of a dearly-beloved but somewhat eccentric old minister, whom she calls *Rev. Mr. Scott* – stories which her uncle had told her.

The *Rev. Mr. Scott* of *The Story Girl* was the Rev. John Sprott, one of the best beloved and most unforgettable of the home-missionary pioneers of the Atlantic provinces of Canada. Mr. Sprott was born in Scotland and came to Canada in 1818. He loved Scotland so dearly that it was difficult for him at first to feel at home in this new world of wide, wild woodlands. Nothing in this country was just what it ought to be. The sun never shone so brightly in Nova Scotia as in Scotland; the birds never sang so sweetly; and even the *parritch* was never anything like it used to be in the old homeland.

When he was contemplating matrimony for the second time (he made three happy ventures of this sort in his life) he wrote in his diary:

"Miss C.L. is a sprig of Caledonia. I love her on that account. The women of this country make good wives, but they have little that is cheerful or playful, and nothing romantic in their disposition. The females of Nova Scotia are second to none for good housewives, and they can be managed with perfect ease, provided they always get their own way. They usually expect a larger share of attention than females in older countries. It is not easy to bend Scotchmen to their manners, and Scotchmen have never been regarded by the females of this country as the most tame and complying husbands."[3]

Clergymen in Mr. Sprott's day were not only meagrely but sometimes amusingly paid. He tells us that he knew some who were paid in buckwheat, shingles, sucking-pigs, and feathers. Some did not fare even so well as these. He says:

"A minister might live in Nova Scotia provided he had Jacob's ladder set up in the midst of his congregation, for on Sabbath evening he could go up to heaven and subsist on spiritual food till next Sabbath morning, and then return to the duties of the day. This would please the congregation for a while, but they would soon begin to complain that he was not visiting during the week."[4]

115

Many are the wise and witty sayings and laughable eccentricities recorded of this noble pioneer, who was a warm friend of Judge Haliburton – Sam Slick.[5] Mr. Sprott's first congregation was in Windsor, Nova Scotia, where Judge Haliburton lived. When Mr. Sprott brought his first bride home, Haliburton was one of the first to call to offer his congratulations.

The Rev. L.G. Macneill, of St. John – Miss Montgomery's uncle, the *Uncle Edward* of "The Story Girl" – many years ago told some amusing things about this worthy pioneer minister. Mr. Macneill says:

"Our first recollection of Mr. Sprott was in the days of our boyhood. He came to our home and our church. It was a warm summer's day when he was preaching for our minister. A large congregation had assembled, and the church windows were open, letting into the crowded building the fresh air and the grateful odour of new-made hay. Ascending the narrow stairs that led up to the bowl of an old wine-glass style of pulpit, to his dismay he found that he could not enter it in the usual way. He was too corpulent for its narrow door, and placing a hand on either side, lifting himself over the aperture, he said in a perfectly audible whisper, 'This pulpit door was made for speerits.' Then having rapidly conducted the preliminary exercises, he opened the Bible, and looking out at the open window, his first words were: 'Ye have a fine place here; ye're no like the thousands that are driven forth from such cities as London, Liverpool, or New York, to escape the noisome exhalations of the place. Ye can sit down under the shade of your own green trees, none daring to make you afraid. Ye've a grand place. You will find my text in Habbakuk.'"[6]

The *Story Girl* makes a passing reference to this amusing incident, but does not give the story in full.[7] It is worthy[8] of mention that Mr. Macneill's home, to which Mr. Sprott came that beautiful summer's day, was for years Miss Montgomery's own home.

One of *Uncle Edward's* stories which the *Story Girl* tells at length relates to the young minister, Mr. Sedgwick, afterwards the distinguished Dr. Robert Sedgwick, father of Mr. Justice Sedgwick, of Ottawa, and of Dr. Thomas Sedgwick, of Tatamagouche, who succeeded Mr. Sprott as pastor of the congregation of Musquodoboit, in Halifax County, Nova Scotia.[9] Mr. Sprott in his old age had retired from the pastorate of that church somewhat reluctantly, and his successor was a little afraid to meet the old minister. The story of how he hid himself in the closet of one of his parishioners when he saw Mr. Sprott approaching the house, and listened to the old minister as he prayed with the family, making special reference to the poor young man hiding in the closet, is told at length in Miss Montgomery's new book: "Oh Lord, bless the poor young man hiding in the closet. Give him courage not to fear the face of man. Make him a burning and a shining light to this sadly abused congregation." In Mr. Macneill's version of this story we are left to imagine how the young minister in the closet acted when the prayer was over; but Miss Montgomery's *Story Girl* has made it all plain: "He came right out like a man, though his face was very red, as soon as Mr. Scott had done praying. And Mr. Scott was lovely to him, and shook hands, and never mentioned the china closet. And they were the best of friends ever afterwards."[10] In Miss Montgomery's book one of the boys asks the *Story Girl* how the old minister knew that the young man was in the closet. The answer given is that it was supposed that he had seen him through the window before he came into the house and guessed he must be in the closet.[11] It seems that Mr. Macneill's suggestion that he had recognised the young minister's waggon in the yard did not appeal convincingly to the novelist.

Almost as many interesting stories have gathered about the name of this brilliant young minister who hid himself in the closet as we find associated with that of the inimitable and eccentric Mr. Sprott himself. At a meeting of the Halifax Presbytery arrangements were being made for supplying vacant fields. One vacant congregation was called Sheet Harbour. There was a minister at the disposal of the court who was looked upon by the brethren as rather lazy and sleepy. There was a hearty laugh when someone proposed that this man be sent to Sheet Harbour. Dr. Sedgwick failed to see the joke; but at the Presbytery dinner that day the light dawned upon him at a most inopportune juncture, just when a brother was saying grace. He burst out into an uncontrollable fit of laughter, to the consternation of the whole grave and reverend body of divinity.

Miss Montgomery includes in her book the story about the devil and the McCloskeys. Mr. Sprott could not be convinced by his brethren in the ministry that Providence had anything to do in compelling him to resign his church. He thought too much of Providence for that. He said that it was the McCloskeys and the devil, or, as Mr. Macneill has it, "the McCurdys and the devil." The efforts of one of the young people to get the *Story Girl*" to substitute "the old Scratch" for the devil are most amusing.[12] When the *Story Girl* repeated the new version of the old story to see how it would sound – "'Twas the McCloskeys and the Old Scratch"

– she felt that it would never do. It didn't sound so well. She must get back to the devil.[13]

The other stories relating to the old minister in *The Story Girl* are all taken from Mr. Macneill's article of the long ago,[14] and are given with very few variations. Miss Montgomery does not include in her book all the stories that her brilliant uncle gathered together. She does not tell about the day the apple peddler came to the manse and how Mr. Sprott overcame the economical scruples of his wife. The minister told the peddler that he would take a bushel, whereupon his wife remonstrated that it was an unnecessary luxury. "I'll take *two* bushels," was his rejoinder. His wife remonstrated more earnestly, saying, "What's the use of getting apples? The boys ate up the last we got, and it's just wasting money." "I'll take *three* bushels," was the reply that sent the good wife from the room in high dudgeon.

Mr. Macneill tells about a visit which Mr. Sprott paid to St. John's, Newfoundland. His son, the late Dr. George Sprott, of Berwick-on-Tweed, was to preach in the kirk, but was detained in Halifax through illness. His father went in his stead. In beginning his sermon, the old minister said: "You came here this morning expecting to hear the melodious tones of the silver trumpet, but ye'll ha' to be satisfied with the tooting of an auld ram's horn. Ye'll bear in mind, however, that the walls of Jericho didna fall at the blowing of silver trumpets, but at the tooting of rams' horns." Nor was the amusement of the congregation lessened when, after preaching for a while, he suddenly stopped, and reaching down over the pulpit, he was seen to tap the precentor's bald head, and ask quite audibly, "D'ye think they're hearing me?"

Mr. Sprott was a missionary-pioneer of whom any country might well be proud, and he left the impress of his strong and broad-minded and winsome personality upon the Christian churches of the Atlantic provinces of Canada.

NOTES

1 Montgomery, 23 May 1911, in *CJLMM*, 2: 405; Montgomery, 1 March 1930, in *SJLMM*, 4: 43; *SG*, 105, 159.
2 A. Wylie Mahon, "A Charming Canadian Book," review of *Anne of the Island*, unidentified and undated clipping, in SR, 82; *AIs*, 37.
3 This quotation fuses together two unrelated extracts from the Sprott volume of *Memorials*. The first three sentences are from a journal entry

dated 22 November 1823, whereas the rest is from a letter "To the Free Press" dated 1847 (Sprott, *Memorials*, 13, 90–91). There is one substantive misquotation and one substantive omission: the phrase "provided they always get their own way" actually reads "provided they get their own way in everything, but the moment you cross their path they are as restive as our unbroken militia." Before the sentence beginning with "It is not easy," another sentence appears: "You treat them like rational beings but here they are almost idolised" (ibid., 90–91).

4 Ibid., 101. This extract is from an item dated 1849. The phrase "that he was not visiting" actually reads "for want of his visitations." In the Hebrew Bible, Jacob dreams of a ladder to heaven after fleeing from his twin brother Esau. See Genesis 28:10–19.

5 Thomas Chandler Haliburton (1796–1865), Canadian politician, judge, and author of *The Clockmaker; The Sayings and Doings of Samuel Slick of Slickville* (1836).

6 In the Hebrew Bible, the Book of Habakkuk – sometimes spelled "Habbakuk," as it is here – is the eighth book of the twelve minor prophets.

7 This anecdote is told in slightly different form in *SG*, 37.

8 I have corrected the original, which reads "Is is worthy."

9 Robert Sedgwick (1804–1885) was minister of the Musquodoboit congregation from 1849 to 1884. His youngest son, Robert Sedgwick (1848–1906), was a lawyer, politician, and judge. His eldest son, Thomas Sedgwick (1838–1921), was the moderator of the Synod of the Presbyterian church in the Maritime provinces in 1886. Their surname is sometimes spelled "Sedgewick."

10 *SG*, 105.

11 *SG*, 105–6.

12 I have corrected the original, which reads "is most amusing."

13 *SG*, 113–14.

14 The source of this article is not known.

20

L.M. Montgomery: Story Writer

—— 1913 ——

MARJORY MACMURCHY

This profile was published in the *Globe* in October 1913, while Montgomery was in Toronto to give a speech for the Women's Canadian Club, an event that received tremendous newspaper coverage (see chapter 21, "L.M. Montgomery at Women's Canadian Club," below). Marjory MacMurchy (1870–1938), who wrote at least four detailed profiles of Montgomery's life and career between 1910 and 1915,[1] was a book reviewer for the Toronto *News* as well as President of the Canadian Women's Press Club. MacMurchy's past comments about Montgomery's work show restrained enthusiasm, to say the least: calling Montgomery's first three novels "transcripts of the out-of-doors of one of the loveliest islands in the world," an article by MacMurchy in *The Canadian Courier* in 1910 continues: "It would be easy to praise Miss Montgomery's books too highly. They are delightfully fresh and simple, with the charm of what is naturally attractive and wholesome, and they are enriched by the play of a poetical fancy … It is not likely that Miss Montgomery has shown all her powers yet. Her stories do not reveal genius, but they are the work of a charming talent. The spirit of goodness in them and the deep spirit of a strong national life ring as clearly as evening bells."[2] Moreover, in a review of *The Story Girl* published in the Toronto *News* within months of the novel's publication, MacMurchy praised the writing style and claimed that "the delineation of these children is probably as near to truth as that of any children who have appeared in fiction for many years," yet she added that the novel "is not likely to be as popular as her Anne stories, since it does not contain any character as winning," and indeed that "the genius of The Story Girl herself is not quite convincing."[3] Although Montgomery visited MacMurchy in Toronto often after her move to Ontario, they were hardly kindred spirits. "There were many fine things about her," Montgomery noted in her journal upon MacMurchy's death in 1938, yet "I never felt at ease in her presence."[4]

The Golden Road, published a few weeks ago, is Miss L.M. Montgomery's sixth book of fiction. By this time we may sum up clearly the qualities of a writer in whose life one of the most influential facts is that she was born in Prince Edward Island. The world that reads her books – for her books are immensely popular, the sales amounting to half a million copies – is a world of good people, everyday and workaday people, who are happy to warm their hearts in the good-will, sunshine and promise-of-good-coming-true which are a great part of the gift of this woman story-writer of Prince Edward Island. We read her stories eagerly because they are true and happy and full of a clear, kind, wholesome northern simplicity. One wonders if other people find in Miss Montgomery's work a certain likeness to the writings of Hans Christian Andersen.[5] He is a northern writer, clear, simple and truth-telling. Miss Montgomery's creative power is less, but in saying so one detracts nothing from the value of her work as it stands. Hans Christian Andersen is a world writer. It is true that by instinct Miss Montgomery is not economical of words as Hans Andersen was. Her *Chronicles of Avonlea* had less of the flowery diction which sometimes threatens her simplicity; but *The Golden Road* has more of it. Pretty strings of words and fanciful names are not to be compared in value with her plain, straightforward, happy telling of a happy story. Her knowledge of northern character is worth its weight in gold; and economy in words is much to ask from anyone, since it is one of the final proofs of greatness in a writer.

To trace the connection between Miss Montgomery's gift as a story-writer and Prince Edward Island is a delightful task. If the fairies live anywhere in Canada, it must be in Prince Edward Island, with its red earth, gentle aspects, loveliness of fields and broken belts of wood in darker green, and the blue sea coming up on every side. The people are shrewd, kind, self-respecting, full of character and thrift, fond of themselves, their Island and their traditions with a certain degree of passion, and very much disposed to play.

"She said to me to take life easy
As the grass grows in the field."[6]

That is Prince Edward Island. It is a dear place.

But more to our present purpose, which is tracing the true descent and inheritance of a story-writer, the Island is crammed with stories – stories of sailors and great storms, stories of ghosts and the devil, stories of lovers and wooing and runaway matches, stories of queer people and witches, stories of the good little people themselves. Even I have seen the silver rim of a water pitcher that was broken one night on the way to the well – but that is another story.

Miss Montgomery was born in Prince Edward Island some time in the seventies or eighties of the nineteenth century. Her mother died when she was very young. Her father went soon to Saskatchewan. The child was given to the care of her mother's father and mother. Her maternal grandfather was postmaster at Cavendish, a circumstance which later was to mean a great deal to the young story-writer. Every budding genius requires reams of blank paper. The yellowy-brown post office forms of the Dominion Government were trove to her.[7] She scribbled on their yellow backs to her heart's content. Thus do governments encourage unaware the genius of young citizens. Later, when manuscripts were sent out to editors, Miss Montgomery is herself authority for the statement that being able to recover the rejected MSS. from the post office without a soul except herself being the wiser made all the difference in the world. She would never have had the courage to keep on sending if the post office had been elsewhere.

Her maternal grandfather's name was Macneill. The Macneills are famous Island people. Also be it recorded, a Scottish poet named Macneill is one of Miss Montgomery's ancestors. He wrote at least three lovely songs which have survived in Scottish poetry – "Saw Ye My Wee Thing, Saw Ye My Ain Thing?" "Come Under My Plaidie" – often wrongly attributed to Burns – and "I Lo'ed Ne'er a Laddie but One."[8] These romantic countryside gleams of genius, of passion, tenderness and fidelity which make Scottish love songs so poignant and exquisite, came fitfully to Canada in emigrant ships. Such a tradition came with the Macneills. There were two brother Macneills, Miss Montgomery's great-uncles, both of whom were poets on the Island. They were noted for their gift of celebrating local happenings in satirical verse. It was then the fashion in Prince Edward Island to take off the foibles of one's neighbors and the incidents of local history in rhyming couplets. These were not committed to paper, but were recited at evening gatherings. When one of these clever gentlemen, the Macneills, was occupied with the work of the farm his mind would be busy putting into rhyme the exploits of neighbor

Angus or neighbor Neil, the election of the local member of Parliament, the courting of Nancy or the runaway match of Peter and Bessie. At that time boiling potatoes – a famous Island product – for equally famous Island porkers took up hours of time, and afforded mental leisure for the poetical efforts of the Island satirist. It was in this incomparable school for a story-writer that the little girl heard Island stories and learned to understand northern characters. By and by, when Grandfather Macneill died, her grandmother was continued in the Government appointment as postmistress. All the neighbors were cousins, or cousins' cousins, uncles and aunts, and the incidents of daily life in the neighborhood came flying into the post office as a flock of hens will to the centre of a barnyard at the call of the mistress when it is time to scatter provender. But before this Miss Montgomery had been at Dalhousie College in Halifax for a year. Again, in another year she did some writing for *The Halifax Chronicle*. But at the end of a year Miss Montgomery had to give up her work in *The Chronicle* office and return to the Island. Her grandmother Macneill was growing old and needed her. From this time on her grandmother could not bear to have her away from the house scarcely for a day. Then, out of years of writing stories came the wonderful success of *Anne of Green Gables*. The Island lady of stories who lived at Cavendish in a few months had friends by the hundreds who lived all over North America. As she said once: "I think every red-haired girl in the world must have written to me." These friendships have meant a great deal to Miss Montgomery. Once before her grandmother's death she visited her publisher, Mr. L.C. Page, in Boston. *Anne of Green Gables* was followed by *Anne of Avonlea* and *Kilmeny*. In the summer of 1911, following her grandmother's death, Miss Montgomery married the Rev. Ewan Macdonald, who is the minister of the Presbyterian church in Leaskdale, Ontario. Since then she has published *The Story Girl, The Chronicles of Avonlea*, and now *The Golden Road*, a sequel to *The Story Girl*.[9] Her gift is too ardent and compelling not to force for itself an outlet in stories. Story-writing is as natural to her as living. Her little son, born on the first Sunday in July, 1912, has made life full to the uttermost. Leaskdale is a quaint, homelike Ontario village seven miles from a railway station. The neighborhood, like most Ontario neighborhoods, is an excellent field for the study of Canadian and Scottish character. But there is not a sign that Miss Montgomery has exhausted her Island studies. She may never even have thought of writing an Ontario story.

So far only one side of Miss Montgomery's ancestry has been mentioned. The Montgomerys of the Island are equally famous with the Macneills.

Miss Montgomery's father's father was Senator Montgomery, who lived to a great age and long represented the Island at Ottawa.[10] There is a story that the Montgomery family came to live in Prince Edward Island by the determination of a woman. On a certain ship from Scotland came a Montgomery and his wife and family. The voyage was long and stormy, and finally the ship's supply of drinking water was almost at an end. Mrs. Montgomery had been constantly seasick for more than six weeks. The captain, pitying her when he sent his sailors ashore to the Island, which was the nearest land, said she might go with them. The lady accepted the captain's offer. But when the sailors were ready to return to the ship she declared that nothing would induce her to set foot on shipboard again. Expostulation was in vain. Mrs. Montgomery remained firm, and, as a matter of necessity, her husband and children had to be landed on Prince Edward Island.[11] There are descendants of this lady living in most of the nine Canadian Provinces to-day.[12] Miss L.M. Montgomery is one of them. The true benefit and blessing which comes to those who read Miss Montgomery's stories is in her delineation of a sane, wholesome and delightful social fabric. Here are standards which have not been confused or broken. Fever and strife do not exist in these stories. Stalwart characters, strength of will, intellectual and moral soundness, good-will, gayety, common sense and happiness are rated simply as the best things in life. There is no preaching. Money is a servant, not a master. Luxury is never mentioned. The foundation of the northern character which Miss Montgomery shows us is well and truly laid. Laughter and happiness and health are accompaniments of good life, which is normal life. Something like this is the interpretation of Miss Montgomery's work as a story-writer, which is, at the same time, an interpretation of Prince Edward Island. No wonder that the hearts of Islanders in their dreams turn home.

NOTES

1 In addition to those included in this volume and the one quoted here, MacMurchy contributed a profile of Montgomery to *The Bookman* (London) in 1915.
2 MacMurchy, "Prince Edward Island's Novelist," 27.
3 Marjory MacMurchy, "Canadian Fiction," the Toronto *News*, undated clipping, in SR, 16.
4 Montgomery, 16 December 1938, in *SJLMM*, 5: 297.
5 Hans Christian Andersen (1805–1875), Danish children's writer and poet.

6 Properly, "She bid me take love easy, as the grass grows on the weirs." From "Down by the Salley Gardens," from *The Wanderings of Oisin and Other Poems* (1889), by William Butler Yeats (1865–1939), Irish dramatist and poet.

7 Here and throughout, I have corrected the original, which reads "postoffice."

8 In "The Alpine Path," Montgomery identifies this poet as Hector Macneill (1746–1818), a cousin of her direct ancestor John Macneill, who had immigrated to PEI from Scotland in 1775 (*AP*, 13–14). Rubio and Waterston state that Hector Macneill's "relationship to the west-coast Macneills has not been definitively established" (*SJLMM*, 5: 396).

9 *The Story Girl* was actually published in spring 1911, after Grandmother Macneill's death but before Montgomery's marriage, honeymoon, and move to Ontario.

10 Senator Donald Montgomery (1808–1893) represented Prince Edward Island in Ottawa from 1874 until his death (Rubio and Waterston, Introduction to *SJLMM*, 1: xiii).

11 The ancestors in question are Montgomery's great-great-grandparents, Hugh Montgomery and Mary McShannon, who arrived in Prince Edward Island in 1769 (ibid., xiii; see also *AP*, 12). Montgomery recycled this story for Hugh Murray and Mary Shipley, ancestors of Emily Byrd Starr in *Emily of New Moon* (*ENM*, 71). Carolyn Strom Collins has recently shown that this family mythology does not match the information found in surviving shipping records about the Montgomerys' journey across the Atlantic Ocean (Collins, "'Bound for Quebec' or 'Journey's End'?").

12 Newfoundland and Labrador would become the tenth Canadian province in 1949.

21

L.M. Montgomery at Women's Canadian Club

—— 1913 ——

In a journal entry dated 1 November 1913, Montgomery wrote that she had consented to give a speech on Prince Edward Island for the Women's Canadian Club of Toronto, even though she had never made in speech in public before. She mentioned that it had appeared to her to be a success, quoting several newspaper articles that attested to the fact, but she neglected to add that she had stated in the speech itself that it was her first. "Everyone was greatly surprised the other day in Toronto when Mrs. Macdonald (L.M. Montgomery) declared that the address she was giving that day before the Women's Canadian Club and the local Women's Press Club, who had been invited, was her very first attempt at public speaking," declared *The Canadian Courier*.[1] A similar article in the *Toronto Daily Star* also quoted Montgomery's description of one of her first literary efforts: "I shed tears over it, and when I attempted to read it to my girl friends they were overcome. It told of the deaths and burials of nine children of a Methodist minister. I followed her all over the continent, from Halifax to Vancouver, leaving graves dotted here and there. I told of the deathbed scenes, and the epitaphs. I had intended to kill the tenth also, but whether my feelings overcame me, or I wearied of so much infanticide, I relented, and allowed him to grow up a hopeless cripple." The *Star* report refers to the speech as a "most characteristically humorous and instructive paper on the glories and benefits of life in her birthplace," and notes that Montgomery "succeeded in creating an intense spirit of discontent in all those who had been unfortunate enough to have been born elsewhere."[2]

A most interesting meeting of the Women's Canadian Club was that held in the Foresters' Hall on Saturday afternoon, when L.M. Montgomery (Mrs. Ewan Macdonald), author of *Anne of Green Gables* and other fascinating tales, gave a most delightful address on "The Garden of the Gulf," Prince Edward Island. To illustrate the loyalty of Prince Edward Islanders to their "garden," Miss Montgomery told of a little lad who, when asked to name the three greatest islands in the world, answered "promptly, glibly and truthfully, Prince Edward Island, the British Isles and Australia." And the speaker went on to vindicate this loyalty so successfully that every listener must surely have felt that her fairy godmother had withheld one of her choicest gifts in not giving her Prince Edward Island for a birthplace. The tales of the sea, visible from almost every point on the Island, of its beauties and its tragedies, might have come from the story books of our childhood and so might the staunch characters of a type cherished and emulated from pioneer days.

"They say we are unprogressive," Miss Montgomery said, and admitted: "In the country districts the women still have quilting bees and sewing circles, instead of bridge and afternoon tea. Fashions are certainly behind those of Paris, and the indecent ones we never adopt. Salacious novels are never to be found on our tables. We are a God-fearing people, holding to the faith of our fathers, so of course we must be unprogressive!"

Then there is always time in Prince Edward Island; time to be as well as to do; time to dream; time to cultivate character. "Nothing really good goes by us, but much that is evil escapes us, by reason of our out-of-the-wayness."

One could not doubt the speaker's claim that Prince Edward Island is a good place for children to grow up.

In concluding, Miss Montgomery told something of the characters and places in her books, and answered the frequent question if this and that one had been drawn from life. "I have never met," she said, "one human being who could be put into a book, as a whole, without injury to the book." The one character in her works who had come nearest to following a living pattern was "Peg" in *The Story Girl*, and even here, she had been forced to "paint the lily."[3] Anne, she said, probably the best beloved of all her book-folk, had "just happened." When a Sunday school paper asked her for a seven-chapter serial she ran through her note-book and picked out a suggestion which read, "Old couple adopt ward – ask for boy, get girl." "I didn't create Anne," we were assured; "like Topsy, she 'just growed,'[4] and soon grew to such proportions that no seven-chapter serial could possibly contain her," and *Anne of Green Gables* was the result.

The Women's Press Club were the guests of the Women's Canadian Club at this meeting, and to tea afterwards to meet Mrs. Macdonald.[5]

NOTES

1 Montgomery, 1 November 1913, in *SJLMM*, 2: 137–38; *The Canadian Courier*, "The Maiden Speech That Wasn't," 16. Although Montgomery quoted from this article in her journal entry, it is worth noting that the article in *The Canadian Courier* was published on 8 November 1913, a week after the journal entry dated 1 November.

2 *The Toronto Daily Star*, "Women's Canadian Club," 10. In "The Alpine Path," she refers to a "certain lugubrious yarn, 'My Graves,'" as her masterpiece (*AP*, 57), as does Anne Shirley in *AIs*, 208.

3 To embellish. From *King John* (1623), by William Shakespeare. Montgomery repeats this assertion in "The Alpine Path," but then refers to her real-life inspiration by her character's name (*AP*, 73, 78–79).

4 See chapter 3, "Origin of Popular Book," note 2, in this volume.

5 A list of prominent women who were also in attendance has been omitted.

22

L.M. Montgomery of the Island

—— 1914 ——

MARJORY MACMURCHY

This second profile by Marjory MacMurchy was published in the *Manitoba Free Press* in April 1914 and, on the same day and in slightly different form, as "'Anne of Green Gables' Is Story of Miss L.M. Montgomery's Childhood" in the *Toronto Star Weekly*. This is also the day that Montgomery began drafting her third novel about Anne, which she finished in November 1914 with the title "Anne of Redmond." It would be published in 1915 as *Anne of the Island*, a title that Page insisted upon "much against my will."[1]

The author of *Anne of Green Gables* still signs her stories "L.M. Montgomery," although in 1911 she married the Rev. Ewan Macdonald, of Leaskdale, Ontario, who at one time had been the Presbyterian minister at the settlement of Cavendish in Prince Edward Island, where he met the writer who was afterwards to become one of the most popular of present day authors.

No Canadian province has any more passionately devoted citizen than Mrs. Montgomery-Macdonald is of Prince Edward Island. She was born at Clifton, P.E.I., in 1877.[2] Her mother died soon after her birth and she was taken to live with her maternal grandparents at Cavendish.[3] Her grandfather, Mr. Macneill,[4] was postmaster of the settlement. As soon as she was able to run about her playmates were cousins and the children of neighbors. Everyone knows who has read Miss Montgomery's stories how common it is in Prince Edward Island for neighborhoods to be closely related. To this day, with the most vivid distinctness, the author will describe every nook and cranny, every pasture field and slope, of her island home. There was one sloping field where every spring they went to look for wild flowers. A day came when the field was plowed, and the little girl thought her heart would break. Near the homestead, she remembers, was their playhouse. Its walls were built only in imagination. But the children had fastened a door to a tree and everyone who came into the playhouse had to come by the door. It is this vivid remembrance of the scenes of her childhood and her passionate attachment to every inch of ground and every memory, which is part of Miss Montgomery's gift as a story writer. Like Robert Louis Stevenson,[5] Miss Montgomery has never wholly lost the spirit of childhood. In her heart she is still the girl who played in Prince Edward Island.

One Year in the West

When she was a child of twelve or so her father sent for her to join him in Saskatchewan, but the little island girl stayed only a year in the west.[6] She was lonely for her home by the sea. The schools of the island are good schools. After leaving the Cavendish school, L.M. Montgomery attended Prince of Wales College in Charlottetown. Later she spent a year at Dalhousie University in Halifax. While she was in Halifax she did some work for one of the Halifax papers. Her university course had to be given up, since after the death of her grandfather, her Grandmother Macneill wanted her at home.[7] When her husband died, Mrs. Macneill was appointed postmistress. Miss Montgomery has often said that she would never have had courage to send out her stories if the post-office had been in a neighbor's house. She could send away manuscripts and get them back again without a soul in Cavendish but herself being any the wiser. When she was a little girl she used to write many stories and the paper she used was the back of the government forms sent to the post-office. Anyone who has read *Anne of Green Gables*, and *Anne of Avonlea*, knows exactly how joyous and delightful Miss Montgomery's girlhood was; it is faithfully described in these stories.

"Anne of Green Gables" One of Immortal Children

Anne of Green Gables had been to a good many publishers before Mr. L.C. Page, of Boston, perceived what a charming creation the little girl was. Mark Twain spoke of Anne as the "sweetest creation of child life" yet written. The Canadian poet, Bliss Carman, called her one of the immortal children of fiction. The author found that she had made friends all over the world. *Anne of Green Gables* had not been her first story. She had published several serials, mostly in Sunday school publications. But when *Anne of Green Gables* charmed the reading public, Miss Montgomery had some stories on hand which she could have disposed of at once without the least difficulty.[8] Her later books have been: *Anne of Avonlea*, (1909); *Kilmeny of the Orchard*, (1910); *The Story Girl*, (1911); *Chronicles of Avonlea*, (1912); *The Golden Road*, a sequel to *The Story Girl*, published in 1913. All these books, with the exception of *The Chronicles of Avonlea*, have been stories of a radiant childhood in Prince Edward Island.[9] *The Chronicles* is a collection of short stories, mainly of grown-up people. These have splendid humor and give an admirable analysis of Island character. They somewhat resemble Miss Jewett's beautiful stories of New England,[10] and they are considered as being probably Miss Montgomery's best work, although scarcely as popular as the delightful Anne stories. Miss Montgomery has written as well a considerable amount of descriptive verse, much of which has appeared in Canadian and American magazines. A few years ago the Christmas number of *Harper's Magazine* contained one of Miss Montgomery's poems.[11]

And the Baby

The manse at Leaskdale has many island treasures. Leaskdale is seven miles from a railway station. It is a little cluster of houses in a typical country neighborhood of Ontario. The little son of the manse has been once down to the sea. "Punchkins" is a beautiful baby.[12] There is a remarkable cat, which travelled up from Prince Edward Island in a crate when his mistress came to Ontario.[13] He is apparently quite reconciled to his new home. On a table in the drawing-room stands a jug about which clings typical Island memories. The story of this jug explains in some measure one of the reasons why Miss Montgomery is a maker of stories. All the winds of the world have blown many stories to Prince Edward Island. It is not to be wondered at that a Prince Edward Island woman has been gifted with the genius of a story-teller. Indeed the Macneills brought the writing gift over from Scotland with them.

The Scottish song-writer who wrote "Saw Ye My Wee Thing, Saw Ye My Ain Thing?" and "Come Under My Plaidie" belonged to the same family of Montgomerys.[14] But the story of the jug which stands on the table in the manse at Leaskdale is as follows: There was a sailor once whose love lived in Scotland, and he had this jug made for her in a foreign country. He had her name painted on the jug in the centre of a nosegay of painted flowers. But on the voyage he was drowned, and when the ship came in to port the captain gave the jug to the sailor's sweetheart. Years afterwards when she died she gave it to her sister, who came out from Scotland to Prince Edward Island, and on the voyage across it was usefully filled with black currant jam. The jug was in the dairy filled with cream when Miss Montgomery begged for it. The sailor's sweetheart's sister was the story-writer's grandmother.[15]

Atmosphere of the Island

Prince Edward Island chronicles are crowded with stories like this, and it was in such an atmosphere that the gift of this writer was fostered. The red earth of the island, the green fields, the blue sea water are a setting for many romantic stories, many a curious chronicle of human nature. It is a lovely country, with a lyrical softness in its beauty. But there have been shipwrecks on the shores. Miss Montgomery says she remembers a shipwrecked crew of foreigners who spent one summer near her grandfather's place. They used to drive about the island in a wagon, shouting as they drove past, exactly as if they had been pirates out of a story by Stevenson. The Island people have been wise. They lead happy lives, with many social enjoyments and recreations; they do not work too hard; they value highly what is most valuable in life. This is the life which Miss Montgomery has painted so joyously for the world. The latest Island romance is the romance of the fox-ranches; but whether or not Mrs. Montgomery Macdonald will write of this time will show. She has only now come, one would judge, into full possession of her powers as a writer of stories.

NOTES

1 Montgomery, 11 April 1915, in *SJLMM*, 2: 163; see also Montgomery to Weber, 12 January 1916, in *AfGG*, 63; Montgomery, 18 April 1914, in *SJLMM*, 2: 146–47; Montgomery, 20 November 1914, in *SJLMM*, 2: 156.
2 This incorrect birth date, three years after Montgomery's actual birth date, would be repeated in later publications, including some obituaries.
3 I have corrected the original text, which reads "grand maternal parents."
4 Here and throughout, I have corrected the original, which reads "MacNeill."

5 Robert Louis Stevenson (1850–1894), Scottish novelist, essayist, and poet. Montgomery recommended one of his best-known books, *Strange Case of Dr. Jekyll and Mr. Hyde* (1886), to Ephraim Weber in a 1905 letter and renamed a cat Dr. Jekyll-and-Mr. Hyde in her novel *Rilla of Ingleside* (Montgomery to Weber, 7 March 1905, in *GGL*, 24–25; *RI*, 7–8).

6 Given that the article lists Montgomery's birth date as 1877, thus subtracting three years from her age, MacMurchy may have surmised that Montgomery had been twelve when she left for Saskatchewan by the fact that this trip occurred in August 1890, when Montgomery was in fact almost sixteen.

7 The article here makes several errors in the chronology of Montgomery's life.

8 See Montgomery to MacMillan, 21 May 1909, in *MDMM*, 46–47.

9 I have restored the phrase "of a radiant childhood in Prince Edward Island. 'The Chronicles' is a collection of short stories," which was inadvertently dropped from this version of the article.

10 Sarah Orne Jewett (1849–1909), American author of "local colour" novels and short stories set in Maine on the border of New Hampshire.

11 I have not been able to locate this item in the online archives of *Harper's Magazine*.

12 Chester had visited Prince Edward Island with Montgomery in July and August 1913.

13 The cat in question, Daffy – actually the third cat of Montgomery's named Daffy – was born in 1905 and died in August 1920. See Montgomery, 7 January 1910, in *SJLMM*, 1: 379–80; Montgomery, 28 January 1912, in *SJLMM*, 2: 92; Montgomery, 22 August 1920, in *SJLMM*, 2: 388–89.

14 Actually, as stated in several other essays in this volume, the relative in question is Hector Macneill, a maternal ancestor.

15 This jug is described in detail in a journal entry dated 1912, and a jug of its description appears in Montgomery's short story "Old Lady Lloyd," published in *Chronicles of Avonlea* the same year (Montgomery, 28 January 1912, in *SJLMM*, 2: 88; *CA*, 27). The jug would become a central motif in her 1931 novel *A Tangled Web*.

23

What Twelve Canadian Women Hope to See
as the Outcome of the War

—— 1915 ——

This article includes contributions from a number of prominent Canadian women, including Emily Murphy (1868–1933), who wrote four popular books of personal sketches under the pseudonym Janey Canuck, including *Janey Canuck in the West* (1910); Zoé Lafontaine (1842–1921), wife of then–Prime Minister Wilfrid Laurier; Marshall Saunders (1861–1947), Canadian author of *Beautiful Joe* (1893) and *'Tilda Jane: An Orphan in Search of a Home* (1901); Flora MacDonald Denison (1867–1921), Honorary President of the Canadian Suffrage Association; Katherine Hale, whose 1927 profile of Montgomery appears later in this volume; and Nellie L. McClung. Montgomery's claim that "there are things that are more horrible still" than war contrasts sharply to the vision of war that she would depict in her 1921 novel *Rilla of Ingleside*.

What do you as a woman hope to see as the outcome of the war: (1) for the world at large, (2) for women in particular?"

In November *Everywoman's World* addressed this question to several prominent Canadian women with the object of getting a national expression of Canadian women's feeling on the result of the war, and of giving this symposium to Canadian women, to all Canadians, to the world, as a representative expression of what Canadian women hope to see as the outcome of the greatest, and, as they all hope, the last world war. The thought of Canadian women would pretty well represent the general thought of Canadian, of American, of women throughout the world on the subject of the war. All of us have the heartfelt hope that it may soon end, and as to what the outcome of the war is to be, there have been many predictions. So far, however, no one has asked or perhaps thought of what she hoped would be the outcome of the war. The contributors who have written for the symposium have frankly said what they *hoped* would be the outcome of the war, and this expression of personal desire is for that reason all the more valuable. What these women, and all the women whom they represent, want, is the object of the symposium to bring to the attention of our readers.

The First National Expression of Opinion by Canadian Women

These Canadian women appreciated what we were trying to do, and responded in such a way that they should have not only our appreciation and thanks – because we want Canadian women to think and feel and write nationally – but they should have, and we think they will get them, the appreciation and thanks of the women of Canada and the country generally. We are proud to have been the means of collecting in one page the public expression of representative Canadian women from coast to coast – the first national public expression by Canadian women on any question.

Some whom we wanted and you would want were not able to contribute – either, as they said, because they were not writers, or because they were so involved in executive patriotic work of the moment that they could not look so far ahead. [* * *]

The majority of our correspondents, however, realized what part in national life public expression of opinion plays; how it is worth while, for themselves and for others to take part in the life of the times and of the nation. [* * *]

A Place for War

War has many aspects. L.M. Montgomery, writer of graceful romances, strikes a sterner note in her message to the readers of *Everywoman's World*:

"You ask me what I hope to see as the outcome of the war, (1) for the world at large, (2) and for women in particular. I am not of those who believe that this war will put an end to war. War is horrible, but there are things that are more horrible still, just as there are fates worse than death. Moral degradation, low ideals, sordid devotion to money-getting, are worse evils than war, and history shows us that these evils invariably overtake a nation which is for a long time at peace. Nothing short of so awful a calamity as a great war can awaken to remembrance a nation that has forgotten God and sold its birthright of aspiration for a mess of pottage.[1]

"But I do hope that, as a result of the war, humanity may re-learn its lesson so thoroughly that it will not need another such drastic schooling for many generations. I hope that the heroism and fortitude evoked may leave a rich legacy of character to races yet unborn; and I hope that a great awakening to high issues, moral, spiritual and intellectual, may follow the agony of conflict.

"In regard to women, I do not expect that the war and its outcome will affect their interests, apart from the general influence upon the race. But I do hope that it will in some measure open the eyes of humanity to the truth that the women who bear and train the nation's sons should have some voice in the political issues that may send those sons to die on battlefields

"'Where thousands die
To lift one hero into fame.'"[2]

[* * *]

NOTES

1 Something of little monetary value. In the Hebrew Bible, Esau, son of Isaac, sells his inheritance to his brother Jacob for a pot of pottage (Genesis 25:29–34); however, the phrase "mess of pottage" has its origins in the sixteenth century.
2 Properly, "On battle-fields where thousands bleed / To lift one hero into fame." From *The Hanging of the Crane* (1874), by Henry Wadsworth Longfellow.

24

The Way to Make a Book

—— 1915 ——

L.M. MONTGOMERY
Author of *Anne of Green Gables*, etc.

This article, published in the same issue of *Everywoman's World* as chapter 23, "What Twelve Canadian Women Hope to See as the Outcome of the War," was rediscovered by Cecily Devereux and was first reprinted in her critical edition of *Anne of Green Gables*, published in 2004.[1] As Devereux notes, here Montgomery is much more explicit in her advice to aspiring female writers than she is in "The Alpine Path," her retrospective account of her life and early career that two years later would also be published in this magazine. Although Montgomery cautions her readers that the three-volume Victorian novel (or "triple-decker") is no longer in fashion, she peppers her article with allusions or references to a number of male writers from England, Scotland, and the United States, including Burns, Tennyson, Scott, Cooper, Jerome, and Byron, most of whom were active before the twentieth century.

An old joke will probably be familiar to all who read this article. A woman who had one child was anxious to train it properly. Feeling herself to be very ignorant of such a subject, she appealed for instruction to a friend who had seven children.

"My dear," said her friend, "there is no use asking me how to bring up children because I really don't know anything more about it than you do. But just ask the first old maid you meet and she will be able to tell you all about it."

And it is just so in regard to the writing of books. Those who never write books can so easily tell how it is done and how it should be done.

It is as easy for them as rolling off a log. For those of us who *have* written books it is an exceedingly hard thing.

My own experience is that books – real "live" books – are *not* written. Like *Topsy*, they "grow."[2] The function of the author is simply to follow the growth and record it.

> "Perhaps it may turn out a song,
> Perhaps turn out a sermon."[3]

Never mind what it turns out. As long as it grows out of your life it will have life in it, and the great pulse of humanity everywhere will thrill and throb to that life.

Before attempting to write a book, be sure you have something to say – something that *demands* to be said. It need not be a very great or lofty or profound something; it is not given to many of us to utter[4]

> "Jewels five words long
> That on the stretched forefinger of all time
> Sparkle for ever."[5]

But if we have something to say that will bring a whiff of fragrance to a tired soul and to a weary heart, or a glint of sunshine to a clouded life, then that something is worth saying, and it is our duty to try to say it as well as in us lies.

A book to be worth anything, must have a good central idea. I do not say a plot, for many very successful books have little or no plot. Certainly, a logical and well-constructed plot adds strength and charm to any book and increases the chances of its success. But a central idea – a purpose of some sort – a book must have. It is not to be flung in the reader's face; it is not to be obtruded in every paragraph or chapter; but it must be there, as the spine is in the human body, to hold the book together; and all that follows, characters, incidents and conversations, must be developed in harmony with this idea or purpose.

One should not try to write a book impulsively or accidentally, as it were. The idea may come by impulse or accident, but it must be worked out with care and skill, or its embodiment will never partake of the essence of true art. Write – and put what you have written away; read it over weeks later; cut, prune, and rewrite. Repeat this process until your work seems to you as good as you can make it. Never mind what outside critics say. They will all differ from each other in their opinions, so there is really not a great deal to be learned from them. Be your own severest critic. Never let a sentence in your work get by you until you are convinced that it is as perfect as you can make it. Somebody else may be able to improve it vastly. Somebody will be sure to think he can. Never mind. Do *your* best – and do it sincerely. Don't try to write like some other author. Don't try to "hit the public taste." The public taste doesn't really like being hit. It prefers to be allured into some fresh pasture, surprised with some unexpected tid-bit.

An accusation is often made against us novelists that we paint our characters – especially our ridiculous or unpleasant characters – "from life." The public seems determined not to allow the smallest particle of creative talent to an author. If you write a book you *must* have drawn your characters "from life." You, yourself, are, of course, the hero or heroine; your unfortunate neighbors supply the other portraits. People will cheerfully tell you that they know this or that character of your books intimately. This will aggravate you at first, but later on you will learn to laugh at it. It is, in reality, a subtle compliment – though it is not always meant to be. It is at least a tribute to the "life-likeness" of your book people.

But no true artist ever draws exactly from life. We must *study* from life, working in hints gathered here and there, bits of character, personal or mental idiosyncrasies, humorous remarks, tales, or legends, making use of the real to perfect the ideal. But our own ideal must be behind it all. A writer must keep his eyes open for material; but in the last analysis his characters must be the creations of his own mind if they are to be consistent and natural.

Right here, let me say that a writer of books must cultivate the "note-book habit." Keep a blank book; jot down in it every helpful idea that comes your way, every amusing or dramatic incident or expression you hear, every bit of apt description that occurs to you. Be all eye and ear in your daily walks and social intercourse. If you meet a quaint personality write down its salient characteristic. If you see a striking face or feature describe it for future use; if you hear a scrap of native wit or unconscious humor or pathos, preserve it; if you see some exquisite, fleeting effect in sky or sea or field, imprison it in words before it can escape you. Some day you may create a character in whose mouth the long-preserved sentence of fun or absurdity may be appropriate – you may stage your story in a landscape where the bit of first-hand description furnishes exactly the necessary touch of reality. I have, time and again, evolved some of my most successful tales or chapters from the germ of some such "bit," hurriedly scribbled in my note-book when I heard or saw or thought it.

Write only of the life you know. This is the only safe rule for most of us. A great genius may, by dint of adding research and study to his genius, be able to write of other ages and other environments than his own. But the chances are that you are not a Scott or a Cooper.[6] So stick to what you know. It is not a narrow field. Human life is thick around us everywhere. Tragedy is being enacted in the next yard; comedy is playing across the street. Plot and incident and coloring are ready to our hands. The country lad at his plough can be made just as interesting a figure as if he were a knight in shining armor; the bent old woman we pass on the road may have been as beautiful in her youth as the daughters of Vere de Vere,[7] and the cause of as many heartaches. The darkest tragedy I ever heard of was enacted by people who lived on a backwoods farm; and funnier than anything I ever read was a dialogue between two old fishermen who were gravely discussing a subject of which they knew absolutely nothing. Unless you are living alone on a desert island you can find plenty of material for writing all around you; and even there, you could find it in your own heart and soul. For it is surprising how much we are all like other people. Jerome K. Jerome says: "Life tastes just the same, whether you drink it out of a stone mug or a golden goblet."[8] There you are! So don't make the mistake of trying to furnish your stories with golden goblets when stone mugs are what your characters are accustomed to use. The public isn't much concerned with your external nothings – your mugs or your goblets. What they want is the fresh, spicy brew that Nature pours for us everywhere.

When you have shaped out your central idea and brooded over your characters until they live and move and have being for you, then write about them. Let them have a good deal of their own way, even if it isn't always your way. Don't try to describe them too fully; let them reveal themselves. As somebody has said, "Don't tell your readers that a certain woman growls; just bring the old lady in and *let her growl*." See to it that your incidents and chapters grow out of one another naturally, as they do in real life. Don't drag some event in, however dramatic or amusing it may be in itself, if it has no real connection with your plot or your idea. This doesn't mean that you must never indulge in any pleasant little by-way excursion to pick primroses. But your by-ways must always lead back to your main road. They must not stop short, leaving you and your readers to jump back.

Write, I beseech you, of things cheerful, of things lovely, of things of good report. Don't write about pig-sties because they are "real."[9] Flower-gardens are just as real and just as plentiful. Write tragedy if you will, for there must be shadow as well as sunlight in any broad presentment of human life; but don't write of vileness, of filth, of unsavory deeds and thoughts. There is no justification of such writing. The big majority of the reading public doesn't want it; it serves not one good end; it debases a God-given talent. Never mind if some *blase* critic sneeringly says that your book will "please the Young Person." You may be justly proud if it does. The Young Person's taste is well worth pleasing because, thank God, it is generally pure and natural, delighting in simplicity, not demanding salaciousness to spur a jaded appetite that has been vitiated by long indulgence in tainted food.

Don't spin your book out too long. The day of the three-volume novel passed with the crinoline skirt and the stage-coach. Don't make anybody too bad or anybody too good. Most people are mixed. Don't make vice attractive and goodness stupid. It's nearly always the other way in real life. Don't be content with writing pretty well; do your best; if you are only describing a stone wall, make your readers *see* that wall, see it yourself first; cut and prune, but – don't make things *too* bare. If you were a genius of the first rank you might present stark facts fascinatingly; but ordinary writers need a few branching sprays of fancy. Study and observe life that you may paint it convincingly; cultivate a sense of dramatic and humorous values; *feel* what you write; love your characters and live with them –

And Keep On Trying!

When you have your book written – what then? Send it to any publishing firm of good repute and standing you prefer. Don't worry over the fact that you are unknown and deduce therefrom the conclusion that your manuscript won't be read. It will be read; it may, and – if it is your first – very likely will, be sent back to you. Don't throw it in the fire; don't sit down and cry; just do it up and send it to the next firm on your list. If there is anything in it, it will find acceptance finally. Don't have anything to do with firms that offer to publish your book if you will pay half the expenses. Arrange to have it published on a royalty basis. On your first book you can't expect more than a ten per cent. royalty. Some firms offer to purchase a manuscript for a certain sum cash down. It is rarely advisable to accept this. If a book is anything of a success it will bring you in more on the royalty basis, and publishers seldom offer to buy a book outright unless they are strongly convinced that it will be a success.[10]

When the book is published your publishers will send you half a dozen copies free. If you want more to present to admiring friends you have to buy them, same as everybody else. But what a day it is when your first book comes to you between covers!

> "'Tis pleasant sure to see one's name in print –
> A book's a book, although there's nothing in it."[11]

But if you have written it "for the joy of the working"[12] there *will* be something in it,[13] and the praise of the Master of all good workmen will be yours.

NOTES

1   See Montgomery, *Anne of Green Gables*, edited by Devereux, 365–70. Most of the literary allusions are first identified in this version of the text.
2   See chapter 3, "Origin of Popular Book," note 2, in this volume.
3   Properly, "a sang." From "Epistle to a Young Friend" (1786), by Robert Burns.
4   I have corrected the original, which reads "many of us utter."
5   From *The Princess: A Medley* (1847), a poem by Alfred, Lord Tennyson.
6   James Fenimore Cooper (1789–1851), popular American novelist best known for *Last of the Mohicans* (1826). In a 1939 version of this article, she replaces Cooper with Rudyard Kipling, who had died in 1936 (Montgomery, "An Author Speaks," 2).
7   An allusion to the poem "Lady Clara Vere de Vere," part of *The Lady of Shalott, and Other Poems* (1842), by Alfred, Lord Tennyson.
8   Properly, "Life tastes much the same, whether we quaff it from a golden goblet or drink it out of a stone mug." From *The Idle Thoughts of an Idle Fellow* (1886), by Jerome K. Jerome (1859–1927), English writer and humorist.
9   Montgomery would continue to use the image of "pig-sties" to denigrate modernist fiction, both in her journals (particularly after reading Morley Callaghan's 1928 novel *Strange Fugitive*) and in her fiction. See Montgomery, 30 December 1928, in *SJLMM*, 3: 387; Montgomery to Weber, 7 April 1929, in *AfGG*, 169–70; *EQ*, 24. See also Lefebvre, "Pigsties and Sunsets."

10 When *Anne of Green Gables* was first accepted in 1907, Montgomery recorded in her journal that they had offered her "a royalty of ten percent on the *wholesale* price," terms that she did not find particularly generous (Montgomery, 16 August 1907, in *SJLMM*, 1: 331; see also Montgomery to Weber, 2 May 1907, in *GGL*, 51). In a letter to G.B. MacMillan over two decades later, she revealed that they had offered her a royalty or "a certain sum outright. I know now they thought I would jump at 'the certain sum' in which case I would have got $500 for *Green Gables*. But green as I was I was not so green as that so I said 'a royalty'" (Montgomery to MacMillan, 10 February 1929, in *MDMM*, 141).

11 From *English Bards and Scotch Reviewers* (1809), by George Gordon, Lord Byron (1788–1824), English poet. Montgomery inserted this quotation in her journal upon the publication of her article "A Western Eden" in the Prince Albert *Times* in June 1891 (see Montgomery, 18 June 1891, in *SJLMM*, 1: 52).

12 See chapter 14, "[Seasons in the Woods]," by L.M. Montgomery, note 92, in this volume.

13 I have corrected the original, which reads "something it in."

25

How I Began

—— 1915 ——

L.M. MONTGOMERY

In this article, published in *The Canadian Bookman* in April 1915, Montgomery mockingly complains that she cannot alter the "facts" about the creation of her first novel (and, by extension, her early writing career). Yet these "facts" change from one version to the other, as do the details she offers to create a snapshot of the writer at work. Many of the details here would eventually be reworked for her longer memoir, "The Alpine Path." A photograph included with the article identifies the author as "Mrs. Ewen Macdonald, known to readers of *Anne of Green Gables*, etc., as 'L.M. Montgomery.'"

The question, "How did you begin to write?" is not an easy one for me to answer. I have no recollection of how I began to write. I never sat me deliberately down and said, "Go to, here is pen and ink; I will write me a book." But as far back as my remembrance goes, I was breathing, reading and writing. My earliest recollection of school-days is of writing a story about my cats on my slate, of being caught at it by my teacher, and – oh, horrors! – being made to "read it out" before the class. It was like tearing the veil from a shrine. That teacher, though he knew it not, committed dire sacrilege towards me.

But even this could not squelch the impulse in me that compelled me to write. I was an indefatigable small scribbler. Generally I wrote prose, and then all the little incidents of my not very exciting existence were described. I wrote descriptions of my favorite haunts, biographies of my cats, and even critical reviews of books I had read. Sometimes I wrote verse about months[1] and flowers, or addressed "lines" to my friends. Most of these productions were written on the blank backs of the long, red letter bills then used in the post offices. It was not easy for me to get all the paper I wanted, and those jolly old "letter bills" were positive boons. My grandparents kept the village post office and three times a week a discarded letter bill came my grateful way.

When I was thirteen, I sent a "poem," painstakingly written on both sides of the paper, to an American magazine. The idea of being paid for it never entered my head. Indeed, I don't think I knew at that time that people ever were paid for writing. People were paid for work. But writing was not, I thought, work. It was a delightful recreation and sally into fairyland, which was its own reward. My early dreams of possible fame were untarnished by any speculations regarding filthy lucre.

Well, the editor of that magazine sent my verses back – although I had *not* enclosed a stamp for their return, being in blissful ignorance of such a requirement. I have forgiven him. But at the time I thought I never could or would. I drained the cup of failure to the dregs. I was crushed in the very dust of humiliation. But as years went on, I found that there were so many similarly hard-hearted editor folk in the world that it was not worth while getting mad with them. Life was too short to wreak vengeance on them all. So the only revenge I took – it was a more cruel one than I then suspected – was to keep on bombarding them with similar stuff.

One day, when I was seventeen, I got a thin letter from the editor of a fourth-rate American periodical. It accepted a poem – on violets – which I had sent, and offered in payment two subscriptions to the magazine. Those magazines, with their vapid little stories, were the first tangible recompense my pen brought me. The second was almost as overwhelming. A floral magazine allowed me to select fifty cents worth of seeds from its firm's catalogue in payment for a poem! After all, it was not such poor recompense, as anyone would have agreed who saw the resulting flower bed's splendor of crimson and gold and blue.

Then followed two lean years. I could not get even magazines and flower seeds for my stories and verses. My stuff invariably came back, save from those periodicals who thought that the glory of seeing one's name in print was sufficient reward. Then came another wonderful day, when I received a check for a short story. It was for five dollars – five whole dollars. I did not squander those beautiful dollars in riotous living. Neither did I invest them in necessary boots and hats. Instead, I hied me to the nearest bookstore and bought five volumes of the standard poets.[2]

I wanted to get something that I could keep forever in memory of having "arrived."

Followed several years of steady magazine work. I wrote hundreds of stories and verses. Every year new magazines opened their portals to the wayfarer on thorny literary paths. I gradually built up a clientele of editors on whom I could depend for a comfortable livelihood if I wrote just what they wanted and sawed it off into suitable lengths. This was much to be thankful for, in a world where one must live; but it was not all I wanted – not what I had dreamed of when I wrote on my red letter bills in years agone.

I have told the story of the genesis of my first book so often that it must be very hackneyed now. I must tell it the same way every time, because I am stating facts, and cannot change or embroider them for the sake of variety. I had always intended to write a book some day. I knew exactly what kind of a book it would be – a very serious affair, with a complicated plot and a Dickensonian wealth of character. But I never seemed to find time for it. Then the editor of a Sunday-school weekly asked me to write a seven-chapter serial for him. I looked through my note book of "ideas" and found an old, faded entry, "Elderly couple apply to orphan asylum for a boy; by mistake a girl is sent them." I thought this would do for a peg to hang my serial on and I blocked out seven Procrustean chapters.[3] I intended to write a nice little yarn about a good little girl, with the usual snug little moral tucked away in it, like a pill in a spoonful of jam; and if I had had time to go on with it at once I suppose that is all it would have been.

But I did not have time, and in the weeks that followed I "brooded" the tale in my mind. *Anne* began to develop in such a fashion that seven chapters could never hold her. So I wrote another little tale for the Sunday-school editor and I let *Anne* do as she would in her own history. The result was my book, *Anne of Green Gables* – a very different sort of book from the one I had fondly dreamed of writing. But perhaps 'tis as well.

> "There's a divinity that shapes our ends,
> Rough-hew them as we will."[4]

NOTES

1 I have corrected the original, which reads "moths."

2 According to her journal, the payment of five dollars was for her second short story, "Our Charivari," published in *Golden Days for Boys and Girls* in 1896 under the pseudonym Maud Cavendish, but she purchased hard-cover volumes of the work of Tennyson, Longfellow, Whittier, and Byron using the prize money for a poem called "Patience" that she had published in the Halifax *Evening Mail* under the pseudonym Belinda Bluegrass. Montgomery makes the same mistake in "The Alpine Path," in which she adds Milton to the list of poets whose work she purchased with her payment from *Golden Days for Boys and Girls*. See Montgomery, 20 February 1896, in *SJLMM*, 1: 158; *AP*, 60–61.

3 Chopped to fit, with enforced conformity.

4 See chapter 13, "How I Began to Write," by L.M. Montgomery, note 14, in this volume.

26

[This Hideous War]

—— 1915 ——

This letter was published in the *Boston Evening Transcript* in early November 1915, only seven months after Montgomery's contribution to the *Everywoman's World* article on Canadian women's hopes for the outcome of the war, but its tone and vision are remarkably different. The contents of the letter may be explained in part by the fact that the United States was not yet involved in the war effort (it would declare war on Germany only in April 1917). At this time, Montgomery was between writing projects: her latest novel, *Anne of the Island*, had been published in July 1915, and she would not start writing her next, *Anne's House of Dreams*, until June 1916, after gathering material for it the preceding winter and spring.[1] In fact, her next book was *The Watchman and Other Poems*, which she dedicated "to the memory of the gallant Canadian soldiers who have laid down their lives for their country and their empire." A later novel, *Rainbow Valley* (1919), would be dedicated to the memory of three of her parishioners had who "made the supreme sacrifice that the happy valleys of their home land might be kept sacred from the ravage of the invader."

That the war is nearer to us than we think, that it concerns us Americans so directly that no man or woman who lives in the present and for the future can be a "neutral," becomes more and more apparent every day. Writing to a friend here in Boston, Miss L.M. Montgomery, author of *Anne of Green Gables*, makes it clear that Europe alone is not involved in the war, that it has reached Canada and is continually reaching into the hearts of the Canadians, our racial and our spiritual kinsfolk. Miss Montgomery is the wife of the Rev. Ewan Macdonald, and she writes from her home at Leaskdale, Ontario: "As for 'the boys' keeping me from literary work – alas it is not the boys.[2] I could manage so far as they are concerned. It is this hideous war. You who live in the comparative calm of the United States do not, I think, realize at all what this means to us in Canada. We are at war – at close grips with a deadly and determined enemy. We live and breathe in its shadows. Never for one moment is the strain lifted. Our land is full of the khaki clad boys. Every week or so another of our young men, to whom we have become attached in our work here, slips away to the country town and enlists.[3] My brother is in the firing line and many cousins and dear friends.[4] My husband even talks of going if the cry for 'more men – more men' keeps sounding. Our Red Cross branches are working and canvassing feverishly. 'The war' is never out of our thoughts. Calm detached work is impossible – at least for me – as long as the present critical situation lasts. If the Balkan campaign results favorably for our allies I may be able to settle down to some work again. Until some such thing happens I cannot do literary work any more than I could if some beloved one were lying critically ill in my home. My nervous and mental strain could not be more severe if it were so. This horrible waiting – waiting – waiting every day for the war news – the dreadful uncertainty – the casualty lists – it all seems to me as if I were crushed under an ever-increasing weight. If ever peace comes again we will not know how to live in it. It seems to me that we have been at war for a hundred years. I watch the poor mothers in our church on Sundays whose sons have gone to the front and see them getting grayer and grayer and older and older week by week. I hear their stifled sobs as my husband prays for the boys on the firing line. I waken in the night and think of my boyish brother in the shell-swept trenches – picture him dying horribly there, far from everyone who loves him. Amid all this think you I can sit me down to calm creation of imaginary people and their imaginary joys and sorrows? No, I cannot. Literature for a while must wait on life and death."

NOTES

1 See Montgomery, 26 July 1915, in *SJLMM*, 2: 170; Montgomery, 17 June 1916, in *SJLMM*, 2: 186.
2 Chester Macdonald was three years old at the time this letter was published. Montgomery's second son, Hugh, had died at birth in August 1914.

Her second surviving son, Stuart, born 7 October 1915, was less than a month old at the time this letter was published.

3　Mary Rubio and Elizabeth Waterston note that Montgomery, as a minister's wife, "was at the nerve centre of the community, responding with uncommon sensibility to the world events that brought deaths and breakdowns to soldiers and their families" (Introduction to *SJLMM*, 2: xv).

4　Montgomery's youngest half-brother, Carl Montgomery, whom she had not yet met in person, enlisted in late 1914. See Montgomery, 1 January 1915, in *SJLMM*, 2: 159.

27

What Are the Greatest Books
in the English Language?

—— 1916 ——

In a poll in which "Well-Known Canadian Authors Write Interestingly on This
Subject" – published in *Bookseller and Stationer*, a Toronto publication, in
January 1916 – Montgomery's contribution regarding the "greatest books" in
English reveals her preference not only for canonical texts of the nineteenth
century but for British literature specifically, a preference that is consistent with
the favourite prose authors that she listed in a 1914 journal entry, including Sir Walter Scott (1771–1832), Charles Dickens (1812–1870), William
Makepeace Thackeray (1811–1863), Wilkie Collins (1824–1889), Anthony
Trollope (1815–1882), "and fifty others."[1] Also included in this survey are
five fellow Canadian authors who were extremely popular during this period:
Arthur Stringer (1874–1950), Stephen Leacock (1869–1944), Agnes C. Laut
(1871–1936), Emily Murphy (1868–1933), and Robert J.C. Stead (1880–
1959). Although like Montgomery many of the respondents insisted that their
lists contained personal favourites rather than objective evaluations of "best"
texts, not a single text by a Canadian author is chosen by the six respondents.
Instead, with a few exceptions – Alexandre Dumas and Victor Hugo from
France, Fyodor Dostoyevsky from Russia, Henry De Vere Stacpoole from Ireland, and Mark Twain and Lew Wallace from the United States – all the texts
chosen are by British authors: William Makepeace Thackeray, Charles Dickens
(all six of Leacock's choices are by Dickens), Charles Reade, George Barrow,
Thomas Hardy, R.D. Blackmore, and Rudyard Kipling. Although the presence
of "foreign authors" is noticed by the unidentified compiler of the piece, there
is no comment on the bias for British literature and literature by men: in fact,
Montgomery is the only one to name a text by a woman.

What are the greatest novels in the English language? This question, hoary with age, has been debated and re-debated by book lovers and will continue to be the inspiration for controversy as long as the taste for good reading continues.

On a question of this kind it is always interesting to get the views of persons who have themselves added to the store of great literature. Accordingly the "Booklover" took it upon itself to secure the views of the best known Canadian authors as to what are the best novels in the literature of the English tongue. As it was necessary to fix certain limits, the number of "Best Novels" was fixed at six. The replies received to date are appended and it is hoped to be able to produce more in the next issue.

The request sent to these writers of distinction was perhaps a little vague in one respect – in limiting the selection to books written in the English tongue. It will be noted that several of the replies list books by foreign authors.

[* * *]

If you had asked me to name the twenty best novels in the English language, or rather – since I cannot arrogate to myself any authority to decide what are the best – the twenty novels I liked most, it would have been an easy task. But, when you ask me to name the six favorites, you put me in the position of the mother of ten children who is asked which three she loves best. She could not tell you and neither can I. To name any six books means treason to the others which I love equally well. However, if I were compelled to save from complete extinction six – and six only – novels, those I would sorrowfully choose will be found in the list herewith appended – not because they give me any greater pleasure than the rest of the aforesaid twenty, but because the characters in them are, to me, more intensely alive and real than in any others: 1. *David Copperfield*; 2. *Pickwick Papers*; 3. *The Mill on the Floss*; 4. *Vanity Fair*; 5. *Jane Eyre*; 6. *Rob Roy*.[2]

You will observe that these are all old books. There *may* be modern novels just as good. "Pigs *may* whistle,"[3] but if so, they lack the ripeness and flavor time alone can give.

Yours sincerely,

L.M. Montgomery Macdonald

NOTES

1 Montgomery, 15 April 1914, in *SJLMM*, 2: 146.
2 *David Copperfield* (1850) and *The Pickwick Papers* (1837), by Charles Dickens; *The Mill on the Floss* (1860), by George Eliot, pseudonym of Mary Ann Evans (1819–1880); *Vanity Fair* (1847–48), by William Makepeace Thackeray; *Jane Eyre* (1847), by Charlotte Brontë; *Rob Roy* (1817), by Sir Walter Scott.
3 "Pigs may whistle, but they hae an ill mouth for't" (Scottish proverb).

28

My Favorite Bookshelf

—— 1917 ——

L.M. MONTGOMERY
Author of *Anne's House of Dreams*, etc.

This article, published in an unidentified periodical around 1917, provides readers with a glimpse of Montgomery's reading life. As her journals and letters also show, she was an omnivorous and rather indiscriminate reader whose public role as a minister's wife had little bearing on her choice of reading materials. Montgomery republished this essay with only minor modifications two decades later, in *The Island Crusader* in 1937, and included a clipping in a letter to G.B. MacMillan the following February.[1] In a promotional blurb for *The Country Kitchen* (1936) by Della T. Lutes (1872–1942) that appeared on the dust wrapper of an early edition of *Jane of Lantern Hill*, Montgomery wrote: "I seemed on every page to be living over again my own childhood in that old P.E. Island kitchen I remember so well. The book is so full of delightful humor and characters. Its people are alive. I've put it away on my 'special bookshelf' where I keep all the books I really love."

There are many books in my library, as I do know well at times of spring housecleaning; and I have a liking for them all – because I never keep a book unless I like it at least a little bit. But the shabby old bookcase in the corner by my desk is the only one I would make a desperate effort to save if the house were on fire. The others could be spared – could be bought over again if need were – but these, never. New copies of them would not take their place – I must have these identical books which I have read and reread so often that they have acquired an aroma and personality all their own, quite irrespective of their contents.

These books are my friends; the books in the other bookcases are merely agreeable acquaintances. Here is a book for my every mood and the white magic of it never fails. I sink wearily into my "lazy" chair, open the worn covers, and presto, change! Everything is different and as it should be.

A motley collection? Verily, yes. There are no class distinctions in my pet bookshelf. If a book has the subtle, intimate, indefinable appeal for me which a book-friend must have I care not whether it come in rags or tags or velvet gown,[2] whether its author be known or unknown, new or old. It is of kin to me and I gladly hail the relationship.

Here is the little book of modern verse into which I like to dip when my mind feels dusty and commonplace and longs for a pleasant bit of starfaring; and here is the Great Poet to whom I turn when I need consolation for some deep grief or expression for some mighty emotion. Here is the book of travel to which I flee when I am desperately weary of well-trodden ways, and here is the quiet, meandering book, pleasing as a daisied meadow, wherein I yearn to browse when life has been too exciting and strenuous. Here is the "girl's book" which I love most when I feel old and sophisticated and too worldly-wise, and want to stray back to the fairy realm of sweet sixteen. And this – yes, it is really a boy's book of adventure which is to me as manna in the wilderness when I grow tired of ordering my household with a due regard for calories and desire wildly to start out with a battle-axe, or go hunting for buried treasure, or shooting grizzly bears.

There is a garden book here, too, which I love best when a snowstorm is howling at my window; and there is a book which brings to me the tang and zest and mystery of the sea when I am prisoned by inland hills. There is a historical novel for the hours when I yearn for the society of kings and queens, and there is a fat biography, garrulous and intimate and savory, such as my soul loveth, which ministers to me when I burn to know what real famous folks have done and said.

History is here for the serious hour of determined self-culture; and essays for the literary, bookish mood; and a book about cats because I love cats in every mood; and a most jolly volume of gruesome, horrible, delicious ghost stories which I must read when midnight is near and the wind is keening round the eaves and the stairs are creaking and anything might be true.

Yes, here they all are, my pets and my darlings. How I love them – how I gloat over them!

Friend, dost thou contemplate giving me a book this Yule? Then I pray thee to select with care. Give me not a book which I will coldly read and put away icily in yonder far-away bookcases. Give me one which belongs to the household of faith, and it will add the beauty of thy friendship to its own. See, there is an empty corner just here yearning for it.

NOTES

1 See Montgomery to MacMillan, 23 February 1938, in *MDMM*, 191. The clipping is found with the handwritten letters to MacMillan, now housed at Library and Archives Canada.
2 Properly, "Some in rags, and some in tags, / And some in velvet gowns." From "Hark Hark the Dogs Do Bark," a popular rhyme originating in thirteenth-century England.

29

The Author of Anne

—— 1919 ——

ETHEL M. CHAPMAN

This article, which appears as part of Chapman's column "Women and Their Work" in *MacLean's* (as it was then spelled) in October 1919, grew out of an interview with Montgomery that took place in late August of the same year, just after she had received copies of her tenth book, *Rainbow Valley*, and had begun her next book, which would be published as *Rilla of Ingleside* in fall 1921. As she reported in her journal, "Miss Chapman ... spent Wednesday here, to get material for an article on me and my 'career.'" Unfortunately, trouble was brewing behind the scenes: Ewan Macdonald had recently developed symptoms of what would be diagnosed as religious melancholia. "I talked brightly and amusingly – and watched Ewan out of the corner of my eye, wondering how he felt."[1] Chapman's enthusiasm about a screen adaptation of *Anne of Green Gables* was marred by more details that Montgomery likewise apparently did not include in the conversation – that in January of that year she had sold all rights to her first seven books to L.C. Page and Company in an attempt to be rid of the firm forever. Because Page waited until all rights had reverted to him before selling film rights of her books, Montgomery received no remuneration from this project and had no creative involvement in it.

There is one heroine of Canadian fiction who will never be criticized as exotic or lacking in inspiration – the winsome, gingery, red-headed girl who grew up through *Anne of Green Gables, Anne of Avonlea, Anne of the Island* and blossomed into full womanhood two years ago in *Anne's House of Dreams*. As an ideal for the young womanhood of the country she has a place all her own, this girl of imagination and wit and dreams, strangely combined with practical common sense, to whom the blossoming cherry-tree outside her window was a "Snow Queen" and the pond across the flats "The Lake of Shining Waters," who found in the woods of silver birches a realm of "kindred spirits" and who could keep house and teach school and help most efficiently in the bringing up of two very human waifs of children.[2] No wonder mothers want their daughters to read the Anne books.

From the first appearance of *Anne of Green Gables* the books "caught on." This winter Anne is going to appear in the movies. The scenario rights to the four books, *Anne of Green Gables*, *Anne of Avonlea*, *Chronicles of Avonlea*, and *Anne of the Island* have been bought by the Famous Players–Lasky Corporation.[3] A Canadian movie with the quaint and beautiful setting of the farms and orchards of Prince Edward Island, written by a Canadian author![4] We have been waiting for this for a long time. But the author herself, now the wife of Rev. Macdonald, the Presbyterian minister at Leaskdale and the mother of two sturdy, quick-brained little boys,[5] doesn't seem to consider it an event of more importance than the next church christening.

It has been said that in the first two Anne books, Miss Montgomery drew from the experiences of her own life. Certainly Anne got her imagination from no one else, but it is not the author's own story. "My places are real places," she says, "but my people are imaginary." They have certain points in common, however. Miss Montgomery's mother died before she was two years old and she went to live with her grandmother, which no doubt gave her her sympathetic understanding of Anne's little problems in a home with only elderly people. What she lacked in the way of companionship with other children, however, seems to have been more than made up by a natural environment uniquely fitted to inspire the imagination. Her home was on a farm near Cavendish on the north shore of the Island and she says "Tourists who travel by train through the Island have no idea of the beauty of its scenery because they do not see the north shore." She has in her home several striking pictures of the rocks and beaches along this coast, one of particular interest being a painting of the sand dunes along a favorite bathing beach – one of the finest bathing beaches in the world, by the way – where the winds had cupped out a hollow that, as children, they used for a dressing-room.

It is not surprising that she loves the sea. "When I was a child," she says, "I practically lived at the shore during the mackerel fishing season.

My grandfather, like all the other farmers around, had a fishing-boat, and from the time the mackerel came in till the end of the season, the men would get up at four o'clock in the morning and go down to the sea. At seven o'clock we children would take their breakfast to them. If the fishing was particularly good they would sometimes stay all day and we would bring all their meals and spend the intervals between wading in the surf and climbing over the rocks ... I get homesick for the sea sometimes yet."

Yet with all her fondness for the outdoors we gather that little Maud must have been "a dark and eerie child,"[6] wandering off by herself to commune with imaginary people or revelling in whatever books were available and already creating her own little stories. "I can imagine," she says, "what it would be to be a drunkard for reading.[7] Fortunately my English grandmother saw to it that I did the practical things as well. There were no lending libraries on the Island at that time and our library at home was a rather unusual collection to satisfy the reading tastes of a child. We had full sets of Dickens, Scott and all the poets; *Pilgrim's Progress* and *Paradise Lost*, which I was allowed to read on Sundays;[8] E.P. Roe's stories, admitted because of their religious setting,[9] and the Pansy books.[10] Personally I was fond of boys' books, adventure and anything dramatic. I don't think I would have liked the kind of books I write."

But neither her early reading nor her picturesque surroundings can be wholly responsible for her literary gifts. Dreamers and writers are born as well as made, and it is not surprising that she is a direct descendant of one of the lesser Scottish poets, the Hector Macneill who wrote "Come Under My Plaidie," "Saw Ye My Wee Thing, Saw Ye My Ain Thing?" and "I Lo'e Ne'er a Laddie but One."[11] She also had a great-uncle – one of the undiscovered poets who composed verse which those who remember it appreciate now as real poetry. Unfortunately he never put his compositions on paper. He created them as he worked about his little Prince Edward Island farm, and at night recited them to the children while they sat around a sugar kettle hung over a fire in the yard where he boiled potatoes for his pigs.

When she grew up, Miss Montgomery taught school for three years. She was already writing stories and this was probably when she did her hardest work, getting up at five o'clock in the morning and writing till seven. "And on winter mornings before the fire had warmed the farm house through, it was some chore," she admits. Later she spent one winter at newspaper work in Halifax, but at the death of her grandfather she went home to be with her grandmother.[12] Perhaps this was a fortunate thing as it led her to give all her time to story writing.

"The first story I was ever paid for," she says, "was published in *Golden Days*, a Philadelphia magazine which has since gone under. I don't know whether my stories killed it or not. They gave me five dollars and I have never been so rich in my life.[13] I had had stories published before this and had received subscriptions to the magazines. It was while I was making my living writing short stories that I sneaked in time to do *Anne of Green Gables* just to please myself. I believe that was the reason for its spontaneity. Five times I sent it out and five times it was returned. The last publisher wrote: 'Our reader has found some merit in it but not enough to warrant publication.' This 'damning with faint praise'[14] was the last straw. I put the story away and left it for a while. One day at housecleaning time I brought it out again and looked it over. As girl's stuff, I thought, that's not too bad, and I tried again. I had an alphabetical list of publishers, had tried everything that seemed possible down to the P's, so I sent it to Page and it was accepted."[15]

Kilmeny of the Orchard had been written before this and published as a serial in the *American Housekeeper*, another defunct magazine.[16] When it appeared in book form one critic wrote that it was obviously a product of the pride of authorship hurriedly gotten out to sell on the merits of the other.

Two years later *Anne of Avonlea* was published. It was about this time that Miss Montgomery was married to the Rev. Macdonald, and came to the manse at Leaskdale. Mr. Macdonald had formerly been the minister in her home church at Cavendish. *Chronicles of Avonlea* had been written before her marriage but was not published until after. Since coming to Ontario she has written *The Golden Road, Anne of the Island, Anne's House of Dreams*, and her latest book *Rainbow Valley* went on the book stands in August.

"I think I'll always write of the Island," she says. And one only needs to hear her talk of the Island, and to see the relics from the Island that she treasures in her Ontario home, to know that her first love has left a lasting impression. She has paintings of "The Lake of Shining Waters" and "The Lover's Lane," which figures especially in *Anne of Avonlea*, and which was really the place where the author used to wander out in the evenings to "think out" her stories ready for writing the next morning.

But we prophesy that some day Mrs. Macdonald will write a shore story with an individuality and color quite as appealing as that of the Anne books.[17] She has a wealth of legend and story of the coast life, for the quiet little island has had its sea tragedies as well as its romances by land. There was "the great American storm of 1851,"[18] and she says "If you have ever seen a storm in the Gulf you'll never forget it. It has a bite and a tang that no land storm could possibly have. At this time American fishing vessels used to come into the gulf for mackerel. This particular storm drove hundreds of these vessels onto the north coast, and for weeks afterwards the men of the Island gathered the bodies from the shore and buried them in the Cavendish churchyard. Many of the graves are there to this day, nameless and unknown."

The author of Anne does not devote herself entirely to the making of books. She is a woman of personal charm and winsomeness, as broad-minded and practical as she is imaginative, with a keen sense of humor, happy in the keeping of her home and the interests of the parish. She is a mother who mothers her children personally; they have always been considered before her books. When she has efficient help in the house she locks herself in her room and writes for two hours every morning; at other times she does her own housekeeping with the skill and despatch of a woman trained to it. She even takes her knitting with her on her pastoral visits; it was soldiers' socks during the war, and since then she has nearly completed a bed spread of the kind you expect to find in some old mahogany, lavender-scented spare bed-room. She is just about what you would expect the author of Anne to be.

NOTES

1 Montgomery, 24 August 1919, in *SJLMM*, 2: 339.

2 In *Anne of Avonlea*, Anne teaches at Avonlea School and Marilla Cuthbert adopts six-year-old twins Davy and Dora Keith, distant relatives of hers, after their mother dies.

3 I have corrected the original, which reads "'Ann of Green Gables.'" The silent film version of *Anne of Green Gables*, directed by Irish-born William Desmond Taylor (1872–1922) and starring Mary Miles Minter (1902–1984) as Anne, would be released in November 1919. Montgomery saw it in February 1920 and liked neither the actors, the plot, nor the scenery (see Montgomery, 22 February 1920, in *SJLMM*, 2: 373). Minter and Taylor had collaborated on several films prior to this one. Because all four books were distilled into the one film, which ended with Anne's engagement to Gilbert, there was no possibility of a sequel despite its popularity. No copies of the film are known to exist today.

Ethel M. Chapman

4 The film was actually set in New England and its script was written by Frances Marion (1888–1973), who had written the screenplay of *Rebecca of Sunnybrook Farm* (1917), starring Mary Pickford. See Karr, *Authors and Audiences*, 173–74; Hammill, *Women, Celebrity, and Literary Culture*, 100–23.

5 Chester Macdonald was seven years old at the time of this interview, whereas Stuart was turning four.

6 From "He Called Her In," by James Whitcomb Riley (1849–1916), American author.

7 Montgomery makes a similar remark in a journal entry dated 1899: "I am simply a 'book drunkard.' *Books* have the same irresistible temptation for me that liquor has for its devotee. I *cannot* withstand them" (Montgomery, 4 April 1899, in *SJLMM*, 1: 235).

8 *The Pilgrim's Progress from This World to That Which Is to Come* (1678), a Christian allegory by John Bunyan (1628–1688), English author; *Paradise Lost* (1667), an epic poem by John Milton (1608–1674), English poet.

9 Edward Payson Roe (1838–1888), popular American writer. In a journal entry dated 1898, Montgomery mentioned that she had reread Roe's Evangelical novel *Opening a Chestnut Burr* (1874) and that it had "bored [her] horribly" (Montgomery, 10 July 1898, in *SJLMM*, 1: 223).

10 Pseudonym of Isabella Macdonald Alden (1841–1930), American author of more than one hundred books, mainly Christian-oriented didactic fiction.

11 I have corrected the original, which reads "MacNeill."

12 Chapman evidently misunderstood the chronology of these events.

13 "Our Charivari," published in *Golden Days for Boys and Girls* in May 1896, was actually her second published short story; see chapter 13, "How I Began to Write," by L.M. Montgomery, note 13, in this volume. She published eight stories and two poems in *Golden Days* from 1896 to 1899.

14 The quotation "damn with faint praise" can be traced to Alexander Pope's 1734 poem "Epistle to Dr. Arbuthnot." See also *EQ*, 10, 49, 148.

15 In her article "Novel Writing Notes" (see chapter 38 in this volume), Montgomery states that this list came from a magazine called *The Editor*.

16 For the origins of "Una of the Garden," see chapter 17, "A Canadian Novelist of Note Interviewed," note 6, above.

17 I have corrected the original, which reads "quite an appealing."

18 As Montgomery stated in a journal entry dated 1909, the story of the "Yankee storm" of October 1851, "so called because hundreds of American fishing vessels out in the gulf were wrecked along the north shore," was one that her maternal grandfather enjoyed telling (Montgomery, 3 June 1909, in *SJLMM*, 1: 352).

30

The Gay Days of Old

—— 1919 ——

L.M. MONTGOMERY

This article, published in *Farmers' Magazine* (Toronto) in December 1919, with a number of photographs and captions not reproduced here, appeared with the following subhead: "A Well-Known Author's Reminiscences of Her Girlhood on a Canadian Farm." Although it revisits some aspects of Montgomery's youth that she had covered before in fiction (*The Story Girl*) and in non-fiction ("The Alpine Path"), it also contains some of the material that Montgomery would soon begin to gather for her later novel, *Emily of New Moon* (1923).[1]

"You know a farm is such a hum-drum place to live on," wrote a little girl of twelve to me not long ago.

But I didn't know. My childhood and young girlhood were lived on a farm, and "humdrum" was the last word I should have thought of applying to my days – if I had thought about them at all. I didn't *think* a great deal about them – I just *lived* them, one after another, vivid, interesting days full of little pleasures and delights, like tiny, opening golden buds on the tree of life. Looking back on them now I realize that they were wonderful days, on that remote little farm, eleven miles from a railroad and four from the nearest store. Life there always tasted good to me – "tasted like more," as the school children say.

It was my good fortune to live in a very beautiful spot – the north shore of Prince Edward Island, where red roads wound like gay satin ribbons in and out among green fields and woods, and where I gazed always on the splendid pageant of the sea – splendid with ever-changing beauty of dawn and noon and midnight, of storm and calm, wind and rain, starlight, moonlight, sunset. I had always an intense pleasure in the loveliness of Nature, and to be alone with the trees and flowers and brooks[2] was to me not solitude but the blithest of companionship. I *loved* the trees around my old home with a personal love; I loved the little ferny nooks along the lanes in the woods; I loved the red roads climbing up amid the dark firs; I loved the farm fields, each individualized by some peculiarity of shape of fence or tree clump. To me they spoke with a thousand voices, each with a new and fascinating tale to tell.

From April to December I lived out-of-doors. The house was then a place to sleep in, eat meals in, and wash dishes in. But out-o'-doors was my home. My playmates and I went fishing up the brooks, picking gum in the spruce copses, berrying in "the stumps" and gypsying to the shore. I think we had more fun at the shore than anywhere else. There were so many things we could do there – wade on the rock shore, and bathe on the sand shore; climb the cliffs and poke sea-swallows out of their nests; gather pebbles, dulse, sea-moss, kelp, "snails" and mussels; run races on the sand, dig "wells" in it, build mounds, climb the shining "sand-hills" and slide down in a merry smother of sand, pile up drift wood, collect and unravel into twine the nets on wrecked lobster-traps, make "shore pies," peep through the sky-glass at the fishing boats – space faileth me to tell of all the things we did on that far-away shore of long ago. It remains a wonder to me to this day why we did not get drowned or break our necks climbing up and down those steep and often slippery cliffs. But we did not. It was predestination, that is all there is to be said of it. And oh, what fun we had!

We did not often get out in the fishing boats – the men were too busy to bother with us, although on rare occasions we got out for a sail. But we had our own fishing excursions up the brooks, armed with a small mackerel hook, a piece of the aforesaid lobster trap twine for line, and a stout switch cut from a maple tree for rod; *and* a tin baking powder can full of big, fat, abominable worms.

I may not be believed, but in those days I could put a worm on my own hook, beholden to no boy of them all. What I felt like while doing it I will not harrow my readers' feelings by describing; my sensations were dreadful but not so dreadful as endurance of the contempt meted out to a girl who had to get one of the boys to put on her worm.

When the worm was finally on, with a nice juicy piece left hanging loose to encourage the trout – and the piece I left was always sufficiently long, you may be sure – we dropped our hooks over the edge of the bridge or the big roots of some tree and watched, in breathless suspense, our hoped-for victims circling around in the clear water. Presently, with a whoop of victory, somebody would have "first catch," and soon the fun grew fast and furious. Brook trout are unsuspicious creatures I think. They always bit so readily. And how good they tasted! They were generally small – not more than four or five inches in length. But sometimes we caught one almost as large as a pond trout. Never shall I forget the pride I felt one day when I caught a trout fully nine inches long and big in proportion. I have never experienced such a maddening thrill of triumph since. The boys looked at me with envy and respect. We carried the trout home and weighed it. It surpassed our expectations. I felt that I was richly repaid for all my agonies in putting on worms.

Berry-picking was another summer delight. We would rise at dawn, pack our lunch baskets with all the goodies we could lay hands on, equip ourselves with cups and pails, and start for "the stumps." In the back lands, beyond the belt of woods, where the clearings were, the berries grew in rosy lavishness. Barefooted, we tramped up over the pastures and hayfields dripping with dew, pausing for a moment as we climbed the last fence on the hill to look out over the panorama of gulf and harbor spread out at the foot of the slope – ah, I can see it now! Then we plunged into the wood lanes where ferns and June-bells and ladies'-lips grew thickly.[3] Do you know what June-bells and ladies'-lips are? If you don't, how I pity you! Then, too, we always had the delightful expectation of seeing a rabbit scuttling under the ferns, or a shy red fox darting through the undergrowth like a streak of tawny light.

Amid the stumps we squatted down among ferns and grasses for the day's work. At noon we foregathered by a brook and ate and drank ambrosia and nectar – that is to say, fried ham, apple pie, bread and jam, and raspberry vinegar, flavored by the appetite of youth, sharpened by sunshine and blue air and wind-whispers.

In the fall came apple-picking time. That was sheer fun. Some of us would climb the trees and shake down apples until the gropers beneath cried for mercy. Then we filled basket after basket and toted them off to bin and cellar, munching as we worked.[4]

There were all kinds of apples. The big, ruddy, "sweet" ones, which only we children and the French hired boys cared for, in the winter evenings we roasted them by the dozen and ate them around the fire; the hard, yellow, sour ones that were only fit for pies; the "little, red apples," scarcely bigger than a crab, deep crimson all over and glossy as satin that had such a sweet, nutty flavor; the "syrup apples" that were boiled whole; the "scabby apples" that looked as if they had leprosy but were of unsurpassed deliciousness under their queerly blotched skin – these and many more, each with their own home name and no other, for they were mostly seedlings and had the inimitable flavor that standard varieties never possess.[5]

The fall evenings, too, had another charm – the boiling of pigs' potatoes. Unromantic name for a most romantic reality. Out under the big, wide-branching spruce tree in the back yard was "the pigs' boiler" – a huge, oblong iron box mounted on a furnace of stones. It was filled to the brim with potatoes and a fire built under it. We children, with our pockets full of apples, sat around it and ate while grandfather or French Elair stirred the potatoes, poked the fire, sending glorious streams of sparks upward into the darkness, and told us

"Tales of land and sea,
And whatsoever might betide
The great, forgotten world outside."[6]

We had to pick potatoes, too, which was not at all a delightful occupation. The only romance of the potato-field came on the night the stalks were burned. They don't burn potato stalks now I am told – they use them for fertilizer. Much wiser, no doubt, but one rapture has gone from the farm. What a delight it was to career over that field on an autumn twilight when great pyres blazed on every hand and great white wreaths of pungent smoke rolled over and around us, through which our own figures and those of the men, as they went from pile to pile, poking and turning, loomed phantom-like.[7]

In winter we were more or less cooped up. For fine days and on occasional moonlight nights we had coasting and sliding and snow-men and horses. But the long evenings were generally spent indoors. Then I sought and found my pleasures in a certain old shelfful of books on the kitchen wall. We had not a great many books so I read and reread what we did have until I knew whole pages and even chapters by heart. That old shelf held a curious assortment wherein I browsed at will. There was a *Pilgrim's Progress* which was a constant delight. Many a time did I walk the strait and narrow path with *Christian* and with *Christiana* – although I never liked *Christiana's* adventures half so well as *Christian's*.

For one thing, there was such a crowd with *Christiana*; she had not half the fascination of that solitary, intrepid figure who faced all alone the shadows of the dark valley and the encounter with Apollyon. They tell me that children do not read *Pilgrim's Progress* nowadays. If this be so, it is a great pity. It is one of the classics of literature and as fascinating as a fairy tale into the bargain. If you do not know *Christian* and *Hopeful* and *Mr. Greatheart* and *Miss Much-Afraid*, dear boys and girls, you have missed delightful companions.[8]

Then I read *Hans Andersen's* beautiful tales, and *Talmage's Sermons* – which charmed me, not, I am afraid, because of their religion, but because of their gorgeous word-painting and dramatic climaxes – and a *History of the World*, with wonderful colored pictures, including Adam and Eve and a very snaky snake in the Garden of Eden; Milton, too – I read his *Paradise Lost* a score of times and felt that I was very wicked because I found his *Satan* a personality far more interesting than any of the denizens of heaven.[9] Then I might dip for a change into the coverless, yellowed copy of *Pickwick Papers*; *Ivanhoe* and *Quentin Durward* and *Campbell's Poems* were there, too, on that wonderful shelf – all mixed up together and read together – a poem here, a chapter there, a sermon on Sundays.[10] There were old school readers which my uncles and aunts had used, full of bits of good literature; there were old almanacs on whose blank faded pages dead hands had written entries of storms and births and deaths and weddings; there was a book or two of travel, and an ancient geography, full of "long s's" that looked like "f's," in which there was a most dramatic and horrifying account of the tortures the Canadian Indians inflicted on each other at the stake – and that was about all there was concerning Canada in it, for the old book was written and published in the reign of one of the Georges.[11]

We have a different Canada to-day – the old geographer would open his eyes could he travel from coast to coast over its glorious leagues – a land to live and die for – a land that calls for sons and daughters to inherit and carry on its noble traditions and its high destiny. The boys and girls growing up on Canadian farms to-day are the ones to whom this call comes most insistently. Hear and heed it, lads and lasses, amid your harvest fields and laden orchards of to-day. Live your lives with zest and courage and wholesome mirth and worthy ambition. No life need be dull or humdrum no matter where it is lived. We get out of life what we put into it everywhere, and we can always find, if we look with desirous eyes, "the unsung beauty" – ay, and the unsung charm, lure, and laughter! – "hid life's common things below."[12]

NOTES

1 See Montgomery, 24 August 1920, in *SJLMM*, 2: 390; Montgomery, 13 December 1920, in *SJLMM*, 2: 391.
2 I have corrected the original, which reads "tree and flowers and brooks."
3 For "June-bells," see chapter 14, "[Seasons in the Woods]," by L.M. Montgomery, note 36. The term "'ladies-lips'" appears in Montgomery, 14 July 1890, in *SJLMM*, 1: 23.
4 See *SG*, 219.
5 See *ENM*, 132–33.
6 Properly, "And tell them tales of land and sea, / And whatsoever may betide / The great, forgotten world outside." From "The Hanging of the Crane" (1875), by Henry Wadsworth Longfellow.
7 See *ENM*, 141–42.
8 See *ENM*, 2–3; see also Montgomery, 7 January 1910, in *SJLMM*, 1: 374.
9 For Montgomery's account of reading the work of Hans Christian Andersen in her childhood, see Montgomery, 1 June 1909, in *SJLMM*, 1: 351. For a detailed account of her reading of *New Tabernacle Sermons* (1886) by Thomas De Witt Talmage (1832–1902) and of a multivolume "Histories of the World," see *AP*, 49–50; Montgomery, 7 January 1910, in *SJLMM*, 1: 374.
10 *Ivanhoe* (1819) and *Quentin Durward* (1823), novels by Sir Walter Scott. *Campbell's Poems* likely refers to the works of Thomas Campbell.
11 King George I of Great Britain took the throne in 1714 and was followed by three successors also named George, the last of whom reigned until 1830.
12 From "Dedication" in *Songs of Labor* (1850), by John Greenleaf Whittier. Montgomery had already used this extract as the epigraph to *Chronicles of Avonlea*.

31

Introduction to *Further Chronicles of Avonlea,* by L.M. Montgomery

—— 1920 ——

NATHAN HASKELL DOLE

When Montgomery sold all remaining rights to her first seven books to L.C. Page in early 1919, she agreed reluctantly to allow him to publish a follow-up to *Chronicles of Avonlea* using stories that had not been selected for inclusion in that volume. Because Montgomery had destroyed these copies of her stories, she went to work revising the versions published in magazines a second time, only to find out later that Page had kept copies of these versions and meant to publish them as they were. According to Mary Henley Rubio, Page had initially invited Bliss Carman to introduce the volume, but Carman refused, possibly balking at Page's request that he do "a little retouching" of Montgomery's stories.[1] Nathan Haskell Dole, the popular American author whom Montgomery had met during her trip to Boston in 1910, is rather excessive in his praise, comparing Montgomery to both Longfellow and Tolstoy, and his quotations from the book are always slightly inaccurate. As well, he ignores two additional Anne sequels published by Frederick A. Stokes, in which Anne matures to her forties. The praise did nothing to dissuade Montgomery from filing suit against Page and his brother, driven by a compulsion to "teach them a lesson" in fair dealing with authors and to keep this book out of print.[2] The lawsuit would not be settled until 1928, and Montgomery would continue to receive inquiries about this book until the end of her life.

Although Montgomery succeeded in getting an injunction against *Further Chronicles of Avonlea* in 1928, a new edition, with substantially revised text and omitting Dole's introduction, appeared in the mid-1950s in Canada, the United States, and the United Kingdom, and this version remains in print today.

It is no exaggeration to say that what Longfellow did for Acadia, Miss Montgomery has done for Prince Edward Island.[3] More than a million readers, young people as well as their parents and uncles and aunts, possess in the picture-galleries of their memories the exquisite landscapes of Avonlea, limned with as poetic a pencil as Longfellow wielded when he told the ever-moving story of Grand Pré.

Only genius of the first water has the ability to conjure up such a character as Anne Shirley, the heroine of Miss Montgomery's first novel, *Anne of Green Gables*, and to surround her with people so distinctive, so real, so true to psychology. Anne is as lovable a child as lives in all fiction. Natasha in Count Tolstoï's great novel, *War and Peace*, dances into our ken, with something of the same buoyancy and naturalness; but into what a commonplace young woman she develops! Anne, whether as the gay little orphan in her conquest of the master and mistress of Green Gables, or as the maturing and self-forgetful maiden of Avonlea, keeps up to concert-pitch in her charm and her winsomeness. There is nothing in her to disappoint hope or imagination.

Part of the power of Miss Montgomery – and the largest part – is due to her skill in compounding humor and pathos. The humor is honest and golden; it never wearies the reader; the pathos is never sentimentalized, never degenerates into bathos, is never morbid. This combination holds throughout all her works, longer or shorter, and is particularly manifest in the present collection of fifteen short stories, which, together with those in the first volume of the Chronicles of Avonlea, present a series of piquant and fascinating pictures of life in Prince Edward Island.

The humor is shown not only in the presentation of quaint and unique characters, but also in the words which fall from their mouths. Aunt Cynthia "always gave you the impression of a full rigged ship coming gallantly on before a favorable wind";[4] no further description is needed – only one such personage could be found in Avonlea. You would recognize her at sight. Ismay Meade's disposition is summed up when we are told that she is "good at having presentiments – after things happen."[5] What cleverer embodiment of innate obstinacy than in Isabella Spencer – "a wisp of a woman who looked as if a breath would sway her but was so set in her ways that a tornado would hardly have caused her to swerve an inch from her chosen path";[6] or than in Mrs. Eben Andrews (in "Sara's Way") who "looked like a woman whose opinions were always very decided and warranted to wear"![7]

This gift of characterization in a few words is lavished also on material objects, as, for instance; what more is needed to describe the forlornness of the home from which Anne was rescued than the statement that even the trees around it "looked like orphans"?[8]

The poetic touch, too, never fails in the right place and is never too frequently introduced in her descriptions. They throw a glamor over that Northern land which otherwise you might imagine as rather cold and barren. What charming Springs they must have there! One sees all the fruit-trees clad in bridal garments of pink and white; and what a translucent sky smiles down on the ponds and the reaches of bay and cove!

"The eastern sky was a great arc of crystal, smitten through with auroral crimsonings."[9]

"She was slim and lithe as a young, white-stemmed birch tree; her hair was like a soft, dusky cloud; and her eyes were as blue as Avonlea Harbor on a fair twilight, when all the sky is abloom over it."[10]

Sentiment with a humorous touch to it prevails in the first two stories of the present book. The one relates the disappearance of a valuable white Persian cat with a blue spot in its tail. "Fatima" is like the apple of her eye to the rich old aunt who leaves her with two nieces, with a stern injunction not to let her out of the house. Of course both Sue and Ismay detest cats; Ismay hates them, Sue loathes them; but Aunt Cynthia's favor is worth preserving. You become as much interested in Fatima's fate as if she were your own pet, and the climax is no less unexpected than it is natural, especially when it is made also the last act of a pretty comedy of love.

Miss Montgomery delights in depicting the romantic episodes hidden in the hearts of elderly spinsters as, for instance, in the case of Charlotte Holmes, whose maid Nancy would have sent for the doctor and subjected her to a porous plaster while waiting for him, had she known that up stairs there was a note-book full of original poems. Rather than bear the stigma of never having had a love-affair, this sentimental lady invents one to tell her mocking young friends. The dramatic and unexpected dénouement is delightful fun.

Another note-book reveals a deeper romance in the case of Miss Emily; this is related by Anne of Green Gables, who once or twice flashes across the scene, though for the most part her friends and neighbors at White Sands or Newbridge or Grafton as well as at Avonlea are the persons involved.

In one story, the last, "Tannis of the Flats," the secret of Elinor Blair's spinsterhood is revealed in an episode which carries the reader from Avonlea to Saskatchewan and shows the unselfish devotion of a half-breed Indian girl. The story is both poignant and dramatic. Its one touch of humor is where Jerome Carey curses his fate in being compelled to live in that desolate land in "the picturesque language permissible in the far Northwest."[11]

Self-sacrifice, as the real basis of happiness, is a favorite theme in Miss Montgomery's fiction. It is raised to the nth power in the story entitled "In Her Selfless Mood," where an ugly, misshapen girl devotes her life and renounces marriage for the sake of looking after her weak and selfish half-brother. The same spirit is found in "Only a Common Fellow," who is haloed with a certain splendor by renouncing the girl he was to marry in favor of his old rival, supposed to have been killed in France, but happily delivered from that tragic fate.

Miss Montgomery loves to introduce a little child or a baby as a solvent of old feuds or domestic quarrels. In "The Dream Child," a foundling boy, drifting in through a storm in a dory, saves a heart-broken mother from insanity. In "Jane's Baby," a baby-cousin brings reconciliation between the two sisters, Rosetta and Carlotta, who had not spoken for twenty years because the "slack-twisted" Jacob married the younger of the two.[12]

Happiness generally lights up the end of her stories, however tragic they may set out to be. In "The Son of His Mother," Thyra is a stern woman, as "immovable as a stone image." She had only one son, whom she worshipped; she "never wanted a daughter, but she pitied and despised all sonless women."[13] She demanded absolute obedience from Chester – not only obedience, but also utter affection, and she hated his dog because the boy loved him: "She could not share her love even with a dumb brute."[14] When Chester falls in love, she is relentless toward the beautiful young girl and forces Chester to give her up. But a terrible sorrow brings the old woman and the young girl into sympathy, and unspeakable joy is born of the trial.

Happiness also comes to "The Brother Who Failed." The Monroes had all been successful in the eyes of the world except Robert: one is a millionaire, another a college president, another a famous singer. Robert overhears the old aunt, Isabel, call him a total failure, but, at the family dinner, one after another stands up and tells how Robert's quiet influence and unselfish aid had started them in their brilliant careers, and the old aunt, wiping the tears from her eyes, exclaims: "I guess … there's a kind of failure that's the best success."[15]

In one story there is an element of the supernatural, when Hester, the hard older sister, comes between Margaret and her lover and, dying, makes her promise never to become Hugh Blair's wife, but she comes back and unites them. In this, Margaret, just like the delightful Anne, lives up to the dictum that "nothing matters in all God's universe, except love."[16] The story of the revival at Avonlea has also a good moral.

There is something in these continued Chronicles of Avonlea, like the delicate art which has made *Cranford* a classic:[17] the characters are so homely and homelike and yet tinged with beautiful romance! You feel that you are made familiar with a real town and its real inhabitants; you learn to love them and sympathize with them. *Further Chronicles of Avonlea* is a book to read; and to know.

NOTES

1 Rubio, *Lucy Maud Montgomery*, 231.
2 Montgomery, 9 April 1920, in *SJLMM*, 2: 375.
3 Among the works of Henry Wadsworth Longfellow is an epic poem, "Evangeline: A Tale of Acadie" (1847).
4 *FCA*, 3.
5 *FCA*, 11.
6 Properly, "a wisp of a woman ... She looked as if a breath would sway her. The truth was that a tornado would hardly have caused her to swerve an inch from her chosen path" (*FCA*, 39, 40).
7 *FCA*, 146.
8 *AGG*, 15.
9 *FCA*, 180.
10 *FCA*, 90.
11 *FCA*, 281.
12 *FCA*, 88.
13 *FCA*, 160, 162.
14 Properly, "She could not share his love with even a dumb brute" (*FCA*, 162).
15 *FCA*, 122.
16 *FCA*, 135.
17 *Cranford*, a novel by Elizabeth Gaskell (1810–1865), English novelist and short story writer, serialized in 1851 and published in book form in 1853.

32

One Little Girl Who Wrote to L.M. Montgomery and Received a Reply

—— 1920 ——

According to this article, published in an unidentified periodical around 1920, a high school teacher was so impressed with the response her pupil had received the year before to a fan letter to L.M. Montgomery that she submitted it, with her pupil's consent (but evidently not with Montgomery's), to be published in a newspaper. What is especially remarkable about this letter is not just its length but its warm tone, given that it was written in the midst of what Montgomery would later term "a *hellish* year." In January 1919, just as she was wrapping up her lawsuit against L.C. Page, her first cousin and closest confidante Frederica Campbell MacFarlane died of flu-pneumonia, leaving Montgomery devastated: as she declared to Ephraim Weber, Frede's death was "the most terrible blow I ever have had to bear in all my life." On 11 March, in the midst of "another day of bitter loneliness for Frede," she began her next novel, which would be published as *Rilla of Ingleside* in 1921 and dedicated to MacFarlane's memory.[1]

This letter is dated April 1919. Yet two events that she manages to mention lightly – the upcoming silent film adaptation of *Anne of Green Gables* and her husband's illness – did not occur until that summer, according to her journals.

The Manse, Leaskdale,
April, 1919.

Dear Ruby, – I suppose you have concluded that you are never going to get an answer to your very nice and much appreciated letter of away back in March, but soon after I received it my husband took very ill and has been ill almost ever since, so that I had to cut out all letter-writing except what was absolutely necessary. I am glad to say he is well again now and I am trying to catch up with a terribly big pile of letters. There are so many of them I can't write very long letters to any one.

Yes, isn't it nice to have a birthday in the spring. Mine is in November, the very worst month in the year, I think, and fifteen is such a nice age – so full of hopes and successes with all the world before one. I hope you will succeed in your ambitions to be a teacher and help your brothers and sisters. There are fine chances nowadays for an ambitious girl who isn't afraid of work.

So you've never been on a train. Well, there is plenty of time for that. I was never on a train either until I was nearly sixteen years old. You will likely be taking a trip in aeroplanes before you are an old woman. It is nice to travel, but don't forget that, as Emerson (or Whittier, I forget which) so beautifully says:

> "The beauty which old Greece and Rome
> Sang, painted, taught, lies close at home;
> We need but eye and ear
> In all our daily walks to trace
> The outlines of incarnate grace,
> The hymns of gods to hear."[2]

And some one else has said:
"If we search the world over for beauty we will not find it unless we take it with us."[3]

I think a quiet life in early youth is a great advantage. Body and mind develop better in such an existence and lay good foundations for a more strenuous life beyond. I lived all my girlhood in a little country settlement eleven miles from a railway, and I am very thankful for it now.

No, Anne Shirley is not a "real" girl.[4] She is just an imaginary character. She has always seemed very real to me. She is to be made into a moving picture, this fall, by a U.S. film corporation, so you may yet see her or some one playing her part on the screen. I must close now, for many duties press onward to be done.

With best wishes for your future and your ambitions, I am, yours very cordially,
L.M. Montgomery Macdonald[5]

NOTES

1 Montgomery, 1 September 1919, in *SJLMM*, 2: 321; Montgomery to
  Weber, 26 May 1919, in *AfGG*, 76; Montgomery, 11 March 1919, in
  SJLMM, 2: 309.
2 Properly, "The beauty which old Greece or Rome / Sung, painted, wrought,
  lies close at home." From "To –" (1851), by John Greenleaf Whittier.
3 Properly, "Though we travel the world over to find the beautiful, we must
  carry it with us, or we find it not." From *Essays: First Series* (1841), by
  Ralph Waldo Emerson (1803–1882), American author.
4 I have corrected the original, which reads "Ann Shirley."
5 I have corrected the original, which reads "MacDonald."

33

A Sextette of Canadian Women Writers

—— 1920 ——

OWEN MCGILLICUDDY

This article, published in *Canadian Home Journal* in June 1920, places Montgomery among her contemporaries at the height of her literary career. It was written by Owen McGillicuddy (1888–1954), the author of two books, *The Little Marshal and Other Poems* (1918) and *The Making of a Premier: An Outline of the Life Story of the Right Hon. W.L. Mackenzie King, C.M.G.* (1922). McGillicuddy here notes that Montgomery was the most popular author in Canada at this time. She is also the only author of the six whose works remain in print today. Montgomery's depiction of herself as a professional author who never shirks her domestic responsibilities as wife and mother is one that she would repeat throughout her career, particularly in her 1925 interview with Norma Phillips Muir, reproduced below in chapter 45, "Famous Author and Simple Mother." Around this time Montgomery had publicly endorsed *Canadian Home Journal*, calling it "a capital magazine," one that "is growing better all the time. It is quite equal to the best of the household magazines published in any country to-day, and I wish every home-maker in Canada could have it regularly. I like your editorial pages especially. They always seem to touch on some vital problem of Canadian womanhood, and to present stimulating views from refreshing angles. A good clean, helpful and – last but decidedly not least – most interesting magazine, this of yours."[1]

Canadians are beginning to take a greater interest in their native literature than they ever did in the past. Of course, it is quite true that such writers as Stephen Leacock, Norman Duncan, Sir Gilbert Parker, and Ralph Connor, have always found a large public in the Dominion.[2] Nevertheless, in the last few years, there have been a number of women who have been winning increasing popularity. At the present time there are at least six women whose books are eagerly awaited by the Canadian public. The writers I refer to are Mrs. Emily Murphy, known to the reading world as "Janey Canuck," Mrs. Grace McLeod Rogers, Mrs. Nellie McClung, Mrs. Evah McKowan, Mrs. Ewan Macdonald, who signs herself "L.M. Montgomery," and Mrs. Isabel Ecclestone Mackay.[3] All of these women are married, the majority of them having children, as well as their literary work, to occupy their attention.

Notwithstanding the many duties of home life, together with community duties assumed in the past few years, this little group have found time to write books and magazine articles and to deliver addresses on a variety of subjects. Wondering how these busy housewives manage to accomplish so much, I was surprised to learn that while their plans and methods of work varied, their one central or guiding purpose was to achieve a certain amount of definite work, no matter what the conditions were. Not one of the six professed to have any leisure worth mentioning, a few of them had hobbies, and their preferences, when they had time to read the works of other writers, were somewhat divergent. In asking them questions concerning their work, I felt that the answers would shed some light on how busy women can do so much and yet find time for other and more diversified endeavors. I was not disappointed.

[* * *]

Mrs. Ewan Macdonald, who is more generally known throughout the States and Canada as "L.M. Montgomery," told me that she made much use of her note books, in which all kinds of ideas are jotted down for use in characters, incidents, bits of description, and dialogue. "I select all I think will harmonize with or develop my central idea," said she, "and then I build a 'skeleton' of my story or book, blocking out each chapter fully as regards incidents and development of character, with suitable bits of description and dialogue. When the 'skeleton' is finished I begin to write the book and generally do it pretty swiftly. When the story is done I lay it aside for as long as possible, then I read it over, revise, preen, amplify, or correct as may be required. Everything I write receives three such revisions. I work two hours every morning when I am home at actual writing, but collect material all day long by keeping a pencil and note book handy, jotting down everything that occurs to me. So far as leisure or holidays are concerned, if I ever had any I would spend it in reading other people's books or doing fancy work. Any preference I have for modern literature is not worth speaking of. I like the older writers best and history is my favorite."

Mrs. Macdonald published her first novel, *Anne of Green Gables*, in 1909,[4] and it achieved an immediate success. Since then she has published *Anne of Avonlea*, *Anne of the Island*, *Anne's House of Dreams*, *Kilmeny of the Orchard*, *Chronicles of Avonlea*, *The Golden Road*, and *Rainbow Valley*. Her books have sold into the tens of thousands and there is no more popular writer throughout the Dominion of Canada.

[* * *]

While Canadian writers of the sterner sex have enjoyed, and doubtless will continue to enjoy, a large demand for their work, the fact remains that in recent years feminine names on publishers' lists have been growing in number and at the present time there are a larger number of successful women novelists than there are men. Probably the answer to the situation is found in the fact that Canada is still busily engaged in developing her great natural resources. The present indications are that for some time to come women will play the preponderant part in any literature developed in the Dominion. At the present time "the opening up of the last frontier" seems to attract the vision of the male population and the writing of books by men is largely confined to professors or preachers.

NOTES

1   "Prominent Canadian Women Commend Canadian Home Journal," unidentified and undated clipping, in SR, 163.

2   Norman Duncan (1871–1916), Ontario-born American writer, journalist, and professor of rhetoric in Pennsylvania and Kansas. Gilbert Parker (1862–1932), popular author of more than thirty books and the British director of American propaganda during the First World War.

3   Grace McLeod Rogers (1865–1958), prominent member of the women's movement in early-twentieth-century Canada and author of several books, including *Stories of the Land of Evangeline* (1891); Evah McKowan (1885–1962), Ontario-born author of two romance novels set in British Columbia, *Janet of Kootenay: Life, Love and Laughter in an Arcady of the West* (1919) and *Graydon of the Windermere* (1920); Isabel Ecclestone Mackay (1875–1928), Vancouver novelist and poet whose books included *Fires of Driftwood* (1922).

4   *Anne of Green Gables* was actually published in June 1908.

34

Blank Verse? "Very Blank," Said Father

—— 1921 ——

L.M. MONTGOMERY

In this short piece, originally published in the *Winnipeg Evening Tribune*, Montgomery reminisces about the publication of her first poem, "On Cape Le Force," which has thirty-nine stanzas of four lines apiece and which was published in the Charlottetown *Patriot* on 26 November 1890, just before the author's sixteenth birthday. Living in Prince Albert, Saskatchewan, at the time, Montgomery had to wait over a week before she received a copy of it in the mail. In her journal, she called it "the proudest day of my life!"[1]

My greatest moment came when I was a girl of fifteen. No, it wasn't the first time I had an "escort-home" from prayer meeting! Guess again.

I had been writing poetry (!) for years. I wrote my first poem when I was ten years old, on the back of an old post-office "letter-bill" – for writing paper was not too plentiful in the Prince Edward Island farm-house where my childhood was passed. It was called "Autumn." I read it to father. Father said it didn't sound much like poetry. "It's blank verse," I cried. "Very blank," said father.

My outraged feelings found vent in tears. But after that I determined to write in rhyme so that no mistake should be made. I began sending "pieces" to the editors of the Island weeklies – and never heard from or of them. Perhaps this was because I wrote on both sides of the paper and didn't send any return stamps – being in blissful ignorance of such a requirement. But, whatever gifts the gods denied me, they had at least given me stick-to-it-iveness. I fainted not, and in due season I reaped.[2]

I had sent a yard – just about – of rhyme, written on one of the tragic legends of the old north shore, to the Charlottetown *Patriot*. And the *Patriot* — may its shadow never grow less![3] – published it. Never, before or since, have I felt as happy and triumphant and uplifted as I felt when I opened that paper and saw my poem in it. It does not at all diminish my feelings of gratitude towards the *Patriot* to remember that there were some fearful printers' mistakes and omissions in it, such as made the flesh creep on my bones. I was as a mother, gazing adoringly at her first-born and finding it all lovely, even if some of its fingers and a piece of its nose have been snipped off!

It was indisputably the greatest moment of my life!

NOTES

1 Montgomery, 7 December 1890, in *SJLMM*, 1: 35.
2 Properly, "in due season we shall reap, if we faint not" (Galatians 6:9 in the Christian Bible).
3 Properly, "May your shadow never grow less!" A Persian phrase first appearing in English in 1824 (*OED*).

35

"I Dwell among My Own People"

—— 1921 ——

L.M. MONTGOMERY

This essay, first published in an unidentified periodical around 1921 and again in the *Manitoba Free Press* in December 1925, positions Montgomery as a writer who is in complete control over the development of her characters and over her choices of subject matter.[1] In explicitly defining "Canadian" as a blend of Celt, Lowlander, English, and Irish, excluding the French, Aboriginal, and black populations of Prince Edward Island, Montgomery is also making an explicit comment about the racial, ethnic, and linguistic limits to that vision.

There are two questions which I am repeatedly asked. They have always exasperated me and always will. Before long I feel that I will throw something – something hard and heavy for choice – at the next person who asks me either of them. These questions are: "Is So-and-So in your books a real person?" and "Why don't you try your hand at a problem novel?"

So-and-So – he, she, or it – is never a "real person" – if by that is meant any unfortunate existing creature whom I have put bodily into any stories. I know many people who have repeatedly asserted that they are acquainted with the "originals" of my characters – there are not lacking those who have said it to my face. Now, for my own part, I have never, during all the years I have studied human nature, as I saw it around me, met one human being who could, *as a whole*, be put into a book without injuring it. Any artist knows that to paint *exactly* from life is to give a false impression of the subject. Study from life we must, copying suitable

heads and arms, appropriating bits of character, personal or mental idiosyncrasies, but the *ideal* must be behind it all. A writer must *create*, not
copy, her characters or they will never be life-like.

I never "try my hand" at a problem novel for four reasons. The first
reason is that a problem novel never yet solved any problem; the second
is that most folks have problems enough in their own lives and want
something different when they seek a little rest and relaxation in a book;
and the third and fourth reasons are – I don't want to.

The people I know best and love best, having lived among them and
been one of them all my life, are not very deeply concerned with what are
known as "present-day problems." Their problems are simple and belong
to yesterday and to-morrow as well as to-day. They live in a land where
nature is neither grudging nor lavish; where faithful work is rewarded by
competence and nobody is very rich and nobody very poor, where everybody knows all about everybody else, so there are few mysteries; where
there is always someone to keep tabs on you and so prevent you from
running amuck with the Decalogue;[2] where the wonderful loveliness of
circling sea and misty river and green, fairy-haunted woods is all around
you; where the Shorter Catechism is not out of date;[3] where there are still
to be found real grandmothers and genuine old maid aunts; where the
sane, simple, wholesome pleasures of life have not lost their tang; where
you are born into a certain political party and live and die in it; where it
is still thought a great feather in a family's cap if it has a minister among
its boys; where it is safer to commit murder than to be caught without
three kinds of cake when company comes to tea; where loyalty and upright dealing and kindness of heart and a sense of responsibility and a
glint of humor and a little decent reserve – great solvents of any and all
problems if given a fair trial – still flower freely on the fine Old Country
stock. Such are my people – with the fire and romance of the Celt, the
canny common sense of the Lowlander, the thrift of the English, the wit
of the Irish, all beginning to be blended[4] into something that is proud to
call itself Canadian.

I love the little island province where I was born – I love the rich red
of its wandering roads,[5] I love the emerald of its uplands and meadows,
I love the radiance of the encircling sea, I love its elusive, subtle charm
of beauty with a hint[6] of austerity; I love its life and its people; and so I
write about them because I want my readers to know and love them, too.

NOTES

1 Montgomery continued to use versions of this speech until at least the early
  1930s: see *The Gazette*, "'Problem' Story Does Not Allure."
2 The Ten Commandments. In the Book of Exodus in the Hebrew Bible,
  Moses is given by the Abrahamic God a list of ten religious and moral
  guidelines, which also form the moral basis of Christianity.
3 Completed in 1647 by English and Scottish theological writers, the West-
  minster Shorter Catechism is a straightforward text that uses the form
  of questions and answers to educate Protestant lay people in matters of
  doctrine and belief.
4 The original reads "pressed," but the word is crossed out in ink and replaced with "blended." This correction and the two that follow appear in
  the 1925 republication of the essay.
5 The original reads "woods," but the word is crossed out in ink and replaced with "roads."
6 The original reads "kind," but the word is crossed out in ink and replaced
  with "hint."

36

Bits from My Mailbag

—— 1922 ——

L.M. MONTGOMERY
Author of *Anne of Green Gables*,
Rilla of Ingleside, etc.

L.M. Montgomery's fan mail was a frequent topic in her journals and her letters as well as in her public speeches. Mentioning the receipt of a letter from an adolescent girl from Australia in a journal entry dated September 1910, she commented that she enjoyed receiving such letters – "Some of them are lovely, all are kind but some are rather monotonous"[1] – but that the volume was becoming unmanageable. In October 1929, a deluge of letters arrived – also from Australia – after a reader published a reply from Montgomery in an Australian newspaper, complete with Montgomery's address.[2] Many of these specific letters are also mentioned in Montgomery's journals, in her correspondence, and in her memoir "The Alpine Path," but with one noticeable difference. She mentions here a "romantic miss of sixteen" who begged her for her photograph and whom she sent a snapshot of herself in an outfit for housecleaning. However, she likely altered the details for comedic effect: in her journals, she mentioned "a pathetic ten-year-old in New York who implores me to send her my photo because she lies awake after she goes to bed wondering what I look like." After wondering whether this reader's illusions would be dashed if she sent a photograph of herself wearing the outfit she had worn that day to clean the furnace, she ultimately sent her "a reprint of my last photo in which I sit rapt in inspiration – apparently – at my desk, with pen in hand, in gown of lace and silk with hair just-so – Amen."[3] This article appeared in the *Manitoba Free Press* in December 1922 as part of the "Free Press Book Supplement," edited by W.T. Allison, to whom she would send her essay "'I Dwell among My Own People,'" appearing in the preceding chapter, in 1925, four years before Allison referred to Montgomery as a "sprightly friend and guide of girls in their teens."[4] Almost a decade later, Montgomery would still be using this anecdote – as well as a new one about a schoolboy who had named Anne of Green Gables "as the second wife of Henry VIII" on an examination paper – in a 1931 address entitled "Freaks of an Author's Mail Bag." The article in the Montreal *Gazette* was picked up by at least two newspapers in Australia and one in South Africa.[5]

I have always been glad that there is something in human nature which makes us feel when we have read a book that we want to tell the author what we think of it. If it were not for this my "literary career" would have been minus much real pleasure and not a little amusement. Ever since the publication of my first book I have received a continuous stream of letters from all over the world. The great majority of these have been kind, appreciative missives from older readers and girlish outpourings of pleasure from the sweet 'teens. But occasionally a letter comes which gives me that choicest gift of the gods of any cult – a good laugh.

One earnest being in tortoise-shell spectacles – he didn't tell me he wore tortoise-shell frames but I know he did – wrote to me last year, solemnly assuring me that my "habit of marrying my characters off" was calculated to bring contempt upon the holy state of matrimony. I seldom take any notice of "freak" letters, but I did send a reply to this – a flippant one, I fear, asking my mentor if he thought I'd better let my characters live together without marrying. I never got any reply to my question.

One letter I received soon after the publication of *Anne of Green Gables* began with the astonishing salutation: "My dear long-lost Uncle," and was signed "Your affectionate niece, Charlotte Montgomery." As far as I could make out, the writer had once had an uncle named Lionel Montgomery, who had disappeared many years previously. She had jumped to the conclusion that I was this missing relative and implored me to write her and tell her what I had been doing in the lost years. She seemed so much in earnest about it that I quite hated to have to write and assure her that I wasn't anybody's uncle, least of all a missing one.[6]

An anonymous letter contained merely the melancholy statement:– "Sad to read books in which no glory is given to God."

In common, I suppose, with most authors, I receive many letters from people who want me to write "the story of their lives" – going fifty-fifty on the proceeds, of course. One such letter was from a young man in the Maritime provinces, who was very urgent and wanted to begin work at once. I wrote him, delicately explaining that I had already sufficient plots and ideas on hand to last me for several years. Nothing daunted, he wrote back that he was "very patient" and that after a few years he would write me again. If my own inventions ever give out, I feel that I can always fall back on what that young man assured me was "a thrilling life-story."[7]

Not long ago I got a letter from a lawyer in a southern state, saying that he felt he ought to tell me that the night before he had dreamed that Paddy was alive again. The said "Paddy" was a gray cat in my book *The Story Girl*, who died in the sequel. That man wrote me three closely typed pages about his dream and Paddy's antics therein. I do wonder what his stenographer thought of the letter.

I get scores of requests for my photograph. As I cannot be continually sending out photographs, I turn a deaf ear to all such requests. But I did break through my rule once last year. A romantic miss of sixteen in one of the New England states wrote me, imploring me to send her my photograph because she "couldn't sleep at night for wondering what I looked like." I took pity on her and sent her a snapshot I happened to have handy, taken in a "housecleaning" rig. It was a weird production and would give her plenty to think about in the night! I haven't heard from her since but I hope she sleeps better now.

Another young damsel wrote me twenty pages and wound up by wishing earnestly that she had "a ream of paper and a gallon of ink" so that she could express all her feelings about my books and my characters. How thankful I was that she hadn't!

Yes, some of the letters a writer gets are very funny, and some are grotesque, and some not worth the time it takes to read them. But when I get a letter, as I did some time ago from a young girl whose mother died before she could remember her, telling me that my books "have been to her the mother she never knew," I feel that after all, there is something very nice in an author's mail-bag.

NOTES

1 Montgomery, 29 September 1910, in *SJLMM*, 2: 18.
2 Montgomery, 13 October 1929, in *SJLMM*, 4: 21. See also "A Letter from L.M. Montgomery," unidentified and undated clipping, in SR, 325.
3 Montgomery, 27 February 1920, in *SJLMM*, 2: 374.

4 Allison, "Canadian Literature of To-Day," 272.
5 *The Gazette*, "Odd Letters Are Sent"; *The Canberra Times*, "Unusual Items"; *The Western Argus*, "Australians as Letter Writers"; see also "Canadian Author's Mailbag," *Natal Mercury* (Durban, South Africa), 18 February 1932, in SR, 367.
6 See *AP*, 77.
7 See *AP*, 77–78. In a short article published in *Books and Authors*, a New York periodical, in 1918, Montgomery also mentions receiving letters from individuals offering their life stories to her: "I have answered only one of these letters, ... that of a young man who enclosed stamps for a reply" ("Getting at 'the Facts,'" *Books and Authors*, February 1918, in SR, 122).

37

From *Fiction Writers on Fiction Writing: Advice, Opinions and a Statement of Their Own Working Methods by More Than One Hundred Authors*

—— 1923 ——

This collection, published by the Bobbs–Merrill Company, includes responses from 115 authors, most of whom are no longer widely known. The book was written, according to editor Arthur Sullivant Hoffman, "not by an author of negligible standing, an editor who can not create, a college professor speaking from the outside, or any other theorist whatsoever, but *by the successful writers themselves*, each telling in detail his [or her] own processes of creation."[1] Montgomery's answers to twelve questions are more detailed than most that appear in the collection, indicating her willingness and generosity in sharing her secrets. In fact, this is likely the most detailed account of Montgomery's writing process that she ever recorded on paper. Her responses indicate not only how she went about crafting a short story or a novel, but her view of "romance" as more popular and more appealing than "realism."

Question I: What is the genesis of a story with you – does it grow from an incident, a character, a trait of character, a situation, setting, a title, or what? That is, what do you mean by an idea for a story?

The genesis of my stories is very varied. Sometimes the character suggests the story. For instance, in my first book, *Anne of Green Gables*, the whole story was modeled around the character of "Anne" and arranged to suit her. Most of my books are similar in origin. The characters seem to grow in my mind, much after the oft-quoted "Topsy" manner, and when they are fully incubated I arrange a setting for them, choosing incidents and surroundings which will harmonize with and develop them.

With short stories it is different. There I generally start with an idea – some incident which I elaborate and invent characters to suit, thus reversing the process I employ in book-writing. A very small germ will sometimes blossom out quite amazingly. One of my most successful short stories owed its origin to the fact that one day I heard a lady – a refined person usually of irreproachable language – use a point-blank "cuss-word" in a moment of great provocation.[2] Again, the fact that I heard of a man forbidding his son to play the violin because he thought it was wicked furnished the idea for the best short story I ever wrote.[3]

Question II: *Do you map it out in advance, or do you start with, say, a character or situation, and let the story tell itself as you write? Do you write it in pieces to be joined together, or straightaway as a whole? Is the ending clearly in mind when you begin? To what extent do you revise?*

I map everything out in advance. When I have developed plot, characters and incidents in my mind I write out a "skeleton" of the story or book. In the case of a book, I divide it into so many "sections" – usually eight or nine – representing the outstanding periods in the story. In each section I write down what characters are necessary, what they do, what their setting is, and quite a bit of what they say. When the skeleton is complete I begin the actual writing, and so thoroughly have I become saturated with the story during the making of the skeleton that I feel as if I were merely describing and setting down something that I have actually seen happening, and the clothing of the dry bones with flesh goes on rapidly and easily. This does not, however, prevent changes taking place as I write. Sometimes an incident I had thought was going to be very minor assumes major proportions or *vice versa*. Sometimes, too, characters grow or dwindle contrary to my first intentions. But on the whole I follow my plan pretty closely and the ending is very often written out quite fully in the last "section" before a single word of the first chapter is written. I revise very extensively and the "notes" with which my completed manuscript is peppered are surely and swiftly bringing down my typist's gray hairs with sorrow to the grave. But these revisions deal only with descriptions and conversation. Characters, plot and incidents are never changed.

Question III:

1 *When you read a story to what extent does your imagination reproduce the story-world of the author – do you actually see in your imagination all the characters, action and setting just as if you were looking at an actual scene? Do you actually hear all sounds described, mentioned and inferred, just as if they were real sounds? Do you taste the flavors in a story, so really that your mouth literally waters to a pleasant one? How real does your imagination make the smells in a story you read? Does your imagination reproduce the sense of touch – of rough or smooth contact, hard or gentle impact or pressure, etc.? Does your imagination make you feel actual physical pain corresponding, though in a slighter degree, to pain presented in a story? Of course you get an intelligent idea from any such mention, but in which of the above cases does your imagination produce the same results on your senses as do the actual stimuli themselves?*

2 *If you can really "see things with your eyes shut," what limitations? Are the pictures you see colored or more in black and white? Are details distinct or blurred?*

3 *If you studied solid geometry, did it give you more trouble than other mathematics?*

4 *Is your response limited to the exact degree to which the author describes and makes vivid, or will the mere concept set you to reproducing just as vividly?*

5 *Do you have stock pictures for, say, a village church or a cowboy, or does each case produce its individual vision?*

6 *Is there any difference in behavior of your imagination when you are reading stories and when writing them?*

7 *Have you ever considered these matters as "tools of your trade"? If so, to what extent and how do you use them?*

Yes, when I read a story I *see* everything, exactly as if I were looking at an actual scene. I *hear* the sounds and *smell* the odors. When I read *Pickwick Papers*[4] I have to make many an extra sneak to the pantry, so hungry do I become through reading of the bacon and eggs and milk punch in which the characters so frequently revel. I never feel *physical* pain when I read a story, no matter how intense the suffering described may be. But I feel *mental* pain so keenly that sometimes I can hardly bear to continue reading. Yet I do not dislike this sensation. On the contrary I like it. If I can have a jolly good howl several times in a book I am its friend for life. Yet, in every-day existence, I am the reverse of a tearful or sentimental person. No book do I love as I love *David Copperfield*.[5] Yet during my many re-readings I must have wept literal quarts over David's boyish tribulations. And ghost stories that make me grow actually cold with fear are such as my soul loveth.

I can "see things," with eyes shut or open, colors and all. Sometimes I see them mentally – that is, I realize that they are produced subjectively and are under the control of my will. But very often, when imagination has been specially stimulated, I seem really to see them objectively. In this case, however, I never see landscapes or anything but *faces* – and generally grotesque or comical faces. I never see a beautiful face. They crowd on my sight in a mob, flashing up for a second, then instantly filled by others. I always enjoy this "seeing things" immensely, but I can not do it at will.

The very name of geometry was a nightmare to me. I decline to discuss the horrible subject at all. Yet I loved algebra and had a mild affection for arithmetic. These things are predestinated.

I have no "stock pictures" as a reader. I generally see things pretty much as the writer describes them – though certainly not as the "movie" people seem to see them! This is especially true of places and things. But very few writers have the power to make me visualize their characters, even where they describe them minutely. Illustrations generally make matters worse. I detest illustrations in a story. It is only when there is some peculiarly striking and restrained bit of description attached to a character that I can *see* it. For example: when R.L. Stevenson in *Dr. Jekyll* says that there was something incredibly evil about "Hyde" – I am not quoting his exact words – I can see "Hyde" as clearly as I ever saw anything in my life.[6] As a rule, I think the ability to describe characters so that readers may see them as clearly as they see their settings is a very rare gift among writers.

Yes, as a reader I *do* resent having too many images formed for me. I don't want too much description of anything or too many details in any description.

When I *read* a story, I *see* people doing things in a certain setting; when I *write* a story I *am* the people myself and *live* their experiences.

Question IV: *When you write do you center your mind on the story itself or do you constantly have your readers in mind? In revising?*

In writing a story I do not think of all these things – at least consciously. I never think of my readers at all. I think of myself. Does this story I am writing interest *me* as I write it – does it satisfy *me*? If so, there are enough people in the world who like what I like to find it interesting and satisfying too. As for the others, I couldn't please them anyhow, so it is of no use to try. I revise to satisfy myself also – not any imaginary literary critic.

Question V: *Have you had a classroom or correspondence course on writing fiction? Books on it? To what extent did this help in the elementary stages? Beyond the elementary stages?*

I never took any kind of a course in writing fiction. Such things may be helpful if the real root of the matter is in you, but I had to get along without them. I was born and brought up in a remote country settlement, twenty-four miles from a town and ten from a railway. There I wrote my first stories and my first four books. So no beginner need feel discouraged because of remote location or lack of literary "atmosphere."

Question VI: *How much of your craft have you learned from reading current authors? The classics?*

I think I owe considerable to my greedy reading and rereading of standard fiction – the old masters – Scott, Dickens, Thackeray, Hawthorne.[7] Occasionally, too, a well-written modern magazine story has been helpful and illuminating. But, as a rule, I think aspiring authors will not reap much benefit from current fiction – except perhaps from a purely commercial point of view in finding out what kind of stories certain magazines take! Most writers, except those of absolute genius, are prone to unconscious imitation of what they read and that is a bad thing.

Question VII: *What is your general feeling on the value of technique?*

I feel that its value is great up to a certain point. But when you become conscious of a writer's technique that writer has reached the point of danger. When you find yourself getting more pleasure from the way a writer says a thing than from the thing itself, that writer has committed a grave error and one that lessens greatly the value of his story. Carried too far, technique becomes as annoying as mannerisms.

Question VIII: *What is most interesting and important to you in your writing – plot, structure, style, material, setting, character, color, etc.?*

In my own writing character is by far the most interesting thing to me – then setting. In the development of the one and the arrangement of the other I find my greatest pleasure and from their letters it is evident that my readers do, too. This, of course, is because my *flair* is for these things. In another writer something else – plot, structure or color would be the vital thing. Only the very great authors combine all these things. For the rank and file of the craft, I think a writer should find out where his strength lies and write his stories along these lines. In my own case I would never attempt to handle complicated plot or large masses of material. I know I should make a dismal failure of them.

Question IX: *What are two or three of the most valuable suggestions you could give to a beginner? To a practised writer?*

As to advising beginners – why, I love to do it. Advice is so cheap and easy. First, I always tell them what an old lady used to say to me: "Don't marry as long as you can help it, for when the right man comes along you can't help it."[8] So – don't write if you can help it; because if you ought to write and have it in you to make a real success of writing you can't help it. If you are *sure* you can't help it, then go ahead. Write – write – write. Revise – revise – revise. Prune – prune – prune. Study stories that are classed as masterpieces and find out *why* they are so classed. Leave your stories alone after they are written long enough to come to them as a stranger. Then read them over as a stranger; you'll see a score of faults and lacks you never noticed when they came hot from your pen. Rewrite them, cutting out the faults and supplying the lacks.

I would advise beginners to cultivate the note-book habit. Jot down every idea that comes to you as you go on living – ideas for plots, characters, descriptions, dialogue, etc. It is amazing how well these bits will fit into a story that wasn't born or thought of when you set them down. And they generally have a poignancy that is lacking in deliberate invention. For example, I was once washing the dinner dishes when a friend happened to quote to me the old saying: "Blessed are they who expect nothing, for they shall not be disappointed." I retorted, "I think it would be worse to expect nothing than to be disappointed." Then I dropped my dish cloth and rushed to "jot it down." It lay in my note-book unused for ten years and then it motivated one of the best chapters in my first book.[9] This illustrates what I mean by the note-book habit.

Practised writers should try to avoid mannerisms and stereotyped style. They won't succeed, of course, but they should try. Also, they shouldn't presume on their success and think that anything goes because they write it.

Question X: *What is the elemental hold of fiction on the human mind?*

The deep desire in every one of us for "something better than we have known." In fiction we ask for things, not as they *are*, but as we feel they *ought* to be. This is why the oft-sneered-at "happy ending" makes the popular novel. Fairy tales are immortal – in some form or other we *must* have them or we die. Fiction redresses the balance of existence and gives us what we can't get in real life. This is why "romance" is, and always will be, and always should be more popular than "realism."

Question XI: *Do you prefer writing in the first person or the third? Why?*

Personally I prefer writing in the first person, because it then seems easier to *live* my story as I write it. Since editors seem to have a prejudice against this, I often write a story in the first person and then rewrite it, shifting it to the third. As a reader, I enjoy a story written in the first person far more than any other kind. It gives me more of a sense of reality – of actually knowing the people in it. The author does not seem to *come between* me and the characters as much as in the third-person stories. Wilkie Collins' *Woman in White*[10] is a fine example of the use of the first person. It could not have been half so effective had he told it in the third. And *Jane Eyre*[11] simply couldn't have been written in any but the first.

Question XII: *Do you lose ideas because your imagination travels faster than your means of recording? Which affords least check – pencil, typewriter or stenographer?*

I don't think many ideas ever get away from me by reason of slowness of recording. My aforesaid note-book habit has been of tremendous value here. I write with a pen and couldn't write with anything else – at least, as far as prose is concerned. When I write verse I always write on an ordinary school slate, because of the facilities for easy erasure. But for prose I want a Waverly pen[12] – this is not an advertisement – I just can't write with any other! a smooth unlined paper and a portfolio I can hold on my knee. Then I can sail straight ahead and keep up with any ideas that present themselves. But these are only personal idiosyncrasies and have nothing to do with a writer's success or non-success. So no aspiring beginner need despair because his or her stationer is not stocked up with Waverly pens!

NOTES

1 Hoffman, "Fiction Writers on Fiction Writing," 2.
2 "A Case of Atavism," published in *The Reader* in 1905, was reworked as "The Winning of Lucinda" for *Chronicles of Avonlea*. The phrase in question is "*You damned idiot!*" (Montgomery, "A Case of Atavism," 665), although in *Chronicles of Avonlea* it reads "*You d – d idiot!*" (*CA*, 92).
3 "Each in His Own Tongue" was published in *The Delineator* in 1910; a revised version appears in *Chronicles of Avonlea*.
4 *The Pickwick Papers* (1837), the first novel by Charles Dickens.
5 *David Copperfield* (1850), a later novel by Charles Dickens.
6 "Edward Hyde, alone in the ranks of mankind, was pure evil." From *Strange Case of Dr. Jekyll and Mr. Hyde* (1886), by Robert Louis Stevenson.
7 Nathaniel Hawthorne (1804–1864), American novelist.
8 See chapter 9, "Want to Know How to Write Books?" by Phoebe Dwight, in this volume.
9 The chapter in question is "The Delights of Anticipation" in *Anne of Green Gables* (see *AGG*, 94). In her critical edition of the novel, Devereux attributes this "old saying" to Alexander Pope. See Montgomery, *Anne of Green Gables*, edited by Devereux, 139n1.
10 *The Woman in White* (1860), an epistolary novel by Wilkie Collins (1824–1889), English author. I have corrected the original, which reads "Wilkie Colliers'."
11 Brontë's *Jane Eyre* (1847) was enormously influential to Montgomery, particularly when she was writing the Emily books at the same time as the publication of this essay.
12 Properly, the Waverley pen, which was manufactured by Macniven and Cameron of Edinburgh and which sported a turned-up rather than a convex point.

38

Novel Writing Notes

—— 1923 ——

L.M. MONTGOMERY

This essay appears as part of a column called "Contemporary Writers and Their Work": "A Series of Autobiographical Letters on the Genesis, Conception, Development, and Writing of Fiction, Poems, and Articles Published in Current Periodicals," in a 1923 issue of *The Editor: The Journal of Information for Literary Workers*. As with her contribution to the *Fiction Writers on Fiction Writing* volume published the same year, she was unusually self-conscious and forthcoming about her writing process, particularly for her most recent book, *Emily of New Moon*.

I'm very glad to send the brief sketch asked for because I owe an old and very big debt to *The Editor*. When I was a struggling writer of magazine stories twenty years ago it was of immense assistance to me. Indeed, I don't see how I could have got along without it at all, for I was living on the north shore of Prince Edward Island, eleven miles from a railroad and twenty-five from a town. It was one of the loveliest spots in the world – but it was absolutely out of the world in a literary sense, and *The Editor* was indispensable to me.

I began to write verse and stories when I was a "district school" teacher in my 'teens. I sent them away to the addresses of the United States magazines I found in *The Editor*. In those days Canadian magazines weren't "on the map" – at least as far as paying a living wage was concerned. In 1908[1] I sent my first book, *Anne of Green Gables*, to a publishing firm whose address was in an invaluable list of book publishers issued by *The*

Editor. The novel was accepted and was immediately successful. Since then I've written and published ten other books. My latest, *Emily of New Moon*, is one of my favorites, because I enjoyed writing it so much.

Very soon after *Green Gables* was published the idea of Emily's character came into my mind – just "came," as all my characters do. But I had no time to develop her then because my publishers and public insisted on "more Anne." During these years I carried her in the background of my mind and when at last I was free to write of her two years ago, there she was all ready to be transferred to paper. There weren't really any "problems" to be met while writing her. She and her environment and adventures were already so clear in my mind that I seemed to be merely copying down on paper a history that had really happened. The creative work was already done in my subconscious mind. Nearly all my writing comes like this. If my books were stories with complicated plots no doubt I should have more problems to solve. But, depending for their interest, as they do, mainly on humor and characterization, they seem to "work themselves out" without a great deal of conscious manipulation on my part.

I might add for the encouragement of young writers that *Anne of Green Gables* was rejected five times before it was accepted. Yet it has sold nearly half a million copies, has been translated into several foreign languages, and was a success from its first appearance. Whether Emily will win as many friends remains to be seen. If I were superstitious I should doubt it. The new moon on her cover is an old moon. I am hoping the omen won't prove an unlucky one. I notice on the cover of Kathleen Norris's new book, *Butterfly*,[2] that there is something probably intended for a new moon which is also an old one. Artists should take a course in moon study. But I can't say much, because I saw the jacket of *Emily* before the book came out and never noticed the mistake in the moon any more than artist and publishers had!

NOTES

1 In Montgomery's copy of this clipping in her scrapbook, "1908" is crossed out and replaced with "Accepted Apr. 8, 1907" scribbled in ink.
2 On the cover image of the first edition of *Butterfly* (1923), by Kathleen Norris (1880–1966), popular American author, a woman stretches her arms out in the direction of the moon, which is just beyond her reach.

39

Proud That Canadian Literature Is Clean

— 1924 —

According to the subhead of this article, published in *Bookseller and Stationer* in March 1924, "L.M. Montgomery Expresses the Opinion That It Is Difficult for Authors to Make Good in Canada – Praises Domestic Literature for Clean Morals – Product of Canadian Authors Compares Very Favorably with Sex Writings from Other Countries." In this reported speech, likely given in Kitchener, Ontario, on 13 February 1924, Montgomery repeated her conviction that literature ought to be concerned with the "betterment" of readers. In urging audience members to ensure that one out of three books purchased was by a Canadian author, she mentioned *Over Prairie Trails*, a volume of nature essays by Frederick Philip Grove and published by McClelland and Stewart in 1922. In an unidentified clipping in her scrapbooks, Montgomery endorsed Grove's book publicly, calling it "one of the few pieces of real and vital literature that Canada has produced. The style is finished and exquisite, the restraint admirable, the atmosphere and close observance of nature wonderful."[1]

"One thing that can be said about Canadian literature, is that it is clean. I am proud to say that it is clean. There are very few stories published in Canada that mothers could not give to their daughters. It is very much different from some of the stories that come into this country from the United States and England. There are too many magazines and books coming into Canada that are not clean, and that cannot help in any way toward the betterment of Canadians, or the development of true domestic literature. I do not talk about 'uplift,' but my mission is to bring a little bit of humor into the lives of people.

"I believe there is a place for sex novels, for adults, but the person who writes them should be a genius. The matter is a very important one and is a delicate one to write about."

These sentiments were recently expressed by L.M. Montgomery, author of *Anne of Green Gables*, and a number of other books and poems, at a recent address delivered before the Women's Canadian Club.

Worth of Domestic Authors

The author, who is now Mrs. Macdonald,[2] wife of an Ontario minister, spoke of Canadian literature as it is to-day. She pointed out that although Canada has no literature like the European countries, still the country is getting it, and will have it.

"We owe all the literature we have to the mistakes, tragedies and joys of human life," said Mrs. Macdonald.[3]

"It is hard for Canadian authors to make good in Canada. Very often, a Canadian's book must be taken up by other countries, before Canadians realize its worth. We would like our Canadian authors to remain Canadians in atmosphere and in flavor. When they go to the United States, however, they lose something they can never regain. They become somewhat Americanized, but we want them to be Canadians. The one way in which we can keep them home is to support them. We have good authors in Canada and the Canadian people should support them.

"Every time you buy, beg, borrow, or steal books, see that one of three is by a Canadian author. In this way you are helping your own people, and you will keep your Canadian authors here."

An Author's Mail Bag

"One of the best pieces of literature Canada has ever produced is *Over Prairie Trails*, by a writer in Winnipeg. It is a book that should be in every library, and every institution that has a library. The title of the book would lead one to believe that it was a wild and woolly west story, but, it is a book of essays, and it is a wonderful one."

Mrs. Macdonald gives the following humorous account of the mail received by an author:

"In one letter I received, a woman asked me to reform my characters in stories, because she objected to one story in which the heroine used slang, and to *Anne of Green Gables* in which Matthew smoked a pipe. She said it did not tend toward strengthening the morals of the younger generation. I answered that I wrote about people just as I found them, and asked her if she would not prefer to have a good book on wicked people, instead of a bad book about good people. This did not seem to satisfy her, and she wrote again telling me I could make my books just as interesting if I left out slang."

NOTES

1 "Books by Frederick Philip Grove," ad for *Over Prairie Trails*, by Frederick Philip Grove, unidentified and undated clipping, in SR, 349. For more on Montgomery and Grove, see Irene Gammel's "'My Secret Garden': Dis/ Pleasure in L.M. Montgomery and F.P. Grove" in Volume 2 of *The L.M. Montgomery Reader*.
2 I have corrected the original, which reads "McDonald."
3 Here and throughout, I have corrected the original, which reads "MacDonald."

40

Canadian Public Cold to Its Own Literature

—— 1924 ——

According to the subhead of this article, published in the *Hamilton Spectator* in November 1924, "L.M. Montgomery, Creator of Lovable Heroines, Charms Business Women's Club – Urges Canadians to Get Behind Their Own Writers." In a similar article published in the *Hamilton Herald*, she is quoted as saying: "If the Canadians only read one book by their own authors out of every three, it would be sufficient to keep the national literature going."[1]

Mrs. Macdonald,[2] known to the hundreds of thousands of her reading public as L.M. Montgomery, creator of *Anne of Green Gables, Anne of Avonlea, Anne of the Island*, the *Story Girl, Kilmeny of the Orchard*, and a score of other books which have made her the adored of thousands, was the speaker last evening at the monthly meeting of the Canadian Business Women's Club. The spacious board room of the Y.W.C.A.[3] was taxed to capacity to hear the distinguished author's charming and delightfully informal address, and many stood in the doorway, being unable to find seating accommodation. As a member of the Canadian Authors' Association,[4] an organization which has for its primary object the advancement of Canadian literature, Mrs. Macdonald made an appeal for the literature of this country. It had often been said – and with some measure of truth, she admitted – that there was no Canadian literature. "Naturally," she said, "our little beginnings cannot compare with the literature of the old lands. I dislike to admit it, but Canada is the hardest country in the world for a young writer to make a start in."

Buy Canadian Books

The young Canadian writer was up against the tremendous competition of thousands of writers in the great country to the south of Canada; and the equally large number of experienced writers' books from England, whose works flooded the country.

"I am not appealing for myself," said the speaker, "for I am one of the older writers; but I make this plea on behalf of the writers of the future."

There was another and a higher way in which to produce a great Canadian literature, said the speaker, one in which the ordinary Canadian woman could assist. Great literature was not, after all, an exotic blossom flung to earth from the gods. Rather it was a growth sprung from the soil of a race. Every great literature had a great people behind it; no really great literature ever sprang from a sordid, mean, materialistic or grasping people. "It should be our privilege to prepare the soil in which this flower may grow," said Mrs. Macdonald.

"We can prepare it by our vision, clear and far-sighted; by our ideals, lofty and enduring, by a culture, deep and profound." Genius, she said, was but the ability to grasp and give expression to those things which had existed in a people.

Her Public's Letters

She told of the many interesting and amusing letters which she received from her public all over the world, and also related an amusing incident in connection with a visit which she had made to her home in Prince Edward Island some years ago with her year-old son. The Charlottetown *Guardian* chronicled the fact that "Miss L.M. Montgomery and her infant son were visiting in town." "I assure you," she said, "I was not at all the sort of modern young woman that the item implied."

NOTES

1 *The Hamilton Herald*, "Girl Now Does," 7.
2 Here and throughout, I have corrected the original, which reads "McDonald."
3 Young Women's Christian Association. The YWCA in Hamilton is still located on MacNab Street South today.
4 For more on the CAA, see the introduction to this volume, note 35, above.

41

Thinks Modern Flapper Will Be Strict Mother

—— 1924 ——

According to the subhead of this article, "L.M. Montgomery, Canadian Writer, Discusses Foibles of Present-Day Youth – Expresses Disgust With Super-Heated Fiction, and Predicts Its Passing." It was published in the *Hamilton Spectator* on the same date and even the same page as "Canadian Public Cold to Its Own Literature," reprinted above. As she noted in her journal, "The reporters descended on me in swarms and all wanted to know what I thought of the present day girl, smoking for women – and *Flaming Youth* ... They reported me with fair accuracy except that one lady wrote me down as saying that smoking did no harm – in moderation."[1] In a similar article in the *Hamilton Herald* that included the comment on smoking in moderation, Montgomery offered the "cheery opinion" that "there is only one difference between the girl of today and the girl of the past generation. The girl of today is doing what her mother wanted to do!" Although she also stated in this article that she had "nothing against the present day girl," she added: "I am a Presbyterian minister's wife and am still old-fashioned enough to live with my husband."[2]

A distinguished guest in Hamilton, for a few hours last evening, was Mrs. Macdonald,[3] better known as Miss L.M. Montgomery. Mrs. Macdonald is known all over the continent and indeed in Europe, too, for her delightful series of Anne books. The eminent author was the guest of the Canadian Business Women's Club, before which organization she spoke.

Often when a woman carves for herself a definite and very prominent place in the world of art, literature or the various professions, the effort by which she has attained that position leaves its mark on her. Mrs. Macdonald is an exception. When she graciously permitted the *Spectator* to interview her in her room at the Connaught,[4] before dinner last evening, the interviewer found her an altogether delightful person – rather above medium height, and with thick hair, slightly graying, which she wore waved and coiled becomingly about her well-shaped head. Her face was unlined and she smiled easily, and to the reporter who had once fancied that the lovable Anne of Green Gables was none other than the author, she seemed indeed the embodiment of that wholesome, refreshing type of Prince Edward Island womanhood.

A delightful conversationalist, Mrs. Macdonald chatted pleasantly about people, her work and things in general, the while she dressed for dinner.

"Was Anne of Green Gables a real girl – someone you really knew in Prince Edward Island?" the author was asked.

"No, Anne, like all the characters in my books, was wholly imaginary, on my part, but none the less real to me," she replied. *Anne of Green Gables* was her first book, Mrs. Macdonald stated, although for years previous to its publication, she had contributed many delightful little stories to magazines, papers and various juvenile publications.

Peg Bowen,[5] whom thousands will remember as the old witch-like woman in *The Story Girl*, Mrs. Macdonald said was the only character drawn from real life – and Peg was a famous old character in a Prince Edward Island village.

When asked her opinion of the modern 'teen age girl – the ultra-modern young person who smoked and went everywhere unchaperoned, and who contrasted rather sadly with Anne of Green Gables, Mrs. Macdonald defended the modern young girl. Anne, she said, was a country girl, but she felt sure that there were just as many sweet girls of character to-day as in previous years. The modern "stepper," she thought, would pass; it was only a phase of the general loosening up which followed the war.

"Indeed, I think," she said, "that the modern flapper, with her fast pace, will make the strictest and best of mothers. She will probably keep her daughters confined in a convent to keep them safe! Every generation, you know, thinks that the present one is bound to perdition, while the scandalized ones were probably the despair of their own parents."

Speaking of the too popular sex novel of the present day which the young girl reads, Mrs. Macdonald admitted that it was not until the other day that she had read *Flaming Youth*,[6] the most flagrant of the fast, "sexty" novels. She had been disgusted by it, for it neither pointed a moral, nor had it any excuse for its existence, like some of the really great sex novels, such as Tolstoi wrote. This type of literature, too, she thought, would pass. She spoke of the influx of disgusting literature which had flooded the restoration period of the Stuarts, which had been immediately followed by the prim, narrow literature of the Victorian period.

Mrs. Macdonald's next book will be the second in the series of Emily books, which she is tentatively calling *Emily Climbs*.[7] In this book, Emily reaches flapperhood.

It was with surprise that one learned that Mrs. Macdonald did not now live in her beloved Prince Edward Island, but now lived with her husband, a Presbyterian minister, and her two small sons, outside the village of Leaskdale, about 50 miles north of Toronto.

NOTES

1 Montgomery, 23 November 1924, in *SJLMM*, 3: 208.

2 *The Hamilton Herald*, "Girl Now Does," 7.

3 Here and throughout, I have corrected the original, which reads "McDonald."

4 The Royal Connaught Hotel was located at King Street East and John Street South in downtown Hamilton, a thirteen-storey building that still stands.

5 I have corrected the original, which reads "Peg Bone."

6 *Flaming Youth* (1923) was the first of two novels by Samuel Hopkins Adams (1871–1958), American author and investigative journalist, but published under the pseudonym Warner Fabian due to its controversy and sexual frankness. This best-selling novel depicted college students in the United States, including "flappers" with short skirts, short hair, and an abundance of sex appeal. The novel was made into a film that same year. In her journals, Montgomery claimed she had told a reporter that "*Flaming Youth* was a book haunted by the imaginations of hell" (Montgomery, 23 November 1924, in *SJLMM*, 3: 208).

7 I have corrected the original, which reads "Emily Clines." The article in the *Hamilton Herald* adds that Montgomery "is already planning yet another Emily book in which she will take her young heroine 'through the love stages,' to quote her own words" (*The Hamilton Herald*, "Girl Now Does," 7).

42

Symposium on Canadian Fiction in Which Canadian Authors Express Their Preferences

—— 1924 ——

This article includes responses from a number of popular authors – including Bliss Carman, Madge Macbeth, Isabel Ecclestone Mackay, Emily Murphy (Janey Canuck), William Arthur Deacon, Robert Watson, Robert Stead, Frederick Philip Grove, Nellie L. McClung, H.A. Cody, and Marian Keith – and appeared with a descriptive subhead: "What They Have Written in Reply to the Question: 'What Are Your Three Favorite Novels by Canadian Writers?' – Their Answers Show a Very Interesting Variety of Opinion and from Them Our Readers Can Compile a Useful Reference List." Montgomery's answers are significant because the three authors she chose are ones that she never included in her lists of favourite authors (most of whom were British or American), either in the essays in this volume or in her journals.[1] Watson named Montgomery as part of a list of several authors whose works could be a third choice, while Cody chose *Anne of Green Gables*, along with Marshall Saunders's *Beautiful Joe*, for their "simplicity and spontaneity of maiden efforts, the thrill of first love, so to speak. Although the authors have done notable work since, they have never quite equalled their first efforts."

It is a somewhat difficult and invidious task to select my three favorite works of fiction by Canadian authors. There are so many other books I like "just as well." And my favorite book of all – *Over Prairie Trails* by Frederick Philip Grove – is not a "work of fiction" at all, but a classic in essays.

However, I have selected three which, in one sense at least, are my favorites. It is easier to pick them out than to give my reasons for doing it.

One can't give reasons for this sort of thing. Fancy asking a lover to give his "reasons" for liking his lady better than anybody else.

(1) *The Heart of the Ancient Wood* by Charles G.D. Roberts[2]
I love this book because it is one of those fairy tales the human heart craves. I love it because its scene is laid in the woods which are and always have been realms of romance for me; and, subtlest and most potent reason of all, I love it because I read it and re-read it first in the magic years of early youth, and every time I open it I find my lost girlhood between its covers, and while I read it am immortally young once more.

(2) *Doctor Luke of the Labrador* by Norman Duncan[3]
I love this book for the simple, heroic lives it depicts, for its gracious humor, for its breath of salt sea and hungry waves, and because it, too, brings back to me a life and a period forever passed away not only from me, but from the world.

(3) *The Child's House* by Marjory MacMurchy[4]
This is a new book and so has no sorcery of old years in it for me. I like it on its merits alone. It is subtle, artistic, altogether delightful.

NOTES

1 See, for instance, Montgomery, 15 April 1914, in *SJLMM*, 2: 146.
2 This animal story by Charles G.D. Roberts, one of the Confederation Poets, was published in 1900. See Montgomery, 7 November 1928, in *SJLMM*, 3: 381.
3 This novel by Norman Duncan was published in 1904.
4 This novel by Marjory MacMurchy was published in 1923. I have corrected the original, which reads "McMurchy."

43

Something about L.M. Montgomery
—— 1925 ——

In October 1924, Montgomery recorded in her journal that she had received a letter from her former publishing house, L.C. Page and Company, asking for her help in putting together a "little brochure" of her career for the benefit of her reading public.[1] Montgomery was amazed by this request because she and her former publishers were then embroiled in a series of lawsuits and counter-suits over their publication of *Further Chronicles of Avonlea*, a conflict that would not be completely settled until 1928. Issued in 1925 apparently without her involvement, presumably to coincide with a new edition of *Anne of Green Gables*, with new plates and new illustrations by Elizabeth R. Withington (at which point the original plates had worn out after nearly 400,000 copies),[2] the pamphlet lifted without attribution several direct quotations from earlier essays and interviews. A revised version appeared in 1938 with a photograph of an older Montgomery on the title page. Neither pamphlet made any mention of Montgomery's career subsequent to her break from L.C. Page and Company. A review of the first pamphlet in the *Los Angeles Times* mentions that "the life of the author of *Anne of Green Gables*, L.M. Montgomery, has always been more or less of a mystery to the many readers of her books, and her publishers, L.C. Page & Co., have received many inquiries about her." Page produced similar pamphlets concerning other popular authors whose works were published by his firm: Eleanor H. Porter (1868–1920), author of *Pollyanna*; Annie Fellows Johnston (1863–1931), author of *The Little Colonel*; and Ilsa May Mullins (1859–1936), author of *Anne of the Blossom Shop*.[3]

Lewis Page remains in many ways an enigmatic figure in Montgomery's professional life. Although Montgomery depicted him as a vindictive villain in her journals, she and Page proved to be "a good match," as Carole Gerson notes, in that he suggested revisions of short stories and serials when Montgomery could not produce novels quickly enough and created a "Montgomery brand" in terms of "the visual consistency of his Montgomery titles."[4] Notwithstanding his vindictive nature, he had cultivated a carefully controlled public persona: in a 1911 article in *The Boston Herald* about current trends in the publishing industry, he spoke eloquently on behalf of his company:

> The book which has in it the worth while quality, rather than the quality of interest alone – for it is quite true that a book may be interesting and still lack the essential of "worth-whileness" – seems to have come into its own. At least the holiday demand for certain titles from our list would seem to indicate this. We attribute the popularity of "quiet" stories, such as L.N. [*sic*] Montgomery's *The Story Girl*, to the fact that the great reading public is coming more than ever to the appreciation of what is best or uplifting in literature. In the selection of juvenile reading, too, there is a lesser tendency on the part of parents to select the book with the more numerous or gaudy illustrations. It is the text matter itself which is given careful consideration nowadays.[5]

The suggestion that Montgomery's life remained a "mystery" during this period is rather curious, given the sheer number of essays, profiles, and interviews included in this volume. However, a number of letters from readers to newspapers throughout the 1930s indicate that even the most basic information about the author was largely unknown: "Please tell me if the person, L.M. Montgomery, who wrote *Anne of Green Gables*, is a man or a woman; also, please tell me something about this person," a reader wrote to the *Salt Lake Tribune* in 1931. "Is L.M. Montgomery a real name or a pen-name?" another reader asked the *North Adams Evening Transcript*, a Massachusetts paper, in 1934. And finally, "Is the author L.M. Montgomery a man?" a reader asked the *Middletown Times–Herald*, a New York newspaper, in 1935.[6]

The Bible tells us the story of a mustard seed that grew into an amazing tree,[7] but not often in modern times do we hear of a package of flower seeds growing into a hundred thousand dollars!

The success of Lucy Maud Montgomery, author of the world-famed *Anne of Green Gables*, is, however, evident proof that such can be the case. When Miss Montgomery visited Boston in 1910, she was at the height of her success; *Anne of Green Gables* had been enthusiastically received, and the author's royalties were mounting steadily. One evening, at the home of her publisher, Mr. L.C. Page, sitting under the portrait of Anne Shirley, Miss Montgomery remarked that the first story she ever sold was paid for by a package of seeds! Since that time the cash returns from her books have amounted to many thousands of dollars, and she is one of the comparatively few writers whose literary success is world-wide. Truly, a case of "great oaks and little acorns!"[8]

L.M. Montgomery, as she prefers to be known, was born in 1874 at Clifton, Prince Edward Island, of fine old Scotch parentage. Her mother, Clara Woolner Macneill,[9] was descended from a race of poets and story-tellers, one of whom was the author of several songs often attributed to Burns.[10] Hugh John Montgomery, the little girl's father, was of one of the oldest and most prominent families on Prince Edward Island.[11] His father for many years represented the Island at Ottawa. From such a background came one of the most talented writers of modern times.

Miss Montgomery's mother died when she was very young. Her father, soon afterward, found it necessary to move to Saskatchewan, leaving his little daughter to the care of her maternal grandparents. The grandfather was postmaster at Cavendish, a circumstance which meant a great deal to the young author. Paper was scarce in Prince Edward Island, so most of Miss Montgomery's early works were scribbled on the backs of the red post-office forms of which there was an ample supply. Later, as the author herself tells, she would never have had the courage to send manuscripts to editors, if she had not been able to recover the many, many rejected ones from the post office without anyone's knowledge.[12] The post office, too, was the center for village gossip, and all the incidents of everybody's daily life, piquant or commonplace, were to be gathered there by any little girl with ears as sharp as little Lucy Montgomery's.

After Grandfather Macneill died, Grandmother Macneill was continued by the government as postmistress. Miss Montgomery was able, during this time, to spend a year at Prince of Wales College, a year at Dalhousie College, and a year in writing for the Halifax *Chronicle*. But her grandmother's advancing age made it necessary for her to give up newspaper work and return to Cavendish. There she lived and wrote until her grandmother died in 1911.

The first bit of Miss Montgomery's writing which was printed (that of the flower seeds fame!) was accepted when she was seventeen.[13] For two lean years the young and persistent author received nothing but numerous rejection slips, but, after her nineteenth birthday, there came a check for five dollars for a short story. In Miss Montgomery's own words: "I did not squander those beautiful dollars in riotous living. Neither did I invest them in necessary boots and hats. Instead I bought five volumes of the standard poets. I wanted to get something that I could keep forever in memory of having 'arrived.'"[14]

For several years Miss Montgomery wrote for magazines, gradually building up a clientele of editors on whom she could depend for a livelihood. Finally one of them, – the editor of a Sunday School weekly – asked her to write a seven chapter serial for him. Looking over her notebook of "Ideas," she found this entry: "Elderly couple apply to orphan asylum for a boy; by mistake a girl is sent them." That was the beginning of *Anne of Green Gables*.

But seven chapters could never have held Anne Shirley, so Miss Montgomery developed the story and wrote it in its present form. It was too long for the Sunday School editor, so she sent him another story, and *Anne* began her journey to the publishing houses.

The same evening that Mr. Page learned about the package of seeds, Miss Montgomery told him that if he had not accepted *Anne of Green Gables*, the manuscript would have gone into the wastebasket. Six other publishing houses had rejected it, and the author sent it to L.C. Page & Company for a last trial. In the light of the remarkable success of the book, this would indicate the value of persistence.[15]

It was in 1908 that *Anne of Green Gables* was published. It was followed the next year by *Anne of Avonlea*, which carried on the adventures of the delightful red-head. As Miss Montgomery herself remarked, "I think every red-haired girl in the world must have written to me," and it was in response to the demand from these girls and thousands of others – not only girls – that Miss Montgomery continued to write "more about Anne."[16]

In 1910 appeared *Kilmeny of the Orchard*, an idyllic love story, with a heroine who was Anne Shirley's opposite (and would have been her ideal), but who was quite as charming. Miss Montgomery's next book was *The Story Girl*, published in 1911. Of this sweet and sincere book the reviewers said: "There is a freshness and a charm about it which will help lift the load of care, or make brighter still the life of the carefree."[17] Miss Montgomery's books always do that; and the success of the *Story Girl* and *Kilmeny* was immediate.

Following her grandmother's death, in the summer of 1911 Miss Montgomery was married to the Reverend Ewan Macdonald,[18] who is minister of the Presbyterian Church in the little town of Leaskdale, Ontario. This little village is in the heart of a beautiful country, five miles from a railroad station, and there Mr. and Mrs. Macdonald still live, with their two sturdy sons.[19] Successful author though she is, having been elected to membership in the Royal Society of Arts, the Author's League of America,[20] and the Canadian Women's Press Club,[21] Miss Montgomery finds her greatest happiness in her home and in the simple beauty around her.

After taking up her new life in Leaskdale in 1912, *Chronicles of Avonlea*, a collection of short stories laid in the Green Gables country, was published. *The Golden Road* (1913), a sequel to *The Story Girl*, came next. It is woven about the theme that "Life was a rose-tipped comrade, with purple flowers dripping from her fingers."[22] Truly, the author's life has been that, and *The Golden Road* gives a little of the joy she has found to her thousands of friends throughout the world.

Meanwhile, the demand for "more about Anne" continued, so, in 1915, appeared *Anne of the Island*, which recounts Anne's adventures through four gay years of college, which she, of course, enjoyed in a different and more enthusiastic way than any one else. It is needless to say that Anne Shirley was welcomed in her new volume; Anne is one of those happy people who will always be welcomed. Particularly was this true when *Anne of Green Gables* appeared in the motion pictures, with Mary Miles Minter playing the title role. So enthusiastic were the audiences who saw the picture-play that the publishers brought out a special "Mary Miles Minter edition" of *Anne of Green Gables*, illustrated from the picture, in 1920.[23]

The original edition of *Further Chronicles of Avonlea* was published in 1920 but subsequently discontinued. A new revision is in preparation. In his preface to this volume, Nathan Haskell Dole said: "It is no exaggeration to say that what Longfellow did for Acadia, Miss Montgomery has done for Prince Edward Island. And there is something in these continued *Chronicles of Avonlea* like the delicate art which has made 'Cranford' a classic."[24]

A successful author is always besieged by the query, "How did you do it?" Miss Montgomery, with a twinkle in her eye, answers thus:

"An old woman once said to me, 'My dear, never get married as long as you can help it, for when the right man comes along, you can't help it.'

"That is just the way with novel writing. Never write as long as you can possibly help it, for when the writing fever seizes you, you can't help it.

"That's my recipe," she smiles.[25]

And, the evidence proves, it is a good one.

NOTES

1 Montgomery, 30 October 1924, in *SJLMM*, 3: 206.

2 Review of *Anne of Green Gables*, by L.M. Montgomery, illustrated by Elizabeth R. Withington, *Every Evening* (Wilmington, DE), 6 June 1925, in SR, 242. According to the Nashville *Banner* in Tennessee (15 March 1925), the Page Company referred to this edition as "the 'Half-A-Million' edition" in light of the fact that close to half a million copies of *Anne of Green Gables* had already been sold, even though the Asheville *Banner* in North Carolina (11 October 1925) specified that a mere 396,000 copies of the novel had been printed. Montgomery pasted these two articles – published in identically named newspapers in cities with highly similar names – side by side in SR, 250.

3 *Los Angeles Times*, "Biography in Miniature," 28.

4 Gerson, "Seven Milestones," 20.

5 *The Boston Herald*, "Publishers' Views of Season's Books," 8. For a 1922 interview with Miss Mae V. Lebert, an employee of the Page Company, about the publisher's decision to keep its focus on "wholesome" books such as Montgomery's, see Pember, "Are Authors Today."

6 *The Salt Lake Tribune*, "Tribune Information," 13; *The North Adams Evening Transcript*, "Ask the Transcript," 14; *Middletown Times–Herald*, "Questions and Answers," 4.

7 See Matthew 13:31, Mark 4:31, and Luke 13:19 in the Christian Bible.

8 Properly, "The greatest Oaks have been little Acorns," an eighteenth-century adage. The first two paragraphs are omitted in the 1938 pamphlet.

9 Here and throughout, I have corrected the original, which reads "MacNeill."

10 See chapter 20, "L.M. Montgomery: Story Writer," by Marjory MacMurchy, in this volume.

11 Here and in the next paragraph, I have corrected the original, which reads "Prince Edward."

12 Here and in the sentence that follows, I have corrected the original, which reads "postoffice."

13 The phrase in parentheses is omitted in the 1938 pamphlet; in its place is the following sentence: "She received in payment of this story a package of flower seeds."

14 See chapter 25, "How I Began," by L.M. Montgomery, in this volume; see also *AP*, 60–61.

15 In the 1938 pamphlet, the preceding sentence is replaced by the following:
Six publishing houses rejected the story, and the author then sent it to L.C. PAGE & COMPANY for a seventh and last trial, for she had

decided to toss the manuscript into the waste basket if PAGE returned the work with a rejection slip. But PAGE was enthusiastic about the story and published ANNE OF GREEN GABLES in 1908. Immediately poets, statesmen, humorists, critics and the great public lost their hearts to the charming ANNE. Mark Twain hailed the red-headed heroine as "the dearest and most moving and delightful child of fiction since the immortal Alice."

16 *Anne of the Island* is dedicated "to all the girls all over the world who have 'wanted more' about ANNE."

17 Properly, "there is a freshness and a sweetness about it which will help to lift the load of care, to cheer the weary and to make brighter still the life of the carefree and the happy." From a review in the Toronto *Globe* included in Volume 3 of *The L.M. Montgomery Reader*.

18 Here and throughout, I have corrected the original, which reads "MacDonald."

19 This claim about the Macdonalds' home in Leaskdale is repeated in the 1938 pamphlet, even though they left Leaskdale in 1926.

20 Montgomery actually joined the League in 1916 at the suggestion of her later publishers McClelland and Stewart. She wrote to the League in 1917 and filed her case against Page concerning unpaid royalties, the first of several years of litigation (Montgomery, 26 April 1916, in *SJLMM*, 2: 183; Montgomery, 7 May 1917, in *SJLMM*, 2: 215).

21 I have corrected the original, which reads "Canadian Women's Press."

22 The quotation is from Montgomery's foreword to *The Golden Road* and was used as an epigraph in the first editions of the novel, signed "The Author."

23 The preceding sentence is omitted in the 1938 pamphlet and replaced with the following: "More recently a talking picture of ANNE OF GREEN GABLES was produced by RKO. When the charming young actress, Dawn O'Day, was awarded the title role of Anne, she was so elated to play the part that she adopted Anne Shirley for her real, as well as her screen, name."

24 See chapter 31 in this volume. A new edition of *Further Chronicles of Avonlea*, minus Dole's introduction, would not be published until 1953. This paragraph is omitted in the 1938 pamphlet and replaced with the following:

> In 1933 to commemorate the twenty-fifth birthday of ANNE OF GREEN GABLES the publishers issued a beautifully illustrated gift book edition, with eight plates in full color from original paintings done by the talented artist, Sybil Tawse.

ANNE OF GREEN GABLES has retained her lead in the best seller class not for months, but for years, more than a million copies having been sold in the United States and Canada. In addition ANNE OF GREEN GABLES has enjoyed tremendous popularity in Great Britain and has been translated into many foreign language, including the Dutch, French, Polish, Norwegian and Swedish.

25 See chapter 9, "Want to Know How to Write Books?" by Phoebe Dwight, in this volume.

44

L.M. Montgomery's *Rilla of Ingleside*: A Reader's Journal

—— 1925 ——

ALTAIR

This short essay appeared in the *Lethbridge Herald* in July 1925, as part of the "Reader's Journal" column signed "Altair" – the pseudonym of journalist Wilfrid Eggleston (1901–1985). As he states in his memoir *While I Still Remember* (1968), the name refers to "a first-magnitude star in the constellation Lyra."[1] Part of the essay's significance, apart from the fact that it provides an in-depth consideration of the historical and cultural significance of *Rilla of Ingleside*, is that it considers Montgomery's depiction of the Great War within a decade of the war's end, at a time when, as Montgomery feared when the novel was published in 1921, "the public are said to be sick of anything connected with the war."[2] Although Eggleston is already well known to the Montgomery community for his edition *The Green Gables Letters from L.M. Montgomery to Ephraim Weber, 1905–1909* (1960) – a book that covers, as he puts it, "the period when *Anne of Green Gables* was evolving from a fleeting inspiration into the most popular girl's book of its time"[3] – what may be a surprise to these same readers is that Eggleston quoted substantially from these letters in at least three articles in his "The Causerie" column in the *Winnipeg Free Press*, in 1956 and 1957.

The war book has boomed to the heights of popularity, slumped to the depths of unsaleability, and now seems definitely to have begun its upward climb again. We are told that the classic of the war has not yet been written. Without knowing for sure how true this is, even the casual reader is aware and was aware that much of the fiction produced by the stimulation of the war was highly ephemeral. So was the great mass of war verse. Most soldiers repudiate the war tales, though I have heard that Thomas Boyd's *Through the Wheat* and one or two novels in other languages have stood the test,[4] – the acid and supreme test, of the actual participants' criticisms, and have come through with flying colors. If a veteran of Mons and the Somme tells you that a war story is true to life, you can pick it up confident that it is a little more than the idealized, sentimentalized story of war that was so common a few years ago, and that was usually written from a safe location in Blighty[5] by a non-participant who had made one or two flying visits to the front.

Anyway, critics tell us that the great classic of the war is not yet:[6] the novel that does for the great European war what *War and Peace*, passages in *Les Miserables*, and *Charles O'Malley* did for the Napoleonic war, or *Micah Clarke* and *Lorna Doone* did for the Monmouth invasion, for example, – gave them an immortal place in fiction.[7]

But there are other ways of recording great wars in fiction. Hundreds of novels and at least one great epic-drama – Hardy's *The Dynasts* – treated the Napoleonic war as a major theme.[8] They gave us the romance and glamour of war, the actual campaigning, the roll of drums and the flash of sabres, so to speak. It remained for that arch satirist, Thackeray, to present another side, to give "the back-door view" of history, to present the great Napoleonic drama by means of a cowardly and sordid escape from the outskirts of the battle; the lubbering Jos Sedley, and the pitiful figure of Amelia praying while George lay dead on the battlefield, with a bullet through his heart. In *Vanity Fair* we see the Napoleonic war not through the spectacles of glory and renown, but through the demeaning glasses of the indifferent, mercenary, callous non-participants.[9] It is the war seen in reflection, the looking-glass (to change the figure) being the hearts of those who did not fight.

I am reminded of these things by a recent reading of *Rilla of Ingleside* by "our own" novelist, L.M. Montgomery. *Rilla of Ingleside*, besides being several other things, is a similar story of the Great War, a back-door view of the recent world struggle. Not that L.M. Montgomery wields the stiletto of social satire, not that she finds the non-participants indifferent, scheming, mercenary, or callous. But *Rilla of Ingleside* is a war story in the same way as *Vanity Fair* is a war story: both give us the dim reflection of the battle front in the hearts of those who did not go.

I do not know what was the primary purpose of L.M. Montgomery in writing this tale. Possibly it was first and foremost to write another fine addition to her shelf of original and clever girls' books. But it is, as well, a historical document of no small importance. When the writers of another day wish to know what Canada went through at home while the fortunes of war rose and fell overseas, it is to such contemporaneous documents as these that they will turn. It is not a perfect historical source book by any means, – 'twould be a poor novel if it were – but it gives an occasional glint of light that even a masterly study like *Main Street* (a historical novel of the present day Mid West) might in its erudition overlook.[10]

It would be a poor review, however, that would leave the reader with the impression that *Rilla of Ingleside* is a mere source book for the historians of another day. That phase of it is merely a thought in passing. Some Sinclair Lewis will arise who will do the thing much more earnestly and thoroughly. It is for other reasons that we admire L.M. Montgomery.

I am surprised that more is not made of her fine gift in the numerous speeches and articles on Canadian books that bloom forth profusely each year around Book Week. When the critic talks about Canadian poetry, he is fluent; when the subject veers around to the Canadian novel, a strange silence falls; he mentions Gilbert Parker, and apologizes for half a dozen others, and passes on with a sigh of relief to Canada's nature writing. The fact is that we have outstanding poetry and natural history, and only second-rate fiction. But something more might be made of L.M. Montgomery. Fiction for girls is perhaps not as dignified a subject for grey bearded critics as fiction for adults, but at least it might be said that L.M. Montgomery towers over Meade and Southworth and Holmes and Porter, yes, and even Kate Douglas Wiggin and Gene Stratton-Porter,[11] of our Southern neighbors, and, in short, would receive a great many notes as the finest writer of girls books alive on the continent today. And it's something to boast of a Canadian the finest novelist even if the field is only girl's fiction. Our adult fiction is about third or fourth rate, mostly; let us rejoice that we can number in our ranks the author of *Anne of Green Gables*.

I have read *Rilla of Ingleside* with mixed feelings. Sometimes I was thrilled with the poetry of it, – Mrs. Montgomery-Macdonald is a fine colorist, both in prose and verse – sometimes I was moved with the idealism of it. Books for youth should be idealistic, I suppose. But what a dreary diet too much idealism would be for the older person, already a realist, past the dreamer stage, and in love with life, stark and hard and disillusioning as it often is. In this critical and carping mood, I ask myself if there ever were such perfect families as the Blythes and the Merediths; I ask myself if Walter Blythe is a creature of flesh and blood, or the product of a glorious dream of the golden ages of Greece, the high water mark of mediaeval chivalry, and the poetic splendour of Rupert Brooke. There may have been Walter, but L.M. has only shown us one face of the gem.

But this is rank heresy, and must not be continued, lest some novel-reading girl chance to see it, and waste time scoffing at the blindness of this reviewer. If one wants stark realism, one must go to some other source than the Anne books, even when they deal with the starkest and realest thing of the last century: the Great War.

There is danger of being misunderstood. The chief criticism that the realist makes of the idealist is not usually that he paints his characters too perfect, too splendid, too impossibly good. Some people seem to think that the heroes of idealistic fiction are always perfect, and the heroes of realistic fiction always flawed, – in fact, that realism has no heroes. In a way this is true, just as true as to say that no live flesh and blood man or woman is flawless. Nevertheless, the chief characters in a realistic novel may, and sometimes do, rise to heights hardly seen in the most impossible idealism; just as fallible and imperfect men in actual life sometimes rise to stranger and nobler heights than fiction is capable of describing. Nothing could be much more uncompromisingly realistic than Hardy's Wessex novels, yet I cannot think of Clym Yeobright as a slighter figure than the hero of any frankly idealistic novel that comes to mind.[12] The criticism, to repeat, that realism hurls at romantic idealism, is that only a small phase of life is selected, as though the rest were too ignoble, too petty, too uninteresting, to appear in fiction. The romanticist looks on life, and finds it possible to select interesting and worth-while fragments; the realist looks on life as a whole and finds the whole at least dignified and worthy of presentation, even if much of it should be painful, disappointing, illogical.

The digression gets rather a long way from *Rilla of Ingleside*. Nevertheless it explains why I should like the dramatis personae of the book much better if a few more of them were a trifle less saintly. Susan and Rilla and Mary Vance escape,[13] but some of the others are dreams of what ought to be and what might be, rather than transcripts from life. If I am wrong, – then, I hope it may be my luck some day to encounter a few such perfect characters. Only, – I am afraid I should be soon bored by their perfection. This is typical of the present age, which lauds Thackeray, and cannot stand King Arthur, (in Tennyson's Idylls,) because he is without savour. Perfection is uninteresting.

Even this criticism of L.M. Montgomery, slight as it is, and which exhausts all the derogatory remarks I have to set down, is hardly fair in that it criticises a book for missing an aim which, perhaps, the author never thought of. You can't criticize *Alice in Wonderland* because it isn't a tragedy, or *Pickwick Papers* because it isn't a book of travel.[14] Perhaps L.M. Montgomery had no idea of making *Rilla* anything but an interesting, idealistic, likeable girls' book. That being the case, everyone must admit her complete success.

I have an idea that if L.M. Montgomery had set out to write social satire a la Jane Austen she would have succeeded remarkably well. Here and there are hints and fragments quite worthy of Rose Macaulay.[15] Here is a specimen of subtle and very effective irony:

"Listen to this, Mrs. Dr. dear. (Susan is the speaker). 'Mrs. Sophia Crawford has given up her house at Lowbridge and will make her home in future with her niece, Mrs. Albert Crawford.' Why that is my own cousin Sophia, Mrs. Dr. dear. We quarrelled when we were children over who should get a Sunday School card with the words 'God is Love,' wreathed in rosebuds, on it, and have never spoken to each other since."[16]

I have already referred to the fact that L.M. Montgomery is a fine poet-artist both in verse and prose. Her poetry is nothing like so well known as her novels, and, as E.J. Hathaway points out, it lacks the human touch, which makes her stories so well loved.[17] Nevertheless a perusal of even a few lines will reveal her mastery of rhythm and diction. Here are a couple of stanzas from "Sunrise along Shore":

> Athwart the harbour lingers yet
> The ashen gleam of breaking day,
> And where the guardian cliffs are set
> The noiseless shadows steal away;
> But all the winnowed eastern sky
> Is flushed with many a tender hue,
> And spears of light are smiting through
> The ranks where huddled sea-mists fly.

> Across the ocean, wan and grey,
> Gay fleets of golden ripples come,
> For at the birth hour of the day
> The roistering, wayward winds are dumb,
> The rocks that stretch to meet the tide
> Are smitten with a ruddy glow,
> And faint reflections come and go
> Where fishing boats at anchor ride.[18]

To me, however, and doubtless to many more, the prose poetry to be found in her novels surpasses her formal poetry, in its power to charm ear and eye. The writer of the following passage, taken almost at random from *Rilla of Ingleside* is a master of poetic description:

"How beautiful the old Glen was, in its August ripeness, with its chain of bowery old homesteads, tilled meadows and quiet gardens. The western sky was like a great golden pearl. Far down the harbour was frosted with a dawning moonlight. The air was full of exquisite sounds – sleepy robin whistles, wonderful, mournful, soft murmurs of wind in the twilit trees, rustle of aspen poplars talking in silvery whispers and shaking their dainty, heart-shaped leaves, lilting young laughter from the windows of rooms where the girls were making ready for the dance. The world was steeped in maddening loveliness of sound and colour."[19]

NOTES

1 Eggleston, *While I Still Remember*, 53.
2 Montgomery, 3 September 1921, in *SJLMM*, 3: 17.
3 Eggleston, *While I Still Remember*, 314.
4 *Through the Wheat* (1923), a novel by Thomas Boyd (1898–1935), American novelist and journalist. I have corrected the original, which reads "Through – The Wheat."
5 Slang term for Britain.
6 I have corrected the original, which reads "critics tells us that the great classics of the war."
7 *War and Peace* (1869), by Leo Tolstoy (1828–1910), Russian author; *Les Misérables* (1862), by Victor Hugo (1802–1885), French author and artist; *Charles O'Malley, the Irish Dragon* (1872), by Charles Lever (1806–1872), Irish novelist; *Micah Clarke* (1889), by Arthur Conan Doyle (1859–1930), Scottish physician and author; *Lorna Doone: A Romance of Exmoor* (1869), by R.D. Blackmore (1825–1900), English novelist. "The Monmouth invasion" refers to the failed attempt of James Scott, 1st Duke of Monmouth (1649–1685) and an illegitimate son of Charles II (1630–1685), to declare himself to be the rightful heir to the throne and to overthrow his uncle James II (1633–1701), in 1685; he was later executed.
8 *The Dynasts*, an early-twentieth-century verse drama by Thomas Hardy (1840–1928), English poet and novelist.
9 *Vanity Fair: A Novel without a Hero* (1847–48), by William Makepeace Thackeray. Jos Sedley, Amelia Sedley, and George Osborne are all

characters from the novel. I have corrected the original, which reads "Joss Sedley."

10 *Main Street: The Story of Carol Kennicott* (1920), by Sinclair Lewis (1885–1951), American author.

11 L.T. Meade, pseudonym of Elizabeth Thomasina Meade Smith (1854–1914), Irish author best known for *A World of Girls* (1886); E.D.E.N. Southworth (1819–1899), American author best known for *The Hidden Hand* (1888); Mary Jane Holmes (1825–1907), American author; Kate Douglas Wiggin (1856–1923), American author and educator best known for *Rebecca of Sunnybrook Farm* (1903); Gene Stratton-Porter (1863–1924), American author and photographer best known for *A Girl of the Limberlost* (1909).

12 Clym Yeobright, a character in *The Return of the Native* (1929), by Thomas Hardy.

13 I have corrected the original, which reads "Susan and Rilla and Mary and Vance."

14 *Alice in Wonderland*, first published as *Alice's Adventures in Wonderland* (1865), a novel by Lewis Carroll, pseudonym of Charles Lutwidge Dodgson (1832–1898), English author and photographer.

15 Dame Emilie Rose Macaulay (1881–1958), English novelist, biographer, and travel writer.

16 *RI*, 15.

17 E.J. Hathaway's comments about Montgomery's poetry and prose appear in John W. Garvin's anthology *Canadian Poets* (1916).

18 "Sunrise along Shore," originally published in *The Youth's Companion* in 1901, also appeared in Garvin's *Canadian Poets*. It also appeared in Montgomery's own *The Watchman and Other Poems*, with a few minor spelling variations and an extra stanza (*WOP*, 29).

19 *RI*, 29–30.

45

Famous Author and Simple Mother

—— 1925 ——

NORMA PHILLIPS MUIR

This article was published in the *Toronto Star Weekly* in November 1925 with the following subhead: "Career and Home Go Together Well For a Woman If She Can Conduct Her Career at Home, Says L.M. Montgomery, Author of *Anne of Green Gables* – This Minister's Wife Writes Three Hours Every Morning, No More." According to Cecily Devereux, who includes an abridged version of this article in her critical edition of *Anne of Green Gables*, it "suggests that Montgomery's views were deeply traditional and arguably anti-feminist in 1925," and it provides evidence of Montgomery's "continued sense of exceptional women who can move beyond conventional boundaries while not disturbing them – indeed, while actually reinforcing them."[1] Indeed, her specific assumptions about heterosexual relationships, marriage, and "normal" girls point to an ideological basis for the "inevitable" romantic endings of her fiction. The assumption that motherhood must supersede a career is not made for the first time, either. In a profile of Montgomery in *Everywoman's World* in 1914, Mary Josephine Trotter cautions that "the author is a mother, and in that small volume her little boy, the lady sees her only great achievement." Also, in an unidentified clipping in Montgomery's scrapbook reporting on a speech she gave to the Women's Canadian Club around 1921, the same reporter concludes that "no feminist, as many know the words, is Lucy Maude [*sic*] Montgomery, but a woman, and a wife and a mother [with a] sane and happy outlook on the vastness of life."[2]

"Make it early Saturday morning, as early as you like," said L.M. Montgomery (Mrs. Macdonald),[3] author of the "Anne of Green Gables" stories. "I'm going to take my son down town for lunch and then on to a movie. He's going to St. Andrew's now you know.[4] I'm down for his football games."

This was in answer to our plea for half an hour of the time of this busy lady who combines the career of author with the no less arduous one of minister's wife and manages to be a pal to her two sons and keep in touch with the ever turning wheels of the world.

Taking her at her word we were there shortly after nine on the Saturday morning, but we were not too early for Mrs. Macdonald. She was ready for us, and had given some time and thought to the matter on which we wanted her opinion: whether women can successfully possess themselves of careers and home lives at the same time.

"There are really two answers to that problem," she said smiling. "One is affirmative and the other is negative. I would say that a woman may successfully combine a profession of her own with the oldest one in the world, that of wifehood and motherhood but only if she be able to pursue the career at home. It doesn't seem to me possible for a mother to be to her children what she should if they are only the recipients of her left over time, and are, for the major part, under the care of paid help.

"The writing of books, plays, poetry, painting and sculpture – even a career in law is possible and consistent with the duties of wife and mother, but I don't think a woman can pursue any career which takes her away from her home, and still be what she should be to her husband and children. I know there are shining examples where women have been successful in the eyes of the world, and whose homes are supposedly ideally happy, but before I could say that the woman was a success in both phases I'm afraid I should demand the unbiased testimony of her husband and children."

"Think of the great actresses," we protested, "the women who have filled high executive positions, famous women doctors – they have not denied themselves husbands and children. Their very successes have made it possible for them to obtain nurses and governesses for their children – given them care and training which is scientifically perfect, and –"

Has Two Sturdy Sons

"I am thinking," said Mrs. Macdonald quietly. "I'm remembering that the mortality rate in institutions which care for children is infinitely higher than it is in even the poorer class homes. Science is wonderful, but it is not as wonderful for a child as mother-love and mother care. Nothing can make up to a child for that. Children have died, and more will die for love. That is why I say give every woman who wants some interest in addition to her home life a hobby. Give her another interest so that the kitchen and the nursery may not pall, but let it be a hobby, an interest or a profession which she can follow at home."

Then, in answer to our questions Mrs. Macdonald smiled and told us, basing it on her own experiences, of how a woman can have her heart's desire, and no heartburnings and heartsearchings with it.

"The secret really is system," she admitted. "If one doesn't try to run one's life along any definite channels it will soon be like seed sown at random – and the harvest will be too difficult to bring in. Just take that homely old adage, 'A place for everything and everything in its place,' and add to it, 'and a time for everything and everything in its time' and you have the nucleus of success in whatever you are planning to undertake."

We pondered over this for a moment, and then, with a query here, a tentative theory there, the story took form.

It was while she was in her teens that L.M. Montgomery began writing, and like others to whom a large measure of success came later, she made her start in Sunday School papers. Then came serials, followed by *Anne of Green Gables*, and with that book came the well deserved laurels. Later on romance, real and not the story book kind, came into the life of the young author, and she married Rev. Ewan Macdonald, and added a home, a husband, the parochial duties of a minister's wife to her authorship. Motherhood was added, and now two sturdy sons tell "mother" their youthful joys and sorrows. Leaskdale and Zephyr are the two charges over which Mr. Macdonald presides, and there are Sunday services, week-day meetings and week-night gatherings at which the minister and his wife are present, yet L.M. Montgomery's publishers are not disappointed or her public disillusioned when another book from her loved pen appears.

Planning Her Housework

"It does keep me busy," she admitted. "But then there is nothing harder to do than nothing, is there? My day starts at seven in the morning and it lasts until twelve at night. There is breakfast to get, and my younger boy's lunch to pack, routine work to see to – I just have a young maid – and then at nine o'clock I am at my desk and there I stay until twelve. Those three hours a day are all I can allow myself for actual writing, for I am connected with the various church organizations of both charges, president or member or committee worker, and that all takes time. Then there are the countless little things that have to be done about a home to keep it running smoothly, and while I do admit that well trained help could do most of these things as well if not better than the wife and mother can, there is still something about the fact that a man's wife, his sons' mother is doing for her family[5] that makes the little acts mean more than if they were twice as efficiently done by someone else. It is the love motif again.

"I think every woman should have an earnest interest outside or rather independent of her home interests, but one which does not take her away from the supervision of her home and the care of her children. The woman who has not children is in another position entirely, but I feel that while a mother is able physically and mentally, the care of her children should not be relegated to outsiders."

"I think there are far too many girls in the world of business to-day for the good of the world of families," she said quaintly. "Girls have, if they be normal women, a desire for marriage in their hearts, and many of them realize that in the world of business they will have a better opportunity of finding for themselves the type of man they admire, and so – they don't spend the time learning to cook and play the piano and sew and be charming hostesses. They take a commercial course and enter an office and many times defeat their own purposes because the young men they meet are earning not much more than are the girls. They see the girls wearing expensive clothes, appearing well groomed and well content, and when they think, 'there's the kind of girl I'd like to marry,' they stop and think, and the result of the thinking is a decision that it is no use asking her to marry him. How can he suggest that they two get along on what she alone is making now?"

Old Ideals Safe

"Maybe he does ask and she says yes, with the proviso that she keep her position and pay for someone to look after the apartment. Maybe she makes another proviso, or maybe she just makes a resolve to herself, but the fact remains that she keeps her position and he keeps his, and when several Christmases have rolled around there are still no little sox to hang up as an enticement to Santa Claus.

"There are many girls working to-day who do not need to work, daughters of well-to-do fathers, girls whose mothers need them at home

227

for companionship, but these girls are not content with the dullness and quietness of home. They want to be out in the world of rush and excitement, and so they go, and not being dependent upon what they make, they can afford to work for less, which means that the girl who is her own sole means of support is compelled to take a lower wage in competition with these other girls, and so the economic structure is shaken.

"There is one good thing about to come out of the license and disorder and horror – yes, to mothers and fathers it is horror – of to-day. The motor car, the dance hall, the remote road-houses, and clubs, the petting parties and flask parties – horrible as these are they will have their use, for the pendulum will swing backward again toward decency and normalcy. The girls and boys who are the fastest and the greatest danger to themselves with their desire to be smart and up to date – they are the fathers and mothers of to-morrow, and knowing the dangers that they encountered, the fine line of margin which they took, they will be stricter and more watchful with their children, and so the pendulum will swing backward."

"The secrets of life have been kept too much secrets," said Mrs. Macdonald gravely, "and when these boys and girls, who because they realize that mystery has not paid and so have gone to the other extreme, have reached maturity and parenthood, they will see to it that youth learns the God-purpose of life in a way different from the way in which they learned it, and that the mind and soul and body of their children shall be kept clean and healthy and happy and whole for the joys and purposes of life.

"This has grown to be a far cry from women and their careers in one way," she smiled as we rose to go, "but after all the relationship is close. Give a woman a profession which she will be interested in and devoted to, give it to her within the four walls of her own home and the knowledge that she is not neglecting her home, her husband or her children will give her greater strength and purpose for the career which will be satisfying her need of self expression, and will bring pride to her family, without any of the pain of renunciation."

NOTES

1 Montgomery, *Anne of Green Gables*, edited by Devereux, 380; see also 379–84.

2 Trotter, "Novelist of the Isle," 11; also in SR, 75; "Tears and Laughter in Prose and Verse," unidentified and undated clipping, in SR, 186. According to the author of this piece, Montgomery's "sane and happy outlook" emerges in a poem entitled "The Choice" (see *WOP*, 104).
3 Here and throughout, I have corrected the original, which reads "MacDonald."
4 Montgomery's eldest son Chester, now thirteen years old, had started attending this private school for boys, located in the Rosedale neighbourhood of Toronto, that fall.
5 I have corrected the original, which reads "mother doing for her family."

46

The Day before Yesterday

— 1927 —

L.M. MONTGOMERY MACDONALD

In this article – published in *The College Times*, the magazine of Prince of Wales College in Charlottetown, in May 1927 – Montgomery reminisces about her year at teacher's college in 1893–94, during which she crammed two years of study into one, gaining a first-class teaching certificate. Looking back in 1910, she recorded in her journal that her time at PWC was the "happiest year" of her life.[1] Here she reminisces about two professors who made a significant impression on her: John Caven (1826–1914), who taught English and school management, and Alexander Anderson (1836–1925), Principal of PWC and an instructor in Latin composition. Mary Rubio and Elizabeth Waterston note that seventy-seven female students and ninety-nine male students were registered at PWC during this year.[2] Central Academy, built in 1834–35, was renamed Prince of Wales College in 1860, in honour of a visit of the future King Edward VII that year, and became coeducational in 1879. It shared a campus with the Normal School, for student teachers, which had opened in 1856. The school became the University of Prince Edward Island in 1969, and the L.M. Montgomery Institute was founded there in 1993.

That is what it seems like to me.[3] And I suppose to the students of Prince of Wales College to-day it must seem like a part of immemorial antiquity. "So runs the round of life from hour to hour."[4] It is really nearly thirty-four years since I, a schoolgirl in an old North Shore farm house, found myself looking, in a rapture of joy and relief, at my name in the "pass list" of a Charlottetown paper,[5] realizing that the dreaded ordeal of "entrance" was safely over and I had the right at last to call myself a student of "old P.W.C."[6]

It *was* "old P.W.C." in those days. For of course it was the old college to which I went. A shabby old building enough – with a still shabbier "Normal" across the green, with a well-worn trail between the two. Inside, inadequate and badly-ventilated class rooms, dark halls and sagging stairs. But we learned something in it for all that. The students of any school of which Dr. Anderson was the head couldn't help learning something. Of all the teachers I have ever "sat under" none was to be compared to Dr. Anderson. I can see him now, standing before us, making the dry bones of Roman History live, and clothing even Greek verbs with charm and "pep" – though I don't think the word "pep" had been invented then. I think we used "go" instead. Yes, that was it – "lots of go." Even the Victorian slang differs from the Georgian.

There stood Dr. Anderson, beaming on us, meticulously groomed, his hair and beard gleaming silver, his bright brown eyes flashing, his sonorous voice booming through the spell-bound class-room. And how erect he held himself – almost too erect. He really bent backward in his effort to be erect. I remember the horror that pervaded us one day when a wretched student tried to "answer back." I don't think he ever tried it again. One didn't – with Dr. Anderson. The good doctor could be bitterly and epigrammatically sarcastic when he chose. He delivered himself of some ironic remarks concerning the ancestry of the miserable youth who had incurred his displeasure, winding up with a statement to the effect that said youth was an unanswerable argument for evolution. There could be no doubt at all that he had descended – very recently – from a monkey.

Whereupon the tortured worm turned. "Well, if I did I didn't curl my tail up into a back-bone," he retorted.

I don't remember whether there was an earthquake or not.

We always nearly froze to death in Dr. Anderson's room, – especially we girls who sat in the row of seats next to the windows.[7] The good doctor had a praiseworthy passion for fresh air and the lower sash of the windows must be opened to the limit. We sat there, often with wind, snow, or rain blowing in on us. Nor was it the least use to protest. The doctor smiled, patted the protestant on the shoulder and assured her that dampness was excellent for the complexion and fresh air for everything.

He also assured us that while we should never study ordinary lessons on Sunday it was quite in order to study Greek, because it would undoubtedly be the language of the next world. Whether of Heaven or Hades we never dared inquire.

We were always glad to escape into Professor Caven's room, which was always warm and unhygienic. No open windows for Professor Caven.

In his methods Professor Caven was a hang-over from a yet older day. Nevertheless, if one wanted, one could learn a good deal from him. That was the difference between him and Dr. Anderson. With the latter one *had* to learn whether one wanted to or not. With Professor Caven, if you did not want to, you could read a novel under cover of the desk, carve your name on the lid, or carry on a mild flirtation with the young gentleman across the aisle from you. I don't say I ever did any of these things. At any rate, as the good Caven taught English, French and Literature and as these were my three favourite subjects I contrived to absorb plenty of information in his classes.

Such stories as he could tell. He would stand on the platform, tugging away at his long, gray, tobacco-stained beard, and begin the class work blamelessly. In a few minutes some literary allusion would suggest a story to him and he was off on the trail of it. When it was told half the hour would be gone and we so far away in spirit that some of us could never get back to conjugations and foot-notes. But there was a certain tang about "Old Caven," as we irreverently called him behind his back, that one could not forget. I remember him very vividly – his jokes, his mannerisms, his rages – when far better and more up-to-date teachers have faded into some dim hinterland of memory.

Professor Caven was given to having "pets." Every year he singled out some girl in the class and favored her shamelessly above all others. Let her do as she listed – it was all right in Caven's eyes. He never turned on her the bitter tongue that occasionally reduced some of the girls to tears and others to fury. I remember him telling one girl, as he danced about the platform in rage, that "a decent pick-pocket would be ashamed to associate with her."

In my year the lot fell on me. It is not mock modesty to say that. I don't know why. There were dozens of prettier girls in the class, many more brilliant students, certainly several who were better behaved. His own explanation was that I had the two most beautiful names in the English nomenclature and he couldn't see how my parents had the amazing good taste to dower me with both of them. I did not like either of my names and I liked them none the better for his unctuous re-iteration of them both.

But I think I was his favourite of the year, because he sensed in me a certain appreciation of the literary quality of his jokes which he may have found lacking in the class at large. He always looked at me across the sea of faces when he perpetrated one and we exchanged a fraternal grin.

The fact that I was his "pet" didn't prevent him from doing a beastly thing one morning. I was the last to enter the class-room and I entered in a hurry. Professor Caven was standing on his platform close to the door. I was wearing my hair in a braid down my back. He bent down as I shot by him and caught the end of the braid firmly in his hand. I was brought up in my head-long career by a jerk that nearly wrenched my head off my shoulders. I turned in fury from the delighted class to see that diabolical old professor, still holding my hair with one hand, tugging at his beard with the other, and grinning like a benevolent monkey.

"One can't help doing that when a girl has hair a yard long, Lucy Maud," he said.

It was weeks before I forgave him – and weeks before my neck ceased to be stiff and sore.

Of course no teacher in Prince of Wales to-day would do such a thing. But I sometimes wonder if any of them can bring home to you such a vital, penetrating sense of "the glory that was Greece and the grandeur that was Rome"[8] – ay, and England and Scotland and Ireland, too, as "Old Caven" could when he really addressed himself to the literatures he was supposed to teach.

That winter what was, I believe, the first college paper of P.W.C. came into being – *The College Record*. A thin little 8-page sheet Monthly. Twenty-five cents in advance. Norman Hunter and Hedley McKinnon (whose death was recently reported) were the editors, and Talmage MacMillan the business manager. It created quite a bit of excitement. Having a fatal reputation even then of "writing for the papers" I was obliged to be one of the "regular contributors" and some of my earliest sketches appeared in that old *Record*.[9]

A barbarous custom obtained in those days, I am told has long since been done away with. It was the one of having the "License Exams" separate from the College exams. At the end of the year we sweated and grilled for three weeks taking the final college exams. And as soon as they were over, tired, played-out, heavy-eyed from late hours of study we were plunged into a week of horrors, where we wrote on the same subjects all over again at the rate of two or three a day. Talk about the third degree! We knew all about it.

Nevertheless some of us passed and I think we deserved to.

Then, of course, we had a grand, bang-up finale in the Opera House (there being no suitable room in the college for it) where speeches were made and diplomas presented and essays read.[10] Then the curtain went down and the lights went out and we were left feeling suddenly a bit bewildered and lost and homesick – with the big, untried world before us and the jolly P.W.C. days behind.

The day before yesterday! But that yesterday was over thirty years ago – thirty years of such progress and the upsetting changes that come with progress as no thirty years of the world's history ever presented before. Think of it! When I went to Prince of Wales College there was not an automobile in the whole world or a traffic cop in America. Nobody but Darius Greene had ever flown.[11] No wireless.[12] No radio. No moving pictures. No X-Ray. No bobbed hair. No Charleston. No jazz. No Lloyd George.[13] No Bolsheviks. A peaceful world with even the Spanish-American war and the Boer unpleasantness far in the future, while the seed of the red harvest of 1914 was not yet even sown.[14] A slow world? Not a bit of it. Mad rushing around in a circle, as so many are doing to-day, isn't getting ahead. We were just as bright and ambitious and full of the joy of life as you are – and with precisely the same tendency to think pityingly of the preceding generation as old fogies who could hardly ever have known they were alive.

Speaking of bobbed hair reminds me that I haven't said a word of the fashions of the day before yesterday. Well, they were very charming. Yes, shriek at that if you will, girls, remembering the photographs your mothers hide out of sight. I repeat it. The "bell" skirts were graceful, the puffed sleeves (not the monstrosities of a few years later) were very pretty, the hats *were* hats and not eclipses. And the faces under them were just as bright and flower-cheeked as yours of to-day. Ask the boys of '94 if they weren't.

I am often asked the question, "What do you think of the young people of to-day?"

Why, I think a whole lot of them. They are just as nice as we were. It is said that it is a sign of old age when you begin to feel that the rising generation is possessed of the devil. So at that rate I am far from old age yet. Because I think youth is much the same from age to age, with the same hopes and dreams and fears and problems – and the same happy confidence that they are speedily going to set right whatever is wrong with the world. Girls wear short skirts and "bobs" where they wore long skirts and "puffs." But they are just like the girls of the day before yesterday. Boys wear Russian cuts where they wore Pompadours, but they have the same smirk for a pretty classmate. Oh, no, youth hasn't changed – never will change. Thank God for it.

When I glance over the P.W.C. Calendar for '94 I always feel a little sad nowadays. Of too many already can be said,

The Day before Yesterday

"By brooks too broad for leaping
Those light-foot boys are laid.
Those rose-lipped girls are sleeping
In fields where roses fade."[15]

But I don't want to end on a minor note. Neither shall I give any good advice. Nobody ever takes advice – least of all those who need it. So I'll just say in closing – try to know as much when you're forty as you know now. This is not sarcasm. Sarcastic people *do* say "Young people know it all."

And they *do*. All that is worth knowing. They know that the world is a beautiful place – that life is a great adventure to be taken gallantly – that something wonderful is just ahead over the crest of the next hill. Older people are apt to have forgotten these things. Hold fast to this knowledge, boys and girls of '27. And then for you your youth will always be just "the day before yesterday."

NOTES

1 Montgomery, 7 January 1910, in *SJLMM*, 1: 388.
2 *SJLMM*, 1: 401.
3 I have corrected the original, which reads "That is what is seems."
4 From "Circumstance" (1830), by Alfred, Lord Tennyson.
5 In Montgomery's era, the results of major examinations were published in local newspapers and were therefore a source of communal scrutiny. This convention became a source of major anxiety for Montgomery throughout the 1930s due to her sons' difficulties at university.
6 In her entrance examinations, Montgomery ranked fifth out of 264 candidates. Montgomery, 18 July 1893, in *SJLMM*, 1: 91.
7 I have corrected the original, which reads "next the windows."
8 From "To Helen" (revised 1845 version), a poem by Edgar Allan Poe (1809–1849), American author.
9 According to the bibliography by Russell, Russell, and Wilmshurst, Montgomery's contributions to *The College Record* included the playlet "The Usual Way," "Extracts from the Diary of a Second-Class Mouse," and "High School Life in Saskatchewan."
10 The Opera House was located on Fitzroy Street. Montgomery's essay on Shakespeare's "Portia" was subsequently published in three Charlottetown papers – the *Guardian*, the *Patriot*, and the *Examiner* – in June 1894.

11 From "Darius Greene and His Flying-Machine" (1869), a poem by John Townsend Trowbridge (1827–1916), American author.

12 The term "wireless" refers to wireless telegraphy, which allowed for Morse code to be transmitted across great distances without a wired connection. The term and its related technology were in vogue at the turn of the twentieth century.

13 David Lloyd George (1863–1945), Prime Minister of the United Kingdom from 1916 to 1922.

14 The term "red harvest," referring to the blood shed during the First World War, appears in "Epilogue, 1914," a poem in *All's Well*, by John Oxenham, pseudonym of William Arthur Dunkerley (1852–1941), English author and journalist.

15 From "With Rue My Heart Is Laden," a poem in *A Shropshire Lad* (1896), by A.E. Housman (1859–1936), English scholar and poet.

47

Who's Who in Canadian Literature:
L.M. Montgomery

—— 1927 ——

V.B. RHODENIZER

This profile by Vernon Blair Rhodenizer (1886–1968), professor of English at Acadia College in Nova Scotia and head of the department from 1918 to 1954, was published in the Toronto-based *Canadian Bookman*, by then an official publication of the Canadian Authors' Association, in August 1927.[1] In referring to *Anne of Green Gables* as a community novel, Rhodenizer echoes a similar claim made by J.D. Logan and Donald French in their book *Highways of Canadian Literature* (1924), in which they note that *Anne*, Marian Keith's *Duncan Polite*, and Nellie L. McClung's *Sowing Seeds in Danny* were part of the "real beginning of the Second Renaissance in Canadian fiction" of 1908. The "Community Novel," they suggest, "presented the adventure, the humor, and the pathos of the daily life of themselves, their neighbors, or their fellow-Canadians in other parts of the country and sometimes of other racial origins."[2] Two unidentified clippings in Montgomery's "Scrapbook of Reviews" provide further context for this piece: the first indicates that Rhodenizer had previously won a cash prize for an essay submitted to the "Why I Like Emily of New Moon" contest sponsored by McClelland and Stewart; the second indicates that he had published an earlier version of this essay before, in an unidentified periodical, shortly after the publication of *Emily Climbs*.[3]

Mrs. Lucy Maud Montgomery Macdonald was born at Clifton, Prince Edward Island, whence, in her early infancy, the family moved to Cavendish. After attending the district school there until she was sixteen years of age, she spent a year each at Prince of Wales College,

Charlottetown, and Dalhousie University, Halifax, Nova Scotia. In 1911 she married and moved to Leaskdale, Ontario, her present home.[4]

She inherited with her Scotch blood a strain of poetry, and has written nature verse, particularly of the sea, characterized by play of fancy rather than by descriptive vividness. There is a deeper poetry of life in her prose than in her verse. In her short stories and in her novels, especially in her treatment of child life, by throwing "a certain coloring of imagination"[5] over the humor and pathos of the incidents of common life as lived in a picturesque rural environment, she achieves a rare combination of truth and beauty that may best be described as poetic realism.

Her most important short stories have been published in two volumes. These are the cameo work or the miniature painting in her house of life. In them she shows a fine sense for the story values in single tragic or comic incidents or episodes in common life, and for idyllic settings and artistic skill in giving her material fictional form.

Her novels come under the classification "community novel." She is distinctive among the authors of this type of Canadian fiction in that she usually links her novels in series by continuing the story of important characters. *Kilmeny of the Orchard*, an idyllic love story, is complete in itself, but *The Story Girl* and *The Golden Road* are linked, the series connected by the character Anne contains six books, and there are two Emily books. Each series pictures realistically the life of young people, and yet there is freshness and originality of treatment in every volume.

The Anne series is a *comédie humaine* unparalleled in Canadian fiction. The first book of the series, *Anne of Green Gables*, is widely known as a fascinating story of the childhood and young girlhood of a remarkably sensitive and highly original character. In it, as the title indicates, the central interest is the influence of Anne upon the home into which she is adopted. *Anne of Avonlea* shows her sphere of influence widened to include the whole community in a special way, for she is now the teacher of the public school. *Anne of the Island* shows the heroine reflecting glory on her native province by her distinctive work in college. The last three of the Anne books give us glimpses of Anne's life as a woman. In *Anne's House of Dreams* she is the young wife of her former schoolmate, now Dr. Gilbert Blythe. In *Rainbow Valley* the interest shifts to Anne's children. She has six of them, and they make things as interesting as we should expect the children of such a mother to do. Moreover, they are ably supported by the four children of the manse. In *Rilla of Ingleside*, Anne's daughter Rilla is the central figure. The mother's personality, nevertheless, exerts an important influence throughout the series. To write such a series is a work of eminent literary distinction.[6]

The Emily series shows an improvement on the Anne series in some respects. Anne's characteristics were not accounted for. Emily's are. She inherits from her father the Starr emotional temperament and sense of beauty; from her mother the Murray strength of will and gift of second sight. In *Emily of New Moon*, the dramatic moments in Emily's life are the logical result of her inherited tendencies and the environment in which she is placed.[7] Characterization and plot are an organic unity. The interest aroused in Emily's literary ambitions is continued in *Emily Climbs*, to the end of her high-school period. Rejection slips make her realize the necessity of continuous practice in writing. A necessary promise to write no fiction for three years corrects her highly imaginative style by confining her to the writing of prose facts, and near the end of the book she is well on the way to literary fame. The characters, both juvenile and adult, are as vividly drawn in this as in the preceding volume, and fit as logically into the situations which constitute the plot.

Skill in logical characterization, as revealed in the Emily books, was a necessary prerequisite for successful fiction dealing primarily with adult characters. This our author first attempted in *The Blue Castle*, the story of a repressed, inhibited, introverted woman who, on being told by mistake at the age of twenty-nine that she will die of heart disease within a year, becomes emancipated and extroverted to the extent of marrying a Muskoka mystery man, author of nature books and son of a patent-remedy millionaire. Though the romantic plot makes the novel less poetically realistic than its predecessors, the characterization fulfills the promise of the Emily books, and the idyllic handling of the setting does justice to the Muskoka country and to the author.[8]

NOTES

1 This profile was updated and woven into Rhodenizer's chapter on "Other Novelists, Historical and Regional," in his book *A Handbook of Canadian Literature* in 1930.

2 Logan and French, *Highways of Canadian Literature*, 299, 298.

3 Unidentified and undated clipping, in SR, 232; V.B. Rhodenizer, "The Writings of L.M. Montgomery," unidentified and undated clipping, in SR, 234–35.

4 I have corrected the original, which reads "Leaksdale." Montgomery and her family had, in fact, left Leaskdale for Norval eighteen months prior to the publication of this article.

5 From "Preface to Lyrical Ballads" (1800), an essay by William Wordsworth.

6 In the earlier version of this article found in Montgomery's scrapbook, the preceding sentence is replaced by the following: "This last book of the Anne series is touched by the tragedy of the Great War. In thus tracing the story of Anne from early childhood to the time when she must be willing to sacrifice her son on the altar of Mars, our author has performed a work of eminent literary distinction" (Rhodenizer, "The Writings of L.M. Montgomery," unidentified and undated clipping, in SR, 234).

7 In the earlier version of this article, the following sentence appears here: "In fact it may be said that in this novel the great single scenes as well as the main and subsidiary plots as a whole are the logical and artistically true outcome of the contact of the various characters in the particular environment in which they live and move and have their being" (ibid.).

8 A "Check-List of First Editions" is appended to the original article, as is the following "Editor's Note": "Since the receipt of this article from Prof. Rhodenizer there has appeared the new Emily book, *Emily's Quest*, which has been added to the foregoing check-list, and which will be reviewed in the next issue of *Canadian Bookman*. It takes up the thread of Emily's story where *Emily Climbs* ended, and tells the love story that started there." Rhodenizer's review appears in Volume 3 of *The L.M. Montgomery Reader*.

48

About Canadian Writers: L.M. Montgomery, the Charming Author of "Anne"

—— 1927 ——

KATHERINE HALE

This article by Katherine Hale – pseudonym of Amelia Beers Warnock (1878–1956), journalist, poet, and short story writer who was also married to anthologist John W. Garvin – appeared in September 1927 in *The Canadian Countryman*, a Toronto farm magazine in which Montgomery's recent novel *The Blue Castle* (1926) was serialized in twenty-two instalments between 17 August 1927 and 14 January 1928. Stanley Baldwin (1867–1947), at the time serving the second of his three non-consecutive terms as Prime Minister of the United Kingdom, had requested to meet Montgomery during a tour of Canada that year. As he was quoted in an article published in *The Christian Science Monitor*, "I learned to love green gables and I wanted to see Anne."[1]

At the Ontario Government House Garden Party for T.R.H.'s, the Prince of Wales and Prince George of England, a few weeks ago, a little court surrounded the Premier of Great Britain and Mrs. Stanley Baldwin.[2] But among the four thousand guests of that afternoon one "literary lady," as certain critics designate us, was sure of more than a hurried handshake, and this was Mrs. Ewan Macdonald of Leaskdale, Ontario. For Mr. Baldwin had written to Miss L.M. Montgomery, Prince Edward Island, and the letter had been forwarded to her Ontario address, to say that he especially desired to meet, while in Canada, the author of *Anne of Green Gables*. And this garden party was the place of meeting.

Friends of this author's books are scattered over the English-speaking world.

Once, lunching with Basil King in Montreal,[3] he told me of a search for an English bookshop one rainy day in a European city. I think it was Florence. He needed a pleasant travelling companion, in the way of a novel, for further journeying. And now he had picked up the first book he saw, which was *Anne of Green Gables*, and opened it carelessly, and was caught up in delight at the opening chapter, which took him back to his beloved Maritime birthplace – "Our Island – The Island." "And I was so proud," he continued, "to return to my hotel and show the English and Americans there, a new book, a charming book, a book that had penetrated away down Europe to a bookshop in Italy, a book about Canada, beautifully written by a Canadian."

It was twenty years ago that Anne appeared upon the scene. It sold in hundreds of thousands, and its immediate successor *Anne of Avonlea*, which appeared in 1909, has had almost as large a sale. To supply the eager demand, eleven other books have followed the first two, the latest of which is *The Blue Castle*, just beginning serially in *The Countryman*.

What of the life story of this, perhaps best loved, of all Canadian fiction writers?

The story of her early life is woven closely with the Island in the Atlantic of which she writes so lovingly. Her first names, always disguised by initials, are Lucy Maud, and she was born at Clifton, Prince Edward Island, but lived in Cavendish nearby. Her father, Hugh John Montgomery, was also a native of Prince Edward Island, and her mother, Clara Woolner Macneill,[4] came from Cavendish – so they were all Island folk.

And the ancestry is unmistakably Scottish. There is at least one poet of note in the line, for Hector Macneill, who wrote those famous lyrics "Saw Ye My Wee Thing" and "Come Under My Plaidie" was a first cousin to her great-great-grandfather.

Miss Montgomery was educated at Cavendish, then at Charlottetown, and later took a special course in English and languages at Dalhousie College, Halifax. It was shortly afterwards, as a young girl, that she began to write her first story whose setting was the Island that was her home; an unaffected, natural, human story, devoid of the abnormal complex of sex that was to descend upon so many of the race of novelists a little later on, and therefore a story that was full of appeal to romantic youth, and to grown-up minds that had not shaken off the glamour of youth and its adventure.

There is no use explaining or describing the books that made this writer famous, for readers of the *Countryman* know and love them all. Because few people know her poetry I am tempted to quote two verses from "When the Dark Comes Down," which are full of the feeling of the sweet Island province which I also have the happiness to know, though, during the weeks I was there, I did not realize who was my near neighbor.

> When the dark comes down, oh, the wind is on the sea,
> With lisping laugh and whimper to the red reefs' threnody,
> The boats are sailing homeward now across the harbor bar
> With many a jest and many a shout from fishing grounds afar.
> So furl your sails and take a rest, ye fisherfolk so brown,
> For task and quest are ended when the dark comes down.

> When the dark comes down, oh, the landward valleys fill
> Like brimming cups of purple, and on every landmark hill
> There shines a star of twilight that is watching evermore
> The low dim-lighted meadows by the long dim-lighted shore,
> For there, where vagrant daisies weave the grass a silver crown,
> The lads and lassies wander when the dark comes down.[5]

NOTES

1 *The Christian Science Monitor*, "Mr. Baldwin Continues," 3.
2 The Prince of Wales (1894–1972), who became King Edward VIII in January 1936; Prince George (1895–1952), who took the throne as King George VI in December 1936, after his brother Edward abdicated; Lucy Baldwin (née Ridsdale) (1869–1945), who married Stanley Baldwin in 1892. For an account of this reception in Toronto in August 1927, see Montgomery, 7 August 1927, in *SJLMM*, 3: 351; *The Lethbridge Herald*, "Author of 'Green Gables.'"
3 Basil King (1859–1928), Charlottetown-born clergyman in Nova Scotia and Massachusetts who became a best-selling novelist after his retirement.
4 Here and throughout, I have corrected the original, which reads "MacNeil."
5 This poem, originally published in *The Youth's Companion* in 1907, appeared in both John W. Garvin's anthology *Canadian Poets* (1916) and in Montgomery's volume *The Watchman and Other Poems* (1916). The first two of three stanzas appear here.

49

On Being of the Tribe of Joseph

—— 1927 ——

AUSTIN BOTHWELL

This article by Austin Bothwell (1885–1928), a graduate of Oxford University whose anthology *English Master Poems* had been published in 1926, appeared in a December 1927 issue of *Saturday Night*. It sought to address the mystery of the term "tribe of Joseph," used in Montgomery's dedication, in her most recent novel *Emily's Quest*, to her first cousin Stella Campbell Keller. It is a variation on the phrase "the race that knows Joseph," coined by Stella's sister Frederica Campbell MacFarlane and attributed to the character Miss Cornelia in *Anne's House of Dreams*. Montgomery found the article amusing: as she commented in her journal and in almost identical form in a letter to Ephraim Weber, "he read a good deal more into it than it could carry ... and he is quite, quite wrong in saying that the real members of the race of Joseph do not *know* they are members. They jolly well know it."[1]

What are the qualifications that mark one as belonging to the tribe of Joseph? The dedication of one of this season's books "To ... of the tribe of Joseph" causes me to wonder. Why is it a distinction to belong to Joseph's rather than to Levi's or Simeon's tribe. It is I suppose due to the fact that Jacob on his death-bed blessed Joseph and his seed forever.[2] This is not to be a sermon but, haply, an essay so I shall content myself with quoting one verse of the dying man's lengthy blessing (they were giants in those days).

"The blessings of thy father have prevailed above the blessings of my progenitors unto the utmost bound of the everlasting hills; they shall be on the head of Joseph, and on the crown of the head of him that was separate from his brethren."[3]

"Separate from his brethren" – there we have it. That is the distinction. The author, who dedicates her book to a friend, who, like herself, belongs to the tribe of Joseph, conceives of herself and her friend as being like the Kangaroo, different from all other animals – as possessing certain qualities which alone are qualifications of tribal value à la Joseph.

Since the author is L.M. Montgomery one might speculate – and one will – as to whether those whom L.M. Montgomery includes in her tribe of Joseph are the same persons as Charles G.D. Roberts would include in his, or Nellie McClung in hers, or Stephen Leacock in his, or Robert Stead in his. At one and the same time, to wear the white ribbon and to be able to appreciate Haig and Haig; to condemn *Empty Hands* and to fill one's own; to mix with the millionaires and to sow seeds in Danny; to esteem Henry James; to be a Whitmaniac; no one person however protean could accomplish.[4] It would appear that the tribes of Joseph are as many as there were colors in his coat.

Well, it depends! If we may regard as belonging to the tribe of Joseph those who share our views, put first the first things we put first, follow in the wake of our enthusiasms – for the work of Marcel Proust or Joseph C. Lincoln; for the poetry of H.D. or Edgar A. Guest as the case may be – share our antipathies for jazz or Beethoven; for Thomas Hardy or Ethel M. Dell; laugh at the jokes we laugh at – not Scotch ones.[5] Then indeed the tribes of Joseph have inherited the earth, they are legion.[6]

But there is something wrong with this conception. Our tribe, Smith's tribe, Robinson's, would be in a continual state of flux, if common views were all, or mutual enthusiasms. Conceive Smith to get on in the world, as he so often does; those things he once put first he doesn't put first any longer. If he had the inclination to do so his wife wouldn't let him.[7] She has not now any time for first things, she is too busy cultivating the first persons. No longer do the Smiths feel that they and their friends are "separate" because of their mutual admiration for the poetry of Keats, or liking for long walks in the unspoiled country. They did have such friends once. But they are now to be designated quondam – hateful word!

The Ode to the Nightingale once inspired them,[8] now constantly engaged in keeping up with the Joneses they are haunted by owed to their creditors and their long walks are in pursuit of a white pellet over the smooth shaven sophisticated lawn of the Country Club. There, the tribe of Joseph is very exclusive. You must at least be in the six cylinder class to belong, for without are Fords. You may wear Joseph's coat of many colors there and it will be quite all right if you do not leave that garment behind which he forsook so perilously.

The idea that common interests constitute those who have them a tribe of Joseph may easily be reduced to absurdity. Bridge sharks are not Josephuses though possibly Bohankuses.[9] To possess the qualifications that entitle one to belong to the tribe of Joseph, it is not enough to share enthusiasms, to have similar views.

Perhaps to share a genuine passion, not a complex, is sufficient qualification. To have music in one's heart, to be so keenly interested in the drama as to be willing to stand hours in the queue for the chance to see "St. Joan,"[10] to starve for poetry's sake. That makes for separateness. When two or three are gathered together who are passionate pilgrims in search of beauty in any art, is there not constituted a tribe of Joseph? Across the abysses of convention, of fashion, of snobbism, that separate man from man, like calls to like when some passionate pursuit is common to each, whether the search for the perfect book or an eagerness to elucidate Egyptian hieroglyphics.

Yet it is plain that the scripture (and here let us be fundamentalists) bases the separateness of the tribe of Joseph on the possession by Ephraim and perhaps also Manasseh of certain moral qualities, of an attitude towards life more admirable than that of the tribe of Dan for instance.[11] "Dan shall be a serpent in the path, an adder in the path, that biteth the horse's heels so that his rider shall fall backward."[12]

There is a communality that holds together people more tightly than any other. Who never ate his bread with tears enters its pale very rarely. To "belong" here you must have gone down into the depths, wrestled for your soul with agony – had your intelligence awakened to a thousand shades and nuances that escape the prosperous, the materially successful. There must have been times in your life when Thought leapt out to wed with Thought – even the highest and best. You must have won through to a serenity of outlook, be above rancor, envy or jealousy, love all beauteous things, seek and adore them – look past the trumpery gauds of place and power to a far-shining goal whatever it may be. Here is the ultimate fellowship – to fare away home therein is to have lived not in vain.

"The point of honor is the simple secret of the few," wrote Alice Meynell.[13] Yet if one is too smugly conscious of belonging to the tribe of Joseph one doesn't remotely glimpse the point of honor. For, at the end of all, those who are of the tribe of Joseph are precisely those who do not think of themselves as so doing.

There is a novelist whom I have been tempted to admire but something has always acted as a drag on my enthusiasm. It is that she is conscious that she is achieving fine writing. It was therefore with some delight that I read a malicious comment upon her by Rebecca West that no one had ever written so pretentiously since St. Rose of Lima who claimed to write with a feather dropped from the wing of the Holy Ghost.[14]

> Modesty is the indispensable.
> "Thou hast cast down the mighty from their seats
> And hast exalted those of low degree."[15]

These lines from a poem popular with the instructors of youth in a pre-jazz age – ours – express exactly what happens to the self-consciously superior. It was Ephraim, the younger son of Joseph, upon whom Jacob laid his hand. It is the younger sons, the not-so-gifted, it is the Marthas often, when one had expected it to be the Marys, to whom the "full fair grace"[16] is given to be indisputably of the Tribe of Joseph. Their separateness is not aloofness, they move among us and their very being among us irradiates life. May their tribe increase.

NOTES

1 Montgomery, 17 December 1927, in *SJLMM*, 3: 361; see also Montgomery to Weber, 7 April 1929, in *AfGG*, 163.

2 In the Hebrew Bible, Jacob, grandson of Abraham, has twelve sons (whose offspring would become the twelve tribes of Israel) but favours his eleventh son, Joseph, who was born of his favourite wife, Rachel.

3 Genesis 49:26 in the Hebrew Bible.

4 Roberts, McClung, Leacock, and Stead, all best-selling authors in Canada during this era; Haig & Haig, the oldest distiller of scotch whisky; *Empty Hands*, a 1924 novel by Arthur Stringer; *Sowing Seeds in Danny*, a 1908 novel by Nellie L. McClung; Henry James (1843–1916) and Walt Whitman (1819–1892), American authors.

5 Marcel Proust (1871–1922), French author and critic; Joseph Crosby Lincoln (1870–1944), American author; H.D., born Hilda Doolittle (1886–1961), American author; Elgar Albert Guest (1881–1959), English-born American poet; Ludwig van Beethoven (1770–1827), German composer and pianist; Ethel M. Dell (1881–1939), English author of popular romance novels.

6 See Psalm 25:13 in the Hebrew Bible.

7 I have corrected the original, which reads "so to do."

8 Properly, "Ode to a Nightingale" (1819), a poem by John Keats (1795–1821), English Romantic poet.

9 From the 1891 American folk song "Bohunkus," about "a farmer who had two sons": "Bohunkus was the name of one / Josephus was the other's."

10 *Saint Joan* (1923), a play about the life of Joan of Arc, by George Bernard Shaw (1856–1960), Irish playwright. Montgomery was influenced by this play when she wrote a chapter on Joan of Arc in her non-fiction book *Courageous Women* (see chapter 59, in this volume).

11 In the Judeo-Christian tradition, Ephraim and Manasseh are sons of Joseph, whereas Dan is one of Joseph's older half-brothers and also father of one of the twelve tribes of Israel. Here and below, I have corrected the original, which reads "Ephriam."

12 Properly, "Dan shall be a serpent by the way, an adder in the path, that biteth the horse heels, so that his rider shall fall backward" (Genesis 49:17 in the Hebrew Bible).

13 From "The Point of Honor," appearing in *Essays* (1914), by Alice Meynell (1847–1922), English author and suffragist. I have corrected the original, which reads "Maynell."

14 Rebecca West, pseudonym of Cicely Isabel Fairfield (1892–1983), English author and critic. The author in question is Eleanor Mildred Sidgwick (1845–1936), Scottish activist for the higher education of women. In a review of Sidgwick's book *Hatchways* in *Daily News* in 1917, West claimed that, "with the possible exception of Angela Carranza (condemned by the Inquisition in Lima in 1684), who claimed to have written her revelations with a quill from the wing of the Holy Ghost, Miss E. Sidgwick is the most pretentious woman writer who ever lived" (West, *The Young Rebecca*, 337).

15 Properly, "He hath put down the mighty from [their] seats, and exalted them of low degree" (Luke 1:52 in the Christian Bible).

16 In the Christian tradition, Martha and Mary are sisters who invite Jesus into their home. Although Martha complains that she has been left with all the preparations and serving, Mary prefers to sit quietly and listen to what Jesus has to say. The phrase "full fair grace" is from *The Canterbury Tales*, a fourteenth-century collection of stories by Geoffrey Chaucer (ca. 1343–1400), English poet.

50

Minister's Wife and Authoress

— 1928 —

C.L. COWAN

In this interview with C.L. Cowan, then minister of St. Andrews Presbyterian Church in Ancaster, Ontario (outside Hamilton), Montgomery chatted amiably about her literary beginnings, her readership, and her views about the present generation. The article was published in the *Toronto Star Weekly* in December 1928, two months after she had finished her novel *Magic for Marigold*, which would be published in September 1929.

Twenty years ago I arrived in this land of promise, Canada. At that time two names loomed large on the literary horizon, that of Ralph Connor (Rev. C.W. Gordon, D.D.), whose domicile was in Winnipeg, the gateway of the far west, and that of L.M. Montgomery, who claimed the far east as her home. Ralph Connor swung into ken by his stirring tales of lumberjacks and rivermen, sky pilots and cowmen; L.M. Montgomery by her delightful, wholesome "Anne" series that depicted a life that profoundly differed in outlook and practice from the former.[1] It was natural that both should find a ready sale for their works for the fields explored were virgin and the writers excellent exponents of their craft. It must be a matter of considerable gratification to each of them that their products are still among Canada's best-sellers, and that each new book from their respective pens is signalled as an event in the literary world.

Some weeks ago the Presbyterian ministers of our city and their wives decided to have a banquet and the speaker chosen was L.M. Montgomery (Mrs. Ewan Macdonald), the manse, Norval, Ontario. She was invited to our home. I had had much experience of ministers' wives (I have lived with one for sixteen years) from Ontario to British Columbia and found them to be noble, self-sacrificing homemakers, hard-working, unpaid curates to their husbands almost without exception, but this was a new experience to meet a literary celebrity who was also a parson's wife. Just a short time before I had read that the Prince of Wales and Premier Baldwin of Great Britain desired to see her when in this country and that she had responded. Mr. Baldwin, according to newspaper report, had declared that one of his anticipated joys on coming to Canada was to meet L.M. Montgomery, the author of one of his favorite books, *Anne of Green Gables*. So it was with some trepidation that we awaited our distinguished guest. Authors are generally reputed to have certain peculiarities, born with them or diligently acquired. One literary genius never knew, never cared about meal hours. Bah! to eat food was a mundane exercise fit only for the common herd! Another was so absent-minded that not until his humiliated wife informed him did he know that he had joined in the applause that followed a speech he had made.

First Book Ran 500,000

However, we need not have been in any way perturbed over the coming of our guest. She quickly made herself at home, and ere many minutes had passed we were comfortably seated about a cheery fire talking like old friends.

She is a comely, comfortable looking lady. The years have dealt kindly with her; she still retains a fair share of her youthful looks, and the fine color swept into her cheeks by the wind of the north shore of Prince Edward Island still adorns her kindly face. Presently I steered the conversation round to her books. She has written fourteen, the last one being just forwarded to her publishers. *The Magic of Marigold* should have a fine reception.

As *Anne of Green Gables* is perhaps her best known work I inquired as to its circulation, and her guess was around 500,000. This must be near to a record for a Canadian story. Just recently I observed that R.E. Knowles, who has an admiring following in *The Toronto Star*, admitted proudly that his *St. Cuthbert's* had reached the 100,000 mark.[2] Perhaps Connor's *Sky Pilot* has reached more readers than *Anne of Green Gables*, but I have not heard.

A singular analogy exists in the matter of Sir Walter Scott's *Waverley* and *Anne of Green Gables* in that Sir Walter had thrown aside the manuscript of *Waverley* and apparently had forgotten all about it until he discovered it when he was searching for some fishing tackle. *Anne of Green Gables*, too, appears to have been cast into the limbo of forgotten things, for L.M. Montgomery found the M.S. in an old trunk or attic and decided that publishers would be given the privilege of looking it over. The results were unanticipated and gratifying, as the figures above reveal.

The publishing of books, especially first books, is largely a gamble. Somewhere I read that out of every thousand books printed six hundred never pay the cost of printing, two hundred just pay expenses, one hundred return a small profit and the remainder show a substantial profit. If these figures are approximately correct, publishing firms assume no small risk when they send forth a new volume. No wonder the colorful "jacket" has become a feature of astute modern book salesmanship. *Anne of Green Gables* came on to the retail counters of booksellers in the days when the aforementioned "clothing" was unthought of, and was almost immediately a best-seller. It had the guinea stamp!

New Generation Is O.K.

Since L.M. Montgomery's appeal is very largely to the young women of to-day, it was natural that she should be asked concerning them. "What is your opinion of girls of this so-called fast age?" she was queried. Her reply was definite, unhesitating: "Just as good as those of any other generation. There is a certain proportion of 'high-flyers' in every generation – the ages do not differ radically. Girls are freer to express themselves now. The pressure is off; that is about all the difference there is between our girls now and those of a bygone day."

"And so you think that the much-powdered and puffed, compacted and barbered, gay and daring young ladies of the present, generally speaking, will ultimately settle down to the humdrum business of marriage and all responsibilities it entails?"

A decided "I do" came from the famous novelist's lips. And as one who has had abundant opportunities for seeing the matter tested out I can corroborate L.M. Montgomery's opinion. Between thirty-five and forty brides stand before me yearly with their grooms. I visit a goodly proportion of their homes afterwards. With ninety-nine per cent. of them the little home is the paramount interest. Canada, I hardly imagine, need not be unduly worried over the nurseries of to-day and to-morrow.

One could see that Mrs. E. Macdonald – or L.M. Montgomery as the world prefers to call her – is a proud mother. She has two fine boys attending St. Andrew's College, near Toronto.[3] A rather embarrassing notice was printed in the society column of a 'way-down-east newspaper a year or two after her marriage. She told it against herself with glee. This paper announced that Miss L.M. Montgomery had arrived in the town for a visit with her young son! Her interest extends to the sports of her lads. We can imagine the tender pride that would light up her face when an extra letter came from one of them with the breath-taking news that he had made the rugby team!

The address of our guest to the Presbyterian ministers of Hamilton was informative and piquant. She told a few thrilling stories of a day that is swiftly passing down in Prince Edward Island. My interest centred in her literary reminiscences. The mail carries to her most interesting letters. They come from all parts of the world.

A Long Lost Uncle

In Australia, perhaps, she has as many admirers as anywhere else. There her books have the greatest sale in proportion to the population. A mother superior in an Australian convent in a letter expressed her thanks for the clean, inspiring note that runs through her books, and expressed the thought that the writer should be a Catholic. The lady further communicated to L.M. Montgomery that every night she knelt in the chapel and prayed that she might come to the light some day.

"I will tell you," confessed the speaker, "that her letter touched me deeply. It is something to know that one person in the world prays for me."

When *Anne of Green Gables* was first published under the name she continues to write under, a reader wrote to express her joy that she had found a lost relative. The letter began, "My dear long-lost uncle!" L.M. Montgomery was the name of the wandering uncle. The novelist was sorry to disillusion the correspondent.

Not all the letters received by L.M. Montgomery are so pleasant. She has not escaped the criticism of the "uncoguid."[4] Although no modern novelist, man or woman, is more careful in the materials that go to make up her stories, the very fact that she has allowed some of her male characters to court the goddess Nicotine brought wrath upon her. Her answer to one of these detractors was a reminder that probably the *Iliad* would not have been written had Helen been a perfect character, and had not Lucifer fallen the blind Milton would not have given to the world his incomparable *Paradise Lost*.[5] But this woman was not to be denied a come-back. She countered with the remark that it would be better to write dull books free from the taint of evil than interesting books smudged with "vice."

I had the pleasure of joining in moving a motion of thanks to L.M. Montgomery, and in the course of my remarks I confessed that my first story, a three-column affair, gained for me the magnificent sum of three dollars! When she responded she drew a laugh by confessing that her first literary effort was not so well rewarded. A florists' trade magazine printed her initial verses, and she was permitted, as a reward, to pick out seeds to the value of fifty cents! "I picked them out," she said, "and planted them in my garden. There was a riot of color for my pains. I have often wished that every ten lines I wrote since that time brought me as much happiness as those ten lines for which I got the seeds."

Every writer, I suppose, has the same thing to confess that there is no joy just quite like that of first breaking into print, and no reward quite as significant as the first, no matter how poor it may appear in comparison with later financial success.

L.M. Montgomery has plans for the future. She hopes some day to step out into the adult field, to write for a more mature class of readers (although even now she does not lack them) than she has done for so long. She has the ability and the temperament to do so, and a host of readers throughout the world will look for a new venture on her part confident that success will be the outcome.[6]

NOTES

1 Here and throughout, I have corrected the original, which reads "Ann."
2 *St. Cuthbert's*, an evangelical novel by R.E. Knowles published in 1905.
3 Stuart Macdonald had joined his brother at boarding school the preceding September.
4 Properly, "'the unco guid,' those who are professedly strict in matters of morals and religion" (*OED*), a term whose etymology derives from "Address to the Unco Guid, or the Rigidly Righteous" (1786), a poem by Robert Burns.
5 *The Iliad*, an ancient Greek epic poem attributed to Homer.
6 Her next novel, *A Tangled Web*, would prove to be a major departure for her in terms of characterization, narration, and plot. She began writing it in May 1929. See Montgomery, 3 May 1929, in *SJLMM*, 3: 396.

51

An Autobiographical Sketch

—— 1929 ——

L.M. MONTGOMERY

This essay, published in *Ontario Library Review* in February 1929,[1] follows a model that Montgomery used several times over the course of her career. Four slightly different versions of this "sketch" have so far been found, and many extracts appear in similar form elsewhere. In "How I Became a Writer," published in 1921 in the *Manitoba Free Press*, and in "Prince Edward Island's Famous Writer," published in 1940 in *The Maritime Advocate and Busy East*, Montgomery limits her ancestry to "Scotch ... with a dash of English,"[2] and her inclusion in this current essay of Irish and French ancestry anticipates an observation that she would make in a journal entry later that year: "I'm a queer mixture racially – the Scotch Macneills, the English Woolners and Penmans, the Irish of Mary McShannon (Hugh Montgomery's wife) and that far-off French descent."[3] (In her contribution to *The Junior Book of Authors*, published in 1935, she writes: "I came of Scotch ancestry with a dash of English, Irish, and French."[4]) Although Montgomery begins this essay by regretting that she cannot alter the facts of her own life to make them "far more interesting" to her readers, she tends to select and emphasize certain facts to tell a particular story about her life and professional origins. One of the only substantial variations in these four pieces is found in the final paragraph, in which she totals up the number of books she has published. In "How I Became a Writer," however, she adds a revealing paragraph about her most recent book: "In my latest story, *Rilla of Ingleside*, I have tried, as far as in me lay, to depict the fine and splendid way in which the girls of Canada reacted to the Great War – their bravery, patience and self-sacrifice. The book is theirs in a sense in which none of my other books have been; for my other books were written for anyone who might like to read them; but *Rilla* was written for the girls of the great young land I love, whose destiny it will be their duty and privilege to shape and share."[5]

I wish it were permissible to write fiction about oneself when asked for "an autobiographical sketch." I get so tired of writing the same old facts over and over. As *Anne* herself said, I could imagine a heap of things about myself far more interesting than what I know![6] Any one of the "dream lives" I have lived by the score would be really thrilling.

I was born – praise to the gods! – in Prince Edward Island – the colourful little land of ruby and emerald and sapphire.[7] I come of Scotch ancestry, with a dash of English and Irish from several "grands" and "greats" and a French origin back in the mists of antiquity. The Montgomerys emigrated from France in the wake of a French Princess who married a Scottish King. But they became so Scotchified eventually that they even had a tartan of their own.[8]

My mother died when I was a baby and I was brought up by my grandparents in the old Macneill homestead at Cavendish – eleven miles from a railway and twenty-four from a town, but only half a mile from one of the finest sea-beaches in the world – the old North Shore.

I went to the "district school" there from six to sixteen. Out of school I lived a simple wholesome happy life on the old farm, ranging through fields and woods, climbing over the rocky "capes" at the shore, picking berries in the "barrens" and apples in the big orchards. I am especially thankful that my childhood was spent in a spot where there were many trees – trees with personalities of their own, planted and tended by hands long dead, bound up with everything of joy and sorrow that visited my life. The old *King* orchard in my books, *The Story Girl*, and *The Golden Road*, was "drawn from life."

My little existence was very simple and quiet. But it never held a dull moment for me. I had in my imagination a passport to fairyland. In a twinkling I could whisk myself into regions of wonderful adventure, unhampered by any restrictions of reality.[9]

For anything I know I might have been born reading and writing. I have no recollection of learning to do either. I devoured every book I could lay my hands on and knew most of *Paradise Lost* and *The Pilgrim's Progress* by heart when I was eight. Novels were taboo, but fortunately there was no ban on poetry. I could revel at will in "the music of the immortals"[10] – Tennyson, Byron, Scott, Milton, Burns.[11] And one wonderful day when I was nine years old I discovered that I could write "poetry" myself!

It was called "Autumn," and I wrote it on the back of an old post-office "letter bill" – for writing paper was not too plentiful in that old farmhouse, where nothing was ever written save an occasional letter. I read it aloud to father. Father said it didn't sound much like poetry. "It's blank verse," I cried. "Very blank," said father.

I determined that my next poem should rhyme. And I wrote yards of verses about flowers and months and trees and stars and sunsets and addressed "Lines" to my friends. When I was thirteen I began sending verses to the Island weekly paper – and never heard either of or from them. Perhaps this was because I did not send any return stamps – being then in blissful ignorance of such a requirement.

Before this, however, when I was eleven years old, I had begun writing stories. I had a boxful of them – many tragic creations in which nearly everybody died. The "happy ending" was a thing unknown to me then. In those tales, "battle, murder and sudden death"[12] were the order of the day.

When I was fifteen I had my first ride on a railway train, and it was a long one. I went out to Prince Albert, Saskatchewan, and spent a year with father who was living there. During that winter I sent a "poem," written around one of the dramatic legends of the old North Shore, down to the Charlottetown *Patriot* – and the *Patriot* printed it – thereby giving me the greatest moment of my life!

Being now, as I thought, fairly launched on a career, I kept on sending verses to various papers and began to plume myself on being quite a literary person. I returned to Prince Edward Island the next summer, attended school for another year, then went to Prince of Wales College, Charlottetown, to qualify for a teacher's license. After that I taught a year. During these years I was writing all sorts of stuff, mainly verses and short stories, but had never succeeded in getting into any periodical that paid anything. All the stuff I sent to other magazines came promptly back. I used to feel woefully discouraged at times over those icy little rejection slips. But I kept on.[13] Whatever gifts the gods had denied me they had at least dowered me with stick-to-it-iveness!

After teaching a year I went to Halifax and spent a winter taking a selected course in English literature at Dalhousie College. One day in that winter I got a letter from the editor of an American juvenile magazine accepting a short story I had sent him and enclosing a check for five whole dollars. Never in all my life have I felt so rich as I did then! Did I spend it for needed boots and gloves? I did not. I wanted to get something I could keep forever in memory of having "arrived." I hied me down town and purchased leather-bound dollar editions of Milton, Byron, Wordsworth, Longfellow and Tennyson. I have repented me of many things rashly bought in my life, but never of those. I have them yet – dingy and shabby now – but with the springs of eternal life still bubbling freshly in them. Not that I do not love many modern poets. I do. But the old magic was good and remains good.

I taught two more years. Then grandfather died and I went home to stay with grandmother. She and I lived there alone together in the old farmhouse for thirteen years, with the exception of one winter which I spent in Halifax working as proof-reader and general handy-man on the staff of the *Daily Echo*. In those years I wrote literally thousands of poems and stories – most of the latter being juveniles for the United States periodicals, the Canadian magazine market at that time being practically non-existent.

I had always hoped to write a book – but I never seemed able to make a beginning. I have always hated beginning a story. When I get the first paragraph written I always feel as if it were half done. To begin a *book* seemed quite a stupendous task. Besides, I did not see how I could get time for it – I could not afford to take time from my regular writing hours. In the end I never deliberately set out to write a book. It just "happened."

In the spring of 1904 I was looking over my note book of plots for an idea for a short serial I had been asked to write for a certain Sunday School paper. I found a faded entry, written many years before, "Elderly couple apply to orphan asylum for boy. By mistake a girl is sent them." I thought this would do. I began to "block out" the chapters, devise incidents, and "brood up" my heroine. *Anne* began to expand in such a fashion that she soon seemed very real to me. I thought it rather a shame to waste her on an ephemeral seven-chapter serial. Then the thought came, "Make a book of it. You have the central idea and the heroine. All you need do is to spread it over enough chapters to amount to a book."

The result was *Anne of Green Gables*. I wrote it in the evenings after my regular day's work was done. The next thing was to find a publisher. I typed it myself on my old second-hand typewriter that never made the capitals plain and wouldn't print "w" at all. Then I began sending it out – and kept on, because the publishers did not jump at it. It came back to me five times. The sixth time it was accepted. *Anne of Green Gables* was published in 1908. I did not dream it would be the success it has been. I thought girls in their teens might like it but that was the only audience I hoped to reach. Yet men and women who are grandparents, boys at school and college, statesmen at the helm of empires, soldiers in the trenches, old pioneers in the Australian bush, missionaries in China, monks in remote monasteries, Mohammedans in Java,[14] and red-headed girls all over the world have written to me of the delight they found in *Anne*.

With the publication of *Green Gables* my long struggle was over. Since then I have published thirteen novels and a volume of poems. Poetry was my first love and I have always regretted being false to it. But one must live.

Seventeen years ago I married a Presbyterian minister and came to Ontario to live. I like Ontario muchly but anyone who has once loved "the only Island there is" never really loves any other place. And so the scene of all my books, except the *Blue Castle*, has been laid there.[15]

The "Blue Castle" is in Muskoka. Muskoka is the only place I've ever been in that could be my Island's rival in my heart. So I wanted to write a story about it.

My new book, *Magic for Marigold*, will be out next summer. I've gone back to "The Island" in it. For there the fairies still abide, despite the raucous shrieks of motor cars. There are still a few hidden spots where one who knows may find them.[16]

NOTES

1 This piece was summarized in a *Mail and Empire* article entitled "Poetry Her First Love Says L.M. Montgomery," whose subhead reads "Revealing Glimpse of Canadian Writer Given by Herself."

2 Montgomery, "How I Became a Writer," 3; Montgomery, "Prince Edward Island's Famous Writer," 44.

3 Montgomery, 27 June 1929, in *SJLMM*, 3: 398.

4 Montgomery, "L.M. Montgomery," 261.

5 Montgomery, "How I Became a Writer," 3.

6 In *Anne of Green Gables*, Anne tells Marilla that "what I *know* about myself isn't really worth telling," but that "if you'll only let me tell you what I *imagine* about myself you'll think it ever so much more interesting" (*AGG*, 38).

7 Montgomery first uses this phrase in a journal entry dated 15 July 1923, in *SJLMM*, 3: 136. It recurs in later essays in this volume.

8 For more on the ancestry of the Montgomery name, see Gray, *The Montgomerys*.

9 This paragraph appears with slight modifications in *AP*, 47.

10 This quotation also appears in *AP*, 49; *RV*, 17.

11 In the 1921 and 1940 versions of this article, this list includes "Longfellow, Tennyson, Whittier, Scott, Byron, Milton, Burns" (Montgomery, "How I Became a Writer," 3; Montgomery, "Prince Edward Island's Famous Writer," 44).

12 From *Hard Times* (1853), a novel by Charles Dickens.

13 In the version of this sketch that appears in *The Junior Book of Authors*, the tone is much more optimistic: "During those and the following years I wrote all kinds of stuff. Most of it was rejected but enough was accepted to encourage me. Eventually I won a place as a writer of stories for young people" (Montgomery, "L.M. Montgomery," 261).

14 Although the term "Mohammedan" refers to "an adherent of the religion of the prophet Mohammad; a follower of Islam, a Muslim," the *OED* adds that "the term is not employed or favoured by Muslims, and its use is now widely seen as depreciatory or offensive."

15 In the 1935 and the 1940 versions of this piece, Montgomery adds a sentence here: "And in my dreams I go back to it" (Montgomery, "L.M. Montgomery," 262; Montgomery, "Prince Edward Island's Famous Writer," 46).

16 A bibliography of Montgomery's books – including *The Watchman and Other Poems* but excluding *Further Chronicles of Avonlea* – appears in the original publication but is omitted here.

52

Modern Girl Defined by Noted Writer

— 1929 —

In this reported speech, published in the *Georgetown Herald* in May 1929, Montgomery addresses faculty and students at the Macdonald Institute and the Ontario Agricultural College, two colleges in Guelph that merged with the Ontario Veterinary College in 1964 to form the University of Guelph, whose library archives now house a sizeable L.M. Montgomery Collection, including journals, scrapbooks, artifacts, and copies of her books from around the world. Although here she notes that the modern girl must change her outlook in order to succeed professionally in a world that has recently opened up to her, the options that she encourages young people to pursue are rarely those that she includes in her fiction and contrast rather noticeably with her statements about working women given in chapter 45, "Famous Author and Simple Mother," by Norma Phillips Muir, earlier in this volume.

Speaking before an audience of over 600 people in the O.A.C. dining hall on a recent evening, Mrs. L.M. Macdonald of Norval,[1] better known to the readers of fiction as L.M. Montgomery, declared that the modern girl was in no respect worse, and in many respects better than the girl of former generations.

The occasion was the final session of one of the most successful Girls' Conferences in the history of the Junior Women's Institute movement when the delegates with the faculty and students of Macdonald Institute, the faculty and fourth year students of the Ontario Agricultural College, and a number of friends, met for a farewell dinner.

The speaker of the evening was Mrs. L.M. Macdonald, who has written several books about girls, and who proceeded to give her opinion of the girl of to-day.

"It used to be the opinion of the parents, some years ago," said Mrs. Macdonald, "that the young people were fools because they would not listen to the advice of their elders, but that opinion is giving way to a better one, namely, that the young people now know a great many things that their parents have forgotten. Girls of the present generation are no different fundamentally, from the girls of twenty or thirty years ago, for they have the same ideals, likes and dislikes that their mothers and grandmothers had."

"Not so very long ago, the vocations open to girls who wanted to earn their own living were very few being chiefly teaching and dressmaking, but to-day there are very few professions that are not practiced by women as well as men, and in order to meet these changed conditions and increased number of opportunities, the modern girl has had to change her whole outlook. Where formerly she had to accept what was given her, she can now go out into the world and compete successfully with the men, which has created in her a new spirit of independence that is often mistaken for degeneration."

In the opinion of Mrs. Macdonald, the making of a home is the greatest of all careers for a girl, and she cannot make too much preparation for the pursuit of that career, and now that the system of education in Canada offers equal advantages to both young men and women, she can take her place in the home without the least feeling of inferiority to her husband.

For the benefit of those who were intending to enter business or professional life, the speaker told the story of how her first book was written and gave a graphic picture of the difficulties she overcame before it was published finally winning out through perseverance.

In conclusion, Mrs. Macdonald[2] extended to the delegates and the faculty and students of MacDonald's her best wishes for success in their chosen fields of endeavor, and assured them that if they kept to their ideals they would not fail in whatever they undertook.

NOTES

1 I have corrected the original, which reads "McDonald."
2 I have corrected the original, which reads "MacDonald."

53

L.M. Montgomery's Ideas

—— 1930 ——

In this set of letters published in the "Public Forum" column of the Charlottetown *Guardian* in August and September 1930, we see a tense discussion of the interplay among fiction, place, and readership. It begins with a letter by a tourist who took issue with Montgomery's depiction of a PEI community in *Magic for Marigold*, which had been published the preceding fall. Four responses appeared before Montgomery herself took the stage. Although she tended normally to be modest about her international success, her response here indicates that she could stand up for herself when attacked. Montgomery's "Scrapbook of Reviews" contains all six letters reprinted here, along with a seventh column of reviews of *Magic for Marigold* published in a variety of newspapers.[1]

Letter 1 – 12 August 1930

Sir:– This is my second summer on the Island. I love it here; appreciate its people and look forward to coming again. As an interested visitor, I was anxious to get some books that intimately spoke of the life and traditions of its people.

I was informed that Miss L.M. Montgomery, a native of the Island has graphically written many books on the Island. This writer is very popular in the States. However I have never read her books and when her name was suggested to me I immediately procured a book.

As I scanned over the pages lazily before commencing to read I was agreeably pleased to see the names of Charlottetown, Summerside and

Harmony mentioned in her book. By the way I was fortunate in getting her latest book, 1930, and so I felt I would get a modern version of the Island and so with a pleasurable emotion sat down to read.

Imagine my wonder and may I also add "laughter" when I read twelve pages of her *Magic for Marigold* to find such peculiar, antiquated customs here. Her assertions were so mosaic – I really must confess they were a revelation to me and of course were delightful and funny, but coming from the States where such customs were never known and such behaviour I put my thinking cap on and began to ask myself a few stern questions.

I should like readers in Charlottetown and nearby to write in to the newspaper advising its foreigners as to whether or not Miss Montgomery is sincere or not. After all outsiders are entitled to know the Island sincerely. If her book is true, then we have no right as strangers to criticize the thoughts and life of its people, but if Miss Montgomery's writings are fictitious and untrue, then this lady has no right using the names of its villages and towns and belittling its inhabitants. After all her books travel here and abroad. If I lived on the Island – belonged to that "purple clan" of aristocracy that she so well emphasizes, I would certainly resent her exposing such bigotry if it were unreal. I would resent her touching on the intimate lives of its pioneers.

I am going to give a few excerpts from her book so that those who have not read it may know. These few incidents ought to start the ball rolling. If the Islanders know of such people as Miss Montgomery describes, in all fairness to her, they should advise us. It will thus clear up a matter for those visiting this Island and seeing it through the eyes of Miss Montgomery's book.

She writes of a family, "born to the purple," all related to one another. They even know the pedigree of their cats.[2] And yet the uncle, an unmarried wealthy man, who has travelled a lot, comes back to the Island and finds its girls unsuitable for marriage. They either have too thick ankles, pudgy hands, ornamental by candlelight but unbearable at breakfast – a purring, blinking, sidling, clawing bunch, gifted with tongues of gossip and temper.[3]

In this well known family, that are all intermarried, a name must be given to the latest offspring and the most prominent relatives are invited to decide upon a fitting name. After hours of debating, everybody's feelings are hurt and the Clan leaves for their respective homes, "tails up" as Miss Montgomery words it, and wives go on hunger strikes because they were slighted – affectionate sisters refuse to talk to one another. There are a dozen marital ruptures. A thirty years of happiness in one home is destroyed and the wife goes home for three weeks. An engagement trembles. Throbbings in the neck of a prominent aunt become more frequent. A poetess even stops writing because the suggestion of a name was unheeded.[4] Now can it be possible that such families are on the Island among the "deep purple." I wonder.

"Hope you eat a good supper before you go visiting aunt Harriet from Charlottetown," says Grandmother Lesley to her children. "You won't get much at Harriet's. She thinks starving her guests is living the simple life. Aunt Harriet always fills the cups too full on purpose so there'll be no room for cream. Harriet can make a pitcher of cream go farther than any woman I know."[5]

Then grandma today remembers how her marital happiness was destroyed by Grandfather who spilled soup over her purple dress because he did not like the color and to this late date she tells her grandchild, Miss 1930 who is 8 years of age, "he has been dead for over 40 years but if he were here now, I'd like to slap his face for that dress."[6]

One cousin in Harmony had quite a lot of children. The mother-in-law felt that her son had to keep to the grindstone and so did not want her daughter-in-law to have such a large family. "I had twins twice just to spite her," this lady says.[7]

Must we outsiders form our opinion of the inner life and circle of this Island through Miss Montgomery's books? She is a real Islander, born to the "purple" and lived here and is her delineation of its people right. I wonder.

I am Sir, etc.

Mrs. Edith Frank Fisher

Letter 2 – 19 August 1930

Sir, – In regard to Mrs. Fisher's criticism of L.M. Montgomery's book, *Magic for Marigold*, I may say that I live in the country and that I never knew of such stupid, ridiculous and monstrous criticisms as those mentioned. In any community in the world you might possibly get one of the Aunt Harriet type, but on the whole our people are hospitable to a fault, ready at all hours to supply the milk of human kindness, their actions brimming over with cream, and more especially this summer when it is at a discount. The old Scotch people had a fashion of calling more than one member of the family by the same name on account of its popularity, and not from a dearth of names; but there never was any family revolutions on account of child naming. This book must be purely fiction, but, if good fiction should depict life in its real sense, then such literature is evil and a source of injury to our Province.

I am Sir, etc.,
Islander

Letter 3 – 22 August 1930

Sir, – I, too, have read *Magic for Marigold* and found it vastly entertaining as Pepys would say.[8] A correspondent of the Public Forum recently condemned this book as derogatory to the people of Prince Edward Island, or, as an alternative, insincere. To my mind it is neither the one nor the other. The authoress writes of what may be termed semi-pioneer days; Marigold is not "Miss 1930," she is "Miss Thirty-years-ago."[9] Old Grandmother, who is really Marigold's great-grandmother, and a worthy companion to the satirical old Lord Saltire of Henry Kingsley's *Ravenshoe*,[10] carries the speech and manner of a still earlier day. In those by-gone times, when ready money was seldom seen, when home comforts were of the crudest, when commercialized amusements were non-existent, the people were more independent of their fellows; and more original in their ways and sayings. Lying away from the beaten track into Canada, they, like Caesar's Belgae, were "horum omnium fortissimi"[11] – of all these most warlike – and for the same reason: they were at the greatest distance from the polite fashions and civilized manners of the capital, and "merchants did not often repair to them and carry in those things which serve to effeminate their spirit." Thus it happened, in the brave days of old, that no festival, election meeting, or "tea party," was exactly normal, if it did not end in a bout of fisticuffs and men still live who performed heroic deeds on such occasions. That the ladies of those times should quarrel at the selection of Marigold's name is not a matter of surprise; such umbrage is not unknown even today.

The bachelor in the story who says that the girls of his acquaintance have thick ankles and pudgy faces, must not be taken too seriously:[12] he is putting up his best bluff in defence of his unhappy position, and after all he marries an Island girl. Doubtless there are girls with thick ankles still to be found on the Island and good luck to them say I, for they are more likely to become the progenitors of a sturdier race than are the "skinny" creatures which the fashion papers hold up as the feminine ideal.

No, Marigold is not of the present day: a dreamer of dreams,[13] an idealist, who looks to a golden future, she differs from "Miss 1930," whose time is the present, and whose view is bounded by the car, the pictures and whatever amusement can be got out of life.

In many other respects the people of this Province have progressed, I had almost said marvellously even during the past two decades. The Great War, deplorable as it was, opened their hearts. Their patriotism was never in question, but previously their views were narrow, and they gave little heed to the rest of the world. But the catastrophe taught them that they also were their brothers' keeper, and money and goods to relieve the suffering of other lands poured out of the Island in amazing quantity. Self faded largely from the picture and a fine sympathy took its place. This sympathy with its twin sister courtesy is surely the trait which your correspondent finds so admirable in the people of today. But it "was not attained by sudden flight,"[14] and little of it existed in "Marigold's" time.

Scott, Barrie, Hall Caine,[15] and a galaxy of other writers, have presented us with characters which at first glimpse may seem derogatory to their countrymen, but are not so when we consider that they are drawn from more primitive times.

The two cats "Lucifer" and "The Witch of Endor" are another "rock of offence"[16] to your correspondent. Read what Sir Walter Scott said to Washington Irving on the subject of the despised felines: "Ah," said he, "these cats are a very mysterious kind of folk. There is always more passing in their minds than we are aware of. Our Grimalkin here reminds me by the airs of sovereignty which he assumes that he may be a great prince incog., and that he may come some time or other to the throne."[17] With such an opinion before her the authoress may neglect the criticism of her pets.

I am, Sir, etc.,
An Outsider

Letter 4 – 25 August 1930

Dear "Outsider" – I am an "Insider" and have just read *Magic for Marigold* by our own Lucy Montgomery. You defend the authoress by saying she is writing of the "semi-pioneer" of thirty years ago. I belong to those mothers of thirty years ago. We hardly called ourselves "semi-pioneer" individuals. Two hundred years ago would sound much better, and so I resent this imputation.[18] I feel we are being caricatured in a very uncharitable vein. You are therefore jumping from the frying pan into the fire.

We were, thirty years ago, a richer body of men and women. There was no stock-market to suppress our saving quality. We certainly were more hospitable than the present generation and it did not need the Great War of 1914 to bring out our sympathetic qualities, or "open our hearts." I doubt if we had any "Aunt Harriets." If a weary traveller stopped at our farm, he was never questioned as to ways and means. He was fed and gladly given a bed; even clothes. Who thought of being paid! I'm afraid our Lucy Montgomery is laughing up her sleeves and using us as a gay "piece de resistence," very uncharitable of her. You call our views narrow and that we "were at the greatest distance from polite fashions and civilized manners." If we had all these qualities as Miss Lucy claims would our present generation of boys and girls be what they are? Aren't they a splendid type of manhood and womanhood? And when they do leave the Island, taking with them all their inherited good qualities, and come back, what do they bring with them? So, dear "Outsider" you again wrong us as to the Island.

You may be an excellent Latin scholar – a thorough Epicurean on food and vitamin, but on "Legs" – thick Legs, dear me "No." Ten times *no*. Hoot man! A Kingdom for a pair of Legs – a dainty pair of fairy feet, dancing their toes into the heart of a man. Mark Antony lost his Empire when he looked at the fair Cleopatra's limbs. I have yet to find a Beauty Contest throughout the world that will award its prize to thick ankles. I do not agree with you "Outsider" that "thick ankles are more likely to become the progenitors of a sturdier race." I do say however, that thanks to the present generation of good physical exercises, long walks, etc., we do have a sturdier race.

I am afraid Miss Lucy Montgomery has a lot to reckon with, if she is poking fun at the "semi-pioneers of thirty years ago."

I am, Sir, etc.
An Insider

Letter 5 – 27 August 1930

Sir, – In your issue of August 12th, there appears a somewhat lengthy epistle under the heading "L.M. Montgomery's Ideas," signed by a lady who resides in the U.S. and who visited our "Garden of the Gulf."

In a somewhat sarcastic manner she undertakes to criticize the latest book *Magic for Marigold* from the pen of our beloved authoress, "L.M. Montgomery." It seems to me it will be quite time enough for our visitors to question the truth of L.M. Montgomery's statements when we begin to do so.

Do not all authors draw somewhat on their imagination?

And many such characters as those mentioned by L.M.M. in her books may be met with today in P.E.I., and could, I am sure, be found in any civilized part of the world. There must always be some difference in the lives and opinions of those dwelling in country villages and those dwelling in the city.

But whether the people of P.E. Island dwell in the city or country, they are the most patriotic people in the world, also I think the most hospitable and many will resent the criticism of the books of our Island authoress.

I am, Sir, etc.

(Mrs.) A.M.C.

Savage Harbor, P.E.I.

Letter 6 – 1 September 1930

Sir, – Recently a letter ... of which the logic and sense of humour appeared to be about on a par ... appeared in your columns, attacking my book, *Magic for Marigold*. I had a good laugh over this letter and had no intention of taking any notice of it. But others have followed it containing statements and insinuations which, in justice to myself, I cannot ignore.

I am accused of "caricaturing" the people of P.E. Island ... of "laughing in my sleeves" at them. I am a daughter of Prince Edward Island and I yield to none, not even affectionate visitors from "the States" in my love and admiration for its people and the land of my birth. And I have never insulted them by supposing that they were so provincial and "back-country" as not to be able to endure a little friendly humour, even at their own expense ... nor do I now suppose it, in spite of some self-evident exceptions as shown by "*Insider's*" letter.

I do not know what one of your correspondents means by speaking of the "customs" in *Magic for Marigold* as being "Mosaic and antiquated." I doubt if she knows herself. The heroine of the book is a little girl, living a very quiet life in a P.E. Island farm community, and I mentioned only such family customs as reacted on her development. P.E. Islanders can afford to be called Mosaic. I consider it a compliment. Moses and his law are still, I am glad to say, considered reasonably up-to-date among us and for that we have no need to be ashamed, even before visitors from the States where the Ten Commandments seem to have been thrown overboard completely. Perhaps our customs are "antiquated." We still have families and family reunions, family loyalties, christening parties ... and we still go to church. We do not have gang murders, lynchings, divorce and companionate marriage,[19] so no doubt we are very old-fashioned, and books about us must to that extent be old-fashioned too.

I was born and brought up in the very heart of three of our old "pioneer" clans, and I know them from A to Z, as not even a lady who has spent two whole summers on the Island can do. I know their virtues and their faults ... for even P.E. Island pioneers and their descendants have faults. I have a few myself. I know instances of tragedy and comedy beside which the fictitious incidents of my books pale into insignificance. I know their fierce spats among themselves and their equally fierce loyalty when any outsider attacks them. Nor does this date only to pioneer days. Last summer when I was on the Island I was regaled with an account of a recent "clan" row which both for tragedy and comedy surpassed anything I ever invented. Human nature does not change. It is the same now as it was in pioneer days.

I am accused of "caricaturing" the Islanders because I make a tormented old bachelor declare that one girl has thick ankles, because I make one clan member say of another that she is very economical with the cream, and because one old lady says that she had twins twice to spite her mother-in-law. Could crossness and provincialism go further? One would suppose that even a person who was absolutely joke-blind could not take that seriously. Twins are not so obligingly subject to order. And I have, it seems, "no right" to use the "real names" of places when I "belittle" the inhabitants. If the poor soul who perpetrated the foregoing absurdity reads in future some novel of life in New York or Toronto wherein some of the inhabitants are "belittled," I suppose she will write straightway to some metropolitan paper arraigning the author. Let Sinclair Lewis, Theodore Dreiser and Mazo de la Roche stand from under in time.[20]

I suppose there is at least one woman in P.E. Island who is mean, and at least one girl who has thick ankles. I avow ... let the consequences be what they may ... that I have known a few myself. Do my fellow-islanders want me to depict them as wingless angels, perfect in every respect ... and as dull and insipid and uninteresting as such creatures would be? No, I have too much respect for their common sense to think that of them. I believe that most of the Island people have outgrown the Elsie books.[21]

There are people ... it may be even in P.E. Island ... who are so "back-country" as to imagine that everything a writer puts into the mouths of her characters is an echo of her own opinions, but I think there are not many of them. Most of our people have sufficient intelligence to distinguish between humour and caricature, and as for the few who cannot, may God have mercy on their souls.

Marigold is not intended to be "Miss 1930" or Miss Any-age. She is ... or is intended to be ... one of those ageless daughters of imagination and vision that are found occasionally in every age of a nation's history. I do not pretend that her type is common, but it exists. As for the other characters in my books, not one of them is "drawn from life" ... though I doubt not that the provincial type of mind aforesaid imagines that I go about with a sort of mental camera photographing my unfortunate friends and acquaintances for immediate use. My characters are "types" that are found wherever human beings congregate and I cannot help it if an occasional cap fits.

Yes, "after all" ... as one of your correspondents so condescendingly remarks ... my books do "travel abroad." My audience is not wholly in Prince Edward Island. And from all over the world thousands of letters come to me annually telling me that my books have filled the writers with a wish to see P.E. Island because I have depicted it as such a charming place. Even ... as some of your readers may recall ... so insignificant a person as the Hon. Stanley Baldwin, then Premier of Great Britain, asked the Dominion Government to include Prince Edward Island in his itinerary of 1927 because he had become so interested in it through reading my books. I do not know of any other province in Canada which was so honoured for a similar reason. But then poor Mr. Baldwin had never enjoyed the inestimable advantage of being a native of "the States."

I do not think I, or my writings, have done my dear island or its people any harm. For proof I quote the concluding paragraph from a review of Marigold published in a prominent literary journal in Great Britain:

"We have only one fault to find with this very charming book. We are afraid that Mrs. Montgomery has idealized the people of Prince Edward Island slightly. We feel sure that not in any country in the world can there be found so many delightful and interesting people to the square mile as Mrs. Montgomery depicts in 'the Island.'"

In view of the foregoing I think neither the anxious lady from the States nor "Insider," need worry as to the impression of P.E. Island and its people made on the world at large by my books.

I write fiction ... not history or biography. And I shall continue to write of P.E. Island and its people as I see them, through loving and sympathetic eyes: but I shall not be deterred from poking a little kindly fun at some[22] of their foibles ... or even their faults ... for fear that I shall offend the susceptibilities of visitors from "the States" or even of ultra thin-skinned islanders themselves.

Thanking you, sir,

I am, Sir, etc.,

L.M. Montgomery Macdonald

NOTES

1 See *The Guardian*, "Some Reviews of 'Magic for Marigold.'"

2 *MM*, 1.

3 *MM*, 7–8.

4 *MM*, 20. Obadiah Lesley's unnamed wife actually goes home for three days.

5 See *MM*, 61. This speech is actually spoken by Old Grandmother, as opposed to Young Grandmother.

6 See *MM*, 69.

7 See *MM*, 71. It actually is Old Grandmother who had twins twice to spite her mother-in-law.

8 Published in 1893–96, *The Diary of Samuel Pepys* records the daily life of a naval administrator in London between 1660 and 1669. Montgomery first read it in 1917. I have corrected the original, which reads "Pepy's."

9 I have corrected the original, which reads "Thirty-year-ago."

10 Lord Saltire, an atheist and close friend of Densil Ravenshoe, the protagonist in *Ravenshoe* (1861), by Henry Kingsley (1830–1876), English novelist.

11 Properly, "horum omnium fortissimi sunt Belgae" ("the Belgae are the bravest"). From *Caesar's Gallic War*, a classical Latin text translated by W.A. McDevitte and W.S. Bohn in 1915.

12 Horace "Klondike" Lesley – "known to be a woman-hater" – comments on one of the eligible women his clan would like him to marry, "But look at the thick ankles of her" (*MM*, 7, 8).

13 The phrase "dreamer of dreams" is from "Ode," a poem by Arthur O'Shaughnessy (1844–1881), English poet of Irish ancestry.

14 Properly, "Were not attained by sudden flight." From "The Ladder of Saint Augustine" (1858), a poem by Henry Wadsworth Longfellow.

15 J.M. Barrie (1860–1937), Scottish novelist and playwright, best known as the creator of Peter Pan; Sir Thomas Henry Hall Caine (1853–1931), English novelist.

16 See Isaiah 8:14 in the Hebrew Bible and Romans 9:33 and 1 Peter 2:8 in the Christian Bible.

17 Properly, "Our grimalkin here ... sometimes reminds me of the story, by the airs of sovereignty which he assumes; and I am apt to treat him with respect from the idea that he may be a great prince incog., and may some time or other come to the throne." From *The Works of Washington Irving*, Volume 2 (1885).

18 I have corrected the original, which reads "and so resent."

19 "A form of marriage which provides for divorce by mutual consent and in which neither partner has any legal responsibilities towards the other," a term that originated in the second half of the 1920s (*OED*). Montgomery, from an earlier generation, believed that this legal option threatened traditional marriage.

20 Sinclair Lewis (1885–1951), the first American novelist to be awarded the Nobel Prize for Literature (1930); Theodore Dreiser (1871–1945), American novelist whose first book was *Sister Carrie* (1900); Mazo de la Roche's third book, *Jalna* (1927), won a major award by the *Atlantic Monthly* and was the basis for a sixteen-volume saga about the Whiteoak family.

21 See chapter 18, "Interviews with Authors," by Anne E. Nias, note 11, in this volume.

22 I have corrected the original, which reads "fun as some."

54

The 'Teen-Age Girl

—— 1931 ——

L.M. MONTGOMERY

This is the first of two articles by Montgomery published in *The Chatelaine* in 1931, this one with a tantalizing deck: "Do you find it hard to understand your daughter? Does she shut you out of her confidence? Do you feel she is 'boy-crazy' – thoughtless – selfish? Read this telling article written for mothers and daughters." As the subhead indicates, "L.M. Montgomery, author of *Anne of Green Gables* and other books, is Canada's most beloved writer for girls. In this penetrating discussion of mothers and daughters, she reveals her sympathy and understanding for the problems of the 'teen-age girl."[1] Once again it reveals a conservative form of feminism, for while it articulates that young women need respect and understanding, it positions that conviction squarely within the domestic realm, as seen most clearly in Montgomery's comment about the desire of "normal girls" for marriage, home, and motherhood.

Just why *The Chatelaine* should have asked me to write an article on the relations between the 'teen age girl and her mother is, as *Lord Dundreary* used to say, "One of thothe thingth no fellow can underthtand."[2] I, alas, have nothing but sons. So what know I about the problems of daughters?

Perhaps it was because I have written books about girls. But, as for girls in books, you can, up to a certain point, make them behave as you want them to. It is probably a very different thing with flesh and blood creatures.

No, my only justification for complying with the editor's request must lie in the fact that I was a girl once myself and have, I believe, managed to retain, even till now a very vivid recollection of what I was, and what I wished to be and how far and why I failed. For girlhood and its problems do not change as much from generation to generation as folks imagine. The outward fashion changes, but underneath they remain basically the same. Therefore do I rush in where angels might fear to tread,[3] unheeding the gibes that may be hurled at the perfect daughters of the daughterless woman. It is, after all, the easiest thing imaginable to tell the world what you would do in some situation in which you'll certainly never find yourself.

Perhaps it is because of long association with a minister that I have a fondness for texts. Anyhow, I do like something to tie to. So this article is just going to be a string of texts with my comments thereon. And the texts are just going to be certain things that have been said to me by mothers and girls at sundry times and in divers places all over Canada. For I want this article to be practical and helpful, dealing with the real perplexities and worries of real people.

I am, of course, taking some things for granted. I am taking it for granted that your girls are normal and that, unless you have utterly failed in your duty as a mother, they have been taught certain basic principles without which no life can be built. That honest work is the finest thing in the universe; that it is better to lose than to win unfairly; that it is a cowardly thing to lie; and that the fundamental immorality of the world from which most if not all of the iniquities and immoralities spring, is trying to get pleasure and success without paying the price the Power and Wisdom we call God put on it – trying to get something for nothing, in short.

Now, dear mother, let us have a little frank talk together about certain things that are troubling mothers today, as they have troubled them for hundreds of years. I will be candid with you and I shall expect you to be candid with me. Above all, don't try to pretend to me that you were a model and perfect creature when you were a young girl yourself. You may have forgotten how silly and flighty you were in your youth. I think people must forget or else their sense of humor would prevent them from saying the things they do say to their children. Your children may believe you but I shall not. Which leads me to my first text.

Only a few weeks ago I heard a mother say to her sixteen-year-old daughter,
   "I never did that when I was a young girl."
I wanted to shout with laughter and I am sure it will be counted unto me for righteousness that I kept a perfectly straight face, not even winking an eye when the daughter looked at me as if seeking confirmation.

But I said afterwards to her mother what now I say to you ... are you so perfectly sure you never did things like that? It seems to me that there was a time when what "he" said and what "he" did made up a very large part of your conversation – pardon me, of our conversation. This seems funny to us now, funny and silly because we have outgrown it. But remember I insisted on candor, wasn't it a fact? And as for "petting" ... well, it isn't an entirely new institution, is it? We called it "spooning." Petting is certainly a much prettier word – so much gain for the cult of the beautiful. But tell me, dear lady, in this heart to heart talk of ours, if "he" never kissed you at the gate after he had "escorted" you home, and if both his arms were continually employed in driving the horse that drew the top buggy of the "gay nineties." If you can answer "no" sincerely then you may be quite truthful in telling your daughter that you never did things like that. But I do not think you will be altogether wise. Because, though your daughter may believe you, she will think that times and manners – and men – have changed mightily in forty years and that you have no comprehension of her problems at all.

"Do you then approve of petting?" demands a scandalized matron. No, I do not. But I cannot see any use in saying, "Don't." You must try to make your daughter see that to be an aristocrat of the body is as fine a thing as to be an aristocrat of the mind or of society and that anything which degrades to amusement or habit that which should be consecrated to the service of love alone is a foolish thing to do or permit, because it means taking the third rate thing and losing the first rate. She must make her choice. She cannot have both.

"The young people of today are so selfish and thoughtless," mourned a mother to me recently.

Selfish? Yes, they are. Just as the middle-aged of today are selfish; just as the old are selfish – and always have been. No more. Selfishness isn't a matter of years. I have known many ghastly instances of selfishness in older people that wrecked lives and ruined careers. Selfishness is an abominable thing but for pity's sake don't imagine it is peculiar to youth.

"Thoughtless"? Ah, I grant you that. The young are thoughtless. Naturally. You have to learn to think. Nobody is born thoughtful. Your daughter doesn't know certain things which might make her thoughtful. What is more, she has no right to know them. She has a right to her unclouded youth, revelling for a few brief, glorious years in thoughtlessness. They will pass all too quickly, dear mother. Don't grudge them to her. Wouldn't it be really nice if we could be thoughtless once again for a little while?

"My daughter doesn't tell me things – she shuts me out of her confidence," was another mother's plaint.

Is that one of your problems? And if so, are you so sure that you are not yourself to blame for it? Do you remember the time – she was much smaller than she is now perhaps – when she came to you to tell you something silly or trivial, at least, you thought it silly and trivial. You laughed at her. And now you make moan that she doesn't confide in you as you hoped for.

If you ever laughed at her I don't blame her for not taking you into her confidence. *Never laugh at her*. Don't blow her little candles out. Youth takes itself so very seriously. And laughter makes scars that never fade. I know. I have forgiven the people of my youth who advised me and scolded me and lectured me. But I have never forgiven the ones who laughed at me.

We will suppose, however, that you have not committed this unpardonable sin. And yet your daughter denies you her full confidence. What then? Why worry over it? Your daughter may be one of the many people who do not find it easy to talk to older people of intimate and personal things. "There are some things," says Ellen Thorneycroft Fowler, "so delicately made that to talk about them destroys them."[4] Your daughter may feel that way about a good many things. You should respect her personality and never try to force her confidence. A girl's confidence is like a rosebud ... "We must not tear the close-shut leaves apart."[5] She has a right to her own secrets, her own inner, unshared life. I think a tremendous lot of harm is done in every relationship by this failure to respect one another's personality and in none more than in that between mother and daughter. The mother who insists that she must know every word and act and thought of her daughter is going to make a dismal wreck of what should be one of the most beautiful of all human ties. I always smile when I hear a mother say, "I know every thought of my daughter." She doesn't. No mother does. God has mercifully arranged it thus in order that mothers may have some peace of mind.

"She had no clothes on," said a sweet old lady to me once, with a gasp of horror.

"No clothes?" I echoed.

"Well, none to speak of. No petticoat I'm certain, no stockings, nothing but a thin dress and, and knickers."

I don't know that many modern mothers are worried as to how their daughters dress but I know that some are. Some think their girls don't wear enough, some think they want too many clothes. There are battles royal waged every day about it. The foolishness of it!

Why not let your daughter dress as she wants to, even if you think it foolish? She probably wants to dress just as the rest of her set are doing and it will be torture to her if she can't. Never shall I forget how I suffered because when a girl I was not allowed to have a "bang" when every other girl had one. And because I had to wear boots and stockings when all the other girls went barefoot to school.

Never mind if you think the things she wears aren't "decent." Personally I ask only one thing about a girl's clothes – are they beautiful and do they add to the beauty of the wearer? If they are not and do not they are indecent. I always loathed too short skirts because they show the ugliest curve in the human body, the in-bend of the knee. Too low backs I dislike because nine out of ten backs are ugly and should be covered up. I have seen sadly few beautiful bare legs – they are generally too scrawny or pimply. But I can't see any other indecency save that of ugliness in them. Girls should want pretty clothes and should have them. "Dowdiness," says Oliver Wendell Holmes, "is clearly an expression of imperfect vitality."[6]

"Oh, she's boy-crazy." So said a woman once in my hearing. I didn't know the girl to whom she referred. Perhaps she was boy-crazy. There are always a few silly girls like that – always have been, and, I fear, always will be. But, dear mother, every normal girl likes boys. "A woman," says Holmes, "would rather talk to a man than to an angel."[7] Which is sweetly reasonable. Why shouldn't she? What point of contact would she have with an angel? I'm sure I wouldn't know what to say to such a being.

Of course there is a year or so in the teens when boys do seem to a girl more wonderful beings than they will ever seem again. This interest is a natural and healthy one and should be acknowledged and directed, not forbidden. At that last word an old memory comes up. I hear a very small girl, wild horses will not drag from me the secret of who that girl was, saying pleadingly,

"Aunty, please forbid us to do it so that it will be fun to do it."

That small girl did not know much but she had got hold of a powerful bit of psychology by the tail. The forbidden thing has a charm. Don't make too many things charming because of a taboo. Especially boys, who are quite charming enough without that to Sweet Sixteen. Don't let your girl pass into womanhood with nothing but starved or stolen youth behind her. Let her have some boy friends and some "dates" – even, to use a real nice, old-timey word, some beaus. If she hasn't a beau or two in her 'teens how on earth is she ever going to learn how to manage the men? I once heard a dear old lady say severely,

"I don't 'old with beaus. Either they means nothing or they means too much."

Her daughters both ran away and married the wrong men. Naturally. They hadn't learned to distinguish for themselves between those who meant nothing or too much.

"I love her so – and I want to save her from making the mistakes that I did."

Of course you love her. Who could help loving her, this palpitant young creature, so sweet and so absurd, as beautiful and mysterious as a summer twilight, with her flower-like face, her great, asking eyes, her body exquisite in its litheness as a lyric of spring, her every step a dance, her every gesture one of grace and virility, believing romance and happiness to be hers of right by the token of the dimple in her chin? But love isn't enough, dear lady. You must understand, too. And understanding is something very much rarer and harder than loving.

Perhaps you find it hard to understand her. Small wonder. She is an enigma – this creature who sometimes has the face of one who listens to fairy music and at other times is austerely intellectual, staggering you with casual remarks about the quantum theory and the planetesimal hypothesis. Who sometimes seems to you like a lonely little rudderless ship drifting over the rim of the world, and anon is only a girl who is a star forward in basket ball and aspires to the championship in bareback riding. Who now is a living flame and again as cool as an April night, with a horror of not seeming hard as nails which a really hard person would never feel. Who is sometimes so near you and sometimes so far away that she might as well be beyond Sirius. Indeed, it is hard to understand her. But just remember what you were twenty years ago, your moods, your whims, your dreams, your aspirations. Perhaps it won't be so hard then.

It's all very well to say you want to save her from the mistakes you made. But you can't do it. And anyway she isn't likely to make the same mistakes. She'll probably make entirely different ones. Why not cultivate that rarest thing in man or woman, toleration, and let her make a few mistakes? Our mistakes teach us more than anything else sometimes. You may be wise with the wisdom of the old. But remember she is wise with the wisdom of the young. Such a thing does exist and sometimes I feel very sorry that I have lost it. Don't try to plan her life out for her. Let her do the planning herself. Don't force her into a mold. Don't make her do something just because someone else – or everybody else – is doing it. Don't give her too much advice. Youth hates advice. Age hates advice. And our attitude to it is generally that of an old man I once knew whose daughter-in-law nagged him terribly. When he was asked why he put up with it he smiled tolerantly.

"Lawful heart, she do enjoy giving advice so much. And it don't hurt me 'cause I never takes it."

Let her alone a good deal. Young things can stand an immense amount of letting alone if we elders could only realize it. As I said, in the beginning, teach her a few basic things and beyond that exercise a little wise forgetfulness. Having done your best don't worry. Keep a sense of proportion. I have known few if any "model" girls who have in later life made women of vitality or magnetism or success. And I have known many harum-scarum girls who turned out to be wonderfully good wives and mothers. Yourself, for example.

But oh, *do* insist that she returns the books she borrows!

This little preachment of mine isn't all for the mothers. Lastly and very briefly (more ministerial influence probably!) I do want to say a word to the girls.

You are all so youthful and charming, dears, and so much, so very much, like the girls of my own generation. You won't quite believe this of course. You can't believe that your mothers and grandmothers were ever girls like you. But it's true.

I'm taking a few things for granted, just as I did when talking to your mothers. I'm taking it for granted that you are not the kind of girl who yowls about living her own life when her mother objects to her staying out most of the night in the company of some youth about whom she knows nothing. I'm taking it for granted that you are not the kind of girl who is always sorry for herself and who calls making life miserable for everybody connected with her "developing her own personality." All that sort of thing has a tendency to make me Dorothy-Dix-minded.[8] No, I'm taking it for granted that you are a girl, very like what I was myself once, eager, ambitious, asking much of life and willing to give all I had to life in return. Full of faults and small vanities and quite mistaken notions about many things, the greatest mistake being that which youth is always so prone to make, in believing that it can pounce on life like a cat on a mouse, play with it awhile, and then devour it at once. And I want, really want, to help you if I can.

"The youth of today is so fearless," said a girl to me not long ago. "We look at life without fear."

The darling thought her generation the only one that had ever done that. But youth is always fearless. It is unafraid because it hasn't found out what life can do to it. And it is always "modern." It is well that it should be so. There would be no progress otherwise. Only don't mistake running around in circles for progress and don't think your mothers were absolute figureheads because they weren't air-minded and didn't talk with what you call, and perhaps believe, "stark sincerity" about certain matters. They weren't "cowards" because of that. Oh, no. Or if they were they were no greater cowards than some of you, who don't, in your secret souls, want to "pet" indiscriminately and smoke and drink but are afraid you'll be laughed at by your set as old-fashioned or "Victorian" if you don't.

"He was the biggest coward there is," I heard a man say once. "He was scared not to do it."

How many of you are cowards of that sort? Answer that question for yourselves.

Oh yes, we girls of that olden day were very much like you. There were rose-leaf girls then where there are sun-tan girls now but the difference is only in the skins. So we understand you better than you think. And I want you to believe that in nine cases out of ten "the old bromide," "your mother is your best friend," is true. Bromides have such an abominable habit of being true. Perhaps that is why we hate them so.

Oh, I know there is a lot of silly fiction of today dealing with "smother love" and all that. There are such cases of abnormal mothers just as there are abnormal daughters. But I'm just talking to normal girls about normal mothers, mothers whom you may think a bit fussy and faddy, as perhaps they are. But don't forget that they love you better than anything in the world and would do far more for you in a pinch than any of your "sophisticated" chums and beaus.

We all love you, dear hearts, with your starry eyes and your belief that life is one endless adventure; with your dreams of all the things that may happen tomorrow; with your thirst for "thrills," and your firm conviction that there are only two complimentary adjectives in the English language, "priceless" and "marvellous." We love you and we want you to have rich full lives, quench your thirst for living at the unknown, enchanted springs we sought and could not find, do all the wonderful things we wanted and failed to do. We want you to have more real freedom, not merely more apparent freedom, than we had to develop and expand. Because, as Holmes says – I'm really quite "nutty" about Holmes and I don't know whether this generation has read a line of his delightful Breakfast Table series ... "The truest lives are those which are cut rose-diamond fashion answering to the many planed aspects of the world about them."[9]

That's the advantage your generation has over mine, you can be cut with more facets. And so you will have more power than we had, the power of the broadened thought, the power of the more unfettered act, the power of the spoken word, and the greatest of these is, I verily believe, the spoken word. Just one word uttered or unuttered and a whole life is changed, even, it may be, the course of history. Suppose Napoleon's mother had said "no" in place of "yes."

"Give us a standard to live by in this age of shifting faiths and ideals, when all the old traditions seem to be going by the board," you say. Ah, but can I? well, here's a try for it. Just another quotation, this time from one of my own books in which a very wise old lady says to the little Marigold,

"Play the game of life according to the rules. It's wiser because you can't cheat life in the long run. Live joyously. Do what you want to do as long as you can go to your mirror afterwards and look yourself in the face."[10]

That isn't as easy as it may sound!

NOTES

1 Because the term "teen" refers specifically to a person whose age is between thirteen and nineteen, the term is spelled here with an apostrophe to indicate that it is a truncated word.

2 Properly, "one of those things that no fellow can find out." From *Lord Dundreary and His Brother Sam: The Strange Story of Their Adventures and Family History* (1863). The character originated in the play *Our American Cousin* (1858), by Tom Taylor (1817–1880), English playwright. Montgomery's version of the quotation was also used in *AIs*, 55.

3 See chapter 11, "Four Questions Answered," by Lucy Maud Montgomery, note 2, in this volume.

4 From *The Subjection of Isabel Carnaby* (1906), by Ellen Thorneycroft Fowler (1860–1929), English author.

5 From "Sometime," in *Sometime and Other Poems* (1892), by May Riley Smith (1842–1927), American poet.

6 Properly, "Dowdyism is clearly an expression of imperfect vitality." From *The Professor at the Breakfast-Table* (1860), by Oliver Wendell Holmes Sr. (1809–1894), American physician and author.

7 Properly, "A woman never forgets her sex. She would rather talk with a man than an angel, any day." From *The Poet at the Breakfast-Table* (1872), by Oliver Wendell Holmes Sr. See also Montgomery, 31 January 1920, in *SJLMM*, 2: 369.

8 Dorothy Dix, a popular syndicated advice columnist, was the pseudonym of Elizabeth Meriwether Gilmer (1861–1951), American journalist.

9 Properly, "the truest lives are those that are cut rose-diamond-fashion, with many facets answering to the many-planed aspects of the world about them." From *The Professor at the Breakfast-Table*, by Oliver Wendell Holmes Sr. His Breakfast Table trilogy began with *The Autocrat at the Breakfast-Table* (1858).

10 Part of Old Grandmother's speech to Marigold the night of her death is actually as follows: "Live joyously, my child. Never mind the old traditions. Traditions don't matter in a day when queens have their pictures in magazine advertisements. But play the game of life according to the rules. You might as well, because you can't cheat life in the end ... Do anything you want to, Marigold – as long as you can go to your looking-glass afterwards and look yourself in the face" (*MM*, 74).

55

Anne of Green Gables at Home

—— 1931 ——

A.V. BROWN

This unidentified interview with A.V. Brown, pastor of St. Andrew's Presbyterian Church in Picton, Ontario, likely published in 1931, does not quote Montgomery directly, but it nevertheless provides a snapshot of her home life from the point of view of an outsider who also has connections to the Presbyterian Church. Although this article is ostensibly about Montgomery as an enduring author, it ends with an "Editor's Note" that identifies her simply as "the wife of Rev. Ewan Macdonald, Norval, Ontario."

It was on a beautiful Sunday afternoon in midsummer that I first saw L.M. Montgomery, the creator of Anne of Green Gables. The manse where she lives is suited to a writer of fiction and poetry – an ideal house of dreams. It is rather antique in design and covered with ivy. Fine trees stand around it; the breezes play over it; the birds twitter under its eaves, and the shadows dance outside on the wide lawn. At the far end of this lawn the church stands like a sentinel at prayer. The sheltered position of this home in a quiet village saves it from the babel and distraction of a great city. Anyone with the mental endowment of L.M. Montgomery should be happy almost anywhere. Her imagination can work miracles with dust and bricks. It can gather grapes of thorns and figs of thistles. One of the finest things she ever wrote was about this princely gift of imagination. "It is better to possess it, living in a garret, than to be the inhabitant of palaces without it."[1] At the same time even poets accept garrets not from choice but from necessity.

As Mr. and Mrs. Macdonald were both at church I was shown for a little time into the parlour. It was clear at the first glance that the house was well furnished. Genius is not supposed to produce first-class housekeeping. But here everything spoke of taste and care and prosperity. Not even Marilla Cuthbert or Rachel Lynde would have found an object to scrub or polish.

Mr. Macdonald came in first, a delightful, cultured, Christian gentleman. And about a minute later his wife came. The only idea I had had of her appearance was from her picture in John Garvin's book, *Canadian Poets*,[2] and I had thought that a sweeter face never looked out of a book, surmounted as it was by a beautiful crown of hair. I hoped to see the same face. I also wondered if the hair would resemble the red hair of Anne, whose glint has shone through our literature from the Atlantic to the Pacific and beyond. And it was the same face; it was older, of course, and rounder, and the splendid crown of hair, not red, had somewhat fallen; but that which made the chief beauty in her look was still there, that is, the light in her eyes; time could not take that away for the soul of Lucy Montgomery was in that light. She was very well dressed, wearing a large hat, and a gown in good and up-to-date fashion. Here again my expectations were upset. Genius is inclined to be timeless, and its style of clothes belongs to the ages. Mrs. Macdonald[3] was not orthodox or traditional in this matter.

While she prepared supper I discussed the doctrine of the Atonement and other subjects congenial to it with her husband.[4] As he is a Presbyterian, I groped about surreptitiously in his theology, seeking to lay my hand, as it were, on the five thorny points of Calvinism.[5] But I could not feel them. No doubt they were there, but a rich growth of honeysuckle covered them up. In an atmosphere of literary humanism great dogmas may change their shape and size. They naturally soften.

At supper the female servant and her child sat at the table with us.[6] That is one way to solve the help problem. The result was real dignity without the faintest taint of snobbery. While we ate a neighbour telephoned to say that a boy, a Scotch immigrant, had been drowned near the village. The entire district was upset. The effect of this news upon a woman, who was the mother of two boys and the author of the greatest child story which Canada, and probably America, has produced, can be understood. She shuddered and turned white as snow. Her whole appearance changed as if, to quote one of her own sentences, "she looked and beheld the seal of the Great Presence."[7] I am sure she was thinking of her own two absent children, and saw them, to quote her again, "as if the white majesty of death had fallen on them and set them apart as crowned."[8] But her self-mastery was as wonderful as her intensity of feeling. By a great effort she subdued her emotion. Fortunately the evil rumour proved to be incorrect.

We did not discuss religion at this meal but it did appear[9] that Mrs. Macdonald opposed church union not because of the circumstance that her husband opposed it, but because of personal conviction.[10] Whatever side she might take in a matter of that kind it was certain that neither narrowness nor spite could affect her decision.

What an excellent supper that was! Everything tasted very good. A large layer cake was the crowning masterpiece of the meal and as I put a slice on my plate I remembered that famous cake of Anne of Green Gables which by mistake was flavored with anodyne liniment instead of vanilla. While eating the cake I did think of the liniment but found it entirely wanting. Liniment cakes are not for everybody.

Emerson says that Nature takes pains to make gifted people and their homes unattractive.[11] The idea is to protect their solitude and to keep the world from their doors, so that they may nurse their genius and fulfil their mission. But in the case of L.M. Montgomery, Nature had departed radically from her settled policy. Her charm lies not only in her pen, dipped in the sunlight though it is, but in her personality and life. How well the words of Whittier apply here:

> "Flowers spring to blossoms where she walks,
> The careful ways of duty,
> Our hard, stiff lines of life with her
> Are flowing curves of beauty."[12]

Throughout this visit I discovered in myself a curious inability to distinguish perfectly between this woman and the children of her mind. If a little girl with a very flaming head and a very freckled face had walked into the room it would have seemed, for the moment, quite a natural thing. And after all do not the most genuine writings tend to be autobiographical? Milton could not help putting his own fortitude even into his Satan and his Samson.[13] L.M. Montgomery's Annes and Emilys are herself. Their circumstances and appearance and age may be different from hers, but that matters little for a true poet never grows old. Authors who write from their souls naturally make their leading characters in their own image.

The last thing Mrs. Macdonald told me was that she hoped to have a new book ready this fall. That will be good news to many. A young country is slow to recognize a writer. It can see very quickly the greatness of the man who builds a railway or a factory, because these things look bigger than a book. *Anne of Green Gables* was rejected by five publishers. If all the publishers had been like the first five, then the book which was described by Mark Twain as the sweetest child-story he had ever read, would never have seen the light. What a murder! How much the world owes to the sixth publisher, who accepted that modest manuscript! Good literature is the biggest business and the best capital of any nation. The stories and poems of L.M. Montgomery are not just pretty playthings, they are messages, and the pulpit has yet to be built in this country that has any better. There is a moral in them; it is not obtrusive nor aggressive, but inevitable as the perfume in the rose. Every book she writes is a voice pleading for the rights of childhood, the sterling worth that is disguised by an ungracious exterior, the love which cannot show itself in speech or look, the tenderness which lives beneath an iron creed, the hearts of gold in casings of granite, and the religion which blooms in unlikely places, like flowers pushing upward through the ice and snow. If anyone would increase his faith in God, in man, in nature, and in all the finest things of life, let him scan the pages of L.M. Montgomery's books.

NOTES

1 *AA*, 128.
2 This anthology was published in 1916 by McClelland, Goodchild, and Stewart, and included three poems by Montgomery.
3 I have corrected the original, which reads "MacDonald."
4 In the Christian tradition, atonement refers to the forgiveness of sin and reconciliation between humans and God, made possible through the crucifixion of Jesus Christ.
5 Within Calvinism, an alternative Protestant tradition and theological system of belief, the five points are as follows: "total depravity," "unconditional election," "limited atonement," "irresistible grace," and "perseverance of the saints."
6 Montgomery's housekeeper in 1929 was Mrs. Mason, who had a four-year-old daughter.
7 Properly, "Anne looked at the still face and there beheld the seal of the Great Presence" (*AGG*, 294).
8 Properly, "the white majesty of death had fallen on him and set him apart as one crowned" (*AGG*, 294).

9 The original reads "it did not appear," but in Montgomery's scrapbook "not" is crossed out in ink.

10 In the mid-1920s, individual Presbyterian, Methodist, and Congregationalist churches voted to merge and form the United Church of Canada, but Montgomery and Macdonald were both opposed to this, and the Leaskdale congregation remained Presbyterian.

11 See "Nature" (1836), by Ralph Waldo Emerson.

12 From *Among the Hills* (1868), by John Greenleaf Whittier. Montgomery had chosen these lines as the epigraph to *Anne of Avonlea*.

13 Satan appears in *Paradise Lost* (1667), whereas *Samson Agonistes* appears in part of *Paradise Regained* (1671), both epic poems by John Milton. I have corrected the original, which reads "Saton."

56

An Open Letter from a Minister's Wife

—— 1931 ——

L.M. MONTGOMERY

According to the subhead of this article, also published in *The Chatelaine* in 1931, "L.M. Montgomery, Author of *Anne of Green Gables*, and one of the most noted minister's wives in the Dominion, answers the question:– '*What does the minister's wife expect from the women of the congregation?*'" Montgomery's detailed answer echoes many of the concerns she had recorded in her journal twenty-five years earlier upon agreeing to marry Ewan Macdonald: "The life of a country minister's wife has always appeared to me as a synonym for respectable slavery – a life in which a woman of any independence in belief or character, must either be a failure, from an 'official' point of view, or must cloak her real self under an assumed orthodoxy and conventionalism that must prove very stifling at times."[1] Although here she is honest enough to admit to some of the community pressures that she has faced in this role, she most certainly does not express publicly the frustrations found in her journals. This article was followed by Nellie McClung's "What Does the Congregation Expect of a Minister's Wife?" in the December 1931 issue, which stated McClung's belief that "the minister's wife does her best service in the congregation by keeping her man fit and happy, thinking well of himself and highly of his calling."[2]

When, twenty years ago, I married a minister, my friends groaned in unison, "So much is expected of a minister's wife!" I was not ignorant of this, having been brought up in a community where I had heard several ministers' wives discussed, favorably and unfavorably. I had, indeed, a pretty clear idea of what was expected of a minister's wife. Moreover, I admitted that I thought the congregation had a right to expect certain things from the mistress of their manse. I have never had any sympathy with the point of view expressed in the statement, "The congregation doesn't pay me a salary, so they have no right to expect anything in particular from me." There are certain things that cannot be expressed in terms of dollars and cents. The leadership which the minister's wife can give, especially in rural communities where it may otherwise be lacking, is one of them. From my viewpoint, the minister's wife has a special opportunity for service which is a privilege and not a duty.

But nothing is one-sided. If the congregation has a right to expect certain things of the minister's wife she has an equal right to expect certain things of them. This is what *The Chatelaine* – May her shadow never grow less![3] – has asked me to write about, and I will try to present as briefly as possible the "minister's wife's" side of the expectations.

In the first place, while a good deal may be expected from a free and unencumbered manse mistress, no congregation should expect anything more from a wife with a young family and no help than from a "lay sister" in the same position. She has a right to this consideration from them. This understands itself, as the French say. And she has a right to expect that if some lynx-eyed mother in Israel discovers a button missing from the ministerial vest on Sunday, she will not be condemned too hastily, but that due allowance will be made for the teething baby or the croupy Junior.

She has a right to expect loyal and intelligent co-operation on the part of the women of her husband's congregation. The minister's wife cannot do it all when it comes to church societies. She can only give a little leadership and guidance. For success and forward marching good team work is necessary for all. It is a joy to work with sweetly reasonable women, but one crank on the executive can embitter the existence of the minister's wife and wreck the work of the organization woefully.

Also I would humbly suggest that she should not have her perfect and incomparable predecessor cast in her teeth too often. In days to come, when she in her turn will be gone and rainbowed with the iridescence of the past, she, too, will be remembered as a flawless and competent creature. But that will not take away the sting of the present comparison.

She expects that the congregation will concede to her a right to her own opinions, tastes, methods of housekeeping and child training. To be the target of endless criticism along these lines would take the joy out of any life.

289

She expects that they will be willing to overlook her blunders and mistakes. She is not flawless any more than they are. She cannot at twenty have the wisdom of sixty. And, after all, the woman who never makes mistakes may be an admirable woman but somehow I think she would be an unlovable one, too. The minister's wife may sometimes fail to recognize the right time to be silent, or she may bungle in trying too hard to be an inspiration. The path of perfection is narrow and few there be that find it. In short, she expects that her husband's people will remember that she is a human being.

She has a right to dress to please herself. This should not worry the women of the parish – or the men either. For women are not the only offenders in this respect. I once heard it asked what a certain good and reverend elder had died of.

"Heart failure," said one neighbor.

"Not at all," said another. "He really died of the minister's wife's bobbed hair."

And I knew of a case where a whole session refused to call a minister who had pleased them in every respect, because his wife, who unwisely accompanied him when he came to "preach for a call,"[4] had a gay red rose in her hat.

Let the minister's wife's clothes alone. It is not likely that on the average minister's salary she will have more pretty things than are good for her. Besides, even if her dress were dowdy and her hat swore at her nose, she wouldn't be a bit the better wife to the minister or help to the congregation.

Then, too, the congregation should remember that the minister's wife likes a little fun, especially if she has been cursed with an inconvenient sense of humor. What agonies I have endured betimes when I was dying to laugh but dared not because I was the minister's wife. How did I keep a straight face when a dear, kindly soul remarked that her husband hadn't been able to attend a certain funeral because he had such a headache that "he knew he wouldn't enjoy himself if he did go!"[5] Or when another equally good and sweet woman groaned behind me at another funeral, as we passed the flower-heaped casket, "Oh, poor man, I hope you are as happy as you look"[6] – more as if she hoped rather than believed it!

She has a right to expect that they will respect her confidences as they expect her to respect theirs. And she has a right to expect that when people tell her about B's faults they will tell her about B's virtues at the same time. But this, I realize, is a counsel of perfection.[7]

If at times the minister's wife is a bit absent-minded or preoccupied or "stiff," the congregation should not imagine that she is unfriendly or uninterested or trying to snub them. She has a right to expect that they make a few excuses for her. Perhaps she is so tired that she is not quite sane; perhaps she is one of those people to whom it is torture to show their feelings – dead and gone generations of sternly repressed forefathers may have laid their unyielding fingers of reserve on her lips; perhaps she is wondering if anyone could sell her a little time; perhaps there are many small worries snapping and snarling at her heels; perhaps she has had one of those awful moments when we catch a glimpse of ourselves as we really are; perhaps she has the odd feeling of not belonging to this or any world, that follows an attack of flu; perhaps she is just pitifully shy at heart. Or her own feelings may have been hurt. Because ministers' wives have feelings that are remarkably like the feelings of other women, and injustice and misunderstanding hurt us very keenly.

For my own part, when I recall the happenings of my own twenty years as mistress of the manse, I conclude that on the whole this is a nice kind of a world even for a minister's wife. The roses have outnumbered the thorns by thousands.

I look back and see many lovely things. They crowd into memory in a curious medley. Charming vanished households from which no one ever went away without feeling better in some way. Homes that were hospitality incarnate. Houses that always seemed pleased to have you come to them. Frank, ungrudging tributes, appreciative, priceless words that cast a sudden rainbow over existence. Dear gentle souls who never once made me feel that I had said the wrong thing. Silent, gentle hand-clasps of sympathy that heartened when life was grey. Camp fires of young folks like fiery roses of night. Little friendly, neighborly offerings now and then – the jar of cream or jelly, the box of eggs, the root of an admired perennial, the bouquet that brought to the manse the loveliness of old-fashioned gardens.

And the dear, dear women I have known! Mrs. A, who was always like a comfortable fire on a warm hearth. Mrs. B, who had something about her capacious maternal bosom that made you want to lay your head on it and whisper your troubles. Mrs. C, whose memory comes as a balm whenever I recall her. Mrs. D, whose words were always of things lovely and of good report. Mrs. E, dear soul, who told me so simply and sweetly, that she had been praying that my lost, beloved pussy might be found. And darling Mrs. F, with ageless sorrow and patience in her eyes, who, when someone remarked to her, "You've had so many troubles, poor-thing," flashed back, "Yes, but think of all the fun I've had between times." A meeting with these women and many more like them always made me feel as if the day had given me a purple gift. I have received far, far more than I expected or had any right to expect from the people among whom it has been my lot and privilege to work.

NOTES

1 Montgomery, 12 October 1906, in *SJLMM*, 1: 321.
2 McClung, "What Does the Congregation Expect," 12.
3 See chapter 34, "Blank Verse? 'Very Blank,' Said Father," by L.M. Montgomery, note 3, in this volume.
4 When a Presbyterian congregation had a vacancy for a new minister, short-listed candidates would be invited to preach once as a trial, and it was on the basis of this trial that a congregation decided on the successful applicant.
5 In *Anne's House of Dreams*, Montgomery attributes this anecdote to Miss Cornelia, who had gone to a funeral the day before. "At first I thought my head was aching so badly I couldn't enjoy myself if I did go" (*AHD*, 45).
6 In *Rainbow Valley*, this anecdote is attributed to Susan Baker (*RV*, 102).
7 In the Christian tradition, chastity, poverty, and obedience are the counsels of perfection, also called "evangelical counsels."

57

Life Has Been Interesting

— 1933 —

MRS. L.M. MACDONALD (L.M. MONTGOMERY)

This short article, published in an unidentified periodical around 1933, shows Montgomery "looking backward" in the final decade of her life. Although she omits any concrete examples to illustrate her points, it is especially intriguing that the light-hearted tone about "manifest destiny," fate, and ambition contrasts sharply with the often despairing tone of her journal entries for the 1930s, in which she frequently comes across as obsessed with the conviction that her life was cursed. In a journal entry dated September 1933, she noted, "I have been told that as you grow older things ceased to hurt so much – you ceased to feel so keenly. I am nearly sixty and this mercy has not yet been vouchsafed to me. Instead, I think I feel *more* keenly and hideously. And I have not the hope of youth now – I have not the years ahead when things may be better – there is no tomorrow for which I can endure today."[1]

Looking backward is not, I think, a peculiarly pleasant business for anybody, but it is an intriguing one. It is, for one thing, amazing to see how values have shifted. Things and events, which at the time seemed of tremendous importance, have shrunk to insignificance and are clearly seen to have had no real influence on my life at all. Whereas, on the other hand, many things which at the time seemed of no importance at all are now seen to have been of cataclysmic influence and to have changed the whole trend and tenor of my existence and career. One lesson that "looking backward" has brought home to me is the power of seeming trifles.
    Another thing that strikes me is the bitter flavour that many old joys have acquired and the strange enchanting sweetness of recollection that

has come to old sorrows. I see humour now in many things that seemed unrelieved tragedy at the time and many comic memories have revealed an inner core of tragedy. I am amazed at the wise things I did which turned out to be foolish and at the foolish things that have turned out to be wise. And I can now trace very clearly a manifest destiny "shaping my ends"[2] in despite of all my futile resistances and struggles.

I was ambitious in youth and I have realized some of my ambition. I had a certain knack of picking friends which I took as a matter of course but can now see to have been a very vital endowment. I wanted to drain the cup of life fully, whether its brewage was bitter or sweet, and I have done it. So I look back on my life with a certain feeling of satisfaction, despite a still unsated thirst.

Yet I would not want to live it again, just as, having finished a book, I do not want to start in and read it over again no matter how interesting it was. I want a different book.

But this one *has* been interesting!

NOTES

1 Montgomery, 23 September 1933, in *SJLMM*, 4: 229.
2 Properly, "a divinity that shapes our ends." See chapter 13, "How I Began to Write," by L.M. Montgomery, note 14, in this volume.

58

The Importance of Beauty in Everything

—— 1933 ——

L.M. MONTGOMERY

This article was published in *The Family Herald and Weekly Star* in July 1933. As its subhead promises, "those who have read *Anne of Green Gables* or any of the 'Anne' books will expect something whimsical and poetic in all that L.M. Montgomery writes. They will not be disappointed in this article." Although the title of this article implies an emphasis on the wonders of the natural world, here Montgomery tackles a decidedly modern problem: the growing availability of post-secondary education in the 1930s was pressuring too many young people to seek specialized training even if they were not intellectually suited for that type of learning. Here she encourages rural young people to consider all options for higher learning and professional training, even though in her own family she was less broad-minded: with her eldest son failing out of engineering at university and her youngest unsure what career path to choose, Montgomery recommended that the former pursue law and the latter medicine at the University of Toronto – which they did, two months after the publication of this essay.

Montgomery was fond of offering advice to young people in print. In a short piece published around 1936 addressing the students of Pembroke Collegiate in Ontario, she stated that she wished for them "all the good things in life – including dreams, whether fulfilled or not. I hope they will make the world a little bit better than the generation before them are leaving it. I know – because I was a student once – that they think they are going to make it a whole big lot better, and that in a brace of shakes. Youth always does – which is part of the delightful condition of being young. And then youth finds out, as we older folks have all found out, that all any generation can do is just to add a little to what has been done before – build one more step up on the stairway that climbs to the stars."[1]

I am afraid I am a bit of a heretic in regard to present day educational methods and aims. There are too many fads and frill. In the rather awful but very expressive "slang" phrase, we have bitten off bigger ... and more ... chunks than we can chew. Education has, too often, become the means of enticing boys and girls away from the farm and small town life and making them dissatisfied with and contemptuous of life there. Too much emphasis is laid on "higher" education. Colleges are flooded with boys and girls who would in the end be better and happier and more useful if they had never gone to college. John, who would have made a good carpenter, thinks a minister has an easier life, goes in for that, and is a failure. Mary who has a positive gift for dressmaking or cooking, develops a hankering for a "career," takes a B.A. course, and teaches rather badly for the rest of her life. Young people are apt to be dazzled by the green of far-off pastures. Of all people farm boys and girls ought to know the fallacy of this, but they don't. There is too little in present day education to correct this optical illusion.

This doesn't mean that I don't believe all boys and girls shouldn't have as good an education as they can get. I do, because real education means discipline and training, broadening and deepening, besides the mere acquiring of knowledge. Education should really "lead out" all our gifts and resources. If a girl really has in her a special fitness for some profession she will feel the urge and make good. If she hasn't, but is only going in for a "career" because it is the fashion or because she doesn't want to stay home or because she wants "freedom," then the higher education is for her only a delusion and a snare.[2]

The boys and girls of the farm and small town need an all-round education, but it seems to me that is just what they don't get at high school. More stress, it seems to me, is laid on pass lists and examinations than on fitting them to live. Of course it is much easier to point this out than to suggest a remedy. But education should deal more with the simple, basic realities of life than it does. It should be a key to unlock the beauties of the past, the possibilities of the present, the problems of the future.

I would like to see our youth taught to keep an open mind in all things and not grow hidebound and prejudiced. I would like to see them taught the importance of beauty in everything ... in character, in relationships, in material surroundings. I would like to see them taught that there is no place like the country for a real home. I would like to see them inspired with the true community spirit ... taught how to live with and get along with other people. Nobody can live to him or herself. That compendium of all wisdom, the Bible, says so and modern consciousness endorses it.[3] Youth must learn to live and work and enjoy and suffer together.

We need leaders for our young people … leaders not coming from outside but among them and of them, understanding their life and problems. I have been reduced to gibbering fury many a time at Sunday School conventions when I heard spruce, glib workers laying down the law as to our rural problems when every word they uttered showed they didn't know a thing about them.

I think the Junior Institutes that are springing up all over Ontario give excellent opportunities for this sort of education.[4] Young people learn more of living and leadership and team play there than they do in the schools.

There is an old rhyme that says:

> "There are lots of things that never go by rule,
>   There's an awful lot of knowledge
>   That we never get at college,
> There are heaps of things we never learn at school."[5]

But youth could and should be fitted to learn them and thus to educate itself. Truth is not a special endowment or possession of any institution of learning. It can be found anywhere if we seek for it sincerely. And I agree with Jerome K. Jerome when he says:

"Life tastes just the same, whether we drink it out of a golden goblet or a stone mug."[6]

The flavor is all in the brewing.

NOTES

1 "From a Real Author," unidentified and undated clipping, in Montgomery, Black Scrapbook, 2: 65.

2 Properly, "a delusion, a mockery, and a snare." From Thomas Denman, British judge and politician, in his judgment on the 1844 case of *Daniel O'Connel vs. The Queen*. See also *RI*, 7.

3 See Romans 14:7 in the Christian Bible.

4 An offshoot of the Women's Institute, started in 1877 by the Ontario Ministry of Agriculture with branches appearing all over Canada, the Junior Institute was formed for rural women aged sixteen to twenty-nine. Its activities promoted homemaking practices, useful citizenship, and leadership.

5 Popular early-twentieth-century rhyme, also appearing in *AIs*, 216.

6 See chapter 24, "The Way to Make a Book," by L.M. Montgomery, note 8, in this volume.

59

From *Courageous Women*

—— 1934 ——

L.M. MONTGOMERY

Published by McClelland and Stewart, Montgomery's Canadian publisher, in 1934, *Courageous Women* was comprised of twenty-one biographies of women who had made substantial contributions to the pioneer movement, literature, education, missions work, health, and activism. The dust jacket referred to the book as "a series of inspiring biographies of girls who grew to be women of courage and achievement. Vivid human interest stories of women leaders in many fields of activity. Fifteen out of the twenty-one sketches in the book deal with Canadian women who have taken a prominent part in pioneer life, in mission work, in education, in literature, and in various spheres of public service. Many of these biographies appear now for the first time in book form." Although Montgomery's name appears first on the title page, her contributions are limited to the first three chapters: on Joan of Arc (ca. 1412–1431), French martyr and Roman Catholic saint; Florence Nightingale (1820–1910), English nurse and writer; and Mary Slessor (1848–1915), Scottish missionary in Nigeria. Her collaborators on the project – Marian Keith, the pseudonym of Mary Esther MacGregor, also the wife of a Presbyterian minister and the author of *Duncan Polite* (1905), and Mabel Burns McKinley, author of *Canadian Heroines of Pioneer Days* (1929) – contributed the remaining essays, whose subjects included Laura Secord (1775–1868), Catharine Parr Traill (1802–1899), Queen Victoria (1819–1901), Madeleine de Verchères (1678–1747), Helen Keller (1880–1968), Ada May Courtice (1860–1923), Edith Cavell (1865–1915), Pauline Johnson (1861–1913), and Marshall Saunders (1861–1947).

Montgomery was less than enthusiastic about her involvement with this project, which she referred to in her journal as "Famous Girls": "I detest it but it will bring in some extra money and that will help out."[1] According to Rubio and Waterston, Montgomery's chapter on Joan of Arc was heavily influenced by George Bernard Shaw's controversial play *Saint Joan* (1924), which she had seen performed in 1924 and which she reread in November 1930.[2] Much of the chapter on Mary Slessor seems to have been lifted from W.P. Livingstone's biography *Mary Slessor of Calabar* (1926).

CHAPTER I

The Maid of France: Joan of Arc

Sometime around the year 1412 a little peasant maid was born in Domremy, a country village of eastern France. Before her was a strange fate. She was to live for a few brief years and in those years she was to change the current of history.

Joan's father was a poor farmer. But there was something in the mother that might partially explain Joan. The wife of James d'Arc was nicknamed Isobel Romée – "the woman who had been to Rome." She had sufficient religious fervor to make the long and dangerous pilgrimage to Rome to see the Pope. What that meant only those who know the condition of Europe at the time can realize.

We do not know what Joan looked like. There are more pictures of her than of any other woman except the Virgin Mary but they are all imaginary. We know she had coal-black hair and she must have been a strapping lass when she could wear the heavy armour of the period and get about in it. No slender, dreamy, ethereal maiden, such as some artists represent her, could have done that. She could plough, too, and tend sheep, as all her chums could. She was normally a gay, gallant little soul, warm-hearted, impulsive, kind to the poor and sick, with a tang of humor and a bit of a temper and a ready tongue. Thus we see the little Joan of that pleasant remote valley, with the long wooded hills on either side, its white sheep, and its white stars of wild strawberry blossoms.

Joan grew up like the other little peasants of her village. She never learned to read or write, but she could spin and sew beautifully. She was a friendly lass, and liked to play with other children in the beautiful woods near the village; only when they hung garlands on the Oak of the Fairies, Joan slipped away and laid hers beneath the statues of the saints in the little village church, especially those of St. Catherine and St. Margaret. When the boys and girls ran races Joan ran, too, and outstripped them all. But times came when she liked to be quiet and pray alone in the church. And the thing she prayed for most earnestly was that God might have pity on France.

France needed it. That unhappy land was torn and distracted. For a hundred years the kings of England had been trying to conquer it. There was no king – only the heir apparent, called the Dauphin. He had never been crowned because eight years before, when Henry of England married the Princess Katherine of France, the French, worn out with ceaseless war, had agreed to accept Henry V's son as their ruler instead of the son of their old king. But all the French were not in favor of this and soon France was divided into two parties. One was for the Dauphin. The other, including the Duke of Burgundy, sided with the English. Civil war ensued, and whichever party was temporarily uppermost, the country people were plundered. The land was full of marauding bands of soldiers. Whole towns fell into decay, and roads grew over with grass. There was no peace anywhere. Even the very children were on opposite sides and fought pitched battles – except in Domremy where everybody was in favor of the Dauphin.

But there were two things that worked against the Dauphin and his chances of ever being firmly seated on the throne of his fathers. The first was that he had never been crowned in Rheims cathedral. No Dauphin was ever held to be really King of France unless he had been anointed with the sacred oil in Rheims cathedral. But Rheims was in the power of the English and there you were. The second, and worst, was the Dauphin himself. He was anything but a hero of romance. He had spindle-shanks and a bulbous nose; he was weak and superstitious, forever blown this way and that way by all the opinions around him. He was a coward and wanted to run away to Spain or Scotland. Hardly a ruler worth fighting for, one would think. But there was something else at stake with him – the rescue of France from foreign bondage. And that was why Joan was praying for him in the little gray church in Domremy.

When Joan was thirteen she began to hear her "voices." Scientific men have been arguing for hundreds of years about those "voices" and coming to no agreement. But there is no doubt whatever that Joan herself firmly believed she heard them. One summer day in her father's garden she saw a great light, like a shining cloud, and a voice told her to go out and save France from the English. Later on she saw St. Catherine and St. Margaret and the Archangel Michael. And they all told her the same thing. This went on for four years.

At first she was terrified and unwilling. Like the child she was, she cried. She did not see what she could do. She was only a poor girl who could not lead soldiers to war. And things were going from bad to worse with the unlucky Dauphin. By this time he held France only south of the Loire. He was so poor he could hardly afford a new pair of boots for his ill-shaped feet. But Orléans was still true to the Dauphin and as long as he held it his case was not hopeless. The English besieged it; if they could take it they would be masters of all France. And nobody knew anything or anybody to prevent them taking it.

Enter Joan!

Joan was seventeen. In far away Domremy she heard of the siege of Orléans. Her voices kept telling her she *must* go and drive the English away. They told her to go to a nearby town, Vaucouleurs, and ask the commander there, Robert de Baudricourt, to send her to the Dauphin. When she saw him she was to tell him she had come to save France. Beautifully simple.

Joan went to an uncle – probably she knew if she went to her father she would be spanked. Girls of seventeen were quite often treated in that way in the France of the middle ages. She told her uncle that she must go to the Dauphin and that Robert de Baudricourt must lend her a small guard of soldiers for the journey. What is strange is that her uncle believed her. What is not strange is that Robert didn't. He laughed at the notion and told her uncle to take the half-witted creature home and box her ears.

Joan did not stay home. She came again. Eventually Robert lent her the guard. Perhaps she had convinced him. Joan had a strange power of convincing people. Or perhaps he thought it the easiest way to get rid of her.

Joan, all through her career, showed herself to be possessed of the sort of glorified common sense which sees the right thing to do and does it. She doffed her red serge dress, cut her black hair short, and donned a boy's suit. It was, as I have said, the sensible thing to do in such a land under such conditions, and consequently it set everyone in church and state by the ears and did more than all else to bring Joan to the stake.

Behold our Joan, then, riding off from Domremy, in her black doublet and cap, her gray tunic and her trunk hose. We are not told what her mother said or felt, but we know she went without her parents' permission, obedient to her voices. She was never to see her wooded hills or her mother's face again.

She was taken to the castle in Chinon and, though she had never seen the Dauphin before, she picked him out among a crowd. Probably this was not the miracle it seemed. Even in Domremy they must have heard of the Dauphin's nose. But Joan clinched the matter by dragging him off into a corner and telling him something he thought she couldn't possibly have known. It convinced him. He was a man very easily convinced. This had not often been a fortunate thing for him but in this case it was.

Then she was taken to Poitiers and badgered and examined for six long weeks by a host of learned priests and lawyers who were not as easily convinced as the Dauphin. They did not doubt that she was advised by spirits, as she claimed, but were they good or evil spirits? The English and the pro-English said she was possessed of devils. They tried to perplex her by their questions but she was too straightforward and common-sensible for them. At last they drew up a report approving of her.

A breath of hope that had long been absent suddenly blew over the French, because they believed in Joan. The Dauphin collected an army to march to the relief of Orléans. White armour was got for Joan and a Scotch painter made her a banner of white cloth sprinkled with gold lilies. The soldiers worshipped her. They even obeyed her when she told them they must not drink or gamble or swear – and they tried to obey her when she told them to pray.

Although Orléans was beleaguered by the English it was really quite possible to get into it by a certain route and Joan got in. This was hailed as another miracle. She headed several sallies so victoriously that confidence returned to the French. As for the English, they were certain she was in league with the devil and they lifted the siege – more from fear of Joan than from any real military set-back. In one of her sallies she was wounded by an arrow and we are told in a quaint old chronicle that she "cried a little." Poor child!

But her voices still guided her and still she obeyed them. She told the Dauphin that she had "only a year," so he must make haste. He was too poor to pay his troops but hundreds kept coming and saying they would serve him for love of the maid. Men and women and little children surged against her stirrups to touch and kiss her mailed hand.

She defeated the whole English army in a great battle in June. The way was now open to Rheims. On the 17th of July the Dauphin was crowned and anointed in the cathedral, Joan standing beside him with her banner in her hand. Her father was there, too. That was her great day. In two months she had driven the English behind the walls of Paris, and the king was king indeed. The king asked her to choose her own reward and she asked that the people of Domremy should be free from paying taxes for-ever. They were free – for three hundred years.

This was the last glad day for Joan the Maid. Her work was done. She was homesick for her own blue hills and the roses in her mother's garden. She wanted to go home but the king would not let her. He was afraid to lose his mascot. But neither he nor his courtiers would be guided by her any longer and everything began to go wrong. When Joan besieged Paris she had every chance of taking it and driving out the English completely. But the cowardly king sent her orders to lift the siege and Joan, broken-hearted, had to obey.

The end of her year was at hand. For many weeks her voices had been predicting evil, telling her she would be taken prisoner by mid-summer. Whatever may be thought of her voices, they told her truly. She was captured during a sally by the Burgundians under Jean de Luxemburg.

Joan could have been ransomed. France was poor but nearly everyone would have given a little for her. Not a penny was paid – no effort was made to ransom her. The coward she had made king left her to her fate.

The rest is pitiful and splendid. Jean de Luxemburg, thrifty creature, sold her to the English, for twenty thousand pounds. It was quite a sum to pay for a few feet of girlish flesh and blood, but the English thought she was cheap at the price. They handed her over to the Inquisition. For three months Joan was kept in chains in a room where five coarse soldiers watched her constantly. For three months her enemies questioned her every day.

She had no advocate to help her defend herself. But she showed she was far wiser than the priests, just as she had shown she was wiser than soldiers and statesmen. She answered all their questions courteously, wisely, even merrily. When they could not get the better of her verbally they threatened her with torture. She did not wince even when they showed her the devilish array of implements.

"What a brave lass. Pity she is not English," said an English lord when he saw her standing up, a slender figure, still in her boy's dress, against the crowd of priests and lawyers.

Even her cruel inquisitors did not go so far as to actually inflict the torture. But in May they brought Joan to a platform in the graveyard of the church at St. Omer and showed her a stake with faggots ready for burning.

Joan's spirit had gradually been broken. She had been very ill. Her gaolers mocked her and jeered at her and made her life a hell. No woman or dear friend was near her. She began to be terribly homesick and longed for the peace and fresh air and open sky of her Domremy. She yielded and put her mark to a paper of confession. She was promised her life and decent treatment. Her judges broke their word. Peter Cauchon, Bishop of Beauvais, whom she had driven from his bishopric, was her bitter enemy. He was determined she should die.

Joan, when she found that she was not to be set free after all but kept in captivity, recanted her confession. "My voices *were* of God," she said.

She was burned in the market-place of Rouen with a guard of eight hundred soldiers to prevent a rescue. On her paper cap was written: "Heretic, Relapsed Apostate." Thus did France reward the girl who had saved her.

Poor little Joan walked to the stake crying and sobbing bitterly. When all was over her ashes were thrown into the Seine, together with her heart, which, strange to say, had not burned. Perhaps – who knows? – having burned so long with spiritual flame, it was proof against earthly fire.

About twenty years after her execution it occurred to her fine king that since she had been burned as a witch he must owe his crown to a witch. The thought was intolerable. Promptly a new trial was arranged for Joan. She was declared innocent, and the sentence against her abolished – which unfortunately could not bring her back to life. In 1919 the Roman Catholic church canonized her as a saint, thus justifying, somewhat tardily, the remark of an English soldier who watched her death: "We are lost. We have burned a saint."

Joan was nineteen when she died. Not many girls of nineteen have saved a kingdom.

CHAPTER II

The Angel of the Crimea: Florence Nightingale

The story of the best loved woman in the world reads like a romance. Her very name smacks of it. Florence Nightingale was born in 1800,[3] the daughter of a wealthy English gentleman. Her childhood and early girlhood, spent in one of the "stately homes of England,"[4] surrounded by meadows of buttercups and clover, with hedges full of wild roses, were just what were to be expected of the Victorian tradition. She was petted, well-educated, protected. It was supposed she would grow up, have a few merry "seasons" in society, make a suitable "match," and settle down to the harmless life of a Victorian gentlewoman. But never did any girl more carefully upset and disarrange the expectations of fond parents.

To be sure, she started out well by being very fond of her dolls. But such dolls! No well, healthy dolls for little Florence. She cared for them only when they were sick or maimed or crippled. Then she nursed them devotedly. She loved animals, too – dogs and ponies especially. And, like the dolls, they were dearer to her if they had something the matter with them. She waited on all the cats that were having kittens and when a shepherd's dog got his leg badly hurt Florence promptly tore up the shepherd's smock and used it as a bandage with hot compresses. The dog got well. It just had to.

Animals did not monopolize her care. Before long the sick villagers were sending for her to ease their sufferings. She had a knack of settling a pillow and rubbing a rheumatic limb – or just simply cheering you up.

Like all the other little girls of her period she could draw and paint, hemstitch, seam, and embroider. She loved flowers and was a good gardener. When she grew up she went to parties and dances, was presented at court, and went for tours on the continent.

So far our Florence with her "pensive" beauty – pensive beauty was a much admired Victorian type – her graceful figure, her shining brown hair, and her "coalscuttle" bonnets, ran true to form. Lovers came a-plenty and she might have picked and chosen.

But she was not content. From her earliest year Florence had felt that she was destined for something else. She must follow her star. She interested herself in the workers of the factories near her home and started a Bible class for the girls. So far, good. Nothing in this that a proper Victorian maiden might not do. But when Florence was twenty-five she wanted to go to Salisbury hospital as a nurse for some months and then set up a sort of Protestant Sisterhood of Nursing.

Her horrified parents squelched this crazy idea promptly. Well-bred young women never did things like that. Nurses, they said, were a most disreputable lot. They were – and not only by Victorian standards, either. Nursing in the early part of the nineteenth century was a very different thing from what it is now. The nurses were all too often coarse, ignorant women, cruel, intemperate, immoral – the kind of women Dickens caricatured in "Sairey Gamp."[5]

Florence obeyed her parents but she did not give up working and planning and gathering knowledge when and where she could. For eight years she studied reports and histories of hospitals. She contrived, during her European tours, to visit all the great hospitals of the continent. These hospitals, run by the Sisters of Mercy, were very different from the unclean, badly-managed hospitals in England. These good Sisters were the only trained nurses in Europe. She even managed three months at Kaiserwerth, a Protestant sisterhood working along the same lines in a modern and enlightened way.

Finally her family yielded to her patient determination and she became superintendent of the Home for Sick Governesses in London.

England was full of governesses. The only way a refined girl could make a living in those days was by going out as a governess. If she had no home or friends what was to become of her if she fell ill? She was sent to this Nursing Home.

But things were in bad shape, partly through lack of means, partly through bad management. The friends of the institution were discouraged but discouragement was a word not found in Florence Nightingale's dictionary. No money? Well, there must be money. She got people interested – money came in – the institution was reorganized – competent nurses were found. But all this meant hard and vexatious work. Her health broke down, and she had to go home to rest.

No doubt her father and mother said, "I told you so."

At this time Florence Nightingale was still young, beautiful, and fascinating – "a perfect woman," somebody called her. Either that somebody didn't know that she knew ancient languages, mathematics, science, and spoke French, German, and Italian fluently – or he was not of the same mind with most of the men of that day regarding the education of women.

In 1854 the Crimean War broke out between Russia and Turkey. England had been at peace for forty years. She and France went into the war on the side of Turkey. Fleets of the allied powers gathered in the Black Sea. The great battle of Alma was fought and the allies were victorious. But, like all great victories, it was bought with the dead and the wounded. And now it became evident that there was gross mismanagement and terrible neglect somewhere. Nobody knew who was to blame for it. Everything was lacking. Food and clothing sent out from England could not be found. No bandages – no medicines – no clean linen – no decency. Appalling stenches – water in the tents a foot deep – snow three feet deep on the level – men dying on the ground – not half enough doctors – *no nurses*. The military authorities had not wanted female nurses – perhaps judging them from the old type. The hospital at Scutari was filled with sick, wounded, dying men, with no one to care for them except a few male orderlies, untrained for the task.

The letters of the war correspondent, William Howard Russell,[6] aroused England and a great cry of anger and sorrow went up from the country.

Sidney Herbert, head of the War Department,[7] knew that only one woman in England had the strength and wisdom and training to grapple with those terrible conditions. Florence Nightingale's great call had come and she was ready for it.

From *Courageous Women*

Mr. Herbert wrote to her asking her to go to Scutari with a band of nurses and take charge of the hospital. A letter of hers crossed his, asking to be allowed to go.

A howl of amazement went up. Nothing like this had ever been known – and the English people do not like novelties. It was not fitting for women to nurse in military hospitals. Their health would be ruined, their morals corrupted.

In six days from the time she accepted the job, Florence Nightingale was ready to start with thirty chosen nurses. The Barrack Hospital at Scutari – that city of mosques and palaces and tombs – was her headquarters and the scene of her labors. Indomitably she confronted the appalling task before her.

Horrors of filth and vermin, cholera and every other plague – fever – only coarse canvas sheets – no bedroom furniture of any kind – wards full to overflowing – corridors crowded with sick and wounded, lying on the floor with rats running over them – dead animals rotting on the grounds outside the windows – no kitchen – no cooks, no laundry – sour bread – filthy butter – meat like leather – no potatoes – no ventilation – no basins, towels, soap, brooms, plates, scissors, knives, forks, spoons, stretchers, splints.

One wonders what there *was*.

And no medical stores to be had! The medical stores were rotting in the warehouse but couldn't be taken out or distributed except by the "proper persons" – and nobody knew who they were. Everything was tied up with red tape. No woman ever before was faced with such a task.

Florence Nightingale was not even welcomed.

The overwrought doctors were suspicious and hostile and furious about a parcel of women coming out "to interfere with their work." Red tape officials were more furious still.

This slender woman in her black dress, her pale beautiful face surmounted by a close-fitting black cap, gave her orders quietly – *and saw that they were obeyed*. People speedily learned that when Florence Nightingale said a thing was to be done it was done. Her voice was low and clear but it was one men had to obey. Few people ever told Florence Nightingale that anything she wanted done couldn't be done.

In ten days a miracle was accomplished. She had established and equipped a kitchen, having had enough foresight to bring out her own stores with her. She had hired a house and set up a laundry. She had distributed clean clothing – she had brought 10,000 shirts with her, among other things. She organized, directed, planned, ordered, made everybody work.

And she worked herself. She would stand on her feet for hours at a time. She superintended all severe operations. She tended – and saved – supposedly hopeless cases herself. There was not always enough chloroform and she stood beside the sufferer and helped him through. She wrote down the dying words of soldiers to send home. Her strength and patience never failed.

As soon as she had the hospital organized she began her battle with the monster, Red Tape. Florence Nightingale was not exactly the creature of unmixed sweetness and light some sentimental biographers have pictured her. Had she been she never could have done the work she did. It took more than sweetness and light to browbeat the fossils of officialdom and compel them to be up and doing. Fortunately Florence had that something. She had a bit of a temper and a somewhat sardonic humor – a sarcasm that lashed unsparingly, and yet, with it all, great tact, judgment, and wisdom. She won over the commander, Lord Raglan, who had at first opposed her coming. She won over doctors and attendants. Everyone carried out her orders willingly, even the men who had growled at her. The sufferers in the wards kissed her shadow as the lady with the lamp went by. When Florence Nightingale went to Scutari the death rate in the Barrack Hospital was 60 per cent. In three months it was reduced to 1 per cent.

In the spring of 1855 Florence Nightingale went to the Crimea to inspect the hospital there. Suddenly she was stricken down with Crimean fever. As she was carried to the sanatorium on a stretcher the rough soldiers wept like children. For several days she lay between life and death. When she recovered her doctors begged her to go home for a rest. But she said her work was not done and back she went to Scutari. Even when the war was over and her name on everybody's lips she did not go home. The hospitals were still full of sick and wounded men. As soon as her strength was restored she went back to the Crimea and took charge of two new camp hospitals. Living in a hut nearby she spent a second winter of hard work and exposure to terrible cold. She established libraries and little reading huts. She got up lectures and classes. She organized cafés where the convalescents could get hot coffee and chocolate in the bitter weather. She even saw that the soldiers wrote home regularly and sent their pay home to their families instead of drinking it away.

On a mountain height above Balaclava towers a great cross of white marble shining like snow against the deep blue sky. This is the "Nightingale Cross," her own tribute to the brave men and devoted nurses who died in the war.

In the spring of 1856 she came home – to realize the bitter truth that she was never going to be strong again. As long as there was work to do her will had ruled her body. Now it sank down broken and exhausted. She had to spend most of the rest of her life in bed or on a sofa. But heart and will and mind were as compassionate and strong as ever. Her sick room was a busy place. All sorts of schemes for reform were worked out there. Under her advice and direction the first training school for nurses was organized and "Sairey Gamp" vanished forever.

In the face of incredible difficulties she got a Royal Commission appointed to inquire into the health of the army and then got its recommendations carried out. Army barracks and hospitals were remodelled, properly ventilated, warmed, lighted. The whole army medical department was re-organized. Then she got a sanitary commission to do the same thing in India. She built hospitals, trained nurses, gave advice to all the governments of Europe. She was nearly ninety-one when the light of her lamp went out. Longfellow has said it all for us:

> A noble type of good
> Heroic Womanhood.[8]

CHAPTER III
The Great White Ma: Mary Slessor of Calabar

To begin life as an uneducated factory girl in a Scottish town and end it as the "uncrowned queen" of an African principality – that is Mary Slessor's life in a sentence. And yet, when she was asked, near the close of her career, to write her autobiography, she couldn't think what she had done that was worth being put in a book. To this woman, of the soft voice and bright, dancing, deep-set eyes, high adventure and jungle explorations, rivers where crocodiles swam, trails where snakes glided, dark, mysterious forests where leopards prowled and elephants trumpeted and boa constrictors roamed at their own sweet will, tornadoes sweeping down from the heights of the Cameroons, the overthrowing of immemorial customs, the rescue of girls who came to her, bleeding and quivering from whips of alligator hide, chumming with and advising and scolding black African kings, brow-beating witch-doctors, building houses and schools and little mud churches with her own hands, cowing mobs, giving six-foot negroes castor oil and Epsom salts and slapping their faces smartly if they objected, solving trade problems, beating off, with a tin basin, hippopotamuses that attacked her canoe, – all these things were such commonplaces of existence that they didn't seem worth writing of! Was there ever such a woman and such a career in the world before?

Mary Slessor was born in a suburb of Aberdeen in December, 1848. Her father was a shoemaker – an intemperate one at that, and she was the second of seven children. Not a great deal is known of her infancy and girlhood. There was poverty, struggle, and hardship in her bare, comfortless home. But the mother sent her children to church every Sunday and saw that they had clean handkerchiefs and knew their catechism. Mary in later life said that she was a "wild lassie." Judging from her career, this probably meant that she saw the funny side of everything, indulged in mischievous pranks now and then, and had a tongue of her own.

The family had moved to Dundee and she worked half-time in a factory until she was fourteen and then she worked full time. Up every morning at five; in the factory weaving monotonously from six to six, with one hour off for breakfast and one for dinner. One wonders how the future pioneer and administrator could endure it.

At this time she had only a slight knowledge of reading and arithmetic. But Mary meant to have an education. She stole time from sleep for study. She read on her way to and from the factory; she worked in a church and taught a class of girls. Later on she taught in a mission for the rough boys and girls of the slums. She taught the "toughs" their place and made them keep it, just as in after years she made chiefs and medicine men toe the mark; and, like the chiefs, if not the witch-doctors, they soon came to love and respect her. She would not tolerate insubordination; but she had a passionate love, even then, for all children, and all the weak and oppressed. The little girl, who often ran sobbing out into the dark, cold streets when her drunken father came home at night, had learned sympathy and understanding in a hard school and its lessons were never forgotten. But her tact and her cheery ways and her unconventional handling of problems were all her own. Some said she was not easy to understand. Geniuses never are. Some said she was eccentric. This meant that she was one of those who "walk where their own nature would be leading."[9]

"Life is so great and grand," she wrote years afterwards. Life is always great and grand to girls with the flame in their souls that was in the soul of Mary Slessor, factory girl in Dundee.

Mary had always been interested in missions, especially in the Calabar mission on the west coast of Africa. Suddenly she began to hope that she might be a missionary herself. At first it seemed a hope impossible of fulfilment. She had to help support her family. For fourteen years she toiled in the factory, studied, prayed, dreamed. And one day the dream came true. Her two sisters became able to support their mother. Mary was free at last, and in 1876 she went to the foreign field as a missionary of the United Presbyterian Church of Scotland.

Of course, some of her friends discouraged her. Or rather, tried to discourage her. There are always people like that. They told her Calabar was frightfully unhealthy – a land of swamps and forests; that it was inhabited by the most lawless and degraded people in Africa; that it was a land of witchcraft and slave markets and skull worshippers and human sacrifices and devil-houses; a land of burning heat and torrential rains and terrific thunderstorms; a land where ants ate your clothing and furniture and cannibals ate you; a land of hunger and fever and death; a land, in short, that was "the white man's grave." What a future for Mary!

"The post of danger is the post of honor," said Mary Slessor; and at the age of twenty-eight she went to seek it.

Green banks – white sands upon which the surf beat – long, grey, dreary levels of mangroves – hot whiffs of tropical odors – brilliant-hued parrots – mud banks – rank, colorful vegetation – flowering trees – tall palms – orchids – pathless forests – gorgeous butterflies – broiling sunshine – luxuriant beauty – filth – vermin – the faint blue Cameroons in the background – this was Calabar. It was peopled by naked blacks, most of whom had never seen a white face; it was not owned or governed by any European power; it was divided into numberless tribes, each one speaking a different dialect, and all perpetually at war with their neighbours. To this land came the plucky little Scotch girl, with her gift of repartee, her inspired common sense, her unyielding determination, her love for all God's creatures. At first very homesick, very timid, often discouraged. At least, we have her own word for it; nobody would guess it from her history.

She learned the language of the natives around her first station at Duketown very soon. From the start she realized that she must minister to the bodies as well as to the souls of these people if she were ever to win them and that the women and children would be her greatest problem. Mary tackled it as only Mary Slessor could. In a very brief time the influence she gained over them was tremendous. On the surface they were not attractive. Lazy, immoral, quarrelsome, dirty, living in hovels surrounded by pools of filth, sending out pestilential odors. Nevertheless, they were women and Mary's heart ached over their sorrows and trials. She entered into all the romance and tragedy of her dark sisters. She bent every energy to alleviating their lot in a land where a man could – and did – do exactly what he liked to his wife – bite her, beat her, divorce her, sell her, kill her. Nobody cared.

To read of Mary Slessor's activities is to feel one's head whirl. She dispensed medicine, she preached, she had a prayer meeting every evening; she taught school to which young and old came, battle-scarred chiefs sitting side by side with little children; she adopted and reared and trained – and *loved* – uncounted numbers of black babies that had been cast out into the jungles to die; she prescribed and bandaged, she taught the girls how to wash and iron and make clothes; she presided over "palavers," she nursed patients covered from head to foot with loathsome sores; she waged war against ants; she saved lives from the "poison" ordeal, she fought with and worsted witch-doctors; she settled all kinds of disputes, she pacified drunken or panic-stricken mobs, she reconciled runaway wives to their husbands, she settled tribal and domestic quarrels; she vaccinated people and married them; and all with unfailing tenderness and good humor, throwing in a little sarcasm and plenty of jokes. Perhaps the natives thought her broad Scotch accent was some peculiarly strong kind of magic. Once when a chief who was a friend of hers died in a smallpox epidemic she made a coffin for him with her own hands, dug his grave, and buried him. No wonder the natives believed she possessed superhuman powers. And may they not have been right?

Much as Mary Slessor was loved by the women and children of that dark land her influence over and success with men were even more marked. She had a wonderful knack of winning the confidence of these wild creatures. She won over the chiefs by her frankness and fearlessness. She won over old men who growled – as old men in all countries and in all times have growled – that "the old customs were better than the new." The young men adored her and called her their "great white ma." Always she was treated by them gallantly and courteously. And when she had finally succeeded in persuading husbands that when twin babies were born one of them was not a demon her victory over them was complete.

Yet this indomitable creature, who bossed native kings and fought witch-doctors to a finish in their own stamping grounds, when she went home to Scotland on furlough, was too timid to speak in public if there were any men in the audience and ran like a hunted thing when she met a harmless cow on the road.

In spite of her spirit her body was a frail tenement. She was often bitterly homesick and hungry for letters from home. She was subject to frequent attacks of fever and rheumatism. And she never took care of herself. Sometimes at night "her only shelter was a mud hut and her only bed a bundle of filthy rags." She starved herself to feed her hungry black babies; she walked barefooted along jungle trails in spite of snakes and "jiggers."

"I often had a lump in my throat," she said, "and my courage repeatedly threatened to fly away though nobody guessed it."

No, nobody would ever have guessed it. Mary was one of those who

> ... always marched breast forward
> Never doubting clouds would break.[10]

She never troubled about conventions but dressed as she liked – lucky woman! She went hatless and bobbed her lank brown hair long years before it became the fashion; she received callers composedly sitting on the roof of her house, repairing it. But those who met her declared she was the most fascinating woman they had ever known.

When Mary Slessor had spent twelve years in and around her first station a great change had come over the people. The local gods were banished, baby murder and human sacrifices were unknown; the people were comparatively civilized and many had become Christians. She might have spent the rest of her life there, still finding plenty to do.

But Mary Slessor was essentially a pioneer. She was one of the order of spirits to which Livingstone belonged.[11] In answer to her plea she was sent to the Okoyong district. "The great adventure of my life," she called it. But in spite of that she didn't sleep very well the night before she left.

Small wonder. The Okoyong people were more deeply sunk in devilry than any she had encountered yet. All kinds of horrors were rampant among them. The teacher who had preceded her had had to flee for his life. Mary has admitted that her heart failed her. She felt a desire to turn and flee. But did she? Not Mary. Like the drummer boy of the immortal story *her* drum had never learned to beat a retreat. She went to the Okoyong – she spent fourteen years there – she subdued and civilized and Christianized it.

When she had been in Okoyong three years she was appointed by the British government to organize and supervise a native court. Her wonderful mastery of the native language was a great asset. It was said she could talk it better than the natives themselves – joke in it, scold in it, harangue in it, as well as preach and pray in it. She had an amazing grip of the most intricate native and political problems of the country. By 1903 she had civilized the Okoyong. Then she went and did it all over again in the Enyong Creek district.

In passing we may note that at the age of sixty she found it would be convenient to ride a bicycle, so she promptly learned to ride one.

The British Government made her a magistrate at Enyong Creek. Behold our Mary sitting on the bench with three local chiefs, deciding murder cases, investigating suicides, dealing with men brought up for branding their wives all over the face and body with a red-hot iron – something they could have done with impunity before her advent. If one of the chiefs who presided with her was obstreperous she thought nothing of giving him a sound cuff on the side of the head. And he bore it meekly.

But even devoted missionaries and fearless pioneers must grow old. She was gradually coming to the end of her strength. And yet, in 1910, when she went to another new place, she said she was the happiest woman in the world. The fire of youth still burned in her eyes. It burned on till 1915, when she died in the little hut she had built for herself on a hill-top, with only her wee black babies and "girls" around her.

Faith – hope – love. These were the secret springs of Mary Slessor's life. "And the greatest of these was Love."[12]

NOTES

1 Montgomery, 30 May 1932, in *SJLMM*, 4: 183.
2 *SJLMM*, 4: 400; see also Montgomery, 18 November 1930, in *SJLMM*, 4: 91.
3 Nightingale's actual birthdate was 1820.
4 From "The Homes of England" (1827), by Felicia Hemans (1793–1835), English poet.
5 Sarah "Sairey" Gamp, an alcoholic nurse and midwife, is a character in *The Life and Adventures of Martin Chuzzlewit* (1844), a novel by Charles Dickens.
6 William Howard Russell (1820–1907), considered one of the first war correspondents, covered the Crimean War for almost two years for the London *Times*.
7 Sidney Herbert, 1st Baron Herbert of Lea (1810–1861), was also a confidant of Florence Nightingale.
8 From "Santa Filomena" (1857), a poem by Henry Wadsworth Longfellow.
9 Properly, "I'll walk where my own nature would be leading." From an untitled and undated poem by Emily Brontë (1818–1848), English novelist and poet.

10 Properly, "One who never turned his back but marched breast forward, / Never doubted clouds would break." From "Epilogue to Asolando" (1889), a poem by Robert Browning (1812–1889), English poet.

11 David Livingstone (1813–1873), Scottish medical missionary.

12 1 Corinthians 13:13 in the Christian Bible. The King James Bible translation of this verse is "but the greatest of these [is] charity," but most other translations read "the greatest of these is love."

60

Author to Get No Profit as *Green Gables* Filmed

—— 1934 ——

In April 1934, Montgomery heard from a correspondent in Hollywood that RKO Radio Pictures was planning a second film adaptation of *Anne of Green Gables*. Because Montgomery had sold all remaining rights to the book to its publisher in 1919, she would not receive any royalties or have any creative involvement in the project. Montgomery's curiosity was nonetheless piqued by the fact that child actor Dawn O'Day (1916–1993), whose birth name was Dawn Paris, had changed both her screen name and her legal name to Anne Shirley after being cast in the film. (She would appear as such in more than thirty additional films until her retirement in 1945.) As Montgomery explained to G.B. MacMillan in 1936 about seeing the name "Anne Shirley" in promotional materials for films that had nothing to do with *Anne of Green Gables*, "I have the weirdest sensation that *Anne* has really come to life."[1] As indicated by the title of this article, published in the *Toronto Daily Star* in September 1934, and by its deck – "L.M. Montgomery Assigned Dramatic Rights to Publishers 15 Years Ago" – its focus is almost solely on Montgomery and provides no details of the actual film. However, it is accompanied by a montage of photographs of Montgomery, "Anne Shirley" in costume, actor O.P. Heggie (who had been cast as Matthew Cuthbert), and Ewan Macdonald – a curious choice, given that, at the time of the interview, Montgomery's husband reportedly was upstairs in his bedroom in the middle of one of his melancholic episodes, which Montgomery referred to as "spells." As Montgomery reported in her journal concerning the interview, "I was in torture all the time, not knowing what Ewan might be doing or feeling. [The reporter] asked so many ridiculous questions I would have liked to throw something at him."[2] In a slightly different version of this article in an undated and unidentified newspaper, an additional paragraph appears immediately after the lead, referring to an incident that had occurred a few weeks earlier: "An almost tragic mishap occurred when her husband, Rev. Ewan Macdonald, was accidentally poisoned. Fortunately, he is now completely recovered."[3]

Anne of Green Gables, written by Mrs. Ewan Macdonald (L.M. Montgomery),[4] which ranks to-day as a novel of world-wide fame, just now is in process of being filmed, a remarkable fact in connection with this logical fate of a great work, being that the author will not derive a cent from the process. Probabilities are that no Canadian ever wrote a book or created a character so famous as *Anne of Green Gables*. The author lives to-day at Norval, Ont., where she is busy on a new novel that may eclipse her former great triumph. She will receive no remuneration from movie producers because she sold the dramatic rights to her book to the publishers in 1919.

Though she will receive no remuneration, Mrs. Macdonald[5] treasures an autographed picture she received from 16-year-old Anne Shirley, who plays the leading role. Mrs. Macdonald thinks the charming girl actress is well chosen to play the part of the red-haired child whom Mark Twain called "the most delightful creation of child life since the immortal Alice."

"Anne" has made Mrs. Macdonald as dear to the hearts of girls as was Louisa May Alcott and the delightful freshness and simplicity of her books gives them a never-failing charm. Sixteen are set in Prince Edward Island, but one, *The Blue Castle*, in which her favorite cat Good Luck is depicted, has its location in Muskoka.

Rejected Five Times

Incredible though it may seem, publishers five times rejected the book that was to make her famous, and for four years the manuscript collected dust in the attic of the Macneill[6] homestead at Cavendish, Prince Edward Island, where she lived with her grandmother. One day while spring cleaning she found it in a corner and became so interested in the story that she completely forgot the work she had come to do. For the sixth time she submitted the book, sending it to a Boston publisher. Fortunately, one of his readers was from Prince Edward Island, and she became so interested in the vivid portrayal of the homesteads and country schools, woods and orchards, wild rose hedges, the song of the salt sea air, long red roads and fieldstone dykes of one of the loveliest islands in the world, that she persuaded him to "take a chance." And on June 29, 1908, *Anne of Green Gables* made her debut.

"Writing a book and making love are alike in that you don't know how it is done," smiled Mrs. Macdonald when asked if she had any "formula" for successful writing. "I just allow the story to grow in my mind, and I am always sorry when I finish a book. Making your characters live is the secret of writing a successful book," she commented.

"The day of horrible realism is over," Mrs. Macdonald continued. "People are finding out that after all the world needs a few fairy tales."

Started at Age of Nine

A firm believer in "happy endings," Mrs. Macdonald, whose kindly face still retains a fair share of her youthful loveliness, started her career by writing verse at the age of nine. There was so little paper available for her ideas that she used the letter bills from the mail bags which went through the post-office kept by her grandfather. As a reward for her first literary effort, a magazine allowed her to pick seeds to the value of 50 cents!

She has just signed a contract for the dramatization of her only love story, *The Blue Castle*, and is now working on a sequel to *Pat of Silver Bush*.[7] After she broke with her original publishers in 1919 she successfully sued them for publishing some of her writings, carrying the case, which lasted nine years, to the supreme court of the United States.

Married 21 years ago and mother of two handsome sons, Chester, who is studying law in Toronto, and Stuart, junior gymnastic champion of Canada, who is in his first year in medicine at Toronto University,[8] Mrs. Macdonald thinks the modern girl is "very much like she used to be; perhaps to-day she says the things we always thought." In every age, she remarked, there is a certain proportion of "high fliers, but present-day girls, generally speaking, will ultimately settle down to the responsibilities of marriage," she felt.

Mrs. Macdonald confessed that when she was a girl she always read boys' books. "I can't stick the pure and simple love story," she exclaimed. "I like to read about adventure."

Criticizes Canadian Authors

The reason Canada appears to neglect some of her native authors is because their books are not interesting enough, she declared. "Too many books are being turned out without any special appeal, but the Canadian public is quick to appreciate a good book."

Mrs. Macdonald worked hard to achieve international renown. Most of her books have been translated into Danish, Swedish, Dutch, Polish, French and Braille. Australia shows as much enthusiasm as Canada and the United States over her work. There is a mother superior in an Australian convent who is so impressed by her books that every night she kneels in the chapel and prays that some day she may become a Roman Catholic. "Her letter touched me deeply," said Mrs. Macdonald.

One of the first of the hundreds of letters which Mrs. Macdonald received after *Anne of Green Gables* was first published was from a Roman Catholic priest who wrote that he was taking the book with him to a retreat for nuns in the south of England. He explained the nuns were not supposed to read secular books, but thinking they would enjoy "Anne," he had secured a special dispensation in order that he might give it to them.

Children Hardest to Please

Children are the hardest readers in the world to write for, in the opinion of Canada's most famous woman novelist. "They are not the kindest of critics, and you can't put things over them," she remarked. "Stories must ring true if they are going to attract children."

Mrs. Macdonald was 13 when her first story was published in a competition run by the Montreal[9]

NOTES

1 Montgomery to MacMillan, 27 December 1936, in *MDMM*, 179. For more on the actor Anne Shirley, see Lefebvre, "What's in a Name?"
2 Montgomery, 4 September 1934, in *SJLMM*, 4: 295, 296.
3 SR, 379; see Montgomery, 17 August 1934, in *SJLMM*, 4: 284–87.
4 I have corrected the original, which reads "Evan MacDonald."
5 Here and throughout, I have corrected the original, which reads "MacDonald."
6 I have corrected the original, which reads "McNeil."
7 Montgomery signed a contract for a dramatization of *The Blue Castle* in August 1934, but by October 1935 the project had petered out. Her next book, *Mistress Pat: A Novel of Silver Bush*, would be published in fall 1935.
8 Montgomery had actually been married twenty-three years previously.
9 The article ends abruptly, and the continuation has not been found.

61

Film Preview of Noted Novel Honors
Canadian Woman Writer

—— 1934 ——

This short article, published in the *Globe* in November 1934, records some
of Montgomery's spontaneous comments after she watched a preview of the
second film version of *Anne of Green Gables* at the Film Exchange Building in
Toronto. In a similar article appearing in the *Toronto Daily Star*, Montgomery
is quoted as being far more emphatic about Mary Miles Minter, who played
Anne in the 1919 silent film, and who "was far too sugary. I felt like getting up
and slapping her." In an article published in the *Toronto Telegram*, she
reminded readers of what happened to that earlier film and its star: "you
may remember Mary Miles Minter was mentioned in a murder scandal when
William Desmond Taylor, film director, was found dead in his apartment – that
of course killed her role and the picture naturally for the time, and so it was
never shown in Europe." As she recorded in her journals, however, her enjoyment of the film was marred by the fact that her husband, seated in front of
her, was in the depths of another spell. "And then to have reporters coming up
to ask 'what I thought of it etc.' I don't know what I said."[1]

In an undated letter sent to Leo Devaney, who is also mentioned in this article, she recorded what was taken up as her official endorsement of the film:

"In the picture of 'Green Gables,' Anne certainly came to life. She is
Anne, and I feel I can never again say, when people ask me if Anne is a
'real girl,' that she has no existence except in the pages of the book.

"Taken all round, I felt that the picture and the dialogue made a very
harmonious whole, with none of the jarring elements which disfigured
the silent picture several years ago. It also gave me a much better sense of
reality than the silent picture."[2]

Yesterday afternoon in a tiny studio theatre in the Film Building, Victoria Street, a book written by a Canadian almost twenty-five years ago, came to life on the screen and took form and sound. The picture was none other than *Anne of Green Gables*, and seated among the audience of eight was a smart, grey-haired, soft-spoken lady, in whose honor the preview was held. She was L.M. Montgomery, or Mrs. E. Macdonald of Norval, Ont.

"For the first two-thirds of the picture it stayed very closely to my book," Mrs. Macdonald told *The Globe* and admitted that the ending, altered in order to bring it into picture-length, did make her "feel a bit teary." And she hastened to explain that the alteration was only natural when it was remembered that the love story of Anne ("spelled with an e") Shirley, the adopted child of Matthew and Marilla Cuthbert, ran through three novels.

To Anne Shirley,[3] leading player, went the full praise of the creator of her role for a splendid interpretation. "She has some ginger, she is peppery, just as I imagined her when the book was written," Mrs. Macdonald commented. "You know the book was filmed in the silent screen in 1919. Mary Miles Minter had the role at that time and she never pleased me. She was far too sugary-sweet.

"Strangely enough I always pictured Matthew as a man with a long white beard, but this Matthew (played by O.P. Heggie) is really very fine.

"The big criticism I can make," said the author, who was raised on the north shores of Prince Edward Island, "is that it is not Prince Edward Island. It is California, and it has not the austere beauty of Prince Edward Island."

Anne Shirley, after playing this, her first leading role, legally adopted the name. She was previously Dawn O'Day.

When questioned if she had ever considered adapting any of her other books for the screen, Mrs. Macdonald laughed. "No, I have not the knack of writing for the screen," she replied. "That, I think, is entirely another business." It was then, however, that she told *The Globe* that she is extremely interested at present in watching the results of her book *The Blue Castle* as a stage play. The adaptation has already begun, she stated.

Anne of Green Gables is to make its first Toronto appearance at the Imperial Theatre on Friday, Dec. 7, Leo M. Devaney, R.K.O. Distributing Corporation Manager, told *The Globe*.[4]

NOTES

1 *The Toronto Daily Star*, "'Anne of Green Gables,' Screened," 19; "'Anne
   of Green Gables' Film Will Be Canadian's Triumph," *The Toronto Telegram*, undated clipping, in SR, 396; Montgomery, 12 November 1934, in
   SJLMM, 4: 319.
2 "A Harmonious Whole," unidentified and undated clipping, in SR, 449.
3 Here and below, I have corrected the original, which reads "Ann Shirley."
4 The Imperial Theatre, first known as the Pantages Theatre when it was
   built in 1920, is now known as the Canon Theatre and is located on
   Victoria Street in Toronto, down the block from the Film Exchange Building.

62

Is This My Anne

—— 1935 ——

L.M. MONTGOMERY

In this article, evidently written shortly after she saw the preview of the *Anne of Green Gables* talkie in November 1934 and published in *The Chatelaine* in January 1935, Montgomery recorded her impressions of two film versions of her novel that were made without her creative involvement or permission. In doing so, while maintaining her sense of humour, she implicitly reasserted her authority as "authoress of the famous *Anne of Green Gables* recently brought to the screen," to quote from this article's deck. Moreover, she was far more diplomatic here than she was in private: "I could have shrieked with rage," she vowed in her journal over the presence of the American flag in the 1919 film.[1]

Many years ago I sat down one spring evening, in the kitchen of an old Prince Edward Island farmhouse, and wrote the first chapter of my first book, *Anne of Green Gables*.

It might be more correct to say that I sat "up." For I climbed up on the high, old-fashioned sofa and sat on the end of the kitchen table, by the west window, to catch the last gleams of sunset. It was one of my favorite roosts for writing. I have always liked to write with my portfolio on my knee and the sofa made a capital footrest. And I could look out into an old apple orchard and a ferny grove of spruces and birches.

Outside it was a warm blossomy May evening. There had been a shower and the leaves of the big maple that almost brushed the window were wet and glistening. I finished one chapter and then, a caller dropping in, I put the work away.[2] I hadn't the most remote idea that I would one day sit in a theatre and see that chapter "come to life" on the screen. At that time "movies" were not even dreamed of; and if they had been, it would never have occurred to me that my simple little story of life in the Maritimes, nine miles from a railroad and twenty miles from a town, would make its appearance in them. Yet the other day I sat with a small group and saw a preview of the film, just before it was released in Canada.

Although I began the story that long-ago night, I had been "brooding" it for some time, waiting until I could find leisure to write it in the intervals of writing the "pot-boilers" by which I made my living. Indeed, *Green Gables* itself was first intended for a pot-boiler, and only escaped that fate because *Anne* simply wouldn't be confined within the limits of a pot-boiler. She demanded more "scope."

People ask me how I came to create *Anne*. I didn't create her. She simply sprang into being in my mind, all ready created – Anne, spelled with an e, red-haired, dreamy-eyed and elfin-faced. Yet she seemed so real to me that when I tell people that she is "entirely fictitious" I have the uncomfortable feeling that I am not telling the truth.

People ask me, too, why I gave her red hair. I didn't. It *was* red. And as I described her long red braids as she sat on the shingle pile at Bright River Station, I did not foresee a curious situation of the future when four prominent lawyers of the Boston Bar would sit around a table piled high with dictionaries and books of engravings, and argue heatedly for three mortal days over the exact tint of Anne's tresses. Were they or were they not Titian red? And if they were, then just what shade exactly *was* Titian red?[3]

In due time *Green Gables* was completed and started out to find a publisher. Eventually one was found and Anne made her bow to a world that took her at once to its heart. To my unbounded surprise I found that my little story seemed to possess universal appeal. Letters soon began to pour in. They have been pouring in ever since. Anne has gone through so many editions that I have lost count of them.[4]

In 1921 Anne appeared in the "silent" pictures.[5] Mary Miles Minter starred as Anne, but I did not like her. She was too "sugary sweet" – not a scrap like my gingery Anne. There was a good Matthew and a good Marilla and a passable Gilbert, but on the whole the picture made me furious. The producers evidently thought it had to be "pepped up," and they introduced a lot of absurdities – among others, Anne at the door of her school, a shotgun in hand, standing off a crowd of infuriated villagers who were bent on mobbing her because she had whipped one of her pupils!

There were two things in the silent film that especially enraged me. One was the fact that in a scene at Queen's Academy, on the occasion of Anne's graduation, the Stars and Stripes was prominently displayed! The other was that on her way to a Sunday-school picnic Anne foregathered with a skunk which she mistook for a kitten!

Now, at that time there were no skunks in Prince Edward Island nor ever had been, and I was jealous for the good name of my fair native land. But "coming events cast their shadows before."[6] A few years afterward some brilliant Island mind conceived the idea of breeding skunks for their fur. Fox farming was profitable. Why not skunk farming? Accordingly some man started a skunk ranch and imported several pairs of skunks. But the ranch did not pay. It was abandoned. The bars were thrown down and the skunks left to wander at their own sweet will. In a few years the Island was overrun with them. They became such a nuisance that the Government was compelled to offer a bounty per snout for deceased skunks. As a result the skunk population has been reduced but some still remain.

The silent film was a huge box-office success but in mid-career it suddenly ceased to be. It had been advertised for release in Great Britain, but it was never shown and Mary Miles Minter disappeared with it. I never knew the reason for years. Then one day in a railway station I bought a book for train reading with the delightful title, *Twelve Unsolved Murder Mysteries*. Among them was that of William Desmond Taylor, the director of Anne, who had been found murdered on the floor of his Hollywood bungalow. The murderer, or murderess, was never discovered. Mary Miles Minter was not suspected of it, though it ruined the careers of two other stars; but the police found in Desmond's desk a packet of letters which proved that the little golden-haired star who was heralded as a rival to Mary Pickford,[7] had been in love with her director – who had a wife somewhere – and the great American public threw back its head and howled. Her career was ended and every film in which she had starred was hastily withdrawn from circulation.[8]

That was thirteen years ago. The other day I sat and watched the "talkie" with mingled feelings. On the whole I liked it much better than the silent picture. Naturally, no picture can, in the very nature of things, reflect the characters and setting just as the author has conceived them. So at times I had the sensation of watching a story written by somebody else.

The little girl who played the part of Anne – whom we must call Anne Shirley, since she has taken that name for the screen – is a good

Anne. There were many moments when she tricked even me into feeling that she *was* Anne. I loved the "rick-rack" braid on her pinafore: it was just what I wore myself once. Matthew, whom I have always seen with a long grey beard, seemed a stranger to me at first, but he was so good that I finally forgave him his clean-shaven face. Oddly enough, both Matthew and Gilbert Blythe were exceedingly like the Matthew and Gilbert of the silent pictures, though entirely different people. Marilla was not the tall, thin, austere Marilla of my conception, but it was impossible to help liking her. I had, for the time being, the conviction that although Marilla was not the least like that, she should have been.

Of all the cast I liked Mrs. Barry the least. They tried to make a composite of Mrs. Barry and Rachel Lynde, and the hybrid result was not satisfactory. And Diana was a washout.

There were no American flags in the picture. Canada and the Island were given some credit for the story. Prince of Wales College was even mentioned by name. Which indicates some faint glimmerings of a sense of geography on the part of Hollywood, which seemed entirely lacking in the silent version. The opening views are real Island pictures but the rest of the setting is California, not Prince Edward Island; and "Green Gables" is New England colonial and not an Island farmhouse. The river where Anne was nearly drowned, while dramatizing *Elaine*,[9] is not my blue Lake of Shining Waters. But how could it be? One must not be unreasonable.

Naturally, the introduction of dialogue into the picture adds to the verisimilitude and is a distinct asset to stories which, like mine, owe much of their interest to the "talk." The producers sent me a copy of the script, but I had no "say" in it in any way or in any features of the story which was bought outright from the publishers. For two-thirds of the film my story was followed with reasonable fidelity. In the remaining third the producers "produced" a narrative of their own for the purpose of providing Anne with a love story. They dragged in the old Montague–Capulet *motif* and everything ended bee-yew-tifully, with Matthew – who died in the book – rescued from the brink of the grave.[10] But I am devoutly thankful that they did *not* end the story with a long lingering kiss between Anne and Gilbert. Had they done so I would have risen up and shrieked!

On the whole, the "talkie" gave me a much greater sense of reality than the silent picture. And I looked back to the evening of long ago, when I began the story of Anne with a smile and a sigh. For it is a "far cry" from those days to these, and the creation of the story and its characters and atmosphere gave to me a delight that Hollywood cannot give or take away.

To see one's own story on the screen certainly provides plenty of "thrills." But one always wonders!

NOTES

1 Montgomery, 22 February 1920, in *SJLMM*, 2: 373.

2 In a journal entry dated 1914, Montgomery revealed that the caller in question was her then-future husband, Ewan Macdonald (Montgomery, 18 April 1914, in *SJLMM*, 2: 147).

3 This discussion took place in June 1920 as part of the lawsuit concerning *Further Chronicles of Avonlea*, which Page had published with an image of a red-haired woman on the cover in violation of his agreement not make the volume look like an "Anne" book (Montgomery, 18 June 1920, in *SJLMM*, 2: 382).

4 Because she stopped receiving any revenue from *Anne of Green Gables* after she sold her remaining rights to Page in early 1919, she stopped keeping track of its sales.

5 The film was released in late 1919; Montgomery saw it in February 1920. See the epilogue to this volume for a "story of the photoplay" of the film.

6 From "Lochiel's Warning" (1801), by Thomas Campbell.

7 Mary Pickford (1892–1979), Toronto-born actor, writer, and producer who would become a sweetheart of early Hollywood cinema. She starred in nearly 250 films between 1909 and 1933, including William Desmond Taylor's three films prior to *Anne of Green Gables* – *Captain Kidd, Jr.*, *Johanna Enlists*, and *How Could You, Jean?* – all released in 1919. All three films had scripts by Frances Marion, who also wrote the script for *Anne of Green Gables*.

8 For more on Montgomery, Minter, and Taylor, see Hammill, *Women, Celebrity, and Literary Culture*, 100–102, 113–18; Lefebvre, "What's in a Name?" 198; Montgomery, 13 October 1929, in *SJLMM*, 4: 20.

9 In this film, in fact, Anne is dramatizing Tennyson's "The Lady of Shalott" after a classroom humiliation involving one of her teacher's former pupils. This substitution of Tennysonian texts recurs in a later television miniseries of *Anne of Green Gables* by Kevin Sullivan (Lefebvre, "Stand by Your Man," 158–59).

10 In a discussion of the "Americanization" of Montgomery's novel in Hollywood, Theodore F. Sheckels notes that the 1934 film is "*Romeo and Juliet* superimposed upon *Anne of Green Gables*" (Sheckels, "Anne in Hollywood," 185).

63

Foreword to *Up Came the Moon,*
by Jessie Findlay Brown
—— 1936 ——

L.M. MONTGOMERY

This volume of poems by Prince Edward Island author Jessie Findlay Brown was self-published in 1936. The foreword is signed "L.M. Montgomery," but the tag "With Introduction by the Author of *Anne of Green Gables*" appears on the title page. As Mary Henley Rubio notes, Montgomery's "courteous (and very tepid)" foreword coincided with a negative review of the book in the *Toronto Daily Star*.[1]

A few years ago I picked up a Toronto paper and came across a poem in praise of Prince Edward Island. It was the name that attracted me to it, but, when I had read it once for the sake of "The Island," I read it over again for its own sake, and clipped it out for my scrapbook.[2] The name signed to it was Jessie Findlay Brown, a name then unknown to me; but since that time I have watched for her work, and I am glad that she is publishing her poems in this collected volume of her verse.

Miss Brown's poems are full of "the unsung beauty hid Life's common things below."[3] She is very close to Nature and interprets the loveliness of the world in a graceful and appealing way. When she writes of "fairy glens where twin-flowers blow," of "the clover leaves saying their prayers at night" and of "snow on hillsides, white and pure and high," we are there with her, seeing them and loving them.[4] She has learned the joy of earth, of winds and woods and "wild brown water singing,"[5] and brings it all to us in her verses; she voices the delight of friendship, of loving, loyal pets – (I like her poems about dogs particularly) – of common, everyday people, living and loving, sorrowing and rejoicing, dreaming and believing.

There is something for every age in this little volume – and a spice of humour to give flavour to the feast. I hope Miss Brown will keep the promise of "Some Day"[6] – and, if she does, I'd like to read the result on "the roof."[7] "Up Came the Moon" is my favourite poem of all in this collection.

NOTES

1 Rubio, *Lucy Maud Montgomery*, 479.

2 Montgomery's Black Scrapbook 1 contains a signed leaflet containing Brown's poem "I Would Return," which appears as "Abegweit" in this volume; see Montgomery, Black Scrapbook, 1: 34.

3 Properly, "The unsung beauty hid life's common things below." "Dedication," from *Songs of Labor* (1850), by John Greenleaf Whittier.

4 From the poems "Abegweit," "Clover Leaves," and "The Lovely Things," in Brown's volume (27, 51, 56).

5 Properly, "wild, brown water sing." From the poem "All in the Red October," in Brown's volume (23).

6 In "Some Day," the final poem in the volume, the speaker outlines her plan to write a book and include both "the nasty people" and "the people that I love," predicting that the inability of both groups of people to recognize themselves will be amusing for both the author and the reader (78).

7 In "Up Came the Moon," the first poem in the volume, the speaker describes the companionship of sitting up on a roof with a friend (7).

64

Come Back with Me to Prince Edward Island
—— 1936 ——

L.M. MONTGOMERY
Author of *Anne of Green Gables*

In a journal entry dated April 1936, Montgomery mentioned that she had been asked to contribute an essay to a special issue of *The Maritime Advocate and Busy East* on Prince Edward Island and that she had decided to write "a condensed form of what I wrote in this journal some years ago on Chas. Macneill's old diary."[1] Montgomery first read this diary in 1923 while visiting Charles Macneill's son and daughter-in-law, Alec and May Macneill (to whom she dedicated *Pat of Silver Bush*), and, according to her journal, they found it so unintentionally funny that they "laughed until the tears poured from [their] eyes."[2] Montgomery copied the diary into her own journal two years later for preservation, calling it "a curious record of the life of a farmer on the North Shore of P.E. Island thirty or forty years ago," one that would "have a certain value in the future" – but, perhaps because she found it "tedious to read and unthinkably tedious to copy," this record was not included in the published *Selected Journals*.[3] In this article, which appeared in spring 1936, Montgomery used this diary as a springboard for a set of reminiscences about rural life in Prince Edward Island – an aspect of the natural world that tends not to be emphasized in her fiction.

Changes come more slowly, I think, in Prince Edward Island than else-where. We are not hidebound or overly conservative ... this word being used in a strictly non-political sense, be it understood ... but we do not rush madly after new fads and fashions simply because they *are* new. We wait calmly until after other parts of the world have tried them out and then, if they have passed the test, we adopt them. But even thus changes come and in the last thirty years they have come more rapidly, even in this last outpost of leisure and dream.

Some time ago an old Prince Edward Island diary fell into my hands ... a diary written by a Prince Edward Island farmer when I was a child. It made me realize as I had never realized before how many changes have come to Abegweit since my youth.[4] In some ... in many ways ... the old Island is changed ... mostly for the better ... in some things, I honestly think, for the worse.

To most readers that old diary would probably have seemed very tedious reading. But to me every sentence in it was a delight. I was back again in a world where simple happiness reigned and problems were nonexistent ... for children at least. The most commonplace entry seemed like a finger touching the keys of an organ and evoking melodies of haunting sweetness. Sights ... sounds ... of that old north shore came back to me. Old friends were alive again to run with me under the moon and together we slipped back into that garden where the sword is set and mortals may not pass – the Eden of childhood.

Yes, every line has its charm for me, even the entries about the weather. It, at least, has not changed. The old diarist writes that it is "raining heavily." In a trice I am standing at his old kitchen door looking out to sea. The rain is coming down steadily over the wide green fields, the dark groves of spruce, the little golden dells between. The long red road grows darker and redder in the wet. White-washed houses gleam out like marble against emerald hills. Far out lies the sea; gray in a mist of rain. Sometimes the diarist adds that it is thundering and I see the huge black clouds riding up and far out to sea a shaft of lightning pierces the sky and the woods have grown dim in their skirts of shadow.

Or he complains that "it is very poor weather for haying." I see the hayfields ... rippling in the wind ... lying in lustrous, fragrant swathes after mowing ... covered with "coils" in the light of July sunsets ... haunted and still on nights of white moon splendor.

Perhaps the rain comes on Sunday when folks are "at preaching." I am back in an old Presbyterian church ... and everybody else is there. Folks dead and buried for a quarter of a century hurry out of their graves and come to fill their accustomed pews just because I read in an old diary that "it rained at preaching." Not one is missing, from the old Scotsman in the front centre pew, who looks like a Hebrew prophet left over from olden time, to the graceless lads of my own generation in the back pews. The minister is preaching ... none of your modern fifteen minute creeds but a solid discourse lasting nearly an hour ... the choir are "up in the gallery," and the rain is streaming against the high, narrow white glass windows. I look out of the one so blessedly near our pew. The pond is gray down in the valley ... the sand dunes can hardly be seen for rain ... the sea beyond moans on its rocky shore. The horses tied to the wooden graveyard fence ... which they have half gnawed away ... don't like the rain. The women are wondering what will happen to their mantles and bustles and bangs and pompadours and quilted satin bonnets and flowered and feathered hats on the way home ... for there are no cars and very few top-buggies. But the wet landscape has a charm all its own. I rather like it when it "rains at preaching."

Or perhaps it is just "blowing hard." The wind may be north. Then it comes swooping up from the shore, whirls through the yard and whistles around the eaves. The gulf is dotted with white caps and near the shore, just beyond the low fields, is a line of breakers under a mist of foam. Or it may be a south or west wind and then it is a lovesome thing, purring softly over the slopes and laughing in the gardens. Or it is east ... sad, mournful, blowing up from a gray and haunted shore. Night comes down in the blackness of a wild autumn storm and my chum, Janie, (she was the daughter of the diarist)[5] and I run into the house laughing and shut the door in its face. Who said Janie was dead? I see her as I read. Kipling says "the Lords of our Life and death shut the doors behind us"[6] ... but sometimes they swing open for a moment and the ghostly hands of winds that blew forty years ago play with our hair again.

Or it is "a fine bright day." Who should know better than I what a fine bright August day on the old shore was? Air crystal and golden. Vast sky gardens where white cloud-flowers bloomed. Fields with the magic of dark spruce woods behind them. Triangles of sea shimmering into violet ... a faint blue loveliness that is the harbour. Yes, it is indeed a "fine bright day." There are days like that here yet. You never have just that kind of a day inland. Only the sea can give them.

A November entry says, "snowed in the night." The first snow of the winter that is to be. At sunset the world was gray and ugly. At sunrise it is a fair white thing, and the sea looks blackly-gray and dour by contrast. The ploughed fields are all dimpled; the spruces and firs are white palms: the apple trees still holding withered leaves are blossom-gay again. Only they are all white ... there are no pink hearts ... for November is not May even in Prince Edward Island.

In December there is "a fine day with squalls of snow by times." Yes, I remember that kind of a day, too. Ground frozen hard. Biting wind in spite of the sunshine. Up comes a big black cloud. A wave of gray shadow rolls over the world. Then the stinging drive of sudden snow. The air is a wild white blur with it. The fields whiten, the hills grow pale. Presto, the cloud is gone! The sun is out. But winter is a little nearer. There comes an entry. "Froze hard last night. Roads very rough."

Bumpy driving over them now. But Janie and I go walking in the wintry twilights and there is something nice tramping along over the hard firm roads. No mud now. Household lights gleaming warmly out along the road. Melody of storm in the wind that is crooning in the spruces. A big round silver moon floating up over a frosty hill. The gnomish beauty of dark lombardies against the sky. Bars of moonlight and shadow on the road under the trees. And Janie laughing beside me ... always laughing. Can the dead laugh?

In January are many "cold" entries. "As the days begin to lengthen the cold begins to strengthen,"[7] says the diarist, quoting a saw of his father's, who doubtless had heard it from *his* father. I wonder who first invented the little rhyme. I recall the odd, sudden childish rebellion that always flared up in my soul when I heard it. I hated it; and yet it *was* true ... for a time. The cold *did* strengthen in January and February, and the storms came whirling over the fields and heaping drifts along the fences and fiercely bombarding the little house crouching against its friendly sheltering "bush." But they died at the door. Inside all was warm and cosy and snug.

But even in January comes sometimes "a mild day" and "a white frost." What a pretty name is white frost! And the thing itself ... lovely as some whim of wildwood god! Every tree a miracle, every dead weed and blade of grass a wonder. The great willows arching over the little house things of silver and pearl. The underbrush in the grove a fairy jungle.

Then in March come the "blustery days." April brings rain ... and in May there is "a foggy day." How I used to love foggy days! For me there was always a beauty and a mystery in the fog of that shore. An evening fog filled me with a strange deep joy ... that mournful, ghostly thing hanging low over the fields and drifting in phantom-like waves through the spruces. But Janie is laughing. I hear her telling a joke. An old man has driven into the yard and greeted her father ... "fogging, sir." We have never heard "fogging" before. We think it is exquisitely funny. Thereafter we never meet each other on a misty day without saying, "fogging, sir." And why not? As well as "raining" and "blowing." Yes, I loved days when it "fogged."

One day the diarist has one brief entry and one alone. "Stumping." After a man had been stumping all day he did not feel much like diary writing. He was thankful to go to bed, feeling that some stumps attempted, some stumps done, had earned a night's repose. People "stumped" a little every summer and cleared a bit more fertile land. But there were always enough stumps left "at the back" to provide berrying grounds for us. Nowhere were there more delightful spots than among the stumps, nowhere where berries were bigger and redder and more abundant than among the long grasses and clumps of fern.

"James went to K... after binder twine." An entry that connotes a certain marked change that had come into farm life, doing away with much hard work and also much romance and beauty. The advent of the self-binder! I do not remember the day of the reaping hook. But when I was a very small girl the first type of mowing machine was in use. On it were two seats, one for the driver, the other for a second man holding a wooden rake in his hand, whose duty it was to rake off the sheaves, using his own judgment as to when enough grain had fallen on the board from the knives to make a sheaf. I have heard the older men say what a wonderful invention they thought this when it first came in. But it was now out of date and the new mowers were coming in with revolving rakes that went round and round until the driver touched a spring. Then one rake fell lower than the others and swept off the sheaf. This was thought the last word in mowers. But the sheaves had still to be bound and for this extra "hands" were hired ... mostly black-eyed French Canadian girls who bound quickly and chattered ceaselessly. I used to find a great fascination in watching them. A girl would catch up a cluster of grain, twist it with another cluster in a special knot, gather up the sheaf and knot the band around it in a twinkling. They did it so quickly my eye could never follow the motion and to this day the secret of that knot is unknown to me. I wonder if anyone living knows it now or has it become one of the "lost arts."

Then came the "self-binder" and the laughing, chattering binders vanished forever from the harvest fields by the gulf. The day of "binder twine" was come and one more bit of poetry was gone. Was anyone a whit the happier for the self binder? Or for all the floods of machinery inventive "genius" has let loose upon the world?

The diarist has several references to "the road farm." This is another phrase, which, quite pithless to most readers, is a master key for me, opening another door into the past. This "road farm" was a "parcel of land" lying along a side road which led through woods and clearings for almost its whole length and was a wild and beautiful spot. Janie and I are walking along it one early spring day. Ferns in clumps and ferns in curly masses and lonely, upstanding brackens. Masses of purple rhododendrons ... "sheep laurel." Mayflower stars along the way. Blue and white violets. Strawberry blossoms. Clumps of young maples. Slender firs. Bird calls. Wild fragrances. Squirrels chattering secrets of Polichinelle.[8] Stipplings of sunlight on the moist red path. Wine of spring in the crystal air. Hill glamor and upland magic. An immortal spirit of beauty brooding over everything. Janie and I faring on together, adventurous and expectant ... no worries ... not a bit afraid of to-morrow. Only a Prince Edward Island side-road ... but a highway into the land of fairy.

One entry ... "got the mill to thrash" revives another host of memories. In those days everybody had his crop thrashed by a little two-horse power threshing machine in place of the gasoline engines of to-day. We small fry were vastly excited when the threshing days came. Generally we had to stay home from school to "tramp straw." One man in the community owned a threshing "mill" and went around all winter thrashing for his neighbours. His job was to "feed the drum." Sometimes he cut the bands also and then someone had to hand him the sheaves one by one from the piles in which they were pitched down from the loft. I often did this and loved to do it. To watch the great ravenous teeth of the drum catch and rend and tear the sheaf as it was fed to it had a terrible fascination for me. So many sheaves made a "rally" and horses and men had a rest for ten minutes or so.

But perhaps I was not passing sheaves but was tramping straw in the loft or in an outside shed. This was gorgeous fun for there were always half a dozen of us. I loved it all ... the whir and roar and dust ... the clouds of grain pouring out of the drum, while the straw was coughed furiously out beyond to the waiting man with the fork who tossed it to us. The only drawback to it all was the mice. There were always legions of them especially when the lower layers of sheaves were reached.

Janie and I used to love to get on the wooden tread of the mill when it would be standing idle before their barn and make it go. We always had to get one of the boys to start it first but once started we could keep it going as long as our legs lasted. If we had been compelled to do this we would have howled in protest ... but when it was play ... why, it was play. And if we had "growing pains" that night when we went to bed ... well, everybody had to have growing pains. One must grow.

The entry "hauling old longers for firewood" reminds me of the fact that I have never heard the rails of fences called "longers" (pronounced "long-gers") in any place outside of Prince Edward Island. I have never come across it in any literature, even in dialect. Yet they were always called so on the island in my youth. The "poles" which the diarist often writes of were much slighter, shorter affairs, used for the ends of the longers to rest on. In that day these pole and longer fences were the only fences known. Board fences came in but were too expensive to oust the longer fences entirely. Then some fiend invented barbed wire.[9]

The old longer fence was a beautiful thing in its way, though wasteful of land. In its deep angles such lovely things grew. Long purple plumed wild grasses, ferns, bracken, strawberry vines, daisies, fireweed, aster ... farewell summers we called them ... yarrow, life-o'-man and great armies of golden rod. Even in winter the gray-headed golden rod stuck up through the drifts that always filled those corners.

There were many stone "dykes" then, too, and these were also lovely things when they grew old. The custom was brought out from Scotland. The dykes were built of layers of the red stones picked off the fields alternated with layers of sod. Soon the grass growing from the sods covered the stones; and if it didn't mosses and lichen did. Then dear things took root in the crevices among the stones ... flowers and ferns and berries. Those old dykes were as beautiful as the rock gardens of today. The strawberries that grew along them were amazing with stems so long that you could pick a "bouquet" of them. Fancy a bouquet of strawberries! And there were always birds' nests in the hollows among the stones. A low fence was built along the top of the dyke or a hedge of young spruce trees planted. If they were not planted they sprang up and grew anyhow. Dykes are never made on the island now but the old ones are still there. To speak of a barbed wire fence in the same breath with one of those exquisite poesy-haunted old dykes was to commit sacrilege.[10] The fields they hold in their embrace have a certain individuality and charm no wire-girdled meadow can ever possess.

The cheapness of things in those days is a constant marvel to me now. One day the diarist went to the shore and bought three large mackerel for which he paid the huge sum of eight cents. They would make a good dinner for his whole family. And a delicious dinner. Nobody knows what mackerel and codfish really taste like who has not eaten them with only an hour between sea and pot. Nothing to equal them save the trout we caught in brook and pond. Codfish dried and broiled was a great breakfast dish. They were spread on constructions called "flakes" and turned carefully until dry. It was an art not to let them get "sunburned," which ruined them.

"Took the sleighs out of stable, box and wood." Our diarist is preparing for winter. There were three kinds of sleighs in common use in those days. The "jaunting sleigh" ... the word cutter was unknown ... which was used for light travelling and always by canoodling couples. The box sleigh ... or pung as it later came to be called ... a rather comfortable affair which might have a seat in the front or might have no seat at all. In that case it was filled with straw covered with a "buffalo" or rug. We all hopped in and squatted down ... half a dozen of us. I've had more fun in those old "box" sleighs than in any other form of conveyance ... especially on moonlit winter nights on the road to some party or "meeting" when everyone in the sleigh was under twenty. The wood sleigh ... so called because used for hauling wood ... was merely a low frame on runners, sometimes with a loose board or two laid on it ... with stakes at the four corners connected with chains. When the sleigh was empty the driver rode standing and it must have been quite an art to balance himself. Later on, "tobogans" became very fashionable ... not quite so "classy" as jaunting sleighs but much classier than the box, and much affected by the junior lads of the family who could not aspire to a jaunting sleigh but wanted some vehicle to drive their lady friends about in.

When the diarist wished to express neighbourly kindness in any way he "said it with wood." When anyone was sick he took them a load of wood. When anyone died he sent the family a load of wood. Well, a load of good dry hardwood was not a bad thing to have on hand ... especially when much cooking had to be done for a funeral! It would really be much more serviceable than an anchor of roses or a pillow of white hyacinths.

One Saturday he "cuts wood for Sunday." Of course that was always done. One might cook a big dinner on Sunday and have half one's clan in to help eat it but it was an unpardonable sin to cut wood on "the Lord's day." I remember a clan story that was told of a certain uncle. He was the soul of hospitality and always had a houseful of guests on Sunday. But one Sunday an appalling discovery was made. By some oversight the wood had not been chopped the night before. Uncle rose to the occasion. "Boys," he said quietly to his two sons, "go out and break a little *with the back of the axe*."

He faithfully records all the bushels of grain sown each spring and harvested in the fall. Of course this "sowing" was done by the seeder then and for many years before. But I well remember the years before the seeder was invented when all the grain was sown by hand. I can recall very vividly seeing the sowers striding across the red fields scattering seed from a particular kind of basket slung from a rope around neck and shoulder. There were people, I believe, who had the knack of "sowing with both hands" but I never saw any of them at work. Such gifted individuals could of course sow a field in just half the time required by the others.

"Janie went after Toms to shear sheep" evokes many quaint old recollections. The sheep shearing was an annual event on the farms and was a mixture of interest and horror to us small fry. Large flocks of sheep were kept in those days and the evening gambols of the lambs around the fields were delightful to see. The "Tom girls" were three elderly maidens who went around shearing. They arrived on the morning of the eventful day carrying their shears and their shearing clothes in a bundle. These they promptly put on ... and very greasy unpleasant garments they were. Shearing unwashed sheep was a dirty job ... and in those days the sheep were never washed before shearing. The Tom girls were not noted for their beauty at the best of times and in their shearing togs they would have been good understudies for Macbeth's witches.

The sheep were driven into the sheep house and a shearing table erected. Susan Tom, with fatal eye, selected and seized a sheep, swung it to the table, hobbled its legs, and began shearing. Clip-clip went the skilled shears. The fleece fell away, so white and clean and silvery on its underside. The sheep emerged from it, an odd bare figure scampering away in amazement at her escape and transformation. I often wondered what a sheep thought about it while she was being shorn. They generally lay very still. Was it the calm of despair? A good shearer never wounded the sheep. But sometimes, even with the most expert, the shears bit too deep and the sheep scampered away with a red stain on her flank. At the end of the day the shearers were paid at the rate of four cents a sheep. Not too much surely. I would not have sheared a sheep, even supposing I had been able to, for four dollars, much less four cents.

The horror of that day centred about the lambs ... their tails were cut off. Those poor pretty frisky lambs who had never known pain. How my heart ached for them ... poor little bleeding lambs bleating pitifully, running to their mothers to be comforted. The wound seemed to heal quickly and next day the lambs would seem normal enough. But I don't think they ever scampered round the fields at sunset quite so light-heartedly again.

After the sheep shearing the wool-washing was a day's work. It was always done outside. A fire was kindled under the big potato boiler, the tubs were taken out and the wool washed and spread on the grass to dry. When dry it was bagged and carried away to the carding mill whence it came back in beautiful soft glossy rolls of floss. The oldest ladies spun them on little spinning wheels. The younger and flightier used the large wheel. Women liked spinning. Then came knitting and weaving. Very few people weave now on the island but when I was a child many did. And it was fascinating to watch them. A good many people hired the Toms to do their weaving for them. As I recall it, those Toms were very useful members of the community. They spun and wove and sheared sheep, planted and picked potatoes, bound sheaves and plaited hats from the wheat straw, washed and white-washed. Somebody was always getting the Toms to do something. I remember their mother … a little old body always at her spinning wheel. She often told me that she had been born in the year 1800 and was a girl of fifteen in Scotland when Napoleon was broken at Waterloo. She always wore a white frilled cap around her face. How odd it would be to see an old lady nowadays with a cap! Yet I do not know that old ladies have gained so much in giving them up. They were quite kind to lined faces and thinning hair. And the caps for state occasions were very "dressy." I remember a great-aunt who was noted for her smart caps. When she went to an evening festivity she always carried her best cap in a box with her. The very old ladies wore little hood-like caps of black net with a black ruching around the face. But these were thought very outmoded by up-to-date old ladies who perched little confections of lace and ribbon on the top of their heads and called them caps, much to the scorn of the still older dames who condemned such new fangled vagaries and predicted dire things for the state of society which permitted them.

"Mercy me!" as those ladies of the last century would have said. Where have I wandered to from my diarist's sheep-pen? Let us get back to our muttons[11] and see if the Toms have finished his sheep. Yes, and been duly paid eighty eight cents, having shorn twenty two sheep. Sweet be their slumbers.

But on that very eve it looks like rain and he predicts "the sheep storm." Evidently it did not come just then but come it certainly would. The "sheep storm" never missed. It had nothing to do with sheep but it was a June storm, invariably coming soon after the sheep were shorn. The wind would set in from the north-east, bitterly cold, and blow hard from that direction two and sometimes three days, with driving, stinging rain. The unlucky sheep, their warm coats reft away, would feel it bitterly and sometimes died from exposure. Hence the name. I am afraid I did not sympathize properly with the poor animals for I always liked the sheep storm. There was such a bite and tang to it.

Frequently our diarist speaks of someone "gone caleying" or "coming for a caley." It is an old Gaelic word for a friendly visit and was a very common expression of long ago. I like it myself and I am sorry it is no longer in use. It has a pleasant home-y sound to me ... perhaps because I heard it so often on the lips of old friends who sleep beneath the Island sod, our diarist among them. For it is long since he wrote the last word of his last entry and laid down his pen for the last time. But it still rains and shines and blows and "fogs" and blossoms on the farm he tilled and still in breeze and flower and meadow the old charm lingers yet. For our Island is still "*the* Island" and what other is there?

NOTES

1 Montgomery, 9 April 1936, in *SJLMM*, 5: 60.
2 Montgomery, 4 August 1923, in *SJLMM*, 3: 140.
3 Montgomery, 1 March 1925, in *SJLMM*, 3: 220; *SJLMM*, 3: 421.
4 Abegweit, the Mi'kmaq name for Prince Edward Island, means "cradle on the waves."
5 As a child, Montgomery was close friends with Charles Macneill's daughter Penzie (1872–1906). For a sample of letters written by Montgomery and addressed to Penzie during the former's year in Saskatchewan, see Bolger, *The Years before "Anne,"* 86–104, 111–33.
6 Properly, "the Lords of Life and Death shut the doors so carefully behind us." From "The Finest Story in the World" (1888), by Rudyard Kipling.
7 Seventeenth-century proverb.
8 Open secrets. In a play, these would take the form of stage whispers to the audience.
9 Lucien B. Smith of Ohio received a patent for barbed wire in 1867.
10 I have corrected the original, which reads "dykes were."
11 A literal translation of the French phrase "Revenons à nos moutons," from the anonymous play *La Farce de Maistre Pierre Pathelin* (ca. 1460), referring to a return to the subject at hand. The phrase appears as "return to my mutton" in *RI*, 13, 111, and as "return to my sheep" in Montgomery, 5 January 1917, in *SJLMM*, 2: 201.

65

Memories of Childhood Days

—— 1936 ——

L.M. MONTGOMERY

In addition to the long article "Come Back with Me to Prince Edward Island," *The Maritime Advocate and Busy East* solicited "a few short paragraphs ... for publicity purposes," according to Montgomery's journal. Only one of the three shorter pieces was published in this periodical, although another later appeared in *The Family Herald and Weekly Star* as an early version of her "Prince Edward Island" piece of 1939, reprinted as chapter 69, below. Montgomery was particularly proud of these three short pieces, noting in her journal that "in one happy moment of inspiration I captured the very essence of P.E. Island-ism."[1] Perhaps for this reason she recycled the article and republished it as "My Childhood in Canada" in the *Brooklyn Daily Eagle* in June 1938.

There are many things in my life for which I am thankful; but the one for which I am most thankful is that it was my good fortune to have been "born and bred" on Abegweit ... that beautiful name for Prince Edward Island which it should never have lost. I know perfectly well that deep down in my heart is a great pity for everyone who was *not* born on Prince Edward Island. Can it ever be made up to them?

It was my further good fortune to have lived on the "north shore" of "the Island," where I could gaze every day and night on the splendid pageant of the St. Lawrence gulf ... splendid in its everchanging beauty of dawn and noon and midnight, of storm and calm, wind and rain, starlight, moonlight, sunset. Sunset! I shall remember in the halls of eternity some sunsets I have seen over New London harbour.

We children of my day almost lived on the shore. There were so many things we could do there ... it was a world in itself. Bathe on the sand beach ... wade around the rocks ... climb the red cliffs and poke sea-swallows out of their nests ... watch the white gulls soaring ... gather pebbles, dulse, sea-moss, kelp, snails, mussels ... run races over the sand ... dig wells in it ... build castles ... climb the shining faces of the dunes ... and slide down in a merry smother of sand ... pile up driftwood ... make shore pies ... peep through the spyglass at the fishing boats ... space faileth me to tell of all the things we did on that far-away shore of long ago.[2]

And the children living there today can do just those things. For that old shore is unchanged amid all the changes of the years.

Empires have toppled ... a world has passed away ... since I, as a child, played on the silver beaches of Prince Edward Island. But they are still there ... still beautiful ... still calling to their exiles with a voice we always hear. And in our dreams we go back to them.

NOTES

1 Montgomery, 9 April 1936, in *SJLMM*, 5: 60; see also Montgomery, "I Have Come Home."
2 Most of this paragraph appears in slightly different form in chapter 30, "The Gay Days of Old," by L.M. Montgomery, in this volume.

66

The Mother of the Anne Series –
Lucy M. Montgomery

—— 1937 ——

EVA-LIS WUORIO
Translated by VAPPU KANNAS

The byline accompanying the original article, published in the Finnish magazine *Sirkka* in 1937, lists the author as "Nameless," but the biographical note identifies "Nameless" as Eva-Lis Wuorio, who was then a student at the University of Toronto. In her journal, Montgomery identifies her as "A Miss Wuari."[1] In this interview – newly translated for this volume by Vappu Kannas, a doctoral student at the University of Helsinki – we see Montgomery as a charming hostess who is so intrigued by her own popularity in Finland that she starts by asking questions of her interviewer. This interview is also unique in that it includes Ewan Macdonald as part of the portrait of the famous author, and provides a glimpse into their home life from the perspective of an outsider a year after the publication of *Anne of Windy Poplars*, a new addition to the overall series.

One night, I was standing on the wide steps of L.M. Montgomery's pretty stone house looking for the doorbell. I couldn't find one, so I knocked three times instead. The door was opened by a tall dark young man who invited me in and admitted that Mrs. Macdonald[2] lived there. While I was still wondering whether I had seen Gilbert or Gilbert's ghost, a rather short, elderly lady with an agreeable air came down the hall stairs. She shook hands with me and welcomed me in, and I introduced myself and reiterated my wish to interview her.

She asked me to sit down on one end of a long sofa in a large, dimly lit room while she sat down on the other. We chatted about this and that: the famous Van Gogh art collection that was presently in Toronto, the weather that had suddenly got chilly, whether I had had trouble finding their house and how long I had been in Canada – until suddenly I realized it was I answering the questions, not the other way around.

So I opened my black notebook, unscrewed my pen and in my best reporter's style asked the most important question, "Mrs. Macdonald, do you know anything about Finland?"

She answered apologetically, "Unfortunately no, I don't know anything about Finland. Of course I studied geography in school and in my mind I can see Finland on a map but that's all."

And again I found myself talking and sharing my little knowledge of Finland in the best possible light. Finally she said, "Finland must be a great country despite its small size." And I assured her that was indeed the case.

We chatted about different languages. Mrs. Macdonald owns books in almost all the languages of the world, but none in Finnish. I explained as best I could that Finnish is not related to German or Swedish as people often think, but is in fact related to Hungarian. Laughing, she told me how she had compared the Swedish version of Anne to the English one and read over the scene where Anne and Diana jump on old Miss Barry. The word "bounded" was translated "klumpi-dumpi" in Swedish. To her it sounded exactly like jumping.

"I was born," said L.M. Montgomery, "in Prince Edward Island, and in my opinion it is the most beautiful place on earth. Although I have lived in Ontario since being married, I spend a month in P.E.I. every year. I have just returned from my month long visit there and I must admit that it only gets prettier with time. The three farms I describe in the Anne series all exist. Of course I have let my imagination run free, so not everything in the book is drawn from real life. Just this year the government has purchased the farmlands with the intent to turn them into a national park, and so Anne's beloved places will always remain the same."

Both the living room and the dining room were full of photos of the "Island" and we admired them together. I saw the real "Lake of Shining Waters," a photo of "Lover's Lane," a picture of the bridge whose piles Anne was clinging on to when Gilbert saved her – and they all seemed so familiar, like in a dream. I admitted that perhaps the "Island" was really the most beautiful place on earth – after Finland. Laughing together we agreed that people who love their birthplace are "kindred spirits."

I asked: "How did you happen to write Anne?"

"It was actually a mistake," L.M. Montgomery smiled. "A Sunday school paper asked me to write a serial approximately seven chapters long, and while I was leafing through my old notebook I saw a note I had once written down: 'Elderly couple apply to orphan asylum for a boy. By mistake a girl is sent them.' I chose this as my subject and thus Anne was born. However, after those seven chapters she didn't want to die, so I wrote a book about her, and another, and another – and there we were. Everybody liked her. But I cannot claim any credit for Anne, since she appeared by herself and refused to disappear. The latest book about her came out this autumn. It is the story of the three years Anne spent teaching in Summerside, waiting for Gilbert. It was quite difficult to go back in time. I found myself using words that didn't even exist back then, but at least it is written now. I hope it will be as well liked as the other Anne books."

"Are all your characters based on imagination alone?" I wanted to know.

"All except old Peg Bowen in *The Story Girl*. (I think it's *Pieni runo-tyttö* [*Emily of New Moon*] in Finnish.[3]) She really lived in the Island and I was quite afraid of her when I was a child."

"How did you like Anne in the movie?"

"The actress who played Anne was excellent, but Matthew and Marilla were not *my* Matthew and Marilla even though the actors were very good. I didn't like Gilbert at all. And the scenery was all wrong of course – it didn't have the feel or soul of the Island," she explained.

I admitted that I too had found the scenery in the movie quite unlike the book. And at that moment I noticed a big, lean grey cat giving me a look, as if he were studying me, from the door. "Hello, cat," I said. Cautiously he stepped in and rubbed up against L.M.M.'s leg. Then he came and purred at my feet. I petted the cat behind the ear and under the chin.

"This is Good Luck," explained L.M.M. "We call him Lucky. He is 13 years old and has lost a lot of weight during the past few years." For the rest of the evening Good Luck sat on L.M.M.'s lap or walked right behind her. Every now and then he graciously granted me the honour to pat him.

We talked about her books: the Emily series, *The Blue Castle*, *Magic for Marigold* and above all, the Anne books. I inquired if her poems had been translated. She explained that she had written poetry since childhood but didn't think they had been translated into other languages.

When I told Montgomery how popular her books were in Finland she was very surprised. She had imagined there being only a few readers in Finland. The publishers of her first books had been unpleasant and she didn't even know that her books had been translated into Finnish.

345

She told me that she received a great deal of letters from all around the world, even from Finland – although she had thought people there read her books in Swedish![4] She replies to all her letters personally – so, dear *Sirkka* readers, I encourage you to write her in your best school English! She has even received several letters from boys who say her books are "awfully good" despite being girls' books. However, girls have always been her "first love." Laughing, I asked why then did she only have two boys. Her answer was that she'd not dared get a girl because the poor thing would have always been compared to Anne or Emily.

After our long chat I got up to leave and asked L.M. Montgomery to send some greetings to the *Sirkka* readers. "Give my warmest regards to all the girls in Finland," she said, "and tell them I am very happy that my books have given them joy." "Perhaps you would be kind enough to write that down yourself?" I asked her, tearing a sheet out of my notebook, and she graciously agreed.

Before I left, I met her husband – an agreeable, grey-haired elderly gentleman who must have resembled Gilbert in his youth. He told me: "It is terrible indeed being the husband of a famous woman – nobody ever says anything about me." But the way he looked at L.M.M. told me another story.

When she saw me to the door, L.M.M. reiterated how happy she was that her books were so well liked in Finland, and as we were shaking hands, Good Luck peeked from under her hem and joined our farewells meowing "good night" and "it was about time."

So, that was L.M. Montgomery – lively, pleasant, funny and amiable. I have not been able to replicate even half of our conversation here, and my words cannot do her justice. Nevertheless, I hope you got to know her a bit better now.

NOTES

1 Montgomery, 16 November 1936, in *SJLMM*, 5: 113.
2 Here and throughout, I have corrected the original, which reads "MacDonald."
3 Wuorio incorrectly guesses *Emily of New Moon*, which had been translated into Finnish in 1928. *The Story Girl* was not translated into Finnish until 1994. My thanks to Vappu Kannas.
4 The first two Anne books in Finnish were actually translations of the Swedish translations. My thanks to Vappu Kannas.

67

The Book and the Film

—— 1937 ——

This short article appeared in September 1937 in *The Canadian Author*, an official publication of the Canadian Authors' Association that was initially published as "Bulletin of the Canadian Authors' Association / Issued Every Little While." Montgomery had been active in the CAA since its founding in 1921 and by 1937 was second vice-president of its Toronto branch. In April 1938, however, she was "elbowed out" during the election of a new executive, a move that was apparently masterminded by her old nemesis, William Arthur Deacon.[1] In February 1941 she had been "elected an Honorary Member of the CAA in recognition of her outstanding contribution to Canadian literature,"[2] yet it was only in September 1944, almost two-and-a-half years after she died, that this periodical – now called *Canadian Author and Bookman* – bothered to publish a detailed notice of her death. Even then, rather than solicit an original tribute, the periodical simply reprinted a Canadian Press report of her death and extracts from a short tribute published in the *Ottawa Journal*.[3]

Mrs. L.M. Macdonald, known to the reading world as L.M. Montgomery, gave the audience some illuminating "Side Lights and High Lights" kindled by her own experience.

"I am the only writer," she remarked, "who ever got an injunction against the publication of her own book. That was in the course of a lawsuit with the first publisher of *Anne of Green Gables*. We finally wound up in the United States Supreme Court, where I won."

The Book and the Film

"What, No Skunks?"

She had been repeatedly asked what she thought of the last moving picture of *Anne*, – so often that she had boiled down her opinion into "With all its faults I liked it better than the silent film of 1921." The earlier producer, in order to "pep up" the play, had invented a number of incidents. These included a very melodramatic scene in which Anne picked up a shot gun to defend herself because the people were going to mob her for whipping one of her pupils. The picture also showed the Stars and Stripes floating over a Canadian school. Then, on her way to a Sunday school picnic, Anne was shown picking up a skunk, which she took for a kitten.

"That was rather more than odd, as there were no skunks in Prince Edward Island. Later on, one of the Islanders had an idea that a skunk ranch would be profitable. He imported the live-stock accordingly, but found it no go and gave up the business, setting the animals free. For a few years the Island was over-run with them. The provincial legislature passed a law forbidding anyone to sell a skunk; but they increased until people couldn't keep chickens, and a girl couldn't go for a walk with her best young man without risk of encountering the little black and white nuisance. The law was rescinded, therefore, and in its stead the legislature offered a bounty of 50 cents for every skunk destroyed."

Contradictory Critics

In her early days as a writer, said L.M.M., she had had touching faith in literary critics, expecting to learn a good deal from them and hoping to correct the defects that they would point out.

"That faith was sadly shaken," the author continued, "by the way in which the critics of my work contradicted each other. While one praised a book to the skies, the next would damn it utterly for the very things the first man had praised. One paper published two reviews in successive issues, the first praising it highly and the second condemning it. The same book was condemned by one reviewer as 'sugary' and commended by another as 'pure and sweet, with no maudlin sentiment,' while a third proclaimed that it 'clearly showed the influence of Swinburne.'"[4]

348

NOTES

1 Montgomery, 8 April 1938, in *SJLMM*, 5: 246; see also Rubio, *Lucy Maud Montgomery*, 529–31.
2 "The Family Circle," 13.
3 "Creator of 'Green Gables'"; "An Estimate." The latter text appears as chapter 73, "L.M. Montgomery's 'Anne,'" below. Prior to this, the December 1942 issue mentioned in its news of the Toronto branch that "Two [members] have been lost by death," one of whom was Montgomery ("From Sea to Sea," 29).
4 The comment about Swinburne appears in the *Montreal News* review of *The Watchman and Other Poems*, in SR, 92.

68

For and about Girls

—— 1937 ——

L.M. MONTGOMERY

Montgomery was asked to review Marjory MacMurchy's latest novel, *The Longest Way Round*, by MacMurchy herself, who had married Sir John Stephen Willison in 1926 (who died a little over a year later) and was henceforth known as Lady Willison. Montgomery felt obligated to do so because MacMurchy had always reviewed her books "so kindly – but I hate to, because I shall have to say insincere things." A week later, in response to a letter she had received from MacMurchy thanking her for her sincerity, Montgomery commented, "That hurt – because it was *not* sincere." She added that she had found the book to be "a terribly commonplace production," especially compared to her "cleverly written" earlier book, *The Child's House* (1923). "Her new one has none of its charm."[1]

Some years ago Lady Willison wrote a very lovely book, *The Child's House*, about a little girl named Vanessa. Now she gives us another book, for, by and about girls of all ages, with another fascinating heroine. *The Longest Way Round* is good reading and old and young will find pleasure in it.

Letty Bye is a cheerful little person with any amount of energy, courage, loyalty, affection, and that most uncommon of all things, real common sense. She seems to me to be typical of all that is best in our Canadian girls. She is a child when the story begins, she is a mature and self-reliant young woman when it ends. We follow her career with unwaning interest from the time she says good-bye to her mother who is going West, through the years in Hiawatha Harbor and Woodycrest ... the exciting basketball game between the Woodycrest A's and the Brownites II is one of the best things in the book ... until the happy day when we leave her dancing with her mother in their own dear home at the end of the long road.

Letty is only one of many charming folks in the book. There is good Mrs. Trant, who doesn't hold with "highfalutin' ways" but is invested with a never-fading glamor because she had seen Queen Victoria in her girlhood, Aunt Alinda who loved to teach but couldn't keep house or remember to put the children to bed at the right time, George Augustus who always knew his own mind and didn't believe in being brought up by women, the twins who locked themselves in the garret and couldn't get out, Doody Hill who could run and Ishbel MacPherson who could dance, Torquil MacPherson who was Torquil only on Sundays but Scotty the rest of the week and who knew who everyone was and where everyone lived because he drove a truck, even Julia O'Connor who was a born actress but wasn't exactly compounded of sweetness and light, not forgetting Joe the canary, and Jim Crow the Woodycrest cat, who climbed trees and couldn't climb down ... you'll love them all.

It may seem ungracious after so much pleasure to carp at a minor grievance. But why, oh, why, did Lady Willison call those delightful people who "neighbored" with Letty the Blanhammers? I have never agreed with Shakespeare ... who luckily isn't alive to worry over the fact ... that a rose by any other name would smell as sweet.[2] It wouldn't. So I ask again ... why Blanhammers? George Augustus will certainly get the Legislature to change it for him when he grows up.

NOTES

1 Montgomery, 2 October 1937, in *SJLMM*, 5: 208; Montgomery, 8 October 1937, in *SJLMM*, 5: 209.
2 Properly, "That which we call a rose / By any other name would smell as sweet." From *Romeo and Juliet* (1597), by William Shakespeare. See also *AGG*, 38.

69

Prince Edward Island

—— 1939 ——

L.M. MONTGOMERY, O.B.E.
Author of *Anne of Green Gables, Anne of Avonlea,*
Anne's House of Dreams, Anne of Windy Poplars, Etc.

In December 1938, Montgomery was invited to contribute a chapter on Prince Edward Island to *The Spirit of Canada*, to be published by the Canadian Pacific Railway as a souvenir album that would be presented to the King and Queen of England during their royal visit to Canada in May 1939. Fittingly, the author is listed as "L.M. Montgomery, O.B.E.," in recognition of her being appointed an Officer of the Order of the British Empire in 1935. While she continues to depict PEI as a place were "it is still possible to believe in fairies," she does acknowledge the Aboriginal and French inhabitants who preceded the predominantly Scots population that she depicts in her books, even paying respect to the island's Mi'kmaq name, "Abegweit." While the essay appears to be self-contained, parts of it were recycled from an earlier source: the last two paragraphs appeared in earlier form as "I Have Come Home," published in 1936. This article was also reprinted in the Charlottetown *Guardian* shortly after her death in 1942.

Somehow, one never thinks of Prince Edward Island in terms of history. It has, of course, had its little history, the echoes of which float faintly down the centuries since the June day of 1534 when Jacques Cartier looked on Abegweit ... that beautiful Indian name, "Floating on the Wave," which it should never have lost, no matter to what saint or prince ... looked and sailed away and did not come again. The French tried to colonize "St. John's Island" ... and we hear of the "exiled Acadians" who came to it from the vale of Evangeline: it was ceded to Britain in

1763.[1] Dim tales come down about forest fires and Indians and invasions from New England and plagues of mice and the heartbreak of terrible storms and homesick emigrants. But it is not in its history that you find the spirit of Prince Edward Island.

Neither is it to be found in the vaunt of "the million acre farm"[2] and of its incomparable black foxes, horses and potatoes. For we do not think of Abegweit in terms of commerce. We think of it in terms of beauty ... charm ... peace. There are beautiful landscapes elsewhere, all over Canada, but they lack the indescribable charm that haunts Abegweit. It is too elusive ... too subtle ... for definition. Is it the touch of austerity in the Island landscape that gives it its distinctive beauty? And in what consists that slight austerity? Is it from the fields with the magic of dark spruce woods behind them? Or in the glimpses of harbours and tidal rivers unbelievably blue? Or does it go deeper still to the very soul of the land? Ay, that it does. For lands have personalities just as human beings have, and the spirit of one land is not the spirit of another nor ever can be. And Destiny once said, "I reserve for myself this colourful little land of ruby and emerald and sapphire as a last refuge for the fairies and the old gods."

The fairies have disappeared from the rest of the world. It has become too noisy and machine-ridden and commercialized for the green folk. Because the fairies can live only by the belief of man. When that dies they die.

But it is still possible to believe in fairies in Abegweit. There are still places there where self-respecting elves can abide ... winding lanes back in the woods ... ferny dells with brooks slipping through them ... eternal green twilights under low-hanging firs ... a clump of silver birches at the turn of some irresponsible path ... a plantation of tiny spruces just beginning to take sly possession of some neglected pasture corner ... a meadow snow-white with daisies lying under a young moon. There you will find the fairies ... almost. Just around that curve ... just over that little rise ... if you can move quickly and silently enough. Only ... you never can. You always just miss them ... but their laughter floats back to you in the sudden whisper of the wind and the puckish rustle of the aspen. And that is your reward. For it is good to hear fairy laughter and forget the world for awhile.

The sons and daughters of Abegweit are a loyal folk. Once there was an old Scotch Islander in the West who was always talking of "the Island." "What island do you mean?" he was asked. With ineffable disdain he answered ... for all of us ... "Why, Prince Edward Island, mon! *What ither island is there?*"

353

None ... none! Deep down in our hearts we are conscious of the most profound pity for those luckless people who were *not* born in Prince Edward Island. We know it can never be made up to them.

Perhaps changes come more slowly in Prince Edward Island than elsewhere. We are not hide-bound or overly conservative, but we do not rush madly after new fads and fashions because they *are* new. We wait calmly until other parts of the world have tried them out for us and then, if they have stood the test, we adopt them. Loyal and upright in dealing, hospitable ... oh, *how* hospitable! ... with a sense of responsibility and a little decent reserve still flowering fully on the fine Old Country stock ... such are the people of Prince Edward Island ... the fire and romance of the Celt, the canny common sense of the Lowlanders, the wit of the Irish, the thrift of the English, the *joie de vivre* of the French, all beginning to be blended into something that is proud to call itself Canadian.

There is still, if you can believe it, a little leisure to be found in Abegweit. People here have not yet forgotten how to *live*. We don't tear through life.[3] There is about existence in Abegweit a certain innate and underlying serenity which is never wholly absent even on days when a church "tea" is in the offing or the hay in the shore field must be got in before it rains. We realize that eternity exists ... we know that "he who believeth shall not make haste"[4] ... shall not run hither and yon, aimlessly chasing will-o'-the-wisps of ambition and fortune and power. We are born knowing that "our own will come to us" ... we have only to wait.

It is a great thing for a land to have this birthright ... this background ... this unfailing "oneness" with the Eternal Spirit of beauty and reality and peace. Peace! You never know what peace is until you walk on the shores or in the fields or along the winding red roads of Abegweit on a summer twilight when the dew is falling and the old, old stars are peeping out and the sea keeps its nightly tryst with the little land it loves. You find your soul then ... you realize that youth is not a vanished thing but something that dwells forever in the heart. And you look around on the dimming landscape of haunted hill and long white sand-beach and murmuring ocean, on homestead lights and old fields tilled by dead and gone generations who loved them – and even if you are not Abegweit-born you will say, "Why ... I have *come home!*"

NOTES

1 See chapter 15, "With Our Next-Door Neighbors: Prince Edward Island," by Thomas F. Anderson, note 4, in this volume.

2 See chapter 6, "A Trio of Women Writers," by Donald B. Sinclair, note 4, in this volume.

3 In the first iteration of this piece, published in 1936, a sentence is added here: "Every time I ... accustomed to the breathless tempo of existence elsewhere ... go back to it I am impressed by this fact" (Montgomery, "I Have Come Home," 47; ellipses in original).

4 Properly, "he that believeth shall not make haste" (Isaiah 28:16, in the Hebrew Bible).

70

Beloved Writer Addresses
Several Aurora Gatherings

— 1940 —

In this report in the *Aurora Era* in February 1940 of a public appearance six
months after the publication of *Anne of Ingleside*, the last of her novels to be
published in her lifetime, the subhead announces that "L.M. Montgomery Tells
of Early Struggles as Young Authoress." It offers today's readers a glimpse of
Montgomery's life and activities after her journal entries cease suddenly at the
end of June 1939. Not surprisingly, the article makes no mention of the trouble
brewing behind the scenes, particularly concerning Chester Macdonald and
Luella Reid, who had married in November 1933 (although in an attempt to
camouflage the scandal of her pregnancy, they claimed they had married secretly the preceding November). They separated soon after, and in March 1938,
sickened by Chester's affairs with other women and by his continued poor
standing at university, Montgomery rewrote her will to leave his portion of her
estate to Luella and her children in the event that Chester and Luella were not
living together at the time of her death (she informed him of her action in April
1938).[1] They reconciled by the end of 1938, and after his graduation from law
school in June 1939, they moved to Aurora, north of Toronto and the location
of his former boarding school, where he settled into a law practice. Although
Montgomery changed her will later in 1939, she changed it back in 1941 after
Chester and Luella's marriage ended for good. When she died in April 1942,
Chester was living in the basement of Montgomery's home, separated from his
wife, and was thus disinherited.

On Friday Mrs. Ewan Macdonald, famous Canadian authoress and poetess, known the world over as L.M. Montgomery, the creator of that delightful fiction character, "Anne of Green Gables," came to Aurora.

In the afternoon she addressed the students at Aurora high school and was besieged with autograph hunters. Following the meeting, the wives of the school board members and the teachers and their wives held a tea in their honor in the board-room.

Mrs. Macdonald next attended a banquet at St. Andrew's Presbyterian church, held by a group known as "the Willing Workers," composed of the members of Mrs. M. Rank's and Mrs. C.C. Macdonald's classes. The president of the group, Norma Mathew, presided over the gathering. Vanetta Maaten gave the toast to the king. Gwen Smith proposed the toast to "our mothers," which was responded to by Mrs. Delmer Barkey. The toast to the visitors was sponsored by Norma Mathew and responded to by Mrs. Macdonald, who spoke briefly.

Following the banquet Mrs. Macdonald spoke to a crowded gathering in St. Andrew's church. Rev. J.K. McCreary gave the address of welcome, while Mrs. J.T. Boad presided. Mrs. Macdonald, in interesting vein, told of her early life in Prince Edward Island, and of her early endeavors in the literary field, many of which had not been successful.

"What a young and aspiring author needs more than anything else is perseverance and plenty of postage stamps. Rejection slips should only spur one on," she said. "When I started to write, we had too few books, but those we had we knew thoroughly. Today, there are almost too many books, and they are only skimmed through."

She told of her mail bag, and her correspondence, and gave humorous and interesting examples. She said that her books were criticized by some because they were of the "sweet" type, but declared herself indifferent to this. "I believe there is a tendency now to stress the sordidness and ugliness of life too much. We pass up much that is beautiful entirely. A mountain top or a rose garden is as interesting as a pig-sty, and is certainly a lot nicer. Let us be uplifting if we can be."

L.M. Montgomery was the maiden name of Mrs. Macdonald and is not a pen name, as many persons suppose. She commenced her writings in her own name and naturally enough did not change after her marriage.

Cordene Mapes presented Mrs. Macdonald with a bouquet of spring flowers. Jean Patterson gave several violin selections, and C.C. Macdonald, Aurora barrister, a member of St. Andrew's church, and the son of L.M. Montgomery, also spoke briefly. It is hoped that Mrs. Macdonald will return to Aurora some time soon again. Her charm and naturalness permeated her whole address, which kept her audiences in constant attention.

NOTES

1 Montgomery, 3 April 1938, in *SJLMM*, 5: 245. See also Devereux, "'See My Journal,'" 241–43.

71

Noted Author Dies Suddenly at Home Here

—— 1942 ——

L.M. Montgomery died at her home in Toronto on Friday, 24 April 1942. The cause of death is not mentioned in this obituary in the *Globe and Mail*, published the following day, but her death was considered by Stuart Macdonald and by her physician to have been a suicide – a belief not made public until 2008, when Macdonald's daughter, Kate Macdonald Butler, broke her silence in an essay also published in the *Globe and Mail*.[1] Most of Montgomery's subsequent obituaries drew on this one, which included the sub-head "Mrs. Ewan Macdonald Wrote Child Life Epic *Anne of Green Gables*."[2] This obituary celebrates rather than minimizes Montgomery's contributions to literature, although there are numerous errors regarding publication details. This obituary also provides a crucial clue to a missing puzzle piece that she left at her death: the manuscript of a final Anne book, *The Blythes Are Quoted*, copies of which turned up in the McClelland and Stewart archives in the 1980s. *The Blythes Are Quoted* was not published in its entirety until 2009.

Mrs. Ewan Macdonald, whose *Anne of Green Gables* was described by Mark Twain as "the sweetest creation of child life yet written," died suddenly yesterday at her Riverside Drive home. The famous Canadian writer was 68.[3] For the past two years she had been in ill health, but during the past winter Mrs. Macdonald compiled a collection of magazine stories she had written many years ago, and these were placed in the hands of a publishing firm only yesterday.

Under the name of L.M. Montgomery, Mrs. Macdonald wrote more than a score of books, and many of them have been translated into Polish, French, Swedish, Dutch and Spanish. Many have been published in Braille. Her most successful work of fiction was the immortal *Anne of Green Gables*. It was adapted twice to the screen, once in the silent days and later as a talkie, and both proved widely successful.

For more than thirty-five years the pen of L.M. Montgomery produced a flow of books that showed no lessening of that freshness and simplicity of style that characterized *Anne of Green Gables*. Many honors came to Mrs. Macdonald. She was made an officer of the Order of the British Empire in 1935 and became a Fellow of the Royal Society of Arts and a member of the Artistes' Institute of France, the Canadian Authors' Association and the Canadian Women's Press Club.[4]

Was Only Child

L.M. Montgomery was born at Clifton, Prince Edward Island, Nov. 30, 1874, the daughter of Clara Woolner Macneill and Hugh John Montgomery, who settled in the island Province to farm. She was an only child, and the mother died about a year after the birth. It was at Cavendish, where she was brought up by grandparents, that the future novelist grew to womanhood. Long before her first book was published by a Boston firm, she displayed convincing proof of her literary talents. At the age of 12 she won a story-writing contest sponsored by the *Montreal Star*.[5] She loved Cavendish and the sea that washed its shores, and in later life she described the farm as "twelve miles from a railroad station, twenty-four miles from the nearest town, but only one-half mile from the sea."[6]

Anne of Green Gables, like so many other splendid novels, was not accepted after first reading. It was rejected three times by publishers before it was sent to a Boston firm and accepted. The book brought immediate fame to the young Canadian. In 1890, after a year at Prince Albert, Sask., with her father, who had married again, she returned to the Maritimes and attended Dalhousie University at Halifax for one winter, taking special courses. Later she taught school at Biddlesford and Ellerslie in Prince Edward Island.[7] At the age of 20, Lucy Maud returned to Cavendish to live with her grandmother. It was while keeping house there that she met Rev. Ewan Macdonald, Presbyterian minister of the district. They were married after the death of the grandmother and moved to Leaskdale, Ont., where Mr. Macdonald was minister of the Presbyterian Church.

Wrote Many Books

The busy life of a minister's wife did not stop Mrs. Macdonald from writing. Her works included *Anne of Avonlea*, 1909; *Kilmeny of the Orchard*, 1910; *The Story Girl*, 1911; *Chronicles of Avonlea*, 1912; *Rilla of Ingleside*, 1921; *The Golden Road*, 1913; *Anne of the Island*, 1915; *Anne's House of Dreams*, 1917; *Rainbow Valley*, 1919; *Emily of New Moon*, 1923; *Emily Climbs*, 1925; *The Blue Castle*, 1926; *Emily's Quest*, 1927; *Magic for Marigold*, 1929; *A Tangled Web*, 1931; *Pat of Silver Bush*, 1933; *Mistress Pat*, 1935; *Anne of Windy Poplars*, 1936; *Jane of Lantern Hill*, 1937; and *Anne of Ingleside*, 1939.[8]

A volume of poems entitled *The Watchman* was published in 1917.[9] Mrs. Macdonald also wrote many magazine stories. An accomplished needlewoman and cook, her home was known for its pleasant hospitality. Mrs. Macdonald moved to Toronto seven years ago from Norval, Ont. She is survived by her husband and two sons, Chester, practicing law in Aurora, and Stuart, an intern at St. Michael's Hospital.

Funeral arrangements have not yet been completed, but burial will take place in the beloved soil of her native Prince Edward Island. The old farm at Cavendish is now a part of the National Park of Prince Edward Island, and spots made famous in her writings have been preserved as they were described in the "Anne" books.

NOTES

1 See Butler, "The Heartbreaking Truth about Anne's Creator."

2 See, for instance, *The Toronto Daily Star*, "'Anne' Books Author Mrs. Macdonald"; *The Guardian*, "Death of Famed Island Writer"; *The Family Herald and Weekly Star*, "*Anne of Green Gables* Creator"; *The Free Press*, "Famous Author Dies Suddenly"; *The Publishers' Weekly*, "L.M. Montgomery"; *The Ottawa Journal*, "L.M. Montgomery, *Anne of Green Gables* Author"; *The New York Times*, "L.M. Montgomery, Canadian Author"; *The Calgary Herald*, "Noted Canadian Authoress Dies"; *The Times Literary Supplement*, "L.M. Montgomery."

3 Born in November 1874, Montgomery was, in fact, still sixty-seven when she died.

4 Montgomery was actually elected to the Literary and Artistic Institute of France in 1935, which was a prestigious honour (see Montgomery, 21 March 1935, in *SJLMM*, 4: 362).

5 According to Russell, Russell, and Wilmshurst's bibliography, the essay in question, "The Wreck of the 'Marco Polo,'" was published in the *Montreal Witness* in February 1891, when Montgomery was sixteen (Russell, Russell, and Wilmshurst, *Lucy Maud Montgomery*, 1655).

6 See *The Globe*, "English Union Hears Author," 9.

7 Montgomery taught in Bideford in 1894–95, attended Dalhousie University in 1895–96, then taught in Belmont in 1896–97 and in Lower Bedeque in 1897–98 until her grandfather's death, which occurred when she was twenty-three. The settlement of Ellerslie is immediately west of Bideford.

8 I have corrected the original, which reads "Rillia of Ingleside" and "Emily of the New Moon." I have also corrected the publication dates of several of her books, which the original lists as follows: *Rilla of Ingleside* (1912), *The Golden Road* (1914), *Anne of the Island* (1916), *Anne's House of Dreams* (1918), *Rainbow Valley* (1920), *Emily of New Moon* (1924), *Emily's Quest* (1928), *Magic for Marigold* (1930), and *A Tangled Web* (1932).

9 *The Watchman and Other Poems* was published in Canada in 1916, in the United States in 1917, and in the United Kingdom in 1920.

72

Lucy Maud Montgomery

—— 1942 ——

It is fitting that the first and most unreserved tribute to Montgomery after
her death, published on 25 April 1942, should appear in the Charlottetown
Guardian, a major newspaper in her home province; it accompanied a version
of the *Globe and Mail* obituary (see chapter 71 in this volume) that appeared
on the front page.[1] Two days later, the Charlottetown *Patriot* published a
"Biographical Sketch" that included much of the same information about
Montgomery's life and career, then added: "Writing was not the only art in
which Mrs. Macdonald excelled. She was an accomplished needlewoman and
cook. Her home was known for its hospitality."[2] On 2 May 1942, a tribute
in the *Patriot* by T.H. MacArthur praised Montgomery's writing ability and
artistry: "In a world gone bankrupt on bunk and hocumb her books fill one's
mind with pure sweet thoughts which should have a great influence in helping
to bridge those dangerous years between adolescence and maturity."[3]

The death yesterday of Mrs. Ewan Macdonald, better known as Lucy
Maud Montgomery, will be felt as a personal loss by every Prince Edward
Islander. Creator of *Anne of Green Gables* and of the delightful series
of "Anne" stories which have popularized Prince Edward Island scenes
and characters throughout the world, Mrs. Macdonald's contribution to
her native Province may well be said to have been priceless. It was given
out of the fullness of a talent inspired by rare humanly sympathies and
understanding.

In achieving fame, she endowed the scenes of her childhood at Clifton and Cavendish with the glamour of immortal youth. The charm of her stories has attracted visitors to our shores from all parts of the world. They come to us every summer – more numerous than ever since the establishment of the National Park – to see "Green Gables" for themselves – to see the sand dunes and the Lake of Shining Waters,[4] the Old Orchard and the Haunted Wood. Mrs. Montgomery changed the locale of the Anne stories from time to time, but there is something perennially fresh about her earlier descriptive scenes, reminiscent of her own childhood days, which makes a universal appeal.

Mrs. Macdonald was a fine poet as well as fiction writer. Her personality was a brilliant and many-talented one, but the chief impression received by those who were privileged to meet her was one of womanly charm and homely culture. She was devoted to her home, and to all the associations which that word invokes. Perhaps that, after all, is why she was able to give us such delightful characters and domestic incidents in her novels.

She also remained devoted to her native Province, and took every opportunity of revisiting the Island and renewing old friendships and making new ones.

To all who knew her, whether personally or through her books, the memory of "Lucy Maud Montgomery" will remain an enduring possession.

NOTES

1 See *The Guardian*, "Death of Famed Island Writer."
2 *The Patriot*, "Biographical Sketch," 5.
3 MacArthur, "Lucy Maud Montgomery," 4.
4 I have corrected the original, which reads "Lake of Shining Water."

73

L.M. Montgomery's "Anne"

—— 1942 ——

This unsigned tribute in the *Ottawa Journal*, published on 27 April 1942, seeks to excuse the continued popularity of *Anne of Green Gables* on account of its old-fashionedness. Yet a similar essay in the *Calgary Herald* published the same day argues that *Anne of Green Gables* was actually "something different – less 'goody-goody' and far more natural" – than the once-popular Elsie books. "With a keen appreciation of the problems of the age in which she lived and their possible reactions upon the lives of those of her own sex in younger age brackets, Mrs. Macdonald through her stories sought to clarify answers to them for the benefit of her readers. That her efforts were appreciated is evidenced by the fact that years after its first publication *Anne of Green Gables* was heralded as an outstanding screen success."[1]

If *Anne of Green Gables* were published today hard-boiled book reviewers would give it little space. A simple thing, they would say, and not without charm, but nothing to set the world afire. *Anne* had its birth in a different age, however, and this gentle little story of a country girl caught the imagination of great numbers of readers, young and old, and shared with some of Ralph Connor's novels written in the same period the honor of attracting a world-wide audience.

Lucy Maud Montgomery,[2] who wrote *Anne of Green Gables* and its various successors over a period of 35 years or so, died in Toronto on Friday. She was Mrs. Ewan Macdonald, wife of a clergyman, in private life, and fiction with her was but a part-time career. But millions knew of

L.M. Montgomery who never had heard of Mrs. Ewan Macdonald, and the author lived to see people making pilgrimages to the old house "Green Gables," in Prince Edward Island, where the first of the Anne books was written. The place now is in the Island's national park, near-by is a golf course which perpetuates the name Green Gables, and the Island's tourist literature makes much of the fact that this celebrated Canadian novelist was born in that province and launched there her distinguished career. For great numbers of persons of L.M. Montgomery's own generation her old home is a literary shrine, and there by the sea they recapture something of the spirit of their own youth.

The Montgomery novels are wholesome, spirited and imaginative, and when we try to value them as literature we should do so by first coming to an understanding of the simpler world in which they had their origin. Millions of readers have loved *Anne of Green Gables*, and that is a tribute from the heart to a great Canadian woman.

NOTES

1 *The Calgary Herald*, "Famous Canadian Author Passes," 4.
2 I have corrected the original, which reads "Lucy Maude Montgomery."

74

Body of Island's Beloved Authoress
Home for Burial

—— 1942 ——

Along with this article, the 29 April 1942 issue of the Charlottetown *Guardian* included a poem, "At Rest," by A.J. MacAdam of Summerside, as well as a reprint of Montgomery's 1939 essay "Prince Edward Island" (see chapter 69, in this volume). Although both Charlottetown papers, the *Patriot* and the *Guardian*, had announced on their front pages two days earlier that Montgomery's funeral would be held at Green Gables the following Wednesday afternoon, both reports made a curious oversight: according to the *Patriot*, Montgomery's husband "and a son, Dr. Stuart Macdonald, will accompany the remains from Toronto."[1] The absence in the earlier report that Montgomery's eldest son Chester would attend may simply have been an oversight, or it may have indicated his initial refusal to attend the funeral after being disinherited – as Mary Rubio notes, he was caught "removing carloads of materials" from his parents' house after Montgomery's death.[2] Whatever the cause behind this omission, Chester did in fact attend his mother's funeral, which was conducted by Rev. John Stirling – who had officiated at Montgomery's wedding in 1911.

The funeral of Mrs. Ewan Macdonald will be held from "Green Gables" house in Cavendish this afternoon at 2.30 to Cavendish United Church. The remains of the famous Island authoress, who wrote more than a score of books under the name of Lucy Maud Montgomery,[3] arrived by train from Toronto last evening.

The body was taken from the station at Hunter River by motor hearse via Rustico to Cavendish. The remains were resting in Green Gables last night – the house made known by her throughout the world in the book *Anne of Green Gables*, published in 1908. The house is situated in the heart of the National Park and overlooks the Gulf of St. Lawrence.

The late Mrs. Macdonald's husband, Rev. Ewan Macdonald and two sons, Dr. Stuart and Chester accompanied the remains home last night.

The service this afternoon will be conducted by Rev. John Stirling.

The motor hearse travelled from Hunter River by pavement to Rustico last evening and had no difficulty reaching Green Gables via the five miles of clay road to Cavendish. The latter stretch of road was put in first class shape this week so that people from various parts of the province would be able to attend the funeral today.

NOTES

1 *The Patriot*, "Funeral from 'Green Gables,'" 1; *The Guardian*, "Funeral from Green Gables on Wednesday," 1; see also *The Gazette*, "Burial to Be in P.E.I.," 22.
2 Rubio, *Lucy Maud Montgomery*, 578.
3 I have corrected the original, which reads "Lucy Maude Montgomery."

75

Island Writer Laid to Rest at Cavendish

—— 1942 ——

"Impressive Funeral Service for Author of *Anne of Green Gables*," declared the subhead to this front-page article published in the Charlottetown *Guardian* on 30 April 1942.[1] Montgomery had chosen her final resting place in 1923; even earlier than that, in 1919, she had recorded in her journal that she had selected the quotation "After life's fitful fever she sleeps well," from Shakespeare's *Hamlet*, for the tombstone of her beloved cousin Frederica Campbell, adding that "it is the one I want on my own when I die."[2] Evidently this wish was not known to her family, and so it does not appear on her tombstone. A rather distressing drama was omitted from the official accounts of the funeral: as Rubio notes in her biography, Ewan Macdonald, in his confusion, kept crying out, "*Who* is dead? *Who* is dead?" and could not seem to register that it was his wife who had died.[3]

The late Mrs. Ewan Macdonald was laid to rest yesterday afternoon in Cavendish Cemetery on a hill overlooking Green Gables and the sand dunes of the shores on the Gulf of St. Lawrence in the distance. The beloved Island authoress was home again – back to the place immortalized by her in the book *Anne of Green Gables* written under the name of Lucy Maud Montgomery.[4]

Hundreds of friends from Cavendish and other parts of Prince Edward Island gathered to pay their last respects to the late Mrs. Macdonald. A short service was held at Green Gables, where the remains rested since Tuesday evening when they arrived from Toronto. Rev. John Stirling,

Kensington, a friend of the deceased and the clergyman who performed the marriage ceremony when she was married to Rev. Ewan Macdonald, conducted the service. The prayer was offered by Rev. Dr. Frank Baird, Superintendent of the Presbyterian Missions in the Maritimes, Chipman, N.B.

The funeral to Cavendish United Church was held at 2.30. The church was filled to the last seat with mourners and friends, and a number stood in the aisles during the funeral service.

The opening prayer was offered by Rev. Mr. Stirling, who was in charge of the service and delivered the eulogy. This was followed by the hymn "The Lord's My Shepherd." A prayer was then offered by Rev. J.R. Skinner, Winsloe, and this was followed by the hymn, "The Old Rugged Cross," sung by a quartette from the Cavendish choir. The Scripture lesson was read by the Rev. G.W. Tilley, pastor of Cavendish Church.

The hymn "Lead Kindly Light" preceded the funeral oration given by Rev. Mr. Stirling. This was followed with a message of sympathy from the Moderator of the Presbyterian Church in Canada which was delivered by Rev. Dr. Baird. The hymn "Nearer My God to Thee" preceded Benediction, pronounced by Dr. Baird.

The service at the grave was conducted by Rev. Mr. Stirling assisted by Rev. A.D. Stirling, Kensington.

The late Mrs. Macdonald's husband, Rev. Ewan Macdonald, and her two sons, Dr. Stuart and Chester, were present. They accompanied her remains from Toronto where she passed away last Friday.

Among those present at the funeral were: His Honour, Lieutenant Governor B.W. LePage and Mrs. LePage; Premier Thane A. Campbell and other members of the Provincial Government.[5]

The pall bearers were: Messrs. Frederick Clark, Cavendish; George Henry Robertson, Mayfield; Alexander McNeill, Cavendish; William Toombs, North Rustico; Joseph Stewart, Bayview; and Jeremiah Simpson, Cavendish.

Pays Tribute

"It was always an event of interest to the people of Cavendish and surrounding districts when Lucy Maud Montgomery came back to visit her native province," Rev. Mr. Stirling said in the opening remarks of the funeral oration. "She was always welcome and her presence brought joy to her friends," he added. "Once again she has come back to the old place" and he wondered if she were looking down at the moment at her friends in Cavendish, the sea shore, the sand dunes and surrounding districts.

"We know how she succeeded, we know how she went far and still remained a friendly individual – a friend to all people," the minister said.

He went on to say that he was not there to "estimate the value of the work she has done in literature." Referring to her brilliant career as a writer, Rev. Mr. Stirling pointed out that her work had been highly praised by men "high in the literary world" such as Mark Twain, Bliss Carman and Earl Baldwin.[6] Although he did not consider himself capable of estimating this work, he could "enjoy it as the humbler people do."

The popularity of her work was manifested when Earl Baldwin, on the occasion of his proposed visit to Prince Edward Island, wrote to say that he was coming here "mainly to meet Lucy Maud Montgomery because of the delight he had got from reading her stories."

Continuing his eulogy, the minister went on to say, "Some felt that her work was largely for girls, perhaps children, but there is another side to her work." Many have failed to estimate the depth of truth and portrayal of character in her work. Her books have given "high ideals for girls and young womanhood.

"The other side of her work touched me most," he asserted. Many did not know her volume of poems, he added. He then read passages from "The Watchman," a poem representing the Resurrection which was composed by the deceased and read by her in Cavendish at a gathering.[7] "It is a powerful thing and shows the depth of character and thought in her work," he declared.

Rev. Mr. Stirling also read passages from the *Chronicles of Avonlea*, written by the deceased. When he concluded he said, "I thought it was better today to let you listen to Lucy Maud Montgomery." What he had just read was "a revelation of forgiveness and she must have touched many with such a message."[8]

Expresses Sympathy

Rev. Dr. Frank Baird, on behalf of Rev. J.B. Skene, Moderator of the Presbyterian Church in Canada, expressed profound sympathy to Rev. Mr. Macdonald, the two sons of the deceased, the community of Cavendish and the whole Island on the loss of one whose reputation was international, world-wide.

"She glorified and immortalized this community," he said, paying tribute to the deceased. In all her writings "there is not a line unworthy and not a syllable that offends Christian teaching," he said.

It was only fitting, he declared, that she should be brought home to rest among those she loved so dearly.

In the whole galaxy of distinguished men and women from this province, he did not think any star outshone that of Lucy Maud Montgomery which will continue to shine down through the ages. "In posterity she will place first," he stated.

NOTES

1 See also *The Patriot*, "Famous Writer Is Laid to Rest"; *The Globe and Mail*, "L.M. Montgomery Rests beside Sea."

2 Montgomery, 21 July 1923, in *SJLMM*, 3: 137–38; Montgomery, 7 December 1919, in *SJLMM*, 2: 356.

3 Rubio, *Lucy Maud Montgomery*, 584.

4 Here and throughout, I have corrected the original, which reads "Lucy Maude Montgomery."

5 Bradford William LePage (1876–1958), Lieutenant Governor of PEI from 1939 to 1945; Harriet Christie (1875–1961), had married LePage in 1897. Thane Alexander Campbell (1895–1978), Premier of PEI from 1936 to 1943.

6 Here and below, the reporter is evidently confusing Earl Grey and Stanley Baldwin.

7 The title poem in *The Watchman and Other Poems* was first published in *Everybody's Magazine* in 1910.

8 The story in question is "Each in His Own Tongue."

76

The Creator of "Anne"

—— 1942 ——

Mary Rubio and Elizabeth Waterston suggest that the author of this unsigned editorial was likely Robertson Davies (1913–1995).[1] Although the author of this piece calls *Anne of Green Gables* "a simple and sentimental work," Davies's own portrayals of small-town Canadian life in a set of novels beginning with *Tempest-Tost* (1951) share a number of similarities with Montgomery's depiction of Avonlea.

Nations grow in the eyes of the world less by the work of their statesmen than their artists. Thousands of people all over the globe are hazy about the exact nature of Canada's government and our relation to the British Empire, but they have clear recollections of *Anne of Green Gables*. The simple story, written when the Dominion was much younger than it is now, and much less troubled, was enormously popular in its day and it may still be read with enjoyment.

Stern critics may be dismayed that what is probably the best-known book to come out of Canada should be such a simple and sentimental work. Admittedly it would have been better if we had produced a *Don Quixote* or a *War and Peace*, but in the world of art we have to be content with what we can get; Canada produced *Anne of Green Gables* and that must suffice us for a while. The book has great charm, and is somewhat reminiscent of the work of Louisa Alcott; *Anne* never set the world on fire, and launched no crusade, but she gave a great deal of happiness of an inoffensive sort.

The Creator of "Anne"

Because of the happiness which her book gave Canadians will be sorry to hear of the death of its author, L.M. Montgomery, who in private life was Mrs. Ewan Macdonald, on the 24th of last month, in Toronto. Apart from her writing, she performed the many duties of a clergyman's wife with dignity and true kindness, and by her death Canada loses a most valuable and beloved citizen.

NOTES

1 Reprinted as "[Happiness of an Inoffensive Sort]," in Montgomery, *Anne of Green Gables*, edited by Rubio and Waterston, 340–41.

77

[L.M. Montgomery's Last Poem]
—— 1942 ——

In early May 1942, a tribute to Montgomery appeared in the same issue of
Saturday Night as her final poem, "The Piper," which she had submitted to this
magazine three weeks before her death. More "poignant additional interest"
is available to us now: Montgomery had included the introductory paragraph
and the poem, with minor variations, in her final book-length manuscript, *The
Blythes Are Quoted*. Montgomery's signature appears in earlier versions of the
typescript but is omitted in the final version that was submitted to her publishers at her death. Given the publication of this poem, it is fitting that the author
of the tribute looks to Montgomery's poem "The Old Home Calls," first published in *The Youth's Companion* in 1909 and included in *The Watchman and
Other Poems*, as evidence of the "spirit of her work."

L.M. Montgomery

Anne of Green Gables brought instant popularity to Lucy Maud
Montgomery. It was a picture of real people in a real place. It was a
view of Prince Edward Island, and of the Islanders, seen through glasses
slightly tinted with rose, but seen in accurate outline. It was the record
of the unfolding loveliness of a young girl's personality. Best of all, it was
an unconscious self-portrait of a sensible, sensitive and gracious lady.

The exalted critics of this day and age look down the nose at her work,
because it dealt with surfaces, instead of psycho-analytic depths; because
it was interesting instead of being a boring essay in abnormal psychology.

But all the things we see in this common life are surfaces, even though life is never superficial. And the dream of beauty which lingers in the background of every normal mind is expressed in surfaces. How else can we account for smiles, and enlightened eyes and pride of gait, and grace of gesture and sweetness of voice? They are indications of the hidden loveliness of the soul.

L.M. Montgomery (in her later name of Mrs. Ewan Macdonald) has passed out of the world, and her mortal frame has gone to mingle with the beloved dust of her Island. Here is the spirit of her work:

> "O children of my love,
> I keep for you all your childhood dreams, your gladness and delights,
> The joy of days in the sun and rain, the sleep of care-free nights;
> All the sweet faiths ye have lost, and sought again, shall be your own.
> Darlings, come to my empty heart. I am old, and still and alone."

L.M. Montgomery's Last Poem

The sudden and lamented death of L.M. Montgomery (Mrs. Ewan Macdonald), the beloved author of *Anne of Green Gables*, lends a poignant additional interest to the verses which *Saturday Night* received from her only three weeks before her death, and which were scheduled for publication in this issue before her death was announced. In the letter which forwarded them the author wrote:

"In one of my books, *Rilla of Ingleside*, a poem is mentioned, supposed to have been written and published by Walter Blythe before his death in the Great War. Although the poem had no real existence hundreds of people have written me asking me where they could get it. It has been written but recently, but seems to me even more appropriate now than then."

The Piper

> One day the Piper came down the glen,
> Sweet and long and low played he ...
> The children followed from door to door
> No matter how those who loved might implore,

[L.M. Montgomery's Last Poem]

So wiling the song of his melody
As the song of a woodland rill.

Some day the Piper will come again
To pipe to the sons of the maple tree ...
You and I will follow from door to door,
Many of us will come back no more!
What matter that if Freedom still
Be the crown of each native hill?

L.M. Montgomery

78

L.M. Montgomery /
Mrs. (Rev.) Ewen Macdonald

—— 1942 ——

Although *Canadian Author and Bookman* made no substantial mention of Montgomery's death until September 1944, *The Presbyterian Record*, "The Official Monthly Record of the Presbyterian Church of Canada," published the following tribute in its June 1942 issue. Perhaps because of Montgomery's role as a minister's wife, this article consistently refers to Montgomery's husband as Ewen Macdonald, as opposed to Montgomery's preference for Ewan.

Well may we cultivate a respectful attitude toward youth in recognition of their possibilities. We know not what the future holds for them. Glints of talent may suggest later attainment or distinction or these gifts may lie latent, entirely undisclosed, awaiting the hour of opportunity. As Thomas Gray in his immortal poem said when musing upon the "rude forefathers of the hamlet" sleeping in the country churchyard:

> Perhaps in this neglected spot is laid
>   Some heart once pregnant with celestial fire;
> Hands that the rod of Empire might have swayed,
>   Or waked to ecstasy the living lyre.

None however were aware of the hidden talents. The hour of opportunity had not come to them and this denial of expression may be the lot of many, to quote Gray again:

L.M. Montgomery / Mrs. (Rev.) Ewen Macdonald

Full many a gem of purest ray serene
> The dark unfathomed caves of ocean bear;
Full many a flower is born to blush unseen,
> And waste its sweetness on the desert air.[1]

We must bear in mind, therefore, that we know not what are the possibilities of the young and treat them accordingly. That consideration justified the respectful gesture of the man who said that he lifted his hat to every youth he met.

When Lucy Maud Montgomery in her teens left the town of Prince Albert on the North Saskatchewan and St. Paul's Presbyterian Church there, of whose Sunday School and Christian Endeavor Society she was a member, no one predicted or even contemplated the distinguished career as a writer that made her name a household word over so wide an area. True, in early girlhood her pen was busy for at the age of twelve she won a story-writing contest conducted by the *Montreal Star*, but this evidence of budding genius was not widely known.

She had lost her own mother and was then living with her father and stepmother. After a brief residence in Prince Albert she left to make her home with her grandmother in Prince Edward Island, where her genius bloomed and flourished and where were the scenes of her winsome stories. She was the author of more than a score of books of fiction and a volume of poems of great merit, besides many magazine articles, a collection of which she had placed in the hands of her publisher on the day of her death. Her first book, *Anne of Green Gables*, described by Mark Twain as "the sweetest creation of childlife yet written" though twice rejected by publishers, won for her a high place in the literary world and introduced her to the Screen. Honors came in due course, such as the Order of the British Empire, membership in the Royal Society of Arts, the Artistes Institute of France, the Canadian Authors' Association, and the Canadian Women's Press Club.

After her grandmother's death she became the wife of Rev. Ewen Macdonald, a minister of our Church and though introduced to the busy life of a minister's wife she did not lay down her pen. Such was the wide appeal of her books that they were translated into Polish, French, Swedish, Dutch and Spanish. They cheered the blind also for many have been published in Braille. She is survived by Mr. Macdonald and two sons, Chester in Law, and Stuart in Medicine, all residing in Toronto where their home has been for the past seven years.

Of the funeral services in Prince Edward Island we have the following report:

It was at Cavendish ("Avonlea" of the novels), Prince Edward Island, that the body of the distinguished authoress was laid to rest on Wednesday afternoon, April twenty-ninth, in the Hill Cemetery overlooking Green Gables, with the sand dunes and lingering patches of snow-white ice on the Gulf of St. Lawrence in the distance to the north. Spring had not yet quite fully come, and snow still held in places where the drifts had been deep; but the wild-geese and the braver of the song-birds had arrived, and while the south-west wind blew strongly, the sun shone, and the wind being toward, not from, the Gulf and the ice, the afternoon was not uncomfortable for the great concourse of people who had come from nearly every section of the Island to look for the last time on a beloved face, clothed now in "the white majesty of death,"[2] and to pay loving tribute to one of themselves who had reached a place of shining pre-eminence in the world of creative literature.

The day previous, Mrs. Macdonald's remains, accompanied by her husband, Rev. Ewen Macdonald of Toronto (by birth of the Island like his distinguished wife), and the two sons, Dr. Stuart and Mr. Chester Macdonald, lawyer, of Toronto, after the train trip from Toronto, and the crossing of Northumberland Strait by ferry, had reached her birth-land. The last stage of the long journey had been the twelve-mile motor drive from Hunter River railway station to Green Gables, the home of the immortal creation, "Anne," and the local setting of one of the most beautiful and appealing works of all fiction.

The service in the Cavendish Church was deeply impressive. The edifice was crowded to capacity, many standing throughout, and some not able to gain admittance. The minister, who had been chosen by the deceased to preside, the Rev. John Stirling of Kensington, and who had officiated when the young organist had married the young minister, came near to being mastered by his emotion as he began his address, which followed the singing of the Twenty-Third Psalm, prayer by Rev. J.B. Skinner of Winsloe, and Scripture reading by Rev. G.W. Tilley, pastor of the Cavendish church.

"It was always an event of interest to the people of Cavendish, and surrounding districts," said Mr. Stirling, "when Lucy Maud Montgomery came back to visit her native province. She was always welcome, and her presence brought joy to her friends ... Once again she has come back to the old place ... We know how she succeeded; we know how she went far, and still remained a friendly individual, a friend to all people."

Proceeding the speaker pointed out how it was an error to suppose that the work of the deceased was superficial, or *for*, or *about*, children only. A lengthy poem on the Resurrection was read, as well as extended extracts from *Chronicles of Avonlea*, in support of the view that she was possessed of a mind of unusual range and soundness, and understood the evangelical as well as the cultural and ethical side of the appeal of the Gospel. "I thought," he concluded, "that it was better for me today to let you listen to Lucy Maud Montgomery herself than to deliver any address of my own."[3]

At the conclusion of his address, Mr. Stirling introduced Rev. Dr. Frank Baird, who had come at the request of the Moderator of the General Assembly of The Presbyterian Church in Canada, Rev. J.B. Skene, to represent him at the funeral.

Dr. Baird began by saying that it had occurred to him that there was a sentence in *Anne of Green Gables*, and in the chapter entitled, "The Reaper Whose Name Is Death," which he considered very beautiful, and also fitting at this time. It was found on page 378 of the book, and it read:

"For the first time shy, quiet Matthew Cuthbert was a person of central importance; the white majesty of death had fallen on him, and set him apart as one crowned."[4]

Proceeding Dr. Baird said: "As citizens of Prince Edward Island, you have not been lacking in names of distinction and importance. I think of your brilliant Sir Louis Davies, of a former day, so distinguished in statesmanship and the law;[5] of Sir Andrew Macphail and his qualities and achievements;[6] of Jacob Gould Schurman the great President of Cornell;[7] of Sir Robert Falconer, the equally great President of Toronto University;[8] of Malcolm James MacLeod who for so long adorned the pulpit of the famous Marble Collegiate Church of Fifth Avenue, New York;[9] of Mr. J.A. MacLeod, the distinguished banker, and present President of the Bank of Nova Scotia; and of many others, great and near-great, recalling such as Hon. Dr. Cyrus MacMillan, M.P., and Dr. John Sutherland Bonnell of the Fifth Avenue Presbyterian Church, New York, both still on the way up;[10] but of the whole galaxy, while one star differeth from another star in glory, I do not think any will outshine the star that shone, and will continue to shine down through the ages in Lucy Maud Montgomery Macdonald. If service to Prince Edward Island be accepted as a criterion of judgment, if I mistake not, and I think posterity will concur – she places first: for I take it, in the language of George Eliot, she has joined 'the choir invisible of the immortal dead, who live again in lives made better by their presence.'[11] Passing through the Valley of Baca, as in the case of the pilgrims of the eighty-fourth Psalm, she made it a well.

"We who live in New Brunswick from which I come, have our Bliss Carman and our Charlie Roberts; we have also and are proud of our Bonar Law, our Baron Beaverbrook and our Viscount Bennett,[12] but in the last analysis, with these and their distinguished deeds considered, and the great figures of Nova Scotia thrown in, I am disposed to think that the judgment of the final assize will be that the palm for all the Maritimes should go to the distinguished authoress robed 'in the white majesty of death' here before us today.

"But it would be untrue to say of her, or to imply that she is dead. She says again of Matthew Cuthbert as he lay in his coffin in Green Gables, and touching the imperishableness of a good life, 'He is just away.'[13] Not dead – 'Just away'; recalling to us that moving little poem of Eugene Field, on the death of his boy, which with the change of a single pronoun, we may apply to today saying of the departed:

> I cannot say, and I will not say
> That she is dead; she is just away.
> With a cheery smile, and a wave of the hand,
> She has wandered into an unknown land;
> And left us dreaming how very fair,
> It needs must be, since she is there.[14]

"Like her character Matthew Cuthbert, 'the white majesty of death' has fallen upon her, and this, the fact of death, as readers of *Anne* will recall, had 'set him apart as one crowned.'

"But long prior to this day, and this event which we mourn so much, she has been 'set apart as one crowned.' She has glorified and immortalized the community which gave her birth, Kingdoms which others laboriously seek to enter and cannot, she came into as by natural inheritance, and there, from the first, from a child, it may be said, she reigned as queen endowed with genius and grace; with shining ability and marvellous gifts; and while her sales ran into millions, there is nowhere a line that is unworthy, a syllable that can offend. She waved her magic wand, and the ugly things fled away, and whatsoever things were true, whatsoever things were honest, whatsoever things were just, whatsoever things were pure, whatsoever things were lovely, whatsoever things were of good report – if there was any virtue, and if there was any praise she thought on these things; and these things came, and found lodgment in her pages, an inheritance for us and for future generations, more precious than gold.

"It is fitting that she should be brought home for burial. Here let her rest among those whom she loved, until the day dawns and the shadows flee away.

"She rests from her labors and her works do follow her.

> "'Now the laborer's task is o'er;
>   Now the battle day is past;
> Now upon the farther shore,
>   Lands the voyager at last.
> Father in Thy gracious keeping,
>   Leave we now Thy servant sleeping.'"[15]

Following the service in the church the body was committed to the Hill Cemetery which looks down on Green Gables to the left, and off toward the sea to the right, with all Avonlea stretching out in front.

"Doubtless in the years to come many will visit the Hill Cemetery, and the hill grave, where rests the dust of the creator of 'Anne' and the interpreter of Avonlea to all the world. To the imaginative, and to those with the seeing eye, and the hearing ear, there will be much to contemplate, and much to enjoy. Not all will see with the keen eye, nor hear with the alert ear of the distinguished sleeper in the hillside grave; but they will be dull of soul and devoid of spiritual sense if, standing there, they do not feel their pulses quicken at the thought of their proximity to the dust of one who painted life so joyously, so full of hope, and of sweetness and light."

NOTES

1 From "Elegy Written in a Country Churchyard" (1751), by Thomas Gray.
2 *AGG*, 294.
3 I have corrected the original, which reads "herself that to deliver."
4 *AGG*, 294.
5 Sir Louis Henry Davies (1845–1924), third Premier of PEI. I have corrected the original, which reads "Davis."
6 See chapter 17, "A Canadian Novelist of Note Interviewed," note 14, in this volume.
7 See chapter 5, "Miss Montgomery, the Author of the 'Anne' Books," by A. Wylie Mahon, note 2, in this volume.

8 Sir Robert Falconer (1867–1943), a Biblical scholar who became president of the University of Toronto in 1907.

9 Malcolm James MacLeod (1867–1940), author of *What God Hath Joined Together* (1915).

10 Cyrus MacMillan (1882–1953), member of the Canadian Parliament for Queen's riding, PEI, from 1940 to 1945; John Sutherland Bonnell (1893–1992), considered a pioneer in pastoral counselling.

11 Properly, "the choir invisible / Of those immortal dead who live again / In minds made better by their presence." From "O May I Join the Choir Invisible" (1867), by George Eliot.

12 Andrew Bonar Law (1858–1923), Prime Minister of Britain from October 1922 to May 1923, before he was succeeded by Stanley Baldwin; William Maxwell Aitken, 1st Baron Beaverbrook (1879–1964), politician and tycoon; Richard Bedford Bennett (1870–1947), Prime Minister of Canada from 1930 to 1935. Law and Bennett were born in New Brunswick, whereas the Ontario-born Aitken moved there as a baby.

13 *AGG*, 297.

14 From "Away," appearing in *Afterwhiles* (1887), by James Whitcomb Riley. It is erroneously attributed here to Eugene Field (1850–1895), American poet and essayist.

15 From "Now the Laborer's Task Is O'er," a nineteeth-century hymn with lyrics by John Ellerton (1826–1893), English hymn writer.

79

L.M. Montgomery as a Letter-Writer

—— 1942 ——

E. WEBER

Six months after Montgomery's death, in October 1942, her longtime cor-respondent Ephraim Weber (1870–1956) published the first of two tribute essays to Montgomery and her work in *The Dalhousie Review*. Here, he draws on forty years of correspondence to piece together a portrait of Montgomery, whom he had met in person only three times. He begins by recounting her visit to his home in Saskatchewan during her trip west in October 1930. While he always appears in awe of his correspondent, Montgomery recorded in her jour-nal that her visit was "only tolerable" and that she found Weber in person "not nearly so interesting" as on paper. Weber had written this essay in 1933 but was unable to find a market for it, a situation to which Montgomery was sym-pathetic: "If I were dead you would have a better chance!!"[1] This essay and the one that followed in 1944 are invaluable sneak peeks at the kind of sustained attention that Montgomery's fiction and life writing would attract in earnest beginning in the 1970s and 1980s. Weber's quotations do not quite match what appears in the two volumes of published letters, however. While some discrep-ancies can be attributed to the difficulty in deciphering Montgomery's hand-writing, it is worth noting that Weber did on occasion take minor liberties with her words – although, given that he showed Montgomery a draft of the essay in the early 1930s, perhaps she requested some minor editorial interventions.

Selections from Montgomery's side of their correspondence were published in two volumes: *The Green Gables Letters from L.M. Montgomery to Ephraim Weber, 1905–1909* (1960), edited by Wilfrid Eggleston, and *After Green Gables: L.M. Montgomery's Letters to Ephraim Weber, 1916–1941* (2006), edited by Hildi Froese Tiessen and Paul Gerard Tiessen.

Ten years ago it was my privilege to introduce L.M. Montgomery to an audience of her readers. In opening her address, she said that she and I had exchanged literary letters for thirty years, though we had never met until the year before, and that, of her many literary correspondents of old, a friend in England and I were the only ones still on her list.[2] This was news to me. And why we two? Were we bolder to strain her good nature, or more patient to decipher her long letters? I hardly dared think we wrote *better* letters. I never found out. In any case, she could easily have squelched us with silence. Of the other survivor I am sorry to know nothing, but as for me, the exchange has been richly in my favor, aside from the honor of it. Surely a famous author needs no obscure schoolmaster.

My respects to L.M. Montgomery's memory are herewith to take form in a few confessions, in which the aim is to show her excellence in the lost and lovely art of letter-writing. As her books are so charming, what may her letters be like? What did she write about, and how? Yes, you are right: her epistolary style carried her personality to her distant friends, for in her case decidedly the style was the man.

Scribbling a bit for second-rate periodicals in my young days, I noticed now and again a "yarnlet" or a snippet of poetry by one L.M. Montgomery, whom by a funny freak I fancied a whiskered sage, "goodly in girth,"[3] one whose thinking and rhyming powers were being liberated into appealing utterance. Trying to do something similar, I was wishing to get in touch with him, but hesitated to write to one of the publishers for his address; "I'd never hear from him anyway."

One day a letter came from a fellow-scribbler in Philadelphia, a stranger, who fancied some little thing of mine in a periodical.[4] In answering I mentioned L.M. Montgomery, whoever he was, as one of my new discoveries in current literature. A reply soon came from Philadelphia with the Montgomery address, urging me to write to my new Canadian writer-friend – "You'll hear from this kindred spirit."

I wrote. In due time a letter came from Cavendish, Prince Edward Island, signed Lucy Maud Montgomery![5] It was a shattering jolt. By instant alchemy the whiskers vanished, and the goodly girth assumed fashionplate length and lankness, but there was now an intellectual nose and a "mild and magnificent eye."[6]

The twentieth century had just seen daylight, and for forty years, up to her illness many months ago, this revised L.M. Montgomery answered my letters with epistles I call classics.

My correspondent's image was changed a second time – how agreeably! – when some years later I saw her picture in a magazine. The lankness shrank into a short and less bony figure; the eye was still magnificent, but now it was the *brow* that was intellectual.

The early Cavendish letters, unlike the later ones, came in ordinary envelopes with single postage. They contained chatty accounts of their writer's activities in the simple life of her Island, her love of cats and flowers and woods and lonely seashore walks at dusk, but mainly of her literary doings: lyric bits in humble monthlies, young people's weeklies, and later, in the *Sunday School Times* of Philadelphia.[7] Many a "faith trip" some of them made before they found asylum in printer's ink. There was constant exploring for new markets, and during her year in Halifax there were sallies for news stories for the *Halifax Echo*. These letters told of ways and means and little helps in the art of writing, gave nerving thoughts on the pain of rejections, and recommended bee-like assiduity in gathering material. They reported how courteous some editors were, and how heartless others; which publications paid on acceptance (only they seldom accepted), and which ones kept your manuscript "on the ticklish balance of suspense"[8] till you were sure they'd print it; then when it was out of season, returned it with those polite regrets in stereotyped print. Such were the chronicles of that dawn time.

Even so, there was hardly ever a letter that had no triumph over the Powers of Rejection to tell of. A triumph was a cheque for five, three, and even two dollars.

In a few more years the lengthening Montgomery letters told of more frequent acceptances with better pay. Montgomery poems were now seen in such classic print as the *Youth's Companion*;[9] Montgomery stories occasionally got into the better magazines, Canadian and American. Whenever, in the remoteness of my homestead near the foothills of the Rockies, I did not have access to the publication containing a sample of my friend's work, she would send me a copy, either of the periodical or of the piece in her own hand. Of course I would report my impressions, hardly ever finding any faults worth showing off my acumen, but it was a delight to dwell on the merits. If it was a poem, what fine fresh fancies, and how her rhymes and metres *sang* around her similies[10] and metaphors! L.M. Montgomery had a lovely lyric knack.

When one of her letters announced she was writing a book, "Great Scott and Caesar's Ghost!" my thoughts exclaimed. "A book! What shall I do now?" I was afraid to read on, lest I might learn she could now get along without my letters. A book! Why, that made an author of her, and authors have no time for the common herd.

No, it made no difference; she retained me.

Still, I had misgivings about the future: some day her completed book would make her famous. I wished her no harm, ye gods! but when she wrote that her manuscript of *Anne of Green Gables* had been rejected five times, the foundation of my hopes seemed to contain more cement. A few months later a letter announced that *Anne* was sold to one of the major American publishers.[11] Even to me that was a thriller. Such an achievement made common drudges of the Empire Builders. But would I survive? "Oh well, perhaps the book won't be a big success," my evil angel comforted in a timid whisper. But *Anne* crashed the gates to the big sellers, outstripped some of them, in fact: spilled over into England, France, Poland, Spain and Finland! Read in five languages, she wore "the million halo." All this I quizzed from her modest creator. Some years later she told me her book was printed in a language one wouldn't guess – braille.

And still it made no difference in my mail: eighteen to thirty largepad loosely-written pages of personal news and views. I never felt I was quite entitled to such expansive, fraternizing responses, happy as I was to get them.

More *Anne* books came along: *Anne of Avonlea*, *Anne of Ingleside*, *Anne of the Island*, *Anne's House of Dreams*, *Anne of Windy Poplars*; also the Emily books and the Pat books, *Marigold*, *Kilmeny*, *The Story Girl*, *A Tangled Web*, *Rainbow Valley* and several others.[12] After the first dozen were out, I felt middling safe, for not even then was there the least deadness in the letters, never a perfunctory line.

If my Montgomery missives have in late years become annuals, they have been requiring indemnifying double fare on the long envelopes. For intimacy, for conversational effect, for stimulating play of thought, one long epistle is surely worth a walletful of hasty notes. The day of long letters has gone with the horse and buggy, but the author of the *Anne*s and the *Emily*s[13] has preserved the liberal epistolary ways of the Queen Anners and the Victorians.

L.M. Montgomery always told me what book she was getting ready next for her world, and whenever she had one published she sent me an autographed copy. A letter announced she had for months been on an adult novel. A Montgomery story that wasn't a girls' novel! What might that be like? The next letter said it was nearly done. Curiosity became suspense. Six months later along it came, in Hodder and Stoughton format: *The Blue Castle*, autographed by the author.

It was avidly read. My wife always read out Montgomery stories to me. We had got to Valancy's marriage proposal to Barney,[14] when, laying the book down to laugh, she caught sight of the flopping leaves, and with an excited voice bade me "Look here!" There on a front page I read:

> To Mr. Ephraim Weber, M.A.,
> Who understands the architecture of Blue Castles.[15]

What! We both scrutinized and made sure. So the new kind of Montgomery fiction was dedicated to me! What for? What had I done, or been? And how could I be said to understand the architecture of Blue Castles when I hardly knew what they were? It demanded a reperusal of the volume with interpretative intent, as well as an enquiry in my next letter. The Oracle answered:

> You, like most people of the House of Joseph, understand "how fair the realms imagination opens to the view."[16]

It was long ago that our letters quit talking shop, for I practically neglected my writing. But there was plenty we exchanged about literature, standard and current, religion and the churches, education and the schools, the changing moral standard (only "it isn't changing," said my friend), the new rising generation (only "it isn't new," she declared), the warless world ("not *this* one ever," she countered).

In talking on serious topics, people seldom give each other time to finish their speeches; but when one party is at Cavendish, P.E.I., the other at Didsbury, Alberta, four-fifths of the continent between, it is not so hard to keep from interrupting. Another advantage of conversing by letter is that we have time to think out better speeches. Once I gave a wee disquisition on the moral constitution of the universe, culminating with this: "We are not punished *for* our sins, but *by* them." The reply had a wee disquisition on the nature of the Bible, culminating with this: "I do not believe the Bible is inspired *by* God, but *with* God."[17] So we exchanged wisdom and epigram, perhaps not so original as we then thought; but so we kept our intellectual souls in clover when the local pickings were scant at either end.

After thirty years of this paper conversing, we met. We almost called for pen and ink! The face-to-face way wasn't the same thing.[18]

What is the source of charm in letters of friendship? Is it that the absence of the physical person stimulates the creation of the friend's ideal personality? And anyway, as absence makes the heart grow fonder, the suspense of anticipating letters almost makes golden texts of half the sentences.

II

But I have not quite shown why I prize the Montgomery letters. Let us see more closely what they contain, and how they read.

My saying I liked tall flowers that sway in the wind brought this:

I like every kind. But I like best the flowers I coax into bloom myself, be they tall or small, white or rosy. It seems as if I were taking a hand in creation – giving life to those unsightly bulbs that hide such rainbow possibilities in their cores. Isn't it strange how such ugly things can give birth to such beauty – the old mystery of good, like the white lily, springing out of the muck and mire of evil? Is it possible that evil is necessary to the blossoming of good, just as the dirty clay and foul smelling fertilizers are necessary to the unfolding of those blossoms? There's a theological problem for you![19]

Here is the poet, stripped of rhyme and metre, though not of fancy's lovely vocabulary, gripping fast the concrete form and fact, then seeing its universal relation.

The letters have many bits of curious, cultured reading. Try this:

A short time ago, a British magazine ran an interesting series of letters on the idea: If you met the ghost of some famous person, and asked him or her *one* question, what would that question be?

A great many questions were asked, none of which appear in my list below. Half of the writers wished they could meet Shakespeare and ask him if he really did write his plays. Well, there's one question I would like to ask Shakespeare, but 'tis not about his plays. I feel absolutely sure he did write them, and the so-called difficulties stump me not a whit. You can't measure a demi-god with a yardstick.

No, if I met Shakespeare's shade I would ask him, "Why did you leave your wife your second-best bed?" Controversies have raged over this. I should really like to know.

Suppose one met St. Paul and asked him, "What was your thorn in the flesh?"

Or Pilate's wife: "What did you dream of the Nazarene?"

Queen Elizabeth: "Were you, or were you not, secretly married to Robert Dudley?"

Mary Queen of Scots: "Did you know about Darnley's murder?"

Dickens: "Was Edwin Drood really murdered or not?"

Homer: "Was there only one or half a dozen of you?"
Mona Lisa: "What are you smiling at like that?"
Abraham: "Just why did you leave Ur?"
Vashti: "Were you ever sorry you didn't obey Ahasuerus?"
Judas Iscariot: "Why did you really betray Him?"
Yes, I think one could have an interesting time among the ghosts.
Can you add any more to the list?[20]

I found it no easy list to extend after St. Paul, Mona Lisa and Iscariot had been taken, though it was fun to try. There are many ghost questions that come to mind, but not many classical cases so specifically puzzling. One would feel like asking any ghost what it feels like to die, but that's too general. I managed to add:

Beethoven: "How did you create those symphonies with a stone-deaf ear?"
Brutus: "Were you never sorry you stabbed Caesar?"
Hamlet: "Which of all the theories about you is right?"
Bishops Ridley and Latimer: "Is it true that in getting burned to death, the nerves are soon seared to insensibility, then easy dying?"
Lucy Gray: "What became of you when you got to the middle of the bridge?"

The reply:

As for questioning ghosts, your question for Ridley and Latimer *would* be interesting. I have read that a hot fire paralyzes the nerves at once, and thereafter no pain is felt. This must be true if the stories of triumphant hymn-singing at the stake are reliable. It was the slow fire that was dreadful. I have read that both Ridley and Latimer had little bags of powder hung from their necks to kill them quickly by explosion.[21]
I, too, want to know what happened to Lucy Gray. The awful intriguing mystery of that phrase, "And further there were none," haunted me all through childhood.[22]

I offered the answer I once got from an extra bright pupil: "Lucy evaporated." The next reply told how Lucy's evaporation tickled this Lucy's risibles.
The poetic descriptions that give the Montgomery stories such freshness and cheery imagery make the letters delightful too. A reviewer in the *New York Tribune*, in lingering appreciation, gets at the secret:

Miss Montgomery at moments has power to recapture and impart the sense of wonder, to present familiar objects in a kind of dawn light as if they were shining new and marvellous.[23]

But just as the describing pen, even though a Carlyle's, must leave it to the camera to bring out the personality behind a face, so the description of an author's style is "without form and void"[24] until we read it. And it takes her Island to liberate L.M. Montgomery's flow of fancies, personifying playfulness, and vital vocabulary.

In a letter I had tried to convey the atmosphere and some immensity of the Canadian prairie, which we were beginning to shred into virgin furrows. Here is the response, October, 1907:

> Though raining now, it was fine this afternoon – oh so fine – sunny and mild as a day in June. I hied me to the woods, away back to the sun-washed alleys carpeted with fallen gold and glades where the moss is green and vivid yet. The woods are *getting ready* to sleep – they are not *yet* asleep, but are disrobing. There are all kinds of little bed-time conferences and whisperings and good-nights. I can more nearly expect to come face to face with a dryad at this time of the year than any other. They are lurking in every tree trunk. A dozen times I wheeled sharply around, convinced that if I could only turn quick enough I could catch one peeping after me. Oh, keep your great, vast prairies, where never a wood-nymph could hide. I am content with my bosky lanes and the purple, peopled shadows under my firs.[25]

Even so, the sea, to this daughter of the Island, has a mightier spell than the woods. It haunts her, as her line of poetry says, "With a voice of gramarye evermore."[26] Or her letter:

> Three evenings ago I went to the shore. We had had a wild storm of wind and rain the day before, but this evening was clear, cold, with an air of marvellous purity. The sunset was lovely beyond words. I drank its beauty in as I walked down the old shore lane, and my soul was filled with a nameless exhilaration. I seemed borne on the wings of an ecstasy into the seventh heaven.
>
> The shore was clean washed after the storm, and not a wind stirred, but there was a silver surf on, dashing on the sands in a splendid white turmoil. Oh! the glory of that far gaze across the tossing waters, which were the only restless thing in all that vast

stillness and peace. It was a moment worth living through weeks of storm and stress for.

There is a great *solitude* about such a shore. The *woods* are never solitary – they are full of whispering, beckoning, friendly life, but the sea is a mighty soul forever moaning of some unsharable sorrow that shuts itself up into itself for all eternity. You can never pierce into its great mystery – you can only wonder, awed and spellbound, on the outer fringe of it. The woods call you with a hundred voices, but the sea has only one – a mighty voice that drowns your soul with its majestic music. The woods are human, but the sea is of the company of the archangels.

Then this daughter of nature, versed in literature, quotes an oracle of Emerson into living meaning:

> The gods talk in the breath of the wold,
> They talk in the shaken pine,
> And they fill the long reach of the old seashore
> With a dialogue divine.
> And the poet who overhears
> Some random word they say
> Is the fated man of men
> Whom the ages must obey.

I shall never hear that random word; my ear is not attuned to its lofty thunder. But I can always *listen*, and haply by times I shall catch the faint, far-off echoes of it, and even that will flood my soul with its supernal joy.[27]

"But I can always listen" – strikingly like Wordsworth listening to the distant waves: "Listen! The Mighty Being is awake."[28]

I had been wanting to describe to this poetic observer of nature the various aspects of the Rocky Mountains seventy to a hundred miles west, as seen from my homestead in various weathers and times of day: the cracked white enamel of their sunward side the morning after a snowfall; the purple gloom of the shady side with a rosy sunset behind them; also as seen from a height among them: the constant shift of sublime scenery from different points and elevations; the thrill of gazing down thousands of feet into valleys with toy townlets strung along a looping, silvery river-ribbon; the jumbled chaos of mountain tops seen through waving curtains of rain at moments glorified by sunbeams – all this with enough detail to make it vivid, for she had never seen the Rockies. But that Indian Summer letter of 1907 discouraged me: I felt unable to match her depth.

Of personal anecdotes these letters have plenty. One problem of famous writers is to keep their mail manageable. But again it takes the author to tell it:

A girl in Australia – may jackals sit on her grandmother's grave – wrote me last fall, and I answered her letter. She published my letter and address in an Australian magazine, something she should not have done without my consent. In mid-winter the deluge began. The first wave was eighty-five letters in one day. The local postmaster wanted to know if I were having a wedding anniversary! This continued until May, when they began to dribble off. I have ceased to count them, but there must have been a thousand. My publishers say, "Oh, answer them, if only by a line ..." But fancy the work! Do you wonder my poor real correspondents are left out in the cold?[29]

A young fellow in Detroit sent a tidy missive with this address:

> Miss Anne Shirley
> Care of Miss Marilla Cuthbert
> Avonlea
> Prince Edward Island
> Canada
> Ontario

Those who know *Anne of Green Gables* and a bit of Canadian geography will be as amused, as L.M.M. was. A post office clerk had written across the envelope, "Try Miss Montgomery, Cavendish."[30] Her getting it implies that her Marilla and her Anne enjoyed no mean fame.

Here's a set of gems from my Montgomery letters:
Poetic awe of a night scene:

Then *the* storm came up, and for half an hour we sat there spellbound, gazing on such a sight as we had never dreamed – the great Canadian Falls (Niagara) lying under the ghostly, shimmering, blue-white gleam of almost constant lightning, while athwart the mist tore zig-zags of living flame, as if some god were amusing himself by hurling thunderbolts into the abyss. No, I shall never see the like of that again. But I have seen it once.[31]

Expecting that her publishers would want "that detestable Anne" written through high-school in a second volume, then through college in a third:

I'm Anne's slave already. The idea makes me sick. I feel like the magician in the eastern story who became the slave of the jinn he had himself conjured out of a bottle.[32]

A weird personal experience:

Mammoth Cave must be terribly full of ghosts. Everyone who goes through it must leave something of himself in it, a little bit of his soul, his personality, and always wants to go back and find it. But does he ever go? I fancy very few people ever revisit Mammoth Cave. It mightn't be safe. *Suppose it kept too much of you?*[33]

How free-verse writers, averse to old forms, strain to be original:

But isn't a beautiful echo more beautiful than the shriek of an automobile?[34]

The characterlessness of the "good mixers":

The only people I ever knew that were worth while were cats who walked by themselves and never pretended to be Maltese if they were tortoise shell.[35]

Immortality of roses:

Henry Ward Beecher said, "Flowers are the sweetest things God ever made and forgot to put souls into." But I believe He didn't forget. I believe they *have* souls. I have known roses that I expect to meet in Heaven.[36]

Playful allusion:

After gardening intensely, and cleaning house ferociously for six weeks, I am taking a breathing spell and intend to put off Martha and put on Mary.[37]

Prevention of profanity:

I never put more than two kinds of flowers together in a bouquet. More would swear at each other.[38]

Kindred spirits:

I wonder if the spirits of all the pussy folk I have loved will meet me with purrs of gladness at the pearly gates.[39]

L.M. Montgomery prefers the warm individuality of the human hand to the cold Roman universality of the typewriter. In the forty years of this literary exchange she never typed me a letter. A typed letter from her would have been the high handshake. No, the handwriting of the well-seasoned correspondent is no matter for an encroaching machine to profane, even when, as in this case, the writing is hard to read; for slow reading allows fond lingering on the lines.

What, then, in sum and substance, are the merits of these letters? Their style is so facile and natural that you forget it isn't conversation. There is open sincerity, clear conviction, free familiarity and a playful original-ity of fancy, with freshness of diction; live subject matter, personal and general, made still more interesting by genial comment; poetic feeling that brings melody and rhythm into the sentences; stimulating thought, strengthened or adorned with bits from lore and legend; and a courteous patience that brought ample replies to my more commonplace news and less adventurous lay experience.

And what were her last words to me? – "We've had a good friendship in our own way," she wrote, explaining that a "hypo" enabled her to hold a pen for a few moments.[40]

This correspondence has made me fonder of the great letters of the masters: Samuel Johnson, Shelley, Cowper, Horace Walpole, Goethe, Lincoln, Carlyle and his wife Jane, for a few; and I still intend to nibble at Madame de Sevigné.[41]

NOTES

1 Montgomery, 2 November 1930, in *SJLMM*, 4: 85; Montgomery to Weber, 18 March 1934, in *AfGG*, 218; see also *AfGG*, 218n15.
2 George Boyd MacMillan was actually from Alloa, Scotland.
3 From "A Consecration" (1915), a poem by John Masefield (1878–1967), English novelist and poet.
4 Miss Miriam Zieber of Philadelphia, attempting to establish a network of writers, introduced Montgomery to both Weber and MacMillan. See Eggleston, "General Introduction," 5.
5 This first letter, dated 29 March 1902 and sent from Halifax, is no longer in existence (Eggleston, "General Introduction," 4). I have corrected the original, which reads "Lucy Maude Montgomery."
6 From "The Lost Leader" (1845), by Robert Browning.
7 Montgomery published four poems between 1901 and 1908, beginning with "The Cure of the Fields," as well as the short story "Their Trip to Town" in 1904, in *The Sunday School Times*.
8 Properly, "Upon the ticklish balance of suspense." From "The Garden" (1785), a poem by William Cowper (1731–1800), English poet.
9 Montgomery published at least fifteen poems in *The Youth's Companion* between 1896 and 1910.
10 An archaic spelling of "similes."
11 Despite what is mentioned here, Montgomery mentioned the book only once she had signed her contract with Page (Montgomery to Weber, 2 May 1907, in *GGL*, 51–52).
12 I have corrected the original, which reads *"Anne of the Islands"* and *"The Tangled Web."*
13 I have corrected the original, which reads "the *Anne*'s and the *Emily*."
14 I have corrected the original, which reads "Valancey."
15 Although it is unclear why, this dedication appeared only in the UK edition of *The Blue Castle* and was omitted from the Canadian and American editions. My thanks to Mary Beth Cavert and Christy Woster.
16 See Montgomery to Weber, 16 November 1927, in *AfGG*, 148. This unidentified quotation also appears in *AA*, 128.
17 See Montgomery to Weber, 8 May 1905, in *GGL*, 30.
18 Weber and Montgomery met for the first time when Weber and his wife visited the Macdonalds in July 1928. See Montgomery, 22 July 1928, in *SJLMM*, 3: 374.
19 See Montgomery to Weber, 16 December 1906, in *GGL*, 48–49.
20 See Montgomery to Weber, 7 April 1929, in *AfGG*, 165.

21 Hildi Froese Tiessen and Paul Gerard Tiessen note that "Nicholas Ridley and Hugh Latimer, Protestant reformers, were burned at the stake in England in 1555" (*AfGG*, 182n31).

22 Montgomery to Weber, 8 June 1930, in *AfGG*, 182–83. From "Lucy Gray, or Solitude" (1799), a poem by William Wordsworth. In her journals, Montgomery stated that Lucy Gray had been the name of one of her imaginary friends in childhood, but that the invention of this friend had predated her reading of Wordsworth's poem (Montgomery, 26 March 1905, in *SJLMM*, 1: 306).

23 See Isabel Paterson's review of *Emily of New Moon* in Volume 3 of *The L.M. Montgomery Reader*.

24 See Genesis 1:2 in the Hebrew Bible.

25 Montgomery to Weber, 10 November 1907, in *GGL*, 56.

26 From Montgomery's poem "The Sea-Spirit," published in *The Criterion* in April 1902 and reprinted as "The Sea Spirit" in *The Watchman and Other Poems*.

27 See Montgomery to Weber, 10 November 1907, in *GGL*, 56–57. The "oracle" in question is "The Poet" (1867), by Ralph Waldo Emerson, whose first line ends with "the breath of the woods." See also *EC*, 10, in which this misquotation also appears.

28 From "It Is a Beauteous Evening" (1807), by William Wordsworth.

29 See Montgomery to Weber, 8 June 1930, in *AfGG*, 176.

30 See Montgomery to Weber, 2 September 1909, in *GGL*, 93. I have corrected the original, which reads "Miss Martha Cuthbert."

31 Montgomery to Weber, 1 November 1924, in *AfGG*, 127.

32 See Montgomery to Weber, 10 September 1908, in *GGL*, 74.

33 See Montgomery to Weber, 1 November 1924, in *AfGG*, 125.

34 See Montgomery to Weber, 17 October 1923, in *AfGG*, 110.

35 See Montgomery to Weber, 17 October 1923, in *AfGG*, 108.

36 See Montgomery to Weber, 8 May 1905, in *GGL*, 29. Henry Beecher Ward (1813–1887), American clergyman and speaker who supported temperance and women's suffrage.

37 See Montgomery to Weber, 8 June 1930, in *AfGG*, 173.

38 See Montgomery to Weber, 28 June 1905, in *GGL*, 33.

39 See Montgomery to Weber, 7 April 1929, in *AfGG*, 164.

40 In a letter dated December 1940, she wrote, "let us thank God for a long and true friendship" (Montgomery to Weber, 31 December 1940, in *AfGG*, 260). Her last letter, dated December 1941, mentions the "hypo" but makes no mention of their friendship (Montgomery to Weber, 26 December 1941, in *AfGG*, 263).

41 Samuel Johnson (1709–1784), English author, critic, and lexicographer; Percy Bysshe Shelley (1792–1822), English poet and husband of Mary Shelley (1797–1851), English author best known for *Frankenstein*; Horace Walpole (1717–1797), English author of *The Castle of Otranto* (see Montgomery to Weber, 1 November 1924, in *AfGG*, 129, in which she recommends Hugh Walpole's 1924 novel *The Old Ladies*); Johann Wolfgang von Goethe (1749–1832), German author of the tragic play *Faust* (see Montgomery to Weber, 25 November 1917, in *AfGG*, 67, in which she comments on Weber's decision to write his doctoral dissertation on "The English Translations of Faust"); Abraham Lincoln (1809–1865), American President from 1861 to his assassination (see Montgomery to Weber, 26 May 1919, in *AfGG*, 79); Thomas Carlyle (1795–1881), Scottish author and historian; Jane Carlyle (1801–1866), whose letters have been published numerous times since her death; Marie de Rabutin-Chantal, marquise de Sauvigné (1626–1696), French aristocrat whose letters were published in the mid-eighteenth century.

80

L.M. Montgomery's "Anne"

—— 1944 ——

E. WEBER

Published in *The Dalhousie Review* in April 1944, a year and a half after "L.M. Montgomery as a Letter-Writer," this second essay by Ephraim Weber marks an attempt to include Montgomery's Anne books in the early conversation about Canadian literature, reading publics, and local colour. Although Weber, here, does not discuss his personal relationship to Montgomery, his observations give us a sense of Montgomery's critical and popular reception, noting that her work was being selected for school systems across Canada in the years surrounding her death.

Not until early in this century did Canadian writers of fiction quite have the realistic eye to see what literary material might be gathered from our commonplace farms, lonely villages and remote frontiers, provided one had the knack of selecting and "processing" it – without over-processing. "They began to realize that life around them was as interesting as Barrie's Thrums or Bret Harte's California," says *Highways of Canadian Literature*. The same writer points out that on reading Ian Maclaren's *Beside the Bonnie Briar Bush*, Adeline M. Teskey declared, "I know just as interesting people in Canada"; and so stimulated, she wrote her *Where the Sugar Maple Grows* – readable sketches of Canadian village characters.[1]

The above authority calls 1908 the real beginning of the Second Renaissance in Canadian fiction, for in that year were published three "community novels" of note: L.M. Montgomery's *Anne of Green Gables*, Marian Keith's *Duncan Polite*, and Nellie McClung's *Sowing Seeds in*

Danny.[2] So strong a start in this experiment doubtless soon brought publishers a grievous lot of manuscripts; though in L.M. Montgomery's case the publishers' trouble later on was not to *read* more of her manuscripts but to *get* more of them fast enough. The five sadder and wiser publishers who had rejected *Anne of Green Gables* evidently saw no future in the community novel, at least when written by an obscure stranger. Out of her twenty-one novels it is the six or seven *Anne* books we are now to re-read and appraise.

To write with third-rate interest about the common people and their daily doings is easy; to write about them with second-rate interest is not extra hard; but to do it with first-rate interest is surprisingly difficult. L.M. Montgomery has depicted the common people of Prince Edward Island with first-rate interest; for, having grown up among them, she knows their ways, their traditions, their souls, as Dickens knows *his* islanders. And yet some of her critics are not won over; one of them, reviewing the later Canadian literature some years ago, called the Montgomery novels "the nadir of Canadian fiction."[3] Of course the thrilling romantic plot is missing. To a reader of the old school, addicted to those far-spun yarns of romance vibrating with heroic excitement, the humbler affairs of the community novel may well be piddling neighborhood fusses. But many of the best late novels, highly rated and widely read, are quite without large-scale plot interest. What, no terrific tenseness between mighty antagonistic forces! No Himalayas scaled in pursuit of the villain! No war over the duchess! Well then, has the community novel any compensating substitute? The compensating substitute in the first-rate community novel is the interest of *reality*.

The interest of reality in the new Canadian novel is mainly *character* interest, heightened by concentrated regional setting; and not far behind is the interest of *incident*. To make up in this way for lack of plot structure is obviously no easy assignment. Before you know it, you have the dry rot of dullness – unless you scrape into unsavory realism. Then, too, this kind of fiction, far more than the heroic romance, attracts the spoiling imitator. Even so, if your author knows his kind and knows his art, the interest of reality fills the bill excellently.

Every day we meet people who have read a few of the Anne books, and there are those who have made a clean sweep of the Montgomery shelf, or have re-read parts of it. As for favorite volumes, many have read *Anne of Green Gables* two, three, and "I don't know how many" times. An ex-collegiate student of ours, now a mother, wrote recently:

Please do not say I *used* to devour the Montgomery books. It is only a few days ago that I contemplated reading them once more. I have lost count of how many times that would be, but each time I get more and more from the reading ... Did you know Guthrie [husband] has been a Montgomery fan for years?

A German Mennonite girl of eleven comes to my study these times twice a week for a next Anne story, because "At the public library Anne books are always out, and the last one I had was all worn out and dirty." I quiz her a bit on these stories; her knowledge is surprising. What is there in them that fascinates this child, who is being brought up in a different social world and on a different language? It is surely her heart's response to the author's friendly human note and the living vividness of it all. "Montgomery girls," reported a bright tenth grade lass I was quizzing, "act just like we girls act; they're just so many of *us*. They just step out of the book and are with us." Her gusto in saying it showed how this middle-'teener enjoyed the illusion of reality. Herein is our author's opportunity: her upward trend and idealization of life is so naturally veiled as entertainment that our girls are off guard against being made better, and so *are* made better. "They just step out of the book and are with us." Is it any wonder that of the hundreds all over the world who wrote their thanks and appreciation to the author, a number of younger girls addressed *Anne Shirley*, Green Gables, Avonlea, P.E.I.?

Anne of Green Gables is getting to be used as story material at school from grade three to first year high-school. In Saskatchewan it is supplementary reading for grade IX, in Manitoba for grade VII, in Ontario for the upper public-school grades, in Alberta for grade VIII and division II of the elementary school, and in practically all the provinces it is recommended for school libraries, though in New Brunswick all the L.M. Montgomery books are thought suitable only "for very young children." In Prince Edward Island, *Rilla of Ingleside* is supplementary reading for grade VII; also in Manitoba, as well as *Magic for Marigold*. The wide age range is striking, and indicates fine literary elasticity in these Anne books. These, Protestant Quebec reports, are all in the school libraries and are quite popular in the high-school grades, *Rainbow Valley* being a favorite. From *Anne of Green Gables* dialogues and scenes are sometimes played in the class-room; here in Saskatoon we have seen it acted full stage throughout, slightly abridged, by a collegiate cast before a large public audience. Small boys read these books above board, big ones on the sly, "to see what scrape this Anne-girl gets into next." Boys with changing voices croak against "that gushy-mushy sentimental stuff about kindred spirits 'n fairies 'n poetry dope," but sometimes sneak back to pick up the discarded volume again. Grandmas absorbed in *Anne* stories brighten up with understanding smiles at spots where their granddaughters giggle. A neighbor borrowed our *Anne of Green Gables* (needs patching and dry-cleaning) for her bed-ridden mother, aged ninety-four, who still is sport enough to fancy she's Marilla; for in a reading circle long ago they said she took the part so well. And here is a thriller: soon after *Green Gables* was published, a missive came to the author from Mark Twain's secretary, a copy of Mark's note to Francis Wilson, famous actor:

Anne of Green Gables is the sweetest creation of child life yet written.

How the great humorist felt Anne's spell! When L.M. Montgomery died, a newspaper pointed out a quotation from him in a booklet on this author:

Anne Shirley, the heroine of *Anne of Green Gables*, is the dearest and most moving and delightful child since the immortal Alice.[4]

Reviewing *Anne of Ingleside*, a belated sequel to several sequels to *Green Gables*, Jane Spence Southron said: "Mark Twain, had he been alive, would have approved of the later Anne. She has worn well; or rather, there is no sign of wear about her."[5]

Not only from the United States came such praise. For the excellence of her literary work and the pleasure it has spread in various lands and languages, King George V, 1935, decorated Lucy Maud Montgomery with the O.B.E. An equal distinction came from another British source. When attending the British Empire Conference at Ottawa, Rt. Hon. Stanley Baldwin, Prime Minister of Great Britain, asked to meet this gifted woman who had so delighted himself and his wife by her literary creations.

Looking back through the years to that great day when she received *Green Gables* from the publishers, L.M. Montgomery wrote:

I did not dream that *Green Gables* would be the success it was. I thought girls in their 'teens might like it, but that was the only audience I hoped to reach. But men and women who are grandparents, boys at school and college, old pioneers in the Australian bush, missionaries in China, monks in remote monasteries, and red-headed girls all over the world have written me telling how they loved Anne and her family ...

The very day on which these words are written has come a letter to me from an English lad of nineteen, totally unknown to me, who writes he is leaving for the front and wants to tell me before he goes how much my books, especially *Anne*, have meant to him. It is in such letters that a writer finds meet reward for all sacrifice and labor.[6]

L.M. Montgomery was rewarded not only by appreciation:

Green Gables, she wrote (*Everywoman's World*, 1917) "has been translated into Swedish and Dutch. My Swedish copy always gives me the inestimable boon of a laugh. The cover design is a full-length figure of Anne wearing a sunbonnet, carrying the famous carpetbag, and with hair literally an intense scarlet!"[7]

II

So, are these Montgomery tales not nearer the zenith than the nadir? Can so many people of so many kinds in so many lands be charmed by *cheap* fiction with its anaemic reality? The adverse critics can still keep their souls in clover on ripping adventure, dashing romance, bigwig intrigue and unlimited realism.

Though it is still the Creator's secret how a talent produces its precise effects, let us visit the Montgomery study and see at least what distinguishing elements, what salt and savor, this creator puts into her characters. No, this is not an interview. Delicately sensitive to personality, she gets sharp impressions of people's inner selves, and is downright happy in exercising her resourceful inventiveness on all kinds of circumstances in which to show their behavior in action and to let us feel their atmosphere. To get us perfectly acquainted with her Island folks, she treats us to a liberal range of incidents, all the more engaging for their local color: Scotch Presbyterian and such. The reason her machinery does not creak is that she never proceeds by a technique she is learning, but just by an original instinct for her characters. Warm with emotion and animated by zest, she enters into them like a dramatist.

How she understands Matthew Cuthbert of *Green Gables*! When this lonely, taciturn soul speaks, he has something to say; his few words, so coolly spoken, make impressions. About such self-suppressing persons there emanates an aura of pathos, which we feel in this rude Scotchman, long-haired old farmer bachelor with a refined soul, a fair type of our pioneering bush-whackers. He has no one to love but a freckled, carrot-haired little thing of an orphan – and is afraid it may be discovered! "For the sweet old-fashioned flowers his mother had planted in the homestead garden in her bridal days he had always had a secret, wordless love." Seldom seen, his presence was felt in the background. But once, "for the first time, this shy quiet Matthew was a person of central importance: the white majesty of death had fallen on him and set him apart as one crowned." The orphan, "in her tearless agony," gathered of the hallowed flowers to put on his coffin; and for years she kept his grave trim and blooming, giving his memory a solitary communing visit there, the last thing on moving away from Green Gables.[8]

Quite as convincing a reality is Marilla, his old-maid sister. Are there, or have there ever been, such stern, dour, uncommunicative Scotch Presbyterians? Well, isn't this their very race-brand back a generation or two? Not on their sleeves but in their deep dense interiors they wear, or wore, their hearts. Added to years of the orphan's softening presence, it took Matthew's funeral to make Marilla confess she loved the child, loved her like her own flesh and blood; and in spite of her crabbed discipline she managed to tell her, "You've been my joy and comfort ever since you came to Green Gables."[9] Her Scotch stubbornness – or shall we graciously call it her dogged consistency with her original grudge against the child for being a girl? – was sturdy stuff, backed up by the traditional asceticism, which supported her hard attitude; backed further by Matthew's secret love of the girl. The complexity is left nicely veiled, and makes good reading for those who know the old Scotch temperament. Though Marilla's earlier scoldings and denials give us heartache, we do not find it hard to forgive her in the end: "It's never been easy for me to say things out of my heart."[10] Even some of us not exactly Scotch might give the old spinster a brotherly handshake on that if we could get ourselves to do it. But what a clean job she made of it once she got round to it! What a mother heart now has room to expand in her bosom! A reader told the author she regretted Matthew's early death; the author replied she had come to feel the same way, explaining her object had been to bring Anne a needed sacrifice.[11] Right or wrong, one fine thing accomplished by it is the highly-due humanization of Marilla.

And now the orphan: the Anne of Green Gables, the Anne of Avonlea, the Anne of the Island, the Anne of Windy Poplars, the Anne of the House of Dreams, the Anne of Ingleside, the mother of Rilla of Ingleside.

After a closer look at her, all this about Marilla and Matthew needs to be re-read. Let us see what kind of energy, what sweetness and light, we can find in this World-Anne, whose major early troubles, next to her homelessness, were her carrot hair, her freckled nose, and the abomination of seeing her name without an *e*.

Anne Shirley, a tall skinny thing of eleven, was so temperamental and emotional that her big light-gray eyes sometimes showed green-gray or a kind of amber glint, according to mood – a fit of anger or a spell of rapture over natural scenery. Imagining things was meat and drink to her soul. The beauty of Green Gables at first sight made her want to live there forever. So here at the very start of the Anne fiction we have first class interest between humble character and humble circumstance: the anguish this sensitive child endures because she is a mistake and is to be driven out of her Eden to make room for a boy. An insipid character in this fine suspense would be boring. At the above-mentioned dramatization of *Green Gables* the audience felt the power of this scene, for already we were all tenderly affectioned toward this individualistic little heroine, and getting adjusted to her. Then her ecstasy on learning she was to stay swung our emotions the other way. Next comes the process of mistress bringing up ward – and ward "bringing up" mistress. "Father" had been brought up while listening to Anne's charming chat during the long buggy ride home. The old ascetic restraint and the new rebellion against it carry on the action, until by degrees the mistress is nine-tenths conquered and doesn't know it, at least hates to own it, even to herself. Not that the ward plotted it; her unconscious influence brought it about. Not Anne's outbreaks, but her quiet innate force liberalized the old-school Calvinist into healthy discipline. Still, the early strictness, though marred by harshness, had the effect of giving the child a compensating appreciation of life's blessings. Interesting reciprocity!

Anne is charming when she gets stormy. The abuses she suffers win her our tender feelings, which make her outbursts all the more startling. When the too neighborly Mrs. Rachel Lynde discharged her blunderbuss at her over her freckles, skinniness and carrot hair, she was "properly horrified" at the response she got;[12] and nobody who was at Avonlea School the day Gilbert Blythe made fun of Anne's hair before the whole room when school was on will ever forget the scene she put up in dealing with him. Small events, these, but character and incident co-operate to make appealing young people's literature of them in their contexts; and appealing young people's literature makes no dull reading for older generations.

The Anne series of the Montgomery novels has as its main interest the development of this scrawny, sensitive orphan into a toughened and enlightened mother. To those who have not read *Green Gables*, the initial volume, this may sound blank and bleak, but only to those. Across the territory of these volumes her personality runs like a power line, distributing energy and light and love, right and left, wherever there is human material that can take the current. Naturally and satisfyingly her presence dominates the whole sequence. In letting such a mite evolve to such a power, the author has nowhere strained the laws and ways of reality to contrive an artificial perfection. Evolution has no grudge against the unlucky. To see Anne through her girlhood, 'teens and mature life is a great way for a girl to learn what unfading satisfaction can be got out of life without either sinking into drudging ambitionlessness or chafing to soar into flighty careering in public life and high society. Here we have that basic middle course which circles enduringly and fulfillingly about a woman's centre of gravity: a childhood home with nature's health and refinement playing about; enough choring to learn housekeeping; preparatory school, then college with its enlarging culture; a spicy nip of public life (school principal); a lovely courtship – such letters! – a fine married life &c. with its creative mystery; and in time that pleasant easing-off into lighter duties.

Logan and French, quoted below, call *Green Gables* a classic and Anne an entirely new character in fiction. A startling statement – no geographic or other limits; but after close study it sounds less wild. Anne's unique originality, live imagination, precocious wisdom, optimistic energy, versatile hearty serviceableness – all these in peculiar combination may well make her stand out:

> The introduction of Anne into the community – Anne, so unconventional, so imaginative, and so altogether different from the staid, prosaic, general attitude of the neighborhood – proved to be the invasion of a peculiar ferment, and the incidents which discover the process of fermentation are most delightfully odd and mirth-provoking ... Others can write plot stories, but most other writers do not hold before us the mirror of Canadian country life.[13]

With her delicate comprehension Anne has unlimited sympathy, and so becomes a helpful confidante to young and old in a variety of predicaments. The catalogue of her own youthful predicaments is long and ridiculous enough to have made her a wise tongue-holding counsellor.

Such a woman can hardly help becoming an incurable match-maker. The intrigue it takes to put hard cases over is irresistible to this active brain, but she never undertakes a match without believing it means happiness, and her successes sweetly reward her. But her major triumph, Alden and Stella, upon which she expends her slyest tact, suddenly suffers such a sheepish deflation that she is cured forever: she learns the pair were blissfully engaged beforehand![14]

III

Reporting to the author on my complimentary copy of *Anne of Ingleside*, I noted how my wife and I were further impressed by her understanding of children, and how at spots our mellow smiles became 'teenish laughs; for the story was a delightfully undulating streak of entertainment. She replied I needn't have been so nice with my compliments; the yarn, spun to order as a fill-gap in Anne's life, was mainly padding.[15] "But yarn and eiderdown, not hay," I retorted, bound to have the last word, "make nice padding." If this story lacks strict organic unity, it has at any rate the continuity of family raising, and such a family! Anne's, of course. One must know them, see them in action, overhear their remarks, be asked their questions, and feel the atmosphere, to get all there is.

As to gap-fillers: the Montgomery novels fall mainly into the *Anne*, the *Emily*, and the *Pat* groups. The first in each is written out of fascination for the dominating heroine, succeeding ones came at the insistence of readers and publishers of the first. L.M.M. did not experience heavenly joy in writing them all. "That detestable Anne!" she wrote on receiving her publishers' demand for a second Anne volume. "I'm her slave already. The idea makes me sick."[16] She wrote not one more Anne volume but six, and wrote some of them *in reverse*: not in chronological order as lived by Anne, but as the publishers kept finding that more Anne books were wanted. So from time to time a gap was discovered in Anne's career big enough to accommodate a book. In *Rilla of Ingleside* Anne is a settled housewife, mother of six, three at the front in World War I. Fancy the awkwardness of having to go back several Anne books and reduce her to an unmarried school principal in *Anne of Windy Poplars*. Again, preparing to write *Anne of Ingleside*, a year before World War II, she mounts a magic mantle and rides annihilatingly backward through the years and through her books to invent Anne-life lived before World War I. It is hard to think the author got no enjoyment out of the writing once she got warmed up to it; there is a live glow in it all.[17]

How tempting it would be to show up the charming style of these tales, which adds so much to the interest, but our conclusion is elbowing in. At L.M. Montgomery's funeral, Rev. Dr. Frank Baird said of her:

Kingdoms which others laboriously seek to enter and cannot, she came into as by natural inheritance, and there ... she reigned as queen endowed with genius and grace, with shining ability and marvellous gifts; and while her sales ran into millions, there is nowhere a line that is unworthy, a syllable that can offend. She waved her magic wand, and the ugly things fled away. – *Presbyterian Record* June '42.[18]

Are not these Anne stories as interesting as the coarse thrillers – to all but the sophisticated Smart Set and their following? The characters, Dog Monday and all, are normal and walk the plane we tread. After re-reading the books, can you imagine Anne as *fiction*? This Anne whose unconscious influence liberated, liberalized Marilla, Mrs. Lynde, Miss Barry; who stood her ground against the Pyes, the Sloanes, the Pringles; who meant so much to groping little Elizabeth and Paul, to gray-haired lonely Matthew, rugged Captain Jim, love-sick Charlotta the Fourth, gruff old Rebecca Dew; this Anne who, while making herself pluck roosters, roamed the Milky Way – can you doubt that if your daughters got to know her well, they would feel a stimulating lift from her toward becoming the girls they would like to be?

Anne Books in Order of Events –
(Not as Written)

Anne of Green Gables: Anne arrives and grows up.
Anne of Avonlea: She teaches Avonlea School.
Anne of the Island: Attends Redmond College.
Anne of Windy Poplars: Principal at Summerside – Love letters to Gilbert Blythe.
Anne's House of Dreams: Settles down married – Jem born.
Anne of Ingleside: Five more Blythes born.
Rainbow Valley: They grow up with the manse children.
Rilla of Ingleside: Anne's three boys in World War I.
(In these last two Anne recedes to the background)

409

NOTES

1 Logan and French, *Highways of Canadian Literature*, 298, 299. Teskey's novel *Where the Sugar Maple Grows: Idylls of a Canadian Village* was published in 1901.
2 Ibid., 299.
3 The phrase "the nadir of Canadian Literature" is actually Montgomery's: it appears in a letter from her to Weber (see Montgomery to Weber, 8 June 1930, in *AfGG*, 180), in reference to William Arthur Deacon. See the introduction to this volume for Deacon's treatment of Montgomery's work.
4 These are both misquotations of Twain's comments to Francis Wilson; see the headnote to chapter 1, "[Such a Delightful Little Person]," as well as chapter 46, "Something about L.M. Montgomery," in this volume.
5 Southron, "After Green Gables," 7.
6 See *AP*, 76.
7 See *AP*, 78.
8 See *AGG*, 294, 295.
9 *AGG*, 296.
10 *AGG*, 296.
11 *AP*, 75.
12 Chapter 9 of *Anne of Green Gables* is entitled "Mrs. Rachel Lynde Is Properly Horrified."
13 See Logan and French, *Highways of Canadian Literature*, 300, 301.
14 See *AIn*, 81–100.
15 See Montgomery's letter to Weber dated May 1939, four months before the publication of *Anne of Ingleside*: "It is just what I have called it – a potboiler" (Montgomery to Weber, 8 May 1939, in *AfGG*, 248).
16 In a 1908 letter, Montgomery mentioned that her second novel, *Anne of Avonlea*, had been her publisher's idea. "I'm awfully afraid if the thing takes, they'll want me to write her through college. The idea makes me sick. I feel like the magician in the Eastern story who became the slave of the 'jinn' he had conjured out of a bottle." In her next letter, dated December 1908, she wrote, "I daresay the most of the letter will be about that detestable *Anne*." Montgomery to Weber, 10 September 1908, in *GGL*, 74; Montgomery to Weber, 22 December 1908, in *GGL*, 77.
17 See Montgomery's comments in her journal, in which she likened writing *Anne of Ingleside* to "going home" (Montgomery, 12 September 1938, in *SJLMM*, 5: 278).
18 See chapter 78, "L.M. Montgomery / Mrs. (Rev.) Ewen Macdonald," in this volume.

Epilogue: *Anne of Green Gables* – The Story of the Photoplay

—— 1920 ——

ARABELLA BOONE

This first volume of *The L.M. Montgomery Reader* concludes with a long-lost early example of an ongoing phenomenon: namely, of the creation of further Montgomery texts written without Montgomery. In her journals, she stated that she was not at all surprised to discover that her first publisher, L.C. Page, had waited until after he had purchased all remaining rights to her books before selling the film rights to *Anne of Green Gables*, *Anne of Avonlea*, *Chronicles of Avonlea*, and *Anne of the Island* to the Realart Pictures Corporation, which released a silent film of *Anne of Green Gables* in November 1919. Indeed, although she mourned the loss of a substantial amount of income that would have otherwise been owed to her, she did not express any anger about the loss of control over her intellectual property. "I do not expect to like the film myself – I never yet have liked any film I have seen that was reproduced from a book I had read," she declared, making no distinction between a book she had read and one she had written. "Nevertheless I am very curious to see it."[1] In fact, her response to this film – both privately and publicly – was emphatically negative (see chapter 62, "Is This My Anne," in this volume).[2]

But even before Montgomery saw the film in Toronto in February 1920, a further extension to the Anne story had already appeared: a short narrative by Arabella Boone, dubbed "the story of the photoplay," was included in the January 1920 issue of *Photoplay Magazine*, a Chicago periodical devoted to articles, photographs, and Hollywood gossip. Given that the 1919 film version of *Anne of Green Gables* was lost long ago, Boone's story serves two crucial functions in our understanding of Montgomery's work and its afterlives: not only does it provide us with at least a partial account of the film's narrative content, but also, as a print adaptation of a screen adaptation of a print text, this story marks an early complication in terms of the authorship of *Anne of Green Gables*: the credit line notes that the story is "narrated, by permission, from the photoplay produced by Realart Pictures Corp., made, in turn, from a scenario by Frances Marion, adapted from the four 'Anne' books by L.M. Montgomery, published by Page & Co., Boston." The shift in tone and subject matter from book to film can also be seen in the subhead that accompanies this story: "Wherein a little orphan girl's happiness is born of this triumvirate: a remarkable imagination, courage in a crisis, and love."

In spite of her loss of income and control, Montgomery nevertheless included in her scrapbook a considerable amount of newspaper and magazine coverage of the film and its star, Mary Miles Minter. Boone's story does not appear in her scrapbook, indicating that she possibly was not aware of its existence. Still, when a new film version of *Anne of Green Gables* was made in 1934, she did record in her journal her impressions of a similar "film story" that had appeared in an English magazine, this time in *Picturegoer Weekly*, by a writer who evidently had never read the novel. "The result is rather curious," she noted, echoing the key term she had used when anticipating the 1919 film.[3]

The creation of new Montgomery texts would only increase in the decades since her death, in terms of a wide number of posthumous volumes, stage and screen adaptations, parodies, abridgments, and extensions of all kinds – one of the most critically acclaimed of these, Budge Wilson's prequel *Before Green Gables*, was published in 2008 to coincide with the centenary anniversary of Montgomery's novel. These new texts are discussed in detail in the remaining two volumes of *The L.M. Montgomery Reader*.

"Land sakes, Marilla," gasped Mrs. Pie, shading her face with her sun-bonnet as she peered down the dusty road. "That ain't a boy Matthew's got with him. It's a girl."

Marilla Cuthbert, gaunt and prim in an immaculate apron, adjusted her spectacles and anxiously followed the pointing finger of her neighbor. Mrs. Pie and Josie, her pretty, affected daughter, had "just run over" conveniently at the time when Marilla was expecting her brother Matthew with the little boy whom she had adopted from the bleak orphan asylum on the hill. All the folks in the neighboring farms agreed that Marilla "took an awful chance," but they admitted that a boy might be useful to help in the fields and do the chores.

The small figure bobbing up and down beside Matthew in the old buggy certainly did not look like a boy. And as it drew nearer and Matthew stopped before the green-gabled farm-house with a hearty "Whoa!" to old Bess, there was no doubt left as to its excessive femininity.

Matthew climbed out heavily and then lifted the child to the ground in his sturdy arms. She was tiny and freckled and frightened in an ill-fitting gingham dress and a funny little straw hat decorated with one stiff quill from the tail of a peacock – evidently her own idea of adornment. But something in her wistful upturned face touched the heart of Marilla even while she was saying in her coldest tones:

"Matthew Cuthbert, will you kindly tell me who that is? And where is our boy, if you please?"

Matthew shifted wretchedly from one foot to another. "There wasn't any boy," he mumbled. "Only her."

Marilla's steely eyes flashed blue fire. "Well, this is a pretty piece of business –" she began, but her reproaches were interrupted by a sob from the orphan who was inconsiderate enough to belong to the wrong sex.

"I might have known it was too beautiful to last," she sobbed. "I might have known nobody would really want me. All the way down the road I've been pretending to be a lady fair on her way home to her castle. And now there won't be any castle or trees or pigs for me after all – just only the orphan asylum."

Marilla tried not to let the smile that had crept into her eyes reach her thin mouth. "I guess we'll have to let you stay a while until we investigate this," she said grudgingly.

At this wonderful news, the uninvited orphan threw both her slim arms about Marilla's neck and kissed her with a resounding smack. Now Marilla's lips were still sticky from the preserves she had just been tasting and the little girl licked her own lips joyously and whispered, "It's plum, isn't it?"

Marilla's twinkle now was unmistakable. But she only reached out one long arm and drew the little girl in front of her like a prisoner before a judge.

"What's your name, child?" she said, severely.

The little girl hesitated for a minute and then said with a rush, "Will you please call me Geraldine Cordelia Fitzgerald?"

"*Call* you Geraldine Cordelia!" exclaimed Marilla. "Is that your name?"

"It isn't exactly my name," the orphan explained gravely. "But I like to imagine it is. My real name's unromantic. It's just plain Anne."

At this, Mrs. Pie, who with Josie had been regarding the scene with critical scorn, broke into the conversation.

"It's romantic enough for you, I guess," she said with a sharp cackle. "They didn't pick you out for your looks, that's certain. Lawful heart, did any one ever see such freckles? And hair as red as carrots!"

The little group turned in astonishment to her and then back again to Anne, who had grown first scarlet and then pale with indignation. She caught her breath with an angry gasp, fixed her huge blue eyes on Mrs. Pie's acid face and answered:

"It's rude to hurt other people's feelings. How would you like to be told that you are fat and clumsy and probably haven't a spark of imagination?"

With well feigned horror, Marilla took Anne sternly by the hand and led her up to the little attic room reserved for the boy she ought to have been. But once up there, her severe expression vanished.

"You hadn't ought to say such things, Anne," she admonished correctly. Then, the smile breaking out from its long imprisonment, "but you said to Elmira Pie what I've been hankering to say for the last thirty years."

Left alone to "tidy up" in the prim little attic bedroom, Anne looked about her with gleaming eyes. "It isn't as dazzling as a castle chamber," she said, half aloud, "but then it isn't a dank and dismal dungeon like the orphan asylum. And there are all the trees outside and the river. I sit by the window and watch the river like the Lady of Shalott with a mirror and everything."

And thus under the green-gabled roof began the first day of a new life for Anne of the orphan asylum – a life which though sorrowful in spots was never gray or monotonous. For Anne possessed God's best gift to humanity, the vivid imagination which can turn this drab everyday life of ours into a brilliant dream world.

Sunlight and leafy tracery and apple-blossoms and underneath it all a little girl in a big pinafore shelling peas. She was pretending that every tenth pea was a caramel and was crushing them with exaggerated pleasure when a large rubber ball came crashing through the branches and bounced heavily on her curly head. As she sprang to her feet and the peas went rolling in every direction, an impish laugh rang out above her and the figure of a freckled, barefoot boy slid down the trunk and sprang out of the reach of her clutching fingers.

Over the fence, into the chicken yard, through the gate and over the haystacks ran the boy with Anne in close pursuit. His legs were longer but Anne had learned to run at the orphan asylum and her wind was better so that she gained on him with every turn. She had just succeeded in tripping him up and was pummeling the exhausted urchin with both fists when Marilla turned the corner with a black-coated ecclesiastical figure beside her. "Anne has improved very much since she has been with us," she was saying. "She is so helpful with the housework. And then she's so quiet and gentle."

At this moment a shriek of victory from the gentle Anne startled both the speaker and her companion. Dusty, disheveled and flushed with triumph, she had both knees on her tormentor's shoulders and was commanding him to "say uncle" before she would release her hold.

"For pity's sake, Anne!" cried Marilla, and the two combatants sprang to their feet and tried to brush the dust from their torn garments.

"This is the Reverend Figtree, Anne," said Marilla severely, turning to the tall figure beside her. "I was just telling him how gentle you were. Stand up and shake hands with that boy like a little lady. He's a neighbor of yours and his name is Gilbert."

The two grimy little paws which had just been pummeling each other met in a handshake which was half shy, half belligerent. But as Gilbert's eyes caught the averted gaze of his little assailant, he suddenly decided that girls were not so bad after all and that there was something in the upturned glance of this one that was mysteriously appealing.

"That's right," said the reverend gentleman approvingly. "And now as a further peace-offering, I invite you both to a Sunday-school picnic in the woods to-morrow."

Anne was thrilled through and through at the prospect of her first picnic. But disaster followed close upon this dazzling prospect.

The day before, she had decked herself out in a gorgeous piano scarf, a sheaf of peacock feathers and Marilla's topaz brooch – the entire costume representing the evening dress of the Countess Geraldine Cordelia Fitzgerald. Marilla had appeared unexpectedly just as she was putting the finishing touches on the costume and had sternly ordered her back to the kitchen and her own prosaic gingham apron. But, on the morning of the picnic when Marilla had gone to search for the brooch, she had found it missing.

Anne had frantically denied having lost the ornament but when Marilla sternly insisted that she confess or stay in her room all day, she admitted with many tears that she had dropped it over the bridge. Marilla, still further infuriated by her carelessness, ordered her to stay home from the picnic and locked her in her room, turning a deaf ear to the child's piteous pleadings.

The events of that day remained in Anne's memory long after more important events had faded. She still laughs at the thought of how she crept out of the window, climbed down the trellis and stumbled through the woods in a frenzied search for the picnic party. On the way she stopped to pet a friendly little animal which looked like a squirrel but seemed far tamer. And then suddenly every one she met on the road seemed to avoid her and turned away from her questions as to the whereabouts of the Sunday-school expedition.

"'Pon my soul," said one deaf old man to another, "but there's been a skunk powerful near this place."

Anne did not know what a skunk was, but she soon found it necessary to pin a clothespin on her nose and in this state met the picnic party. They, too, scattered at her approach and she was forced to eat her lunch in melancholy solitude on the grass. She wandered home, a desolate little figure and sobbed herself to sleep on a haystack in the barn.

And here Matthew found her just after Marilla had discovered the missing brooch under the bureau scarf. He carried her into the house, where Marilla burned the offending picnic finery and comforted her with bread and jam and much affectionate scolding.

"But for mercy's sake, child," stormed Marilla, "why did you tell me you lost the brooch, when you hadn't?"

"You said I had to confess," murmured Anne sleepily. "I thought mebbe if I told a real good confession, you would let me go. And then I prayed to the Lord to let me there somehow. And He did, but I don't think much of His way of doing it," and her drowsy head sunk lower on Marilla's shoulder.

These, and other memories of her later schooldays, formed the medley of recollections that remained with Anne whenever she recalled the house with the Green Gables. Among them was the near-tragedy of the funeral barge which almost terminated Anne's career as a weaver of dreams.

She had been reading the "Idylls of the King" and her imagination had been caught by the tragic story of "Elaine."

"Why can't we act it out on the river?" she suggested to the other girls at recess. "There is an old raft in the boat-house that would do for a barge and we could deck it out with flowers so that the wood wouldn't show."

So afternoon found them busy with their improvised stage properties on the bank of the placid river. Anne, by common consent, was "Elaine." She had slipped a white nightgown of Marilla's over her blue checked dress and her head bore the virginal crown of lilies which is always the property of this mournful maiden.

A little group of school-boys from the village had come to scoff at this amateur play-acting but remained to direct and advise with calm masculine superiority. Among them was Gilbert. "Better look out, Anne – Elaine, I mean," he warned her. "That old raft looks mighty leaky to me."

Now if Anne had felt any doubt as to the safety of the expedition before, wild horses would not have drawn an admission of fear from her after Gilbert's admonition. She refused to answer him but calmly settled herself on the barge, lying flat on her back with her hands crossed on her breast in the conventional funereal fashion, while the girls covered her with flowers from the Green Gables garden.

Slowly they pushed her off from the bank while they chanted the lyrical measures of the "Idylls." All went well until the raft swung around the bend in the river and caught the eddies that swirled at the turn. Then suddenly the lily maid of Astelot came to life with a scream, shook her flowers from her bier and stood swaying on the spinning barge. "It's leaking," she shrieked. "Help me! I'm sinking!"

The girls, knowing that they could not save her, rushed to the house for help. But Gilbert in one bound reached the river's bend, tore off his coat and plunged in after the half-fainting heroine. He caught her just as she was sinking and made his way to the shore with a few powerful strokes.

As he lifted her to the bank and saw that her eyes were half closed with weakness and terror, he stooped and gently kissed her cheek. Whereupon, the dying maiden's eyes suddenly flew open and she became a very indignant little girl. She blinked for a moment and then shook her head at her rescuer in mute reproach.

"How dare you!" she sputtered, brushing the water from her eyes. But she neglected to remove her head from his shoulder and somehow Gilbert kissed her again.

Safely home again, and under the ministration of Marilla's hot tea and blankets, Anne decided that the episode must have been a dream. Her musings were cut short by the entrance of Matthew, whom she could hear talking excitedly in the next room. Marilla seemed to be trying to calm him but he refused to listen.

"They are dragging the river, I tell you," he shouted it. "They are hunting for the body of our little girl."

Dragging the blanket behind her, Anne made three bounds into the kitchen and flew into the arms of the astonished Matthew. "You can't kill me that way, uncle," she laughed. "I was never born to be drowned."

"But they found a body," Matthew stammered, utterly dazed with relief and bewilderment.

"Oh, that thing," sniffed Anne, "that was the scare-crow who played the part of the old boatman. Did they think that was me? I am flattered."

At this moment Gilbert knocked and entered. The two old people vanished as if by magic and left him standing shyly before Anne with a small glistening object in his hand.

"It's an engagement ring," he whispered. "It was the best one they had at the jewelry store. I'll have it all paid for a year from next June if all goes well. But it isn't half good enough for you, Anne."

Anne slipped the sparkling wonder on her finger and cast her adoring eyes up to his. "I wasn't really angry when you kissed me," she told him. "I won't ever pretend to be any more. Try it, Gilbert, and see."

And Gilbert tried – and saw.

High school days faded into graduation and Anne in the glory of her white organdie and carnations was ready to face her first term in college when a sudden blow crushed all her rosy dreams. Matthew, whose health had been gradually failing through the past year, died suddenly at the close of one August day, with his eyes fixed on the sunset and his hand in Anne's. And the young girl, only lately emerged from the short skirts of her orphan days, found the burden of Green Gables' support transferred to her slender shoulders.

She applied for the post of teacher at the little red schoolhouse where she herself had been taught. Somewhat to her surprise, she was elected without any opposition except from Abednego Pie, father of Josie Pie, who had always cherished a lurking grudge against the young orphan. This natural antagonism had not been mitigated by the fact that Josie had set her cap very vigorously for Gilbert. But for all this, the Pies' opposition had been voted down and Anne became the village schoolmarm.

If Josie's father had failed her in her attempt to injure Anne's prospects, she found another and stronger ally in her small brother, Anthony. He was an unpleasant, pasty-faced child whose fits of ill-temper had been encouraged by an adoring family on the grounds that he was "delicate."

"I hate teachers and I won't mind that Anne Shirley," he confided to his sister.

"You don't have to mind her," Josie assured him. "She can't boss a brother of mine. Go ahead, Tony, and be just as mean as you can."

Now Anthony's genius for meanness was unlimited. Anne's patience was tried to the breaking point day after day by his malicious attempts to break up the order of her little class-room. The limit was reached one day when she found him twisting the head of her own white kitten which he had caught under his desk and held for torture.

In the presence of all her pupils who were amazed at such spirit on the part of their gentle teacher, she seized a birch switch and whipped the urchin until he threw himself on the ground howling and kicking. Then, utterly unnerved by the scene, she dismissed the class and went home to Marilla, who was confined to her bed after an operation on her eyes. The operation had been successful but the doctor had warned Anne that the slightest excitement might react fatally on the spent nerves.

That evening, Anthony limped down the main street of the village with his arm hanging from his sleeve. His face was bruised, his coat was torn and he had every evidence of being brutally handled.

"The teacher did it," he was screaming at the top of his lungs. "She knocked me down and beat me and broke my arm."

One of those sudden village mobs, headed by Abednego Pie, gathered in an indignation meeting. "If she'd do that to little Anthony she might kill our own children," one mother screamed and was answered by an excited shout from the mob.

"Shoot her – Tar and feather her – Run her out of town" rose in a frenzied chorus from the mob as the infuriated villagers turned as one man and started in a half run to the house with the green gables.

Anne, who had been bending over Marilla, making sure that all was well for the night, was startled by a crash from a handful of pebbles thrown against the pane. It was her first hint that the mob was gathering out side the window but as she rushed forward and looked out, she saw a sea of angry faces. Her one thought was to protect the sleeping woman to whom a shock might mean blindness. So, choking down her natural terror, she grasped the shot-gun that always hung in the hall and faced the crowd – ordering them back into the road in no uncertain terms.

Dazed by this unexpected move, the mob obeyed, although the muttering grew louder. How long could she have held them alone and single-handed is a question which was never decided for suddenly down the road appeared the long, spare figure of the Rev. Figtree.

He mounted the stump of a fallen tree by the roadside and motioned to the crowd which gathered around him.

"My friends," he began, "I know all about your indignation and what inspired it. But you must take the word of your pastor that it is utterly unfounded.

"This unfortunate child," he went on, waving a long hand at the cringing Anthony, "has been guilty of a base falsehood. His injuries were not caused by the schoolteacher but by a fall from a moving hay-wagon. I myself saw the fall and knew that he would use it to gratify his childish revenge. I beg you now to go back to your homes and leave the Pie family to administer reproof where it is really deserved."

419

Shamefaced and in silence, the villagers drifted away leaving Anne, pale and shaking, to be guided up the road by the old pastor whose tone of righteous indignation had changed to solicitous tenderness.

So Marilla's eyes were saved and a new life of friendly neighborliness was opened up to Anne in the village. But better than all this, Gilbert returned to the village from a trip to a neighboring town with an excited tale of a new job which would support two, even three with its munificent salary.

So late one night, in a dark corner of the porch shaded by honeysuckles, Gilbert told Anne of another house down the road, a smaller house with no green gables but with room for both of them and a comfortable corner for Marilla. "We might as well move in it right away," he said pleadingly. "I can tell the Rev. Figtree tomorrow. There needn't be anybody there but us and the folks and your white kitten. Will you Anne, beloved? What do you say?"

But what Anne said was lost in the honeysuckle vines of the house with the green gables. And the wise old house kept their secret as it had kept many other secrets before them.

NOTES

1 Montgomery, 18 December 1919, in *SJLMM*, 2: 358.
2 Montgomery, 22 February 1920, in *SJLMM*, 2: 373.
3 Montgomery, 17 September 1935, in *SJLMM*, 5: 38. See also Marjory Williams, "Anne of Green Gables: The Story of the Film," *Picturegoer Weekly*, undated clipping, in SR, 420–25.

Sources

The items included in this volume were originally published as follows:

"[Such a Delightful Little Person]," excerpted from "Literature: Recent Publications; Literary Notes," *Illinois State Register* (Springfield, IL), 21 September 1908, 4; also, with minor variations, in "Literary," *The San Antonio Light* (San Antonio, TX), 4 October 1908, 20.

"Author Tells How He Wrote His Story," *The Boston Journal* (Boston, MA), 21 November 1908, 6.

"Origin of Popular Book," *The Brooklyn Daily Eagle* (Brooklyn, NY), 21 December 1908, 3; also, with minor variations, as part of "Books and Authors," *The Sun* (New York, NY), 11 January 1909, 5.

"The Author of 'Anne of Avonlea,'" *Zion's Herald* (Boston, MA), 6 October 1909, 1264.

"Miss Montgomery, the Author of the 'Anne' Books," by A. Wylie Mahon, *The Canadian Bookman* (Toronto, ON), November 1909, 175–76; also in *Bookseller and Stationer* (Toronto, ON), November 1909, 37–38.

"A Trio of Women Writers," by Donald B. Sinclair, *The Canadian Courier* (Toronto, ON), 27 November 1909, 14.

"Canadian Writers on Canadian Literature – A Symposium," *The Globe* (Toronto, ON), 1 January 1910, 8, 14.

"Says Woman's Place Is Home," *The Boston Post* (Boston, MA), 12 November 1910, 8; also in Montgomery, Red Scrapbook, 1: 11.

"Want to Know How to Write Book [*sic*]? Well Here's a Real Recipe," by Phoebe Dwight, *The Boston Traveler* (Boston, MA), 14 November 1910, 5; also in Montgomery, Red Scrapbook, 1: 11–12.

"Miss Montgomery's Visit to Boston," *The Boston Herald* (Boston, MA), 16 November 1910, 5; also in Montgomery, Red Scrapbook, 1: 11.

"Four Questions Answered," by Lucy Maud Montgomery, *The Boston Herald* (Boston, MA), 18 November 1910, 6; also in Montgomery, Red Scrapbook, 1: 21.

"Miss L.M. Montgomery, Author of 'Anne of Green Gables,'" *The Republic* (Boston, MA), 19 November 1910, 5; also in Montgomery, Red Scrapbook, 1: 13.

"How I Began to Write," by L.M. Montgomery, *The Globe* (Toronto, ON), 7 January 1911, 10; also in SR, 19–20.

"[Seasons in the Woods]" consists of four articles by L.M. Montgomery published in *The Canadian Magazine* (Toronto, ON): "Spring in the Woods," May 1911, 59–62; "The Woods in Summer," September 1911, 399–402; "The Woods in Autumn," October 1911, 574–77; "The Woods in Winter," December 1911, 162–64.

"With Our Next-Door Neighbors: Prince Edward Island," by Thomas F. Anderson, *The Boston Sunday Globe* (Boston, MA), 7 May 1911, SM12; the extract in this volume also appears in SR, 23.

"[The Marriage of L.M. Montgomery]" consists of two unrelated items: an excerpt from "Important Reading Matter Selected from This Week's News for the Guardian's Saturday Subscribers," *The Guardian* (Charlottetown, PE), 8 July 1911, 7, and an excerpt from "News of Books and Authors," *The Boston Herald* (Boston, MA), 22 July 1911, 7.

"A Canadian Novelist of Note Interviewed," *The Morning Leader* (Regina, SK), 21 October 1911, Second Section, 10. Also, with minor variations, as "A Canadian Novelist," by Christian Richardson, unidentified and undated clipping, in SR, 25.

"Interviews with Authors," by Anne E. Nias [Jean Graham], *Saturday Night* (Toronto, ON), 28 October 1911, 5; also in SR, 26–27.

"The Old Minister in 'The Story Girl,'" by A. Wylie Mahon, *The Canadian Magazine* (Toronto, ON), March 1912, 452–54; also in SR, 31–32.

"L.M. Montgomery: Story Writer," by Marjory MacMurchy, *The Globe* (Toronto, ON), 25 October 1913, 3; also in SR, 50–51. Also, with minor variations, as "L.M. Montgomery – Story Writer," *The Patriot* (Charlottetown, PE), 1 November 1913, 7. Also, with minor variations, as "L.M. Montgomery" and signed "Marjorie MacMurchy," unidentified and undated clipping, in SR, 68–69.

"L.M. Montgomery at Women's Canadian Club," *The Globe* (Toronto, ON), 27 October 1913, 5; also in Montgomery, Red Scrapbook, 1: 104.

"L.M. Montgomery of the Island," by Marjory MacMurchy, *Manitoba Free Press* (Winnipeg, MB), 18 April 1914, Women's Section, 1. Also, with minor variations, as "'Anne of Green Gables' Is Story of Miss L.M. Montgomery's Childhood," *The Toronto Star Weekly* (Toronto, ON), 18 April 1914, 19; also in SR, 66–67.

"What Twelve Canadian Women Hope to See as the Outcome of the War," *Everywoman's World* (Toronto, ON), April 1915, 6–7, 33–34; Montgomery's response also appears in SR, 89.

"The Way to Make a Book," by L.M. Montgomery, *Everywoman's World* (Toronto, ON), April 1915, 24, 26–27; also in SR, 86–87.

"How I Began," by L.M. Montgomery, *The Canadian Bookman* (Toronto, ON), 1 April 1915, 6–7; also in SR, 70–72.

"[This Hideous War]," excerpted from "Writers and Books," *Boston Evening Transcript* (Boston, MA), 3 November 1915, 25; also in SR, 81.

"What Are the Greatest Books in the English Language?" *Bookseller and Stationer* (Toronto, ON), January 1916, 31–32; Montgomery's letter also appears in SR, 88.

"My Favorite Bookshelf," by L.M. Montgomery, unidentified and undated periodical (ca. 1917), in SR, 95. Also, with minor variations, in *The Island Crusader* (Charlottetown, PE), December 1937, 7.

"The Author of Anne," by Ethel M. Chapman, *MacLean's Magazine* (Toronto, ON), October 1919, 102, 104, 106; also in SR, 170–72; reprinted by permission of the periodical.

"The Gay Days of Old," by L.M. Montgomery, *Farmers' Magazine* (Toronto, ON), 15 December 1919, 18, 46; also in SR, 176–79.

Introduction, by Nathan Haskell Dole, to *Further Chronicles of Avonlea*, by L.M. Montgomery (Boston: The Page Company, 1920), v–xi.

"One Little Girl Who Wrote to L.M. Montgomery and Received a Reply," unidentified and undated clipping (ca. 1920), in SR, 175.

"A Sextette of Canadian Women Writers," by Owen McGillicuddy, *Canadian Home Journal* (Toronto, ON), June 1920, 8, 72.

"Blank Verse? 'Very Blank,' Said Father," by L.M. Montgomery, *The Winnipeg Evening Tribune* (Winnipeg, MB), 3 December 1921, Magazine Section, 3. Also, with minor variations, as "My Greatest Moment," unidentified and undated clipping (ca. 1921), in SR, 195.

"'I Dwell among My Own People,'" by L.M. Montgomery, unidentified and undated clipping (ca. 1921), in SR, 195. Also, with minor variations and by Lucy M. Montgomery, in *Manitoba Free Press* (Winnipeg, MB), 7 December 1925, 6; also in SR, 241.

"Bits from My Mailbag," by L.M. Montgomery, *Manitoba Free Press* (Winnipeg, MB), 9 December 1922, Christmas Book Section, 5; also in SR, 198–99.

Excerpts from *Fiction Writers on Fiction Writing: Advice, Opinions and a Statement of Their Own Working Methods by More Than One Hundred Authors*, edited by Arthur Sullivant Hoffman (Indianapolis: The Bobbs–Merrill Company, 1923), 9, 30, 44, 68–69, 87–88, 160–61, 211, 225, 238, 252, 268, 279–80, 290, 303, 317, 326, 334, 355–56, 373, 382, 390, 400–401, 408, 420.

"Novel Writing Notes," by L.M. Montgomery, *The Editor: The Journal of Information for Literary Workers* (Highland Falls, NY), 17 November 1923, 53–54; also in SR, 230.

"Proud That Canadian Literature Is Clean," *Bookseller and Stationer* (Toronto, ON), March 1924, 54.

"Canadian Public Cold to Its Own Literature," *The Hamilton Spectator* (Hamilton, ON), 21 November 1924, 16; also in Montgomery, Red Scrapbook, 2: 90.

"Thinks Modern Flapper Will Be Strict Mother," *The Hamilton Spectator* (Hamilton, ON), 21 November 1924, 16; also in Montgomery, Red Scrapbook, 2: 92.

"Symposium on Canadian Fiction in Which Canadian Authors Express Their Preferences," *Manitoba Free Press* (Winnipeg, MB), 8 December 1924, Book Supplement, 6.

Something about L.M. Montgomery (Boston: L.C. Page and Company, 1925); also in SR, 281. Copyright, 1925, by L.C. Page and Company (Inc.).

"L.M. Montgomery's 'Rilla of Ingleside': A Reader's Journal," by Altair [Wilfred Eggleston], *The Lethbridge Herald* (Lethbridge, AB), 4 July 1925, 4; reprinted by permission of the periodical.

"Famous Author and Simple Mother," by Norma Phillips Muir, *The Toronto Star Weekly* (Toronto, ON), 28 November 1925, 44.

"The Day before Yesterday," by L.M. Montgomery MacDonald [*sic*], *The College Times* 3, no. 3 (May 1927): 29–34.

"Who's Who in Canadian Literature: L.M. Montgomery," by V.B. Rhodenizer, *The Canadian Bookman* (Toronto, ON), August 1927, 227–28; also in SR, 312–13. Earlier version, as "The Writings of L.M. Montgomery," unidentified and undated clipping (ca. 1925), in SR, 234–35.

"About Canadian Writers: L.M. Montgomery, the Charming Author of 'Anne,'" by Katherine Hale, *The Canadian Countryman* (Toronto, ON), 10 September 1927, 11, 17; also in SR, 319.

"On Being of the Tribe of Joseph," by Austin Bothwell, *Saturday Night* (Toronto, ON), 17 December 1927, 5; also in SR, 311–12.

"Minister's Wife and Authoress," by C.L. Cowan, *The Toronto Star Weekly* (Toronto, ON), 29 December 1928, 28; also in SR, 320–22.

"An Autobiographical Sketch," by L.M. Montgomery, *Ontario Library Review* 13, no. 3 (February 1929): 94–96.

"Modern Girl Defined by Noted Writer," *The Georgetown Herald* (Georgetown, ON), 29 May 1929, 1.

"L.M. Montgomery's Ideas" consists of a series of letters published in *The Guardian* (Charlottetown, PE): Letter 1, by Mrs. Edith Frank Fisher, 12 August 1930, 4; Letter 2, by "Islander," 19 August 1930, 4; Letter 3, by "An Outsider," 22 August 1930, 4; Letter 4, by "An Insider," 25 August 1930, 4; Letter 5, by (Mrs.) A.M.C., Savage Harbor, PE, 27 August 1930, 3; Letter 6, by L.M. Montgomery Macdonald, 1 September 1930, 4; also in SR, 463–68. Montgomery's letter also appears in Montgomery, Black Scrapbook, 2: 38.

"The 'Teen-Age Girl," by L.M. Montgomery, *The Chatelaine* (Toronto, ON), March 1931, 9, 32, 37.

"Anne of Green Gables at Home," by A.V. Brown, unidentified and undated clipping (ca. 1931), in Montgomery, Black Scrapbook, 2: 7; also in SR, 364–65.

"An Open Letter from a Minister's Wife," by L.M. Montgomery, *The Chatelaine* (Toronto, ON), October 1931, 8, 53.

"Life Has Been Interesting," by Mrs. L.M. Macdonald (L.M. Montgomery), unidentified and undated clipping (ca. 1933), in Campbell Family Scrapbook, Park Corner, PE.

"The Importance of Beauty in Everything," by L.M. Montgomery, *The Family Herald and Weekly Star* (Montreal, QC), 19 July 1933, 5; also in SR, 395.

Extracts by L.M. Montgomery from *Courageous Women*, by L.M. Montgomery, Marian Keith, and Mabel Burns McKinley (Toronto: McClelland and Stewart, 1934), 1–31.

"Author to Get No Profit as 'Green Gables' Filmed," *The Toronto Daily Star* (Toronto, ON), 8 September 1934, 27; also in SR, 377, 379.

"Film Preview of Noted Novel Honors Canadian Woman Writer," *The Globe* (Toronto, ON), 13 November 1934, 5; also in SR, 394. Also, with minor variations, as "Author of 'Anne of Green Gables' Approves Version," *The Calgary Herald* (Calgary, AB), 14 November 1934, 8.

"Is This My Anne," by L.M. Montgomery, *The Chatelaine* (Toronto, ON), January 1935, 18, 22; also in SR, 408–9.

Foreword, by L.M. Montgomery, to *Up Came the Moon*, by Jessie Findlay Brown (N.p.: n.p., 1936), n.pag.

"Come Back with Me to Prince Edward Island," by L.M. Montgomery, in *The Maritime Advocate and Busy East* (Sackville, NB), May–June 1936, 3–8, 37. Also in *The Maritime Advocate and Busy East* (Sackville, NB), June 1939, 16–21, 34–37.

"Memories of Childhood Days," by L.M. Montgomery, *The Maritime Advocate and Busy East* (Sackville, NB), May–June 1936, 35.

"The Mother of the Anne Series," by Eva-Lis Wuorio, *Sirkka: Illustrated Magazine for Children* (Porvoosa, Finland), 1 (1937): 4–5, 10. Translated for this volume by Vappu Kannas.

"The Book and the Film," *The Canadian Author* 15, no. 1 (September 1937): 21.

"For and about Girls," by L.M. Montgomery, review of *The Longest Way Round*, by Lady Willison (Marjory MacMurchy), *Saturday Night* (Toronto, ON), 23 October 1937, 15.

"Prince Edward Island," by L.M. Montgomery, *The Spirit of Canada: Dominion and Provinces, a Souvenir of Welcome to H.M. King George VI and H.M. Queen Elizabeth* (N.p.: Canadian Pacific Railway, 1939), 16, 18–19.

"Beloved Writer Addresses Several Aurora Gatherings," *The Aurora Era* (Aurora, ON), 22 February 1940, 1.

"Noted Author Dies Suddenly at Home Here," *The Globe and Mail* (Toronto, ON), 25 April 1942, 5.

"Lucy Maud Montgomery," *The Guardian* (Charlottetown, PE), 25 April 1942, 4.

"L.M. Montgomery's 'Anne,'" *The Ottawa Journal* (Ottawa, ON), 27 April 1942, 8.

"Body of Island's Beloved Authoress Home for Burial," *The Guardian* (Charlottetown, PE), 29 April 1942, 1.

"Island Writer Laid to Rest at Cavendish," *The Guardian* (Charlottetown, PE), 30 April 1942, 1, 11.

"The Creator of 'Anne,'" *The Peterborough Examiner* (Peterborough, ON), 2 May 1942, 4.

"[L.M. Montgomery's Last Poem]" consists of two separate articles in *Saturday Night* (Toronto, ON): "L.M. Montgomery," 2 May 1942, 3; "L.M. Montgomery's Last Poem," 2 May 1942, 25.

"L.M. Montgomery / Mrs. (Rev.) Ewen Macdonald," *The Presbyterian Record* (Toronto, ON), June 1942, 165–68.

"L.M. Montgomery as a Letter-Writer," by E. Weber, *The Dalhousie Review* 22, no. 3 (October 1942): 300–10; reprinted by permission of the journal.

"L.M. Montgomery's 'Anne,'" by E. Weber, *The Dalhousie Review* 24, no. 1 (April 1944): 64–73; reprinted by permission of the journal.

"*Anne of Green Gables* – The Story of the Photoplay," by Arabella Boone, first published as "Anne of Green Gables," *Photoplay Magazine* (Chicago, IL), January 1920, 52–55, 156.

Bibliography

Åhmansson, Gabriella. *A Life and Its Mirrors: A Feminist Reading of L.M. Montgomery's Fiction*, Volume 1: *An Introduction to Lucy Maud Montgomery, Anne Shirley*. Uppsala: Uppsala University, 1991.

Allison, W.T. "Canadian Literature of To-Day." *The Bookman* (London, UK), February 1929, 270–74.

Anne of Green Gables. Directed by George Nicholls Jr. Screen Play by Sam Mintz. RKO Radio Pictures, 1934.

Anne of Green Gables. Directed by Kevin Sullivan. Screen adaptation by Kevin Sullivan and Joe Wiesenfeld. Sullivan Films, 1985.

Anne of Green Gables. Directed by William Desmond Taylor. Written by Frances Marion. Realart Pictures Corporation, 1919.

Baker, Ray Palmer. *A History of English-Canadian Literature to the Confederation: Its Relation to the Literature of Great Britain and the United States*. Cambridge, MA: Harvard University Press, 1920.

Bolger, Francis W.P. *The Years before "Anne."* 1974. Halifax: Nimbus Publishing, 1991.

The Bookseller, Newsdealer and Stationer (New York, NY). "About Authors." 15 August 1911, 103.

Books for Boys and Girls, Being a List of Two Thousand Books Which the Librarians of the Boys and Girls Division of the Toronto Public Library Deem to Be of Definite and Permanent Interest. Toronto: Boys and Girls House, Public Library of Toronto, 1927.

The Boston Herald (Boston, MA). "Authors' Club Reception." 12 November 1910, 7.

———. "From Page's List." 30 January 1909, 7.

———. "Mid-Week Book Notes." 9 December 1908, 7.

———. "Personal and Social News." 12 November 1910, 7.

———. "Publishers' Views of Season's Books." 9 December 1911, 8.

———. "Week-End Book Notes." 24 October 1908, 9.

———. "With Books and Authors." 13 May 1912, 4.

The Boston Journal (Boston, MA). "Canadian Writer Is Authors' Club Guest." 12 November 1910, 6.

Brown, Jessie Findlay. *Up Came the Moon.* N.p.: n.p., 1936.

Butler, Kate Macdonald. "The Heartbreaking Truth about Anne's Creator." *The Globe and Mail* (Toronto, ON), 20 September 2008, F1, F6.

The Calgary Herald (Calgary, AB). "Famous Canadian Author Passes." 27 April 1942, 4.

———. "Noted Canadian Authoress Dies." 25 April 1942, 1.

The Canadian Courier (Toronto, ON). "The Maiden Speech That Wasn't." 8 November 1913, 16.

The Canberra Times (Canberra, Australia). "Unusual Items in Author's Mail Bag." 8 March 1932, 3.

Chesterfield. "Men and Women We Read About." *The Family Herald and Weekly Star* (Montreal, QC), 25 December 1912, 4.

The Christian Science Monitor (Boston, MA). "Among Books and Their Writers." 24 July 1911, 7.

———. "Mr. Baldwin Continues Visit to Maritimes." 17 August 1927, 3.

Clemens, Rudolf A. "Sweet Singers of Canada." *The Methodist Review* (New York, NY), July 1920, 610–21.

Collins, Carolyn Strom. "'Bound for Quebec' or 'Journey's End'? Conflicting Stories about the Montgomery Family's Arrival in Prince Edward Island." In *Storm and Dissonance: L.M. Montgomery and Conflict*, edited by Jean Mitchell, 363–72. Newcastle: Cambridge Scholars Publishing, 2008.

"Creator of 'Green Gables.'" *The Canadian Author and Bookman* 20, no. 3 (September 1944): 24.

Deacon, William Arthur. *Poteen: A Pot-Pourri of Canadian Essays.* Ottawa: The Graphic Publishers, 1926.

Devereux, Cecily. "A Note on the Text." In Montgomery, *Anne of Green Gables*, edited by Devereux, 42–50.

———. "'See My Journal for the Full Story': Fictions of Truth in *Anne of Green Gables* and L.M. Montgomery's Journals." In Gammel, *The Intimate Life of L.M. Montgomery*, 241–57.

Eggleston, Wilfred. "The Causerie." *Winnipeg Free Press* (Winnipeg, MB), 21 July 1956, 1; 15 September 1956, 1; 5 January 1957, 1.

———. "General Introduction." In Montgomery, *The Green Gables Letters*, 1–22.

———. *While I Still Remember: A Personal Record*. Toronto: The Ryerson Press, 1968.

Epperly, Elizabeth Rollins. "L.M. Montgomery and the Changing Times." *Acadiensis* 17, no. 2 (Spring 1988): 177–85.

———. *Through Lover's Lane: L.M. Montgomery's Photography and Visual Imagination*. Toronto: University of Toronto Press, 2007.

"An Estimate." *The Canadian Author and Bookman* 20, no. 3 (September 1944): 24.

"The Family Circle." *The Canadian Author and Bookman* 17, no. 4 (February 1941): 12–13.

The Family Herald and Weekly Star (Montreal, QC). "*Anne of Green Gables* Creator Is Dead." 6 May 1942, 39.

———. "Five Favorite Books – Prize Winners." 17 March 1937, 23.

Ford, Sydney. "Women's Work, Women's Clubs." *Los Angeles Times* (Los Angeles, CA), 21 July 1912, Part III, 16.

Fort Williams Daily Times–Journal (Fort Williams, ON). "Lawyer Son Tells about Writing of Authoress Mother." 23 July 1946, 10.

The Free Press (London, ON). "Famous Author Dies Suddenly." 25 April 1942, 18.

French, Donald Graham. "Rilla, Daughter of 'Anne.'" *The Globe* (Toronto, ON), 8 October 1921, 19.

———, comp. and ed. *Standard Canadian Reciter: A Book of the Best Readings and Recitations from Canadian Literature*. Toronto: McClelland and Stewart, 1921.

"From Sea to Sea." *The Canadian Author and Bookman* 18, no. 2–4 (December 1942): 26–31.

Gammel, Irene, ed. *The Intimate Life of L.M. Montgomery*. Toronto: University of Toronto Press, 2005.

———. "Introduction: Life Writing as Masquerade: The Many Faces of L.M. Montgomery." In Gammel, *The Intimate Life of L.M. Montgomery*, 3–15.

———. *Looking for Anne: How Lucy Maud Montgomery Dreamed Up a Literary Classic*. 2008. Toronto: Key Porter Books, 2009.

———. "Making Avonlea: An Introduction." In Gammel, *Making Avonlea*, 3–13.

———, ed. *Making Avonlea: L.M. Montgomery and Popular Culture*. Toronto: University of Toronto Press, 2002.

Gammel, Irene, and Elizabeth Epperly, eds. *L.M. Montgomery and Canadian Culture*. Toronto: University of Toronto Press, 1999.

Gammel, Irene, and Benjamin Lefebvre, eds. *Anne's World: A New Century of Anne of Green Gables*. Toronto: University of Toronto Press, 2010.

Garvin, John W., ed. *Canadian Poems of the Great War*. Toronto: McClelland and Stewart, 1918.

———, ed. *Canadian Poets*. Toronto: McClelland, Goodchild, and Stewart, 1916. Also as *Canadian Poets and Poetry*. New York: Frederick A. Stokes Company, 1916.

———, ed. *Canadian Verse for Boys and Girls*. Toronto: Thomas Nelson and Sons, 1930.

The Gazette (Montreal, QC). "Author Revisits P.E.I." 5 October 1936, 9.

———. "Burial to Be in P.E.I." 27 April 1942, 22.

———. "Odd Letters Are Sent to Author." 25 November 1931, 3.

———. "'Problem' Story Does Not Allure." 25 November 1931, 3.

Gerson, Carole. "*Anne of Green Gables* Goes to University: L.M. Montgomery and Academic Culture." In Gammel, *Making Avonlea*, 17–31.

———. "'Dragged at Anne's Chariot Wheels': The Triangle of Author, Publisher, and Fictional Character." In Gammel and Epperly, *L.M. Montgomery and Canadian Culture*, 49–63.

———. "Seven Milestones: How *Anne of Green Gables* Became a Canadian Icon." In Gammel and Lefebvre, *Anne's World*, 17–34.

Gillen, Mollie. *The Wheel of Things: A Biography of L.M. Montgomery, Author of* Anne of Green Gables. Don Mills, ON: Fitzhenry and Whiteside, 1975.

The Globe (Toronto, ON). "Anne of Windy Poplars." 7 November 1936, 21.

———. "English Union Hears Author of Noted Book." 4 October 1935, 9.

———. "Women in Canadian Literature." 1 March 1919, 20.

The Globe and Mail (Toronto, ON). "L.M. Montgomery Rests beside Sea." 30 April 1942, 11.

———. "Old-Timers' Stories Source for Author." 11 November 1937, 5.

Gray, Iain. *The Montgomerys*. Glasgow: LangSyne Publishing, 2006.

The Guardian (Charlottetown, PE). "Death of Famed Island Writer." 25 April 1942, 1, 11.

———. "Famous Island Authoress Visits in Charlottetown." 5 October 1936, 3.

———. "Funeral from Green Gables on Wednesday." 27 April 1942, 1.

———. "Some Reviews of 'Magic for Marigold.'" 15 September 1930, 7.

Halifax Herald (Halifax, NS). "Author of 'Anne of Green Gables' Writes to the Rainbow Club." 24 March 1927, 7.

The Hamilton Herald (Hamilton, ON). "Girl Now Does What Mother Wished to Do." 21 November 1924, 7.

Hammill, Faye. *Women, Celebrity, and Literary Culture between the Wars*. Austin: University of Texas Press, 2007.

Hathaway, E.J. "How Canadian Novelists Are Using Canadian Opportunities."
  The Canadian Bookman (Ste. Anne de Bellevue, QC), July 1919, 18–22.
———. "L.M. Montgomery." In Garvin, *Canadian Poets*, 353.
Hoffman, Arthur Sullivant. "Fiction Writers on Fiction Writing: How This
  Book Came into Being." In *Fiction Writers on Fiction Writing: Advice,
  Opinions and a Statement of Their Own Working Methods by More
  Than One Hundred Authors*, edited by Arthur Sullivant Hoffman, 1–6.
  Indianapolis: The Bobbs–Merrill Company, 1923.
The House of Stokes, 1881–1926: A Record. New York: Frederick A. Stokes
  Company, 1926.
Karr, Clarence. *Authors and Audiences: Popular Canadian Fiction in the Early
  Twentieth Century*. Montreal: McGill–Queen's University Press, 2000.
Kennedy, Roderick. "Authors of Today: 'Our Anne.'" *The Family Herald and
  Weekly Star* (Montreal, QC), 5 May 1937, 38.
Lefebvre, Benjamin. "Pigsties and Sunsets: L.M. Montgomery, *A Tangled Web*,
  and a Modernism of Her Own." *English Studies in Canada* 31, no. 4
  (December 2005): 123–46.
———. "Stand by Your Man: Adapting L.M. Montgomery's *Anne of Green
  Gables*." *Essays on Canadian Writing* 76 (Spring 2002): 149–69.
———. "What's in a Name? Towards a Theory of the Anne Brand." In Gammel
  and Lefebvre, *Anne's World*, 192–211.
The Lethbridge Herald (Lethbridge, AB). "Author of 'Green Gables' Will Meet
  Premier Baldwin." 2 September 1927, 18.
Logan, J.D., and Donald G. French. *Highways of Canadian Literature: A
  Synoptic Introduction to the Literary History of Canada (English) from
  1760 to 1924*. 1924. 2nd ed. Toronto: McClelland and Stewart, 1928.
Los Angeles Times (Los Angeles, CA). "Biography in Miniature." 20 September
  1925, 28.
MacAdam, A.J. "At Rest." *The Guardian* (Charlottetown, PE), 29 April 1942,
  4.
MacArthur, T.H. "Lucy Maud Montgomery." *The Patriot* (Charlottetown, PE),
  2 May 1942, 4.
Macdonald, Chester C. "Journal of Chester Cameron Macdonald, March 29,
  1945–Nov. 22, 1945." XZ1 MS A098111, L.M. Montgomery Collection,
  University of Guelph archives.
———. Letter to the Editor. *The Tillsonburg News* (Tillsonburg, ON), 30
  August 1945, 9.
———. "Literary Mss. and Typescripts of Chester Cameron Macdonald."
  XZ1 MS A1000004, L.M. Montgomery Collection, University of Guelph
  archives.

MacMechan, Archibald. *The Headwaters of Canadian Literature.* 1924. Toronto: Canadiana House, 1968.

MacMurchy, Marjory. "The Bookman Gallery: L.M. Montgomery." *The Bookman* (London, UK), September 1915, 155–56.

———. "Prince Edward Island's Novelist." *The Canadian Courier* (Toronto, ON), 18 June 1910, 27.

The Mail and Empire (Toronto, ON). "Poetry Her First Love Says L.M. Montgomery." 19 March 1929, 12.

Manitoba Free Press (Winnipeg, MB). "Authoress Weds." 8 July 1911, 11.

———. "Bright Future for Canadian Letters." 14 May 1910, 16.

Marquis, Thomas Guthrie. *English-Canadian Literature.* Toronto: Glasgow, Brook, and Company, 1913.

Mason, Laura. "Do We Canadians Need a School of Manners?" *The Morning Leader* (Regina, SK), 9 June 1923, Magazine Section, 1.

McAnn, Aida B. "Life and Works of L.M. Montgomery." *The Maritime Advocate and Busy East* (Sackville, NB), June–July 1942, 19–22.

McCabe, Kevin, comp. *The Lucy Maud Montgomery Album.* Edited by Alexandra Heilbron. Toronto: Fitzhenry and Whiteside, 1999.

———. "Lucy Maud Montgomery's Table Talk." In McCabe, *The Lucy Maud Montgomery Album,* 160–67.

McClung, Nellie. "What Does the Congregation Expect of a Minister's Wife?" *The Chatelaine* (Toronto, ON), December 1931, 12, 39.

McGrath, Leslie. "Reading with Blitheness: *Anne of Green Gables* in Toronto Public Library's Children's Collections." In Gammel and Lefebvre, *Anne's World,* 100–16.

Middletown Times-Herald (Middletown, NY). "Questions and Answers." 18 January 1935, 4.

Montgomery, L.M. *After Green Gables: L.M. Montgomery's Letters to Ephraim Weber, 1916–1941.* Edited by Hildi Froese Tiessen and Paul Gerard Tiessen. Toronto: University of Toronto Press, 2006.

———. *The Alpine Path: The Story of My Career.* 1917. Don Mills, ON: Fitzhenry and Whiteside, n.d.

———. "The Alpine Path: The Story of My Career." *Everywoman's World* (Toronto, ON), June 1917, 38–39, 41; July 1917, 16, 32–33, 35; August 1917, 16, 32–33; September 1917, 8, 49; October 1917, 8, 58; November 1917, 25, 38, 40.

———. *Anne of Avonlea.* 1909. Toronto: Seal Books, 1996.

———. *Anne of Green Gables.* 1908. Toronto: Seal Books, 1996.

———. *Anne of Green Gables.* 1908. Edited by Cecily Devereux. Peterborough, ON: Broadview Editions, 2004.

————. *Anne of Green Gables*. 1908. Edited by Mary Henley Rubio and Elizabeth Waterston. New York: W.W. Norton and Company, 2007.

————. *Anne of Ingleside*. 1939. Toronto: Seal Books, 1996.

————. *Anne of the Island*. 1915. Toronto: Seal Books, 1996.

————. *Anne of Windy Poplars*. 1936. Toronto: Seal Books, 1996.

————. *Anne's House of Dreams*. 1917. Toronto: Seal Books, 1996.

————. "An April Night." *The Canadian Magazine* (Toronto, ON), April 1911, 538. Also in Montgomery, *The Watchman and Other Poems*, 46.

————. "An Author Speaks." *Dalhousie Gazette* (Halifax, NS), 24 February 1939, 2.

———— [Maud Cavendish, pseud.]. "A Baking of Gingersnaps." *The Ladies' Journal* (Toronto, ON), July 1895. Also in *The American Farmer* (Baltimore, ML), September 1895, 7.

————, comp. Black Scrapbook 1 and 2. In "Scrapbooks of Clippings, Programs and Other Memorabilia, compiled by L.M. Montgomery, ca. 1910–1936." XZ5 MS A002, L.M. Montgomery Collection, University of Guelph archives.

————. *The Blue Castle*. 1926. Toronto: Seal Books, 1988.

————. "The Blue Castle." *The Canadian Countryman* (Toronto, ON), 27 August 1927, 11, 15–17; 3 September 1927, 11–14; 10 September 1927, 13–16; 17 September 1927, 12–16; 24 September 1927, 12–15; 1 October 1927, 14–18; 8 October 1927, 9, 15–16; 15 October 1927, 7, 12–13; 22 October 1927, 9, 13–14; 29 October 1927, 9, 14–15; 5 November 1927, 14–18; 12 November 1927, 14–18; 19 November 1927, 14–16; 26 November 1927, 9, 17–18; 3 December 1927, 9, 16; 10 December 1927, 19, 47; 17 December 1927, 9, 30–31; 24 December 1927, 13–14; 31 December 1927, 9, 13; 7 January 1928, 9, 21–22; 14 January 1928, 13–15.

————. *The Blythes Are Quoted*. Edited by Benjamin Lefebvre. Toronto: Viking Canada, 2009.

————. "Canadian Twilight." In Garvin, *Canadian Verse for Boys and Girls*, 139. Also as "Twilight in Abegweit" in Montgomery, *The Poetry of Lucy Maud Montgomery*, 53. Also in Montgomery, *The Blythes Are Quoted*, 476–77.

————. "Captain Jim's Enjoyment." In French, *Standard Canadian Reciter*, 259.

————. "A Case of Atavism." *The Reader* (Indianapolis, IN), November 1905, 658–66.

————. *Chronicles of Avonlea*. 1912. Toronto: Seal Books, 1993.

————. *The Complete Journals of L.M. Montgomery: The PEI Years, 1889–1900*. Edited by Mary Henley Rubio and Elizabeth Hillman Waterston. Don Mills, ON: Oxford University Press, 2012.

———. *The Complete Journals of L.M. Montgomery: The PEI Years, 1901–1911*. Edited by Mary Henley Rubio and Elizabeth Hillman Waterston. Don Mills, ON: Oxford University Press, 2013.

———. "The Cure of the Fields." *The Sunday School Times* (Philadelphia, PA), 4 October 1901, 638.

———. "A Disappointment." In French, *Standard Canadian Reciter*, 41.

———. "Dog Monday's Vigil." In *Our Canadian Literature: Representative Prose and Verse*, chosen by Albert Durrant Watson and Lorne Albert Pierce, 381–88. Toronto: The Ryerson Press, 1922.

———. "Each in His Own Tongue." *The Delineator* (New York, NY), October 1910, 247, 324–28.

———. *Emily Climbs*. 1925. Toronto: Seal Books, 1998.

———. *Emily of New Moon*. 1923. Toronto: Seal Books, 1998.

———. "Emily of New Moon." In *The Voice of Canada: Canadian Prose and Poetry*, selected by A.M. Stephen, 97–100. Toronto: J.M. Dent, 1926.

———. *Emily's Quest*. 1927. Toronto: Seal Books, 1998.

———. *Further Chronicles of Avonlea*. Boston: The Page Company, 1920.

———. "Genius." *The Canadian Courier* (Toronto, ON), 25 June 1910, 20. Also in Montgomery, *The Watchman and Other Poems*, 132.

———. *The Golden Road*. 1913. Toronto: Seal Books, 1987.

———. "The Great Actor's Part." *The Canadian Courier* (Toronto, ON), 17 July 1909, 14, 20.

———. *The Green Gables Letters from L.M. Montgomery to Ephraim Weber, 1905–1909*. Edited by Wilfred Eggleston. 1960. Ottawa: Borealis Press, 1981.

———. "A Helping Hand." *Zion's Herald* (Boston, MA), 4 July 1900, 849.

———. "How I Became a Writer." *Manitoba Free Press* (Winnipeg, MB), 3 December 1921, Christmas Book Section, 3.

———. "I Have Come Home." *The Family Herald and Weekly Star* (Montreal, QC), 15 June 1936, 47.

———. *Jane of Lantern Hill*. Toronto: McClelland and Stewart, 1937.

——— [Lucy Maud Montgomery]. "June!" *The Patriot* (Charlottetown, PE), 12 June 1891, 4. Also as "June" in Bolger, *The Years before "Anne,"* 47–48. Also in Montgomery, *The Poetry of Lucy Maud Montgomery*, 140–41.

———. "Letters from the Literati." *The Editor: The Journal of Information for Literary Workers* (Fort Montgomery, NY), July 1912, 4–5.

———. "L.M. Montgomery." In *The Junior Book of Authors*, edited by Stanley J. Kunitz and Howard Haycraft, 261–62. New York: The H.W. Wilson Company, 1935.

———. "Love's Prayer." In *Canadian Singers and Their Songs: A Collection of Portraits and Autograph Poems*, compiled by Edward S. Caswell, 89. Toronto: McClelland and Stewart, 1919. Also in *Canadian Singers and Their Songs: A Collection of Portraits, Autograph Poems and Brief Biographies*, compiled by Edward S. Caswell, 107. Toronto: McClelland and Stewart, 1925.

———. *Magic for Marigold*. 1929. Toronto: Seal Books, 1988.

———. "Miss Cornelia Makes a Call." In French, *Standard Canadian Reciter*, 115–27.

———. "Miss Cornelia's Startling Announcement." In French, *Standard Canadian Reciter*, 128–33.

———. "Miss Marietta's Jersey." *The Household* (Topeka, KS), July 1899, 5–6.

———. *Mistress Pat*. 1935. Toronto: Seal Books, 1988.

———. "My Childhood in Canada." *The Brooklyn Daily Eagle* (Brooklyn, NY), 12 June 1938, 6D.

———. *My Dear Mr. M: Letters to G.B. MacMillan from L.M. Montgomery*. Edited by Francis W.P. Bolger and Elizabeth R. Epperly. 1980. Toronto: Oxford University Press, 1992.

———. "A Narrow Escape." *Zion's Herald* (Boston, MA), 6 October 1909, 1266–67.

———. "Off to the Fishing Ground." *The Youth's Companion* (Boston, MA), 3 November 1904, 556. Also in Garvin, *Canadian Poets*, 356–57. Also in Montgomery, *The Watchman and Other Poems*, 25–26. Also in French, *Standard Canadian Reciter*, 149–50.

———. "Oh, We Will Walk with Spring To-Day!" In Garvin, *Canadian Verse for Boys and Girls*, 140. Also as "Oh, We Will Walk with Spring Today" in Montgomery, *The Blythes Are Quoted*, 478–79.

———. "The Old Home Calls." *The Youth's Companion* (Boston, MA), 1 April 1909, 160. Also in Garvin, *Canadian Poets*, 358. Also in Montgomery, *The Watchman and Other Poems*, 130–31. Also in *Woman's Century* (Toronto, ON), 7 June 1921, 2.

———. "An Old Man's Grave." *The Youth's Companion* (Boston, MA), 6 December 1906, 628. Also as "The Old Man's Grave" in Garvin, *Canadian Poets*, 357–58. Also as "The Old Man's Grave" in Montgomery, *The Watchman and Other Poems*, 156.

——— [Lucy Maud Montgomery]. "On Cape Le Force." *The Patriot* (Charlottetown, PE), 26 November 1890, 1. Also in Bolger, *The Years before "Anne,"* 28–32. Also in Montgomery, *The Poetry of Lucy Maud Montgomery*, 135–39.

———. "One Clear Call." *The Household* (Boston, MA), August 1928, 6–7, 21.

———. "On the Hills." *Zion's Herald* (Boston, MA), 6 October 1909, 1265. Also in Montgomery, *The Watchman and Other Poems*, 73–74.

——— [Maud Cavendish, pseud.]. "Our Charivari." *Golden Days for Boys and Girls* (Philadelphia, PA), 9 May 1896, 396. Also in Bolger, *The Years before "Anne,"* 147–50, 157–58.

———. "Our Women." In Garvin, *Canadian Poems of the Great War*, 158. Also as "Our Women (Written in War-Time)" in *Songs of the Maritimes: An Anthology of the Poetry of the Maritime Provinces of Canada*, edited by Eliza Ritchie, 113. Toronto: McClelland and Stewart, 1931. Also in Montgomery, *Rilla of Ingleside*, 352.

——— [Belinda Bluegrass, pseud.]. "Patience." *Evening Mail* (Halifax, NS), February 1896. Also in Bolger, *The Years before "Anne,"* 159. Also as "Which Has More Patience – Man or Woman?" in Montgomery, *The Poetry of Lucy Maud Montgomery*, 120–21.

———. *The Poetry of Lucy Maud Montgomery*. Selected by John Ferns and Kevin McCabe. Markham, ON: Fitzhenry and Whiteside, 1987.

——— [Lucy Maud Montgomery]. "Portia." *The Patriot* (Charlottetown, PE), 11 June 1894, 2.

———. "Prince Edward Island." *The Guardian* (Charlottetown, PE), 29 April 1942, 4.

———. "Prince Edward Island's Famous Writer." *The Maritime Advocate and Busy East* (Sackville, NB), May–June 1940, 44–46.

———. *Rainbow Valley*. 1919. Toronto: Seal Books, 1996.

———, comp. Red Scrapbook 1 and 2. In "Scrapbooks of Clippings, Programs and Other Memorabilia, compiled by L.M. Montgomery, ca. 1910–1936." XZ5 MS A002, L.M. Montgomery Collection, University of Guelph archives.

———. *Rilla of Ingleside*. 1921. Edited by Benjamin Lefebvre and Andrea McKenzie. Toronto: Viking Canada, 2010.

———, comp. "Scrapbook of Reviews from Around the World Which L.M. Montgomery's Clipping Service Sent to Her, 1910–1935." XZ5 MS A003, L.M. Montgomery Collection, University of Guelph archives.

———. "The Sea-Spirit." *The Criterion* (New York, NY), April 1902, 12. Also as "The Sea Spirit" in Montgomery, *The Watchman and Other Poems*, 31.

———. *The Selected Journals of L.M. Montgomery*, Volume 1: *1889–1910*; Volume 2: *1910–1921*; Volume 3: *1921–1929*; Volume 4: *1929–1935*; Volume 5: *1935–1942*. Edited by Mary Rubio and Elizabeth Waterston. Toronto: Oxford University Press, 1985, 1987, 1992, 1998, 2004.

———. "Some Fools and a Saint." *The Family Herald and Weekly Star* (Montreal, QC), 20 May 1931, 19–20; 27 May 1931, 19–20, 41; 3 June 1931, 19–20; 10 June 1931, 21–22.

———. "Southernwood." *Zion's Herald* (Boston, MA), 4 September 1901, 1136. Also in Montgomery, *The Poetry of Lucy Maud Montgomery*, 77.

———. *The Story Girl*. 1911. Toronto: Seal Books, 1987.

———. "The Story of a Love." *Holland's Magazine* (Dallas, TX), November 1906, 24. Also in *The Canadian Magazine*, March 1911, 487–89.

———. "Sunrise along Shore." *The Youth's Companion* (Boston, MA), 28 November 1901, 630. Also in Garvin, *Canadian Poets*, 355–56. Also in Montgomery, *The Watchman and Other Poems*, 29–30. Also in Montgomery, *The Poetry of Lucy Maud Montgomery*, 48–49.

———. "Their Trip to Town." *The Sunday School Times* (Philadelphia, PA), 30 April 1904, 249.

———. "Una of the Garden." *The Housekeeper* (Minneapolis, MN), December 1908, 7, 18; January 1909, 11–12; February 1909, 8–9, 16; March 1909, 7, 17; April 1909, 8–9, 32.

——— [Lucy Maud Montgomery]. "The Violet's Spell." *The Ladies' World* (New York, NY), July 1894, 5. Also in Bolger, *The Years before "Anne,"* 143–44.

———. "The Watchman." *Everybody's Magazine* (New York, NY), December 1910, 778–83. Also in Montgomery, *The Watchman and Other Poems*, 3–7. Also in Montgomery, *The Poetry of Lucy Maud Montgomery*, 148–51.

———. *The Watchman and Other Poems*. Toronto: McClelland, Goodchild, and Stewart, 1916.

———. "The Way to Slumbertown." *Holland's Magazine* (Dallas, TX), April 1916, 56. Also in Garvin, *Canadian Verse for Boys and Girls*, 137–39.

——— [Lucy Maud Montgomery]. "A Western Eden." *The Prince Albert Times and Saskatchewan Review* (Prince Albert, SK), 17 June 1891, 4. Also in Bolger, *The Years before "Anne,"* 37–40, 47.

———. "When the Dark Comes Down." *The Youth's Companion* (Boston, MA), 7 November 1907, 564. Also in Garvin, *Canadian Poets*, 355. Also in Montgomery, *The Watchman and Other Poems*, 14–15.

"Montgomery, Lucy Maude [*sic*]." In *Twentieth Century Authors: A Biographical Dictionary of Modern Literature*, edited by Stanley J. Kunitz and Howard Kaycraft, 974–75. New York: The H.W. Wilson Company, 1942.

Morgan, Henry James, ed. *The Canadian Men and Women of the Time: A Hand-Book of Canadian Biography of Living Characters*. Toronto: William Briggs, 1912.

New, W.H. *A History of Canadian Literature*. 2nd ed. Montreal: McGill–Queen's University Press, 2003.

The New York Times (New York, NY). "L.M. Montgomery, Canadian Author." 25 April 1942, 13.

———. "The Week's News of Boston Books: Essays, Fiction and Children's Books Forthcoming." 21 November 1908, SR692.

The North Adams Evening Transcript (North Adams, MA). "Ask the Transcript." 5 July 1934, 14.

"Notes on Contributors." In *The Spirit of Canada: Dominion and Provinces, a Souvenir of Welcome to H.M. King George VI and H.M. Queen Elizabeth*, 58–59. N.p.: Canadian Pacific Railway, 1939.

The Ottawa Journal (Ottawa, ON). "L.M. Montgomery, *Anne of Green Gables* Author, Dies." 25 April 1942, 6.

Paterson, Isabel. "The Absentee Novelists of Canada." *The Bookman* (New York, NY), April 1922, 133–38.

The Patriot (Charlottetown, PE). "The Author of Anne of Green Gables." 10 October 1911, 4.

———. "Biographical Sketch of Mrs. Ewan Macdonald (Lucy Maud Montgomery)." 27 April 1942, 5.

———. "Famous Writer Is Laid to Rest." 30 April 1942, 4.

———. "Funeral from 'Green Gables.'" 27 April 1942, 1.

———. "Our Island Poets." 5 March 1901, 2.

Pember, John E. "Are Authors Today as Good as Those of the Past?" *The Boston Herald* (Boston, MA), 3 December 1922, C12, C15.

Pierce, Lorne. *An Outline of Canadian Literature (French and English)*. Montreal: Louis Carrier and Company, 1927.

Pike, E. Holly. "Mass Marketing, Popular Culture, and the Canadian Celebrity Author." In Gammel, *Making Avonlea*, 238–51.

"Publisher's Postscript." In *The Story of L.M. Montgomery*, by Hilda M. Ridley, 141–43. London: George G. Harrap and Company, 1956.

The Publishers' Weekly (New York, NY). "L.M. Montgomery." 2 May 1942, 1675.

Reimer, Mavis. "Introduction: The Anne-Girl and the Anne Book." In *Such a Simple Little Tale: Critical Responses to L.M. Montgomery's* Anne of Green Gables, edited by Mavis Reimer, 1–10. Metuchen: Children's Literature Association and Scarecrow Press, 1992.

Rhodenizer, Vernon Blair. *A Handbook of Canadian Literature*. Ottawa: Graphic Publishers, 1930.

Rubio, Mary Henley. "Introduction: Harvesting Thistles in Montgomery's Textual Garden." In *Harvesting Thistles: The Textual Garden of L.M.*

Montgomery; Essays on Her Novels and Journals, edited by Mary Henley
Rubio, 1–13. Guelph: Canadian Children's Press, 1994.

———. *Lucy Maud Montgomery: The Gift of Wings*. 2008. N.p.: Anchor
Canada, 2010.

———. "Why L.M. Montgomery's Journals Came to Guelph." In McCabe, *The
Lucy Maud Montgomery Album*, 473–78.

Rubio, Mary, and Elizabeth Waterston. Introduction to Montgomery, *The
Selected Journals of L.M. Montgomery*, 1: xiii–xxiv.

———. Introduction to Montgomery, *The Selected Journals of L.M.
Montgomery*, 2: ix–xx.

———. *Writing a Life: L.M. Montgomery*. Toronto: ECW Press, 1995.

Russell, Ruth Weber, D.W. Russell, and Rea Wilmshurst. *Lucy Maud
Montgomery: A Preliminary Bibliography*. Waterloo: University of
Waterloo Library, 1986.

The Salt Lake Tribune (Salt Lake City, UT). "Tribune Information." 9 January
1931, 13.

The Saskatoon Star–Phoenix (Saskatoon, SK). "Author of 'Anne' Books Visits
Girlhood Friend in City for Few Days." 3 October 1930, 8.

Sheard, Virna. "The Young Knights." In Garvin, *Canadian Poems of the Great
War*, 219–20. Also in Montgomery, *Rilla of Ingleside*, 352–53.

Sheckels, Theodore F. "Anne in Hollywood: The Americanization of a
Canadian Icon." In Gammel and Epperly, *L.M. Montgomery and Canadian
Culture*, 183–91.

Something about L.M. Montgomery. [Revised ed.] Boston: L.C. Page and
Company, 1938.

Southron, Jane Spence. "After Green Gables." Review of *Anne of Ingleside*, by
L.M. Montgomery. *The New York Times Book Review* (New York, NY),
30 July 1939, 7.

Sprott, George W., ed. *Memorials of the Rev. John Sprott*. Edinburgh: George
A. Morton, 1906.

Steffler, Margaret. "Anne in a 'Globalized' World: Nation, Nostalgia, and
Postcolonial Perspectives of Home." In Gammel and Lefebvre, *Anne's
World*, 150–65.

Stevenson, Lionel. *Appraisals of Canadian Literature*. Toronto: The Macmillan
Company of Canada, 1926.

———. "Overseas Literature: From a Canadian Point of View." *English
Review*, December 1924, 876–86.

*Successful Authorship: A Handbook Introducing to the Aspiring Writer
Constructive, Practical and Authoritative Home Study Courses of
Instruction in Story Writing*. Toronto: Shaw Schools, n.d.

The Sun (New York, NY). Ad for *Anne of Green Gables*, by L.M. Montgomery. 24 October 1908, 8.

The Tillsonburg News (Tillsonburg, ON). "Green Gables Included in P.E.I. National Park." 23 August 1945, 7.

The Times Literary Supplement (London, UK). "L.M. Montgomery." 2 May 1942, 220.

The Toronto Daily Star (Toronto, ON). "'Anne' Books Author Mrs. Macdonald Dies." 25 April 1942, 28.

———. "'Anne of Green Gables,' Screened, Author Cries a Little Herself." 13 November 1934, 19.

———. "Women's Canadian Club." 27 October 1913, 10.

Toronto Women's Press Club, comp. *Canadian Days: Selections for Every Day in the Year from the Works of Canadian Authors*. Toronto: The Musson Book Company, n.d.

Trotter, Mary Josephine. "The Novelist of the Isle: L.M. Montgomery." *Everywoman's World* (Toronto, ON), September 1914, 11.

Vipond, Mary. "Best Sellers in English Canada, 1899–1918: An Overview." *Journal of Canadian Fiction* 24 (1979): 96–119.

Waterston, Elizabeth. *Kindling Spirit: L.M. Montgomery's* Anne of Green Gables. Toronto: ECW Press, 1993.

West, Rebecca. *The Young Rebecca: Writings of Rebecca West 1911–17*. Selected by Jane Marcus. London: Macmillan, 1982.

The Western Argus (Kalgoorlie, Australia). "Australians as Letter Writers." 15 March 1932, 4.

The Western Mail (Perth, Australia). "Miss Montgomery's Methods." 29 June 1912, 36.

Who's Who 1934: An Annual Biographical Dictionary with Which Is Incorporated "Men and Women of the Time." London: A and C Black, 1934.

Wilson, Budge. *Before Green Gables*. Toronto: Penguin Canada, 2008.

Wrenshall, Irene B. "Jean Graham." *Canada Monthly* (London, ON), July 1915, 161, 172.

The Writer: A Monthly Magazine to Interest and Help All Literary Workers (Boston, MA). "Montgomery." June 1912, 92.

York, Lorraine. *Literary Celebrity in Canada*. Toronto: University of Toronto Press, 2007.

Zion's Herald (Boston, MA). "Noteworthy Books of the Year." 23 December 1908, 1637–38.

———. Review of *Anne of Avonlea*, by L.M. Montgomery. 6 October 1909, 1265.

Index

Adams, Charles Follen, 51, 52n8
Adams, Samuel Hopkins: *Flaming Youth*,
  204, 205–6, 206n6
Aitken, William Maxwell, 382, 384n12
Alcott, Louisa May, 317, 373; *Little
  Women*, 112, 133n11
Allison, W.T., 185–86
American Farmer, The (Baltimore, ML),
  72n13
Andersen, Hans Christian, 121, 124n5,
  167, 168n9
Anne of Avonlea (Montgomery), 10, 37,
  41, 46, 49, 51, 53, 57, 59, 62, 66n5,
  72n9, 161n2, 212, 238, 346n4, 361,
  388, 410n16, 411; critical responses,
  39n7; sales, 44, 46n1, 63
Anne of Green Gables (Montgomery),
  4, 10, 18, 20, 21, 23, 31–32, 38, 41,
  47n6, 49, 51, 52n6, 53, 56n4, 57,
  59, 62, 66n4, 97n98, 98–99, 105–6,
  108n2, 130–31, 170, 171, 189–90,
  195, 196n9, 205, 209, 212, 217, 238,
  242, 258n6, 284–85, 346n4, 375, 381,
  382, 402
– contract, 143n10
– critical editions, 137, 142n1
– critical responses, 7–9, 37, 63, 237–39,
  373–74, 400–401, 404–7

– endorsements, 31–32, 45, 130–31,
  215n15, 286, 317, 359, 371, 379, 403,
  410n4
– origins, 10, 15, 33–34, 35–36,
  38–39, 45–46, 55, 71, 106, 109n6,
  127–28, 146–47, 160, 197–98, 212,
  214–15n15, 250–51, 257–58, 261,
  286, 317–18, 323–24, 344–45, 360,
  387–88, 397n11
– sales, 44, 46n1, 63, 198, 214n2,
  216n24, 250, 324, 327n4
– screen adaptations, 3–4, 157, 158,
  161n3–162n4, 174, 175, 213, 215n23,
  316–317, 320–21, 323–27, 327n5,
  345, 348, 360, 411–20
– target audience, 32, 63, 257–58
– in translation, 198, 216n24, 344, 404
Anne of Ingleside (Montgomery), 72n9,
  74, 92n10, 94n38, 96n69, 356, 361,
  388, 408, 410n15, 410n17; review of,
  403
Anne of the Island (Montgomery), 93n15,
  95n59, 96n65, 104n5, 104n11, 114,
  128n2, 129, 148, 213, 238, 361, 388,
  411; dedication, 215n16
Anne of Windy Poplars (Montgomery),
  94nn43–44, 95n58, 96n74, 97n88,
  343, 345, 361, 388, 408

Anne's House of Dreams (Montgomery), 22, 94n31, 148, 238, 244, 292n5, 361, 388
Arc, Joan of, 248n10, 298, 299–304
Aurora Era (Aurora, ON), 356–58
Austen, Jane, 16, 26n33, 221

Bacon, Francis, 111, 113n8
Baird, Frank, 370, 371–72, 381–83, 409
Baker, Ray Palmer, 17
Baldwin, Lucy Ridsdale, 241, 243n2
Baldwin, Stanley, 241, 243n2, 250, 270, 371, 372n6, 384n12, 403
Barrie, J.M., 266, 272n15, 400
Beecher, Henry Ward, 395, 398n36
Bennett, Richard Bedford, 382, 384n12
Bible, Judeo-Christian, 23, 61n4, 94n42, 95n64, 97n85, 119n4, 119n6, 136n1, 181n2, 184n2, 210, 214n7, 244–47, 247nn2–3, 248n6, 248nn11–12, 248nn15–16, 272n16, 296, 297n2, 315n12, 355n4, 382, 389, 398n24
Bindloss, Harold Edward, 19
Blackmore, R.D., 151; *Lorna Doone*, 218, 222n7
Blake, William, 96n77
Blue Castle, The (Montgomery), 21, 73–74, 92n10, 93n19, 93n21, 93n23, 94nn32–33, 94n35, 94n41, 96n75, 97n86, 97n88, 97n91, 97nn93–94, 239, 258, 317, 361, 388–89; dedication, 389, 397n15; serialization, 241, 242; stage adaptation, 318, 319n7, 321
Blythes Are Quoted, The (Montgomery), 72n9, 93n28, 113n5, 359, 375
Bonar Law, Andrew, 382
Books and Authors (New York, NY), 188n7
Bookseller and Stationer (Toronto, ON), 40, 151–52, 199–201
Bookseller, Newsdealer and Stationer, The (New York, NY), 101
Boston Evening Transcript (Boston, MA), 148–49
Boston Globe, The (Boston, MA), 98–99
Boston Herald, The (Boston, MA), 8–9, 11, 57–58, 59–60, 101, 102–3, 210

Boston Journal, The (Boston, MA), 8, 33–34
Boston Post, The (Boston, MA), 50–52
Boston Traveler (Boston, MA), 53–55
Boyd, Thomas: *Through the Wheat*, 218, 222n4
Brontë, Charlotte, 63, 66n8, 153n2; *Jane Eyre*, 152, 195, 196n11
Brontë, Emily, 314n9
Brooke, Rupert, 220
Brooklyn Daily Eagle (Brooklyn, NY), 8, 35–36, 341
Brown, E.K., 3
Brown, Jessie Findlay, 328–29, 329n2, 329nn4–7
Browning, Robert, 315n10, 397n6
Bunyan, John: *The Pilgrim's Progress*, 159, 162n8, 166–67, 255
Burns, Robert, 95n63, 102–3, 104n9–10, 122, 137, 142n3, 211, 253n4, 255, 259n11
Butler, Kate Macdonald, 359
Byron, George Gordon, 137, 143n11, 147n2, 255, 257, 259n11

Caine, Hall, 266, 272n15
Calgary Herald, The (Calgary, AB), 365
Callaghan, Morley, 142n9
Campbell, Thane A., 370, 372n5
Campbell, Thomas, 61n5, 167, 168n10, 327n6
Campbell, Wilfred, 21
Canadian Author, The, 27n35, 347–48
Canadian Author and Bookman, 35, 347, 378
Canadian Authors' Association, 17, 20, 27n35, 202, 203n4, 237, 347
Canadian Bookman, The, 17, 20, 27n35, 40–43, 144–47, 237–39, 240n8
Canadian Countryman, The (Toronto, ON), 241–43
Canadian Courier, The (Toronto, ON), 44–46, 120, 126, 128n1
Canadian Home Journal (Toronto, ON), 177–79
Canadian literature, 3, 12, 18–19, 21, 48–49, 177–78, 202–3, 207–8, 237, 318–19, 400–409

Index

Canadian Magazine, The (Toronto, ON), 40, 73–92, 114–18

Carlyle, Jane, 396, 399n41

Carlyle, Thomas, 396, 399n41

Carman, Bliss, 21, 31, 32, 169, 207, 371, 382; endorsement of *Anne of Green Gables*, 31–32, 130–31

Carroll, Lewis (Charles Lutwidge Dodgson): *Alice in Wonderland*, 31, 221, 223n14

Caswell, Edward S., 22

Cavendish, Prince Edward Island, 24, 25n12, 38, 41, 64, 73, 107, 158; remoteness of, 8, 15, 54, 163, 175, 193, 197, 255, 360

Cervantes, Miguel de: *Don Quixote*, 373

Chatelaine, The (Toronto, ON), 273–81, 288–92, 323–27

Chaucer, Geoffrey, 248n16

Christian Science Monitor, The (Boston, MA), 101, 241

Chronicles of Avonlea (Montgomery), 10, 121, 131, 133n15, 168n12, 169, 196nn2–3, 213, 361, 371, 381, 411

Clemens, Rudolf A., 21–22, 27–28n50

Cody, H.A., 207

College Times, The, 230–35

Collins, Carolyn Strom, 125n11

Collins, Wilkie, 151; *The Woman in White*, 195, 196n10

Connor, Ralph (Charles W. Gordon), 19, 20, 27n41, 113n4, 178, 249, 365; *Sky Pilot*, 250

Cooper, James Fenimore, 137, 140, 142n6

Corelli, Marie, 45, 46n3

Courageous Women (Montgomery, Keith, and McKinley), 248n10

Cowper, William, 396, 397n8

Criterion, The (New York, NY), 398n26

Dalhousie Review, The, 385–96, 400–409

Davies, Robertson, 373

Davies, Louis Henry, 32, 381, 383n5

de la Roche, Mazo, 269, 272n20

Deacon, William Arthur, 3, 5, 20, 207, 347, 410n3

Deland, Ellen Douglas, 45, 46n3

Deland, Margaret, 45, 46n3

Delineator, The (New York, NY), 196n3

Dell, Ethel M., 245, 247n5

Denison, Flora MacDonald, 134

Devereux, Cecily, 36n2, 137, 142n1, 196n9, 224

Dickens, Charles, 151, 159, 168n10, 193, 390, 401; *David Copperfield*, 23, 152, 153n2, 192, 196n5; *Hard Times*, 259n12; *The Life and Adventures of Martin Chuzzlewit*, 314n5; *The Pickwick Papers*, 152, 153n2, 167, 191, 196n4, 221

Dole, Nathan Haskell, 51, 52n8, 213, 215n24

Doyle, Arthur Conan: *Micah Clarke*, 218, 222n7

Dreiser, Theodore, 269, 272n20

Duncan, Norman, 177, 179n2; *Doctor Luke of the Labrador*, 208, 208n3

Editor, The (Highland Falls, NY), 9–10, 162n15, 197–98

Eggleston, Wilfrid, 217, 385

Eliot, George (Mary Ann Evans), 381, 384n11; *The Mill on the Floss*, 152, 153n2

Ellerton, John, 384n15

Elsie. *See* Finley, Martha

Emerson, Ralph Waldo, 175, 176n3, 285, 287n11, 393, 398n27

Emily Climbs (Montgomery), 19, 93n18, 94n40, 96n71, 96n73, 96n75, 96n77, 97nn82–83, 97nn96–97, 206, 206n7, 239, 361

Emily of New Moon (Montgomery), 19, 72n4, 95n57, 125n11, 163, 198, 239, 240n7, 346n3, 361, 388

Emily's Quest (Montgomery), 21, 94n45, 96n73, 240n8, 361; dedication, 244

Epperly, Elizabeth Rollins, 73–74

Evening Mail (Halifax, NS), 147n2

Everywoman's World (Toronto, ON), 9, 29, 134–36, 137–42, 148, 224, 404

Examiner, The (Charlottetown, PE), 72n8, 235n10

Falconer, Sir Robert, 381, 384n8
Family Herald and Weekly Star, The (Montreal, QC), 10, 23, 295–97, 341
Farmers' Magazine (Toronto, ON), 163–67
Field, Eugene, 382, 384n14
Fielding, Henry, 93n20
Finley, Martha: Elsie books, 112, 113n12, 269, 365
First World War, 14, 48, 134–36, 148–49, 161, 217–22, 346n14, 240n6, 254–55, 266, 267, 376, 408, 409
Fort Williams Daily Times–Journal (Fort Williams, ON), 28n57
Fowler, Ellen Thorneycroft, 276, 281n4
Fraser, Daniel James, 41, 42n3
Frederick A. Stokes Company, 13, 26n26, 169
French, Donald Graham, 17–18, 22, 27n41, 237, 400, 407
Further Chronicles of Avonlea (Montgomery), 52n8, 93n22, 169–73, 209, 213, 215n24, 259n16, 327n3, 347

Gammel, Irene, 5, 36n3
Garvin, John W., 22, 27–28n50, 223nn17–18, 241, 243n5, 284
Gaskell, Elizabeth, 173n17
Georgetown Herald (Georgetown, ON), 260–61
Gerson, Carole, 3–4, 12, 210
Glentworth, Marguerite Linton, 31–32
Globe, The (Toronto, ON), 11–12, 17–18, 48–49, 67–72, 120–24, 215n17, 320–21
Globe and Mail, The (Toronto, ON), 12, 20, 359–61, 363
Goethe, Johann Wolfgang von, 396, 399n41
Golden Days for Boys and Girls (Philadelphia, PA), 54, 56n6, 147n2, 160, 162n13
Golden Road, The (Montgomery), 74, 92n10, 93nn13–14, 93n16, 93nn23–28, 94n30, 94n34, 94n37, 94n39, 94n46, 95nn48–49, 95nn51–56, 95nn60–63, 96nn65–68, 96n70, 96n75, 96nn78–79, 97n85, 97n88, 97n98, 121, 123, 131, 160, 179, 187, 213, 215n22, 238, 255, 361, 362n8
Goldsmith, Oliver, 66n12
Gray, Thomas, 113n14, 378–79, 383n1
Grey, Earl, 106, 108, 108n4, 372n6
Grove, Frederick Philip, 207; *Over Prairie Trails*, 199, 200, 207
Guardian, The (Charlottetown, PE), 101–2, 203, 235n10, 262–71, 352, 363, 367–68, 369–72
Guest, Edgar A., 245, 247n5

H.D. (Hilda Doolittle), 245, 247n5
Hale, Katherine (Amelia Beers Warnock), 134, 241
Haliburton, Thomas Chandler, 116, 119n5
Halifax Herald (Halifax, NS), 13–14
Hamilton Herald, The (Hamilton, ON), 202, 204, 206n7
Hamilton Spectator, The (Hamilton, ON), 202–3, 204–6
Hardy, Thomas, 151, 245; *The Dynasts*, 218, 222n8; *The Return of the Native*, 220, 223n12
Harper's Magazine (New York, NY), 131, 133n11
Harte, Bret, 400
Hathaway, E.J., 17, 27–28n50, 221, 223n17
Hawthorne, Nathaniel, 193, 196n7
Heggie, O.P., 316, 321
Hemans, Felicia, 314n4
Herbert, Henry William, 95n62
Hoffman, Arthur Sullivant, 189
Holmes, Mary Jane, 219, 223n11
Holmes, Oliver Wendell Sr., 277, 281, 282nn6–7, 282n9
Homer: *The Iliad*, 252, 253n5
Household, The (Topeka, KS), 69–70, 72n7
Housekeeper, The (Minneapolis, MN), 109n6, 160
Housman, A.E., 236n15
Hugo, Victor, 151; *Les Misérables*, 218, 222n7

Ibsen, Henrik, 112, 113n9
Irving, Washington, 266, 272n17

James, Henry, 245, 247n4
Jane of Lantern Hill (Montgomery), 154, 361
Jerningham, Edward, 104n7
Jerome, Jerome K., 137, 140, 142n8, 297
Jewett, Sarah Orne, 131, 133n10
Johnson, Pauline, 21, 298
Johnson, Samuel, 396, 399n41
Johnston, Annie Fellows, 209

Keats, John, 245, 248n8
Keble, John, 104n4
Keith, Marian (Mary Esther MacGregor), 113n4, 207, 298; *Duncan Polite*, 237, 298, 400
Keller, Stella Campbell, 104n4, 244
Kennedy, Roderick, 23
Kilmeny of the Orchard (Montgomery), 10, 43n9, 50, 51, 53, 57, 59, 62, 99, 102, 106, 109n6, 123, 131, 160, 179, 212, 238, 361, 388
King, Basil, 242, 243n3
Kingsley, Charles, 41, 43n8
Kingsley, Henry: *Ravenshoe*, 265, 271n10
Kipling, Rudyard, 97n92, 142n6, 151, 332, 340n6
Knowles, R.E., 112–13nn3–4; *St. Cuthbert's*, 250, 253n2

L.C. Page and Company, 13, 31, 32, 57, 63, 157, 160, 169, 209–13, 214n5, 316, 317, 327n4, 397n11, 412; lawsuits against, 13, 174, 209, 215n20, 318, 327n3, 327n4, 347, 397n11. *See also* Page, Lewis
Ladies' Journal, The (Toronto, ON), 72nn12–13
Ladies' World, The (New York, NY), 39n5, 72n11
Lafontaine, Zoé, 134
Lampman, Archibald, 45, 46n5
Laut, Agnes C., 151
Leacock, Stephen, 151, 177, 245, 247n4
Lethbridge Herald, The (Lethbridge, AB), 217–22

Lever, Charles: *Charles O'Malley, the Irish Dragon*, 218, 222n7
Leveridge, Lillian, 16–17
Lewis, Sinclair, 219, 269, 272n20; *Main Street*, 219, 223n10
Lincoln, Abraham, 396, 399n41
Lincoln, Joseph C., 245, 247n5
Livingstone, W.P.: *Mary Slessor of Calabar*, 299
Lloyd George, David, 234, 234n13
Logan, J.D., 17–18, 27n41, 237, 400, 407
Longfellow, Henry Wadsworth, 97n80, 136n2, 147n2, 168n6, 169, 170, 173n3, 213, 257, 259n11, 271n14, 309, 314n8
Los Angeles Times (Los Angeles, CA), 11, 209
Lutes, Della T., 154
Luther, Mark Lee: *The Sovereign Power*, 113n7

MacAdam, A.J., 367
MacArthur, T.H., 363
Macaulay, Rose, 221, 223n15
Macbeth, Madge, 207
Macdonald, Chester, 24, 28n57, 123, 131, 133n12, 149, 149n2, 158, 162n5, 225, 229n4, 251–52, 295, 318, 356, 357, 361, 367, 368, 370, 379, 380
Macdonald, Ewan, 43n10, 59, 101–3, 108, 123, 129, 149, 157, 158, 160, 174, 175, 212, 226, 258, 283, 284–85, 288, 295, 316–17, 320, 327n2, 343, 346, 360, 368, 369, 370, 378, 379, 380
Macdonald, Luella Reid, 356, 357
Macdonald, Stuart, 149, 150n2, 158, 162n5, 226, 251–52, 253n3, 295, 318, 359, 361, 367, 368, 370, 379, 380
MacFarlane, Frederica Campbell, 174, 244
Mackay, Isabel Ecclestone, 178, 179n3, 207
Maclaren, Ian: *Beside the Bonnie Briar Bush*, 400
MacLean's Magazine (Toronto, ON), 157–61

MacLeod, Malcolm James, 381, 384n9
MacMechan, Archibald, 3, 5, 18–19, 27n41
MacMillan, Cyrus, 381, 384n10
MacMillan, G.B., 7, 40, 51, 73, 104n9, 105, 143n10, 154, 156n1, 316, 397n2, 397n4
MacMurchy, Marjory, 27n50, 120–21, 124n1, 208n4, 350; *The Child's House*, 208, 350; *The Longest Way Round*, 350–51
Macneill, Alexander, 38, 68, 107, 122, 123, 129, 130, 132, 159, 162n18, 166, 211, 257, 318, 362n7
Macneill, Charles, 330–40
Macneill, Chester, 41, 43n6
Macneill, Hector, 122, 125n8, 131, 133n14, 159, 211, 242
Macneill, Leander, 41, 43n6, 114, 116–18
Macneill, Lucy Woolner, 7, 38, 39n5, 43n10, 50, 64, 68, 73, 101, 107, 108, 109n8, 122, 123, 125n9, 130, 158, 159, 160, 211, 257, 317, 360, 379
Macneill, Murray, 41, 43n6
Macneill, Penzie, 340n5
Macphail, Andrew, 48, 108, 109n14, 381
Magic for Marigold (Montgomery), 249, 250, 258, 262–71, 271nn4–5, 271n7, 271n12, 281, 282n10, 345, 361, 362n8, 388, 402
Mail and Empire, The (Toronto, ON), 12, 20, 258n1
Manitoba Free Press (Winnipeg, MB), 16, 101, 129–32, 182, 185–87, 254
Marion, Frances, 162n4, 327n7, 412
Maritime Advocate and Busy East, The (Sackville, NB), 24, 254, 330–40, 341–42
Marquis, Thomas Guthrie, 16
Masefield, Jon, 397n3
McAnn, Aida B., 24
McClelland and Stewart, 199, 215n20, 237, 286n2, 298, 359
McClung, Nellie L., 44, 48, 134, 178, 207, 245, 247n4, 288; *Sowing Seeds in Danny*, 44, 46n1, 237, 245, 247n4, 400–401
McGrath, Leslie, 21

McKinley, Mabel Burns, 298
McKowan, Evah, 178, 179n3
Meade, L.T., 219, 223n11
Methodist Review, The (New York, NY), 21–22
Meynell, Alice, 246, 248n13
Middletown Times–Herald (Middletown, NY), 210
Milton, John, 147n2, 167, 255, 257, 259n11, 285; *Paradise Lost*, 159, 162n8, 167, 252, 255, 287n13
Minter, Mary Miles, 161n3, 213, 320, 321, 324, 325, 327n8
Mistress Pat (Montgomery), 92n11, 97n84, 97n87, 97n95, 318, 319n7, 361
Montgomery, Clara Macneill, 38, 39n4, 107, 122, 129, 158, 211, 242, 255, 360, 379
Montgomery, Donald, 124, 125n10
Montgomery, Hugh John, 6, 38, 107, 122, 130, 180, 211, 242, 256, 360, 379
Montgomery, L.M.:
– ancestry, 124, 254, 255, 258n8
– authorship, pressures of, 7–8
– biographical information, 38, 45, 107, 122–24, 211–13, 237–38, 242, 254, 255–57, 344, 360, 363, 379
– birth dates, mistakes in, 16, 129, 132n2, 133n6
– books. *See* individual titles
– and Canadian literature, 12, 18, 48–49, 199–201, 202–3, 207–8, 318–19
– as celebrity author, 4–5, 6, 8, 10–12, 50, 50–52
– characters, inspiration for, 10, 34, 41, 42, 42–43n5, 55, 64, 107, 109n13, 114, 127, 139, 158, 175, 182–83, 205, 270, 285
– death and funeral, 23, 347, 349n3, 359–61, 361n2, 363–76, 378–83, 380–83, 409
– early literary work, 41, 54, 67–71, 122, 126, 130, 131, 144–47, 159–60, 180–81, 197, 205, 210–11, 226, 242, 255–57, 318, 357, 379

– early publications, 37–38, 39n5, 51, 54–55, 62, 65–66n2, 70–71, 145–47, 160, 181, 211–12, 235nn9–10, 253, 256–57, 319, 360, 386

– education, 18, 38, 45, 123, 130, 211, 230–35, 237–38, 242, 255, 256, 360, 362n7

– entries in reference books, 23, 254, 259n13, 259n15

– essays, 5, 9–10, 23, 59–60, 67–72, 73–92, 137–42, 144–47, 154–56, 163–67, 180–81, 182–83, 186–87, 197–98, 230–35, 255–58, 273–81, 288–92, 293–94, 296–97, 299–314, 323–27, 330–40, 341–42, 352–54; "How I Became a Writer," 254, 259n11; "I Have Come Home," 352, 355n3; "My Childhood in Canada," 341; "Prince Edward Island's Famous Writer," 254, 259n11, 259n15; "A Western Eden," 143n11; "The Wreck of the 'Marco Polo,'" 362n5

– fan mail, 8–9, 14–15, 99, 100n2, 185–87, 200–201, 203, 212, 252–53, 319, 346, 357, 394, 402

– and the First World War, 135–36, 148–49

– honours, 213, 352, 360, 361n4, 379, 403

– interviews, 5, 9, 15, 51–52, 53–55, 62–65, 105–8, 110–12, 157–61, 225–28, 249–53, 317–19, 320, 321, 343–46

– journals, 8, 9, 10, 11, 13, 15, 18, 19, 24, 25n12, 35, 42n2, 44, 48, 50, 53, 56n4, 56n6, 57, 62, 66n9, 66n11, 67, 72n6, 72n8, 94n36, 101, 104n4, 114, 121, 126, 128n1, 133n15, 142n9, 143nn10–11, 147n2, 151, 157, 162n7, 162n9, 162n18, 174, 180, 185, 204, 206n6, 207, 209–10, 230, 244, 254, 258n7, 288, 293, 298–99, 316, 320, 323, 327n2, 330, 341, 343, 356, 369, 385, 398n22, 410n17; significance of, 3–4, 5, 6, 7

– letters, 5, 7, 8, 10, 13–15, 33–34, 35–36, 38–39, 40, 49, 50, 51, 73, 100n2, 103, 105, 133n5, 135–36, 143n10, 148–49, 152, 156n1, 174–75, 217, 244, 268–71, 316, 340n5, 385–96

– marriage notices, 101–3

– memoirs: "The Alpine Path: The Story of My Career," 9, 29, 67, 96n72, 125n8, 128nn2–3, 137, 144, 147n2, 163, 185

– as minister's wife, 5, 9, 10, 12, 19, 110, 150n3, 154, 158, 204, 224, 225–27, 249–53, 274, 283–86, 288–92, 361, 378, 379

– and the modern girl, 204–6, 205, 251, 260–61, 273–81, 295–97, 318

– and modernist fiction, 142n9

– name, 6, 40, 232

– newspaper work, 38, 59, 123, 159, 211, 257, 387

– paratexts, 328–29

– physical descriptions of, 54, 63–64, 106, 205, 250, 284, 386

– poems, 6–7, 18, 21–22, 72n11, 131, 221–22, 345, 387; "An April Night," 73; "Autumn," 68, 180, 256; "Canadian Twilight," 28n53; "The Choice," 229n2; "The Cure of the Fields," 397n7; "Evening Dreams," 69–70, 72n1; "Genius," 44; "June!" 70, 72n10; "Love's Prayer," 22; "Off to the Fishing Ground," 22, 28n53; "Oh, We Will Walk with Spring To-Day!" 28n53; "The Old Home Calls," 21, 27–28n50, 28n53, 375, 376; "An Old Man's Grave," 28n53; "On Cape Le Force," 70, 72n9, 180, 181, 256; "On the Hills," 39n7; "Patience," 147n2; "The Piper," 375, 376–77; "The Sea-Spirit," 398n26; "Southernwood," 37; "Sunrise along Shore," 28n53, 221, 223n18; "The Violet's Spell," 38, 39n5, 71, 72n11, 145; "The Watchman," 371, 372n7, 381; "The Way to Slumbertown," 28n53; "When the Dark Comes Down," 21, 27–28n50, 28n53, 243, 243n5

– and problem novels, 54, 56n5, 63, 183

- profiles, 37–39, 40–42, 45–46, 98–99, 121–24, 129–32, 178–79, 237–40, 241–43, 283–86, 356–58
- pseudonyms: "Belinda Bluegrass," 147n2; "Cynthia," 59; "Maud Cavendish," 56n6, 72n13, 147n2
- public persona, 8–10, 11–12, 33, 65, 293–94
- reading tastes, 154–56, 159, 162n7, 166–67, 318
- and retrospection, 293–94, 330–40, 341–42
- reviews by, 350–51
- reviews of, 6, 22–23, 348
- scrapbooks, 6, 15, 27n41, 29, 48, 105, 110, 199, 224, 240n6, 328
- and sequels, 47n6, 64, 111–12, 395
- short stories and serials, 131, 387; "A Baking of Gingersnaps," 72n13, 256; "A Case of Atavism," 196n2; "Dog Monday's Vigil," 22; "Each in His Own Tongue," 196n3, 372n8; "The Great Actor's Part," 44; "A Helping Hand," 37; "Miss Marietta's Jersey," 72n7; "A Narrow Escape," 39n7; "One Clear Call," 72n7; "Our Charivari," 56n6, 147n2, 162n13; "The Story of a Love," 73; "Their Trip to Town," 397n7; "Una of the Garden," 43n9, 109n6, 160, 162n16
- speeches, 12, 13, 15, 126–28, 184n1, 185, 199–201, 202–3, 204–6, 260–61, 347–49
- teaching career, 25n12, 38, 44, 45, 98, 159, 256, 257, 360, 362n7
- tributes, 363–66, 375–76, 378–83
- and women's suffrage, 50–52, 53, 54, 60, 65, 224–28
- work: in anthologies, 22; critical responses, 3–4, 7–9, 16–24, 37, 63, 237–39, 373–74, 400–409; reader responses, 401–3; target audience, 16, 218–19; textual studies, 28n51; in translation, 319, 344–46, 346nn3–4, 360, 379, 388, 404
- writing process, 8–9, 10, 11, 33–34, 35, 52, 53–55, 57–58, 107, 137–42, 178, 182–83, 189–96, 198, 213, 318

Moore, Thomas, 94n37
Morgan, Henry James, 16
Morning Leader, The (Regina, SK), 12–13, 105–8
Mullins, Ilsa May, 209
Murphy, Emily, 134, 151, 178, 207

New, W.H., 17
New York Times, The (New York, NY), 31
Nightingale, Florence, 298, 304–9, 314n3
Norris, Kathleen: Butterfly, 198, 198n2
North Adams Evening Transcript, The (North Adams, MA), 210

O'Day, Dawn. See Shirley, Anne (actor)
Ontario Library Review, 254–58
O'Shaughnessy, Arthur, 271n13
Ottawa Journal, The (Ottawa, ON), 347, 365–66
Oxenham, John (William Arthur Dunkerley), 236n14

Pacey, Desmond, 3
Page, Lewis, 37, 47n6, 50, 52n7, 57, 62, 63, 103, 123, 129, 130, 157, 169, 174, 209–10, 211, 212, 411. See also L.C. Page and Company
Page, Mildred, 51, 52n7, 62
Pansy (Isabella Macdonald Alden), 159, 162n10
Parker, Gilbert, 177, 179n2, 219
Paterson, Isabel, 19
Pat of Silver Bush (Montgomery), 110, 318, 361, 388; dedication, 330
Patriot, The (Charlottetown, PE), 6–7, 72n10, 180, 181, 235n10, 256, 363, 367
Pepys, Samuel, 265, 271n8
Phelps, Arthur L., 3
Photoplay Magazine (Chicago, IL), 411–20
Pickford, Mary, 162n4, 325, 327n7
Pickthall, Marjorie, 48
Pierce, Lorne, 20, 22
Pike, E. Holly, 9
Poe, Edgar Allan, 235n8
Pope, Alexander, 61n2, 162n14, 196n9

Porter, Eleanor H., 209, 219
Presbyterian Record, The (Toronto, ON), 23, 378–83, 409
Prince Edward Island, 121–22, 127–28, 129–30, 132–33, 160–61, 163–67, 183, 262–71, 330–40, 341–42, 352–54; history of name, 100n4; Mi'kmaq name for, 331, 340n4, 341, 352–54; tourism, 24, 111, 158, 364, 366
Prince Edward Island National Park, 11–12
Proust, Marcel, 245, 247n5

Rainbow Valley (Montgomery), 94n33, 104n11, 157, 160, 179, 238, 292n6, 361, 362n8, 388, 402, 409; dedication, 148
Reader, The (Indianapolis, IN), 196n2
Realart Pictures Corporation, 411, 412
Reid, Luella. *See* Macdonald, Luella Reid
Republic, The (Boston, MA), 62–65
Rhodenizer, Vernon Blair, 20–21
Riley, James Whitcomb, 162n6, 384n14
Rilla of Ingleside (Montgomery), 17–18, 22, 48, 72n9, 97n81, 133n5, 134, 157, 174, 217–22, 238, 240n6, 254–55, 340n11, 361, 362n8, 376, 402, 408, 409
Ritchie, Eliza, 22
RKO Radio Pictures, 215n23, 316
Roberts, Charles G.D., 21, 245, 247n4, 382; *The Heart of the Ancient Wood*, 208, 208n2
Roche, James Jeffrey, 64, 66n10
Roe, E.P., 159, 162n9
Rogers, Grace McLeod, 178, 179n3
Rubio, Mary Henley, 3, 4, 20, 34n1, 109n10, 109n14, 125n8, 150n3, 169, 230, 299, 328, 367, 369, 373
Russell, D.W., 25n6, 235n9, 362n5
Russell, Ruth Weber, 25n6, 235n9, 362n5

Salt Lake Tribune, The (Salt Lake City, UT), 210
Saskatoon Star–Phoenix, The (Saskatoon, SK), 9
Saturday Night (Toronto, ON), 20, 23, 110–12, 244–47, 375–77

Saunders, Marshall, 134, 298; *Beautiful Joe*, 207
Schurman, Jacob Gould, 41, 42n2, 381
Scott, Walter, 41, 43n7, 94n47, 137, 140, 151, 159, 168n10, 193, 250–51, 255, 259n11, 266, 272n17; *Ivanhoe*, 167, 168n10; *Quentin Durward*, 167, 168n10; *Rob Roy*, 152, 153n2; *Waverley*, 250–51
Shakespeare, William, 49n2, 72n14, 111–12, 113n8, 113n13, 128n3, 235, 351, 351n2, 369, 390
Shaw, George Bernard: *Saint Joan*, 246, 248n10, 299
Sheard, Virna, 48
Sheckels, Theodore F., 327n10
Shelley, Mary, 396, 399n41
Shelley, Percy Bysshe, 396, 399n41
Shirley, Anne (actor), 215n23, 316–17, 319n1, 321, 325–26
Slessor, Mary, 298, 299, 309–14
Smith, May Riley, 282n5
Southron, Jane Spence, 403
Southworth, E.D.E.N., 219, 223n11
Sprott, George W., 114, 118
Sprott, John, 114–18
Stead, Robert J.C., 151, 207, 245, 247n4
Stephen, A.M., 22
Stevenson, Lionel, 19, 21, 27n43
Stevenson, Robert Louis, 130, 132, 133n5; *Strange Case of Dr. Jekyll and Mr. Hyde*, 192, 196n6
Stirling, John, 101, 104n5, 367, 368, 369–71, 380–81
Stokes, Frederick A. *See* Frederick A. Stokes Company
Story Girl, The (Montgomery), 10, 43n9, 50, 51, 54, 57, 63, 72n9, 98, 102, 103, 106, 107, 109n13, 114–18, 120, 123, 125n9, 127, 131, 163, 187, 202, 205, 210, 212, 238, 255, 345, 346n3, 361, 388
Stowe, Harriet Beecher, 36n2; "Topsy," 36, 36n2, 39, 46, 127, 138, 189–90
Stratton-Porter, Gene, 219, 223n11
Stringer, Arthur, 48, 151; *Empty Hands*, 245, 247n4
Sullivan, Kevin, 3–4, 327n9

Sunday School Times, The (Philadelphia, PA), 387, 397n7

Talmage, Thomas De Witt, 167, 168n9
Tangled Web, A (Montgomery), 133n15, 253n6, 361, 362n8, 388
Tawse, Sybil, 215n24
Taylor, Tom, 281n2
Taylor, William Desmond, 161n3, 320, 325, 327nn7–8
Tennyson, Alfred, 13, 93–94n28, 94n45, 95n50, 95n61, 96n79, 137, 142n5, 142n7, 147n2, 220, 235n4, 255, 257, 259n11, 327n9
Teskey, Adeline M.: *Where the Sugar Maple Grows*, 400, 410n1
Thackeray, William Makepeace, 151, 193, 218, 220; *Vanity Fair*, 152, 153n2, 218, 222–23n9
Thomson, James, 68, 72n3
Tiessen, Hildi Froese, 385, 398n21
Tiessen, Paul Gerard, 385, 398n21
Tillsonburg News (Tillsonburg, ON), 24
Tolstoy, Leo, 206; *War and Peace*, 170, 218, 222n7, 373
Toronto Daily Star (Toronto, ON), 126, 316–19, 320, 328
Toronto Star Weekly (Toronto, ON), 129, 224–28, 249–53
Toronto Telegram, The (Toronto, ON), 320
Toronto World (Toronto, ON), 10
Townley, Alice Ashworth: *Opinions of Mary*, 44
Trollope, Anthony, 151
Trotter, Mary Josephine, 224
Trowbridge, John Townsend, 236n11
Twain, Mark (Samuel Clemens), 99n1, 151; endorsement of *Anne of Green Gables*, 31, 45, 130, 215n15, 286, 317, 359, 371, 379, 403, 410n4

Vipond, Mary, 46n1

Walpole, Horace, 396, 399n41
Ward, Mrs. Humphry, 45, 46n1, 46n3
Warner, Charles Dudley, 98, 99n1
Watchman and Other Poems, The (Montgomery), 20, 148, 243n5, 258, 259n16, 349n4, 361, 362n9, 371, 372n7, 375, 398n26
Waterston, Elizabeth Hillman, 3, 4, 6, 18, 19, 34n1, 125n8, 150n3, 230, 299, 373
Watson, Albert Durrant, 22
Watson, Robert, 207
Weber, Ephraim, 7, 35, 50, 73, 100n2, 133n5, 174, 217, 244, 385, 397n4, 397n18, 410n3, 410n15
West, Rebecca (Cicely Isabel Fairfield), 247, 248n14
Western Mail, The (Perth, Australia), 11
Wetherald, Ethelwyn, 48
Wharton, Edith, 45, 46n3
Whitman, Walt, 245, 247n4
Whitney, James, 111, 113n6
Whittier, John Greenleaf, 96n76, 97n90, 147n2, 168n12, 175, 176n2, 259n11, 285, 287n12, 329n3
Wiggin, Kate Douglas, 219, 223n11
Wilmshurst, Rea, 25n6, 235n9, 352n5
Wilson, Budge: *Before Green Gables*, 412
Wilson, Francis, 31, 32n1, 403, 410n4
Winnipeg Free Press (Winnipeg, MB), 217
Withington, Elizabeth R., 209
women's suffrage, 50–52, 52n9, 54, 60, 65
Wordsworth, William, 97n98, 240n5, 257, 393, 398n22, 398n28
Writer, The (Boston, MA), 11

Yeats, William Butler, 125n6
York, Lorraine, 11
Youth's Companion, The (Boston, MA), 223n18, 243n5, 375, 387, 397n9

Zieber, Miriam, 397n4
Zion's Herald (Boston, MA), 37–39